About the Authors

Henry B. Reiling is the Eli Goldston Professor of Business Administration at the Harvard School of Business Administration, where he has administrative responsibilities for and shares in the teaching of the school's legal offerings. The recipient of an M.B.A. from Harvard and a J.D. from Columbia, he has practiced law in New York and been active as a committee member for the Bar Association of the City of New York and as a task-force chairman for the American Bar Association. A former trustee of Riverside Church in New York and cofounder of a successful financial services company, he is presently a director of a publicly owned oceanography company. Professor Reiling taught at Columbia and visited at Stanford before joining the Harvard faculty. He has taught in the executive education programs of all three schools and in the management development programs of such companies as IBM, Hewlett-Packard, Westinghouse, Morgan Guaranty, First National City Bank, and Merrill Lynch, White-Weld. He has received a variety of awards for excellence in teaching. Professor Reiling has served as a member and committee chairman of the Columbia Faculty Senate and chairman of Harvard University's Advisory Committee on Shareholder Responsibility. His articles have appeared in such publications as the *Michigan Law Review* and the *Harvard Business Review*.

George C. Thompson holds a B.A., an M.S., and a LL.B. from Columbia University, where he is now the James L. Dohr Professor of Business Law and Accounting in the Graduate School of Business. He has published extensively in many journals and has coauthored the following books: *Accounting and the Law, Law in an Economic Environment, Antitrust Fundamentals,* and *The Shortened CPA Law Review,* now in its fifth edition. He is an active member of the New York Bar. Professor Thompson has wide experience in business law, resulting from his work as a business consultant, his service as a director of several corporations and foundations, and his over thirty years of teaching experience.

Gerald P. Brady received his B.A., M.S., and LL.B. degrees from Columbia University. He is currently, and has been for twenty-three years, a Professor of Business Law in the Business Law and Taxation Division of the Graduate School of Business at Columbia. He has frequently served as the divisional representative of the division. He has authored seven books, most of them with George C. Thompson, including the *Shortened CPA Law Review*, now in its fifth edition, originally published by Wadsworth Publishing and now published by Kent Publishing, and *Antitrust Fundamentals*, third edition, published by West Publishing Company. Professor Brady was a Harlan Fiske Stone Scholar and a student member of the Legislative Drafting Research Fund while in law school. He is a member of Beta Gamma Sigma.

Frank J. Macchiarola received his LL.B. and Ph.D. degrees from Columbia University. He has taught business law at the Columbia University Graduate School of Business, the City College of New York, and Baruch College of the City University of New York. Dr. Macchiarola has been admitted to the New York State Bar, the Federal Bar, and the United States Supreme Court Bar. He has also published extensively in the fields of business, law, and education. Dr. Macchiarola served as Counsel to the Committee on Codes of the New York State Assembly, Vice President of the Graduate School and University Center of City University of New York, Assistant Vice President of Columbia University, President of the Northeastern Regional Business Law Association, and President of the Dirigible Society of America.

Preface

Business Law: Text and Cases had its genesis more than a decade ago as a project of the members of the Law Division of the Columbia Business School. The interdisciplinary needs of students and the authors' interdisciplinary backgrounds combined to produce materials with a bit different emphasis than the standard business law texts (see the section in the preface describing special features). These early supplementary, mimeographed materials were shaped in the crucible of the classroom. They were expanded and evolved with changes in the law, with the evolution in the authors' teaching experience (now totaling seventy-six years), and with the expert criticism of academics, lawyers, and businesspersons. The materials have been used with considerable success in a variety of undergraduate, graduate, and corporate settings.

The book's underlying premise is that with a maturing U.S. economy and an increasingly litigious society, business students must understand the workings of the legal mind and be in command of basic legal principles as they apply to business just as they must have basic information about, and an appreciation of, the mental processes involved in finance, marketing, and production. In short, the fiduciary responsibilities discussed in *Guth* v. *Loft* are as vital to a businessperson in the 1980s as a grasp of the capital asset pricing model.

CONTENT AND ORGANIZATION

Content has two subdivisions: breadth and depth. The topics presented are those that academics and practitioners generally agree are important for the general manager or the professional, such as an accountant, who must have a knowledge of a broad array of legal subjects. The depth of coverage should be adequate for the student with well-defined employment objectives (e.g., accounting, consumer marketing, investment banking, real estate). Most of these students have comparable needs for knowledge about such topics as agency, contracts, corporations, legal method, or procedure. Where topics become specialized, we have tried to meet the need of the student working in the particular field. For example, the coverage of commercial paper and negotiable instruments coincides with that given in several major commercial bank management training programs. Similarly, the coverage of sales should meet the needs of one entering either consumer or industrial marketing. One result of this treatment is that instructors may not assign a topic, such as suretyship, or may delete substantial portions. Our premise has been that it is easier for the instructor to delete unneeded material than to create supplementary material.

The book's twelve parts and forty-four chapters subdivide into six natural clusters. The first cluster of four parts consists of those topics usually included in the first term of a multiterm course offering. The two chapters on jurisprudence and procedure constitute Part I and form the foundation on which the subsequent forty-two chapters build. Part II consists of one chapter on torts, specifically negligence. The inclusion of torts reflects its importance as one of the three main areas of U.S. civil law. The modest coverage reflects its limited importance in business law (except for strict liability in tort) due in part to the emergence of specialized areas to supercede common law business torts: unfair methods of competition are subsumed in antitrust; many individual duties under common law are addressed in agency; other common law duties are superceded by corporate law (e.g., corporate opportunity doctrine) or federal securities law (e.g., insider trading). Part III, Contracts, with nine chapters, is the largest part of the book. Its length reflects the importance of this topic in most business law programs. Part IV, Agency is discussed in three chapters containing the private law principles common to both manufacturing and service businesses. Three alternative configurations of agency material are possible. Government regulation of employment and the employer-employee relationship (a section in Chapter 34) might be assigned as a supplement to Part IV. This would be particularly appropriate if the instructor does not wish to emphasize government regulation. Independent of this question is whether to follow agency with corporations and partnerships, two areas where agency is especially important, or with sales and commercial paper, the arrangement that most instructors appear to prefer.

The second cluster encompasses the more important materials based on the Uniform Commercial Code: Part V, Sales (eight chapters), and Part VI, Commercial Paper (three chapters). Chapter 40, on secured transactions, appears in cluster six along with other miscellaneous subjects. We considered putting all UCC material in one place and having secured transactions follow sales and commercial transactions. We concluded, however, that importance and the normal teaching sequence should be emphasized over conceptual tidiness. The interaction between common law contracts and the sale of goods has been handled by addressing major UCC sales innovations in the chapters on contracts but briefly summarizing the earlier discussions in the first chapter of sales. This approach strengthens the contracts material while avoiding both omission from sales and needless double coverage. Pedagogically the subsequent remarks on statutes, hypothetical situations, and examples are especially germane to this cluster.

Cluster three addresses business organizations and consists of Part VII, Partnerships (three chapters), and Part VIII, Corporations (four chapters, including one on federal securities regulation). State law, which articulates the basic rights, duties, and relationships of the country's 5 million businesses, is the focus of six of these seven chapters. A large chapter on federal securities law, is included in the corporate material for two reasons: First, since most of the productive power in the U.S. is controlled by publicly traded companies, the material has considerable relevance to this economic majority. Second, modern finance makes much of efficient market theories. The disclosure requirements of federal law are central to the quantum, quality, and timing of information upon which these theories and their practical implications depend. "Hybrid" organizations — i.e., limited partnerships and those corporations making the Subchapter S election — are considered in this cluster. Comparisons of partnerships to corporations are made.

Cluster four coincides with Part IX, Government Regulation, and consists of two chapters. The first chapter introduces the increasingly important basic principles of administrative law. The balance of that chapter addresses government regulation of employment and the employer-employee relationship. The instructor's preference will dictate whether to emphasize the government regulations or agency aspect of this material. Antitrust, i.e., government regulation of competition, is the second chapter in Part IX.

Cluster five coincides with Part X and the four chapters on the control and transfer of property. In addition to traditional material on the concept of property, note is taken of the number of new personal property rights created by governmental action (licenses, etc.) and the increasing restrictions on historic property rights also emanating from the government. Patents, copyrights, and trademarks are emphasized as examples of property rights of a personal property nature created or enhanced by the government. Reflecting the evolution in real property practices, our coverage gives meaningful attention to leasing, condominiums, cooperatives, and the increasing warranty protection courts are granting consumers. Reflecting standard practice, bailments is covered in this property cluster. Instructor preference varies regarding wills, trusts, and estates. We have placed it in a cluster of miscellaneous topics, but instructors may wish to assign it as a fifth property chapter.

Cluster six consists of Parts XI and XII and includes the five topics whose importance varies the most from one school's program to the next: secured transactions, suretyship, the recently amended bankruptcy law, insurance, and wills, trusts, and estates.

SPECIAL FEATURES

Cases

We agree with those who argue that studying United States law, and business law in particular, without reading cases is like philosophizing about apples without taking a bite of one. All cases represent the application of particularly important or troublesome concepts or a frequently recurring problem. However, cases in this book are more than examples. The judge's opinion is woven into the text and supplements the authors' observations.

Pedagogical and professional judgment rather than a mechanistic formula has been used to determine the density of cases by chapter. Case density is a function of the nature of the area (jurisprudence has no cases since cases tend to demonstrate jurisprudence rather than discuss it), the newness of the area, and the degree to which the area is a creature of statutory as opposed to case law. For example, the Uniform Commercial Code is sufficiently clear on risk of loss that litigation has been limited and has tended to focus on minor points. No case is presented in that short chapter. Instead, a colorful fact situation from pre-UCC litigation is used to demonstrate UCC principles in operation.

The artful task has been to edit cases so as to avoid the pitfall of sterile one paragraph summaries on the one hand and extraneous substantive and procedural reading on the other. Cases are 1,000 words or fewer with a few exceptions, most of which are in the chapter on federal securities regulation, where fact situations are especially complex and multiple parties are involved.

Where options existed, we chose the more colorful fact situation for purposes of student interest. Thus, while many cases could make the point involved in *Webster* v. *Blue Ship Tea Room,* the colorful fact situation and unexpected authorities cited will make it easier for the student to associate facts and legal principle.

Evidencing the book's emphasis on basic principles and a broad "national law" view, cases are drawn from more than forty states. Naturally, though, since litigation, and therefore, the pool of court decisions from which we can select, is a function of population and business activity, decisions from California and New York, our most populous states, appear with greatest frequency. Some cases are included because they resolve important issues and are landmarks. Despite their antiquity, the included ancients remain good law. Moreover, such cases give a flavor for the continuity in much of our law. On the other hand, in areas of rapid development, such as those under Title VII, cases are necessarily of recent vintage. Of the approximately one hundred and sixty-five cases, approximately thirty-nine were decided during the 1970s and eleven were decided in 1978 or later.

Statutes

Considerations of space and the wish to preserve reading continuity and avoid repetition of some sections persuaded us to place major statutes in appendices rather than dispersing extensive quotations throughout the text. This practice permits the full statute to be presented, thereby enhancing the book's utility for future reference. The four statutes reprinted are the Uniform Commercial Code (1972 version), Uniform Partnership Act, Uniform Limited Partnership Act, and Model Business Corporation Act. Citations to the pertinent sections will be found in the text.

Problems and Questions

Depending on the size and importance of the material, a minimum of ten to a maximum of fifteen problems and questions appear at the end of each chapter. The inquiries fall into three categories. Many are straightforward review questions testing the student's mastery of the specific substantive information provided. A second type requires a synthesis of one or more principles from the text and cases. The student can usually make a confident application of princples to the facts. A third type of exercise is more conceptual and has no right answer. Here students can only identify competing legal principles, but cannot predict with a high level of certainty the judicial resolution of the matter. Each type is important. The first tests for grasp of material and builds confidence. The second tests for grasp of material but goes further and emphasizes the importance of facts. The third ensures that students do not fall into the mistaken belief that all questions have a right answer, that a lawyer can provide it, and that compromise is unnecesary.

Hypothetical Situations and Diagrams

Examples and hypothetical situations are frequently used to provide clarity and reinforce the notion of relevance. The art illustrating the check written on a squash not only enlivens the discussion of commercial paper, but makes a point about the writing requirement for a negotiable instrument. The hypotheticals tend to be more elaborate and more frequently used as the information is less likely to be familiar to the student. For example, the material on suretyship and secured transactions — two areas generally acclaimed by students to be dry and difficult — is developed against the unifying theme represented by the business evolution of Ultrasound, a hypothetical company. Diagrams are used to clarify complicated relationships.

Legal Method

One major and one minor example of the law's evolutionary character are provided. These are exceptions to our general approach, which stresses breadth of coverage rather than depth as appropriate for the business student. The major example is presented in the sales area and consists of a module on product liability that traces the evolution from negligence actions through the collapse of privity to the emergence of strict liability in tort. The minor example appears in Chapter 3, where Holmes's famous (infamous) "stop, look, and listen" opinion is juxtaposed to Cardozo's opinion overruling Holmes.

Business and Student Relevance

Experience teaches that students are more interested and work harder when they appreciate the relevance of a topic. Consequently we provide examples, discussion, and background designed to demonstrate the material's relevance. Choices between alternative cases are resolved in favor of those emphasizing business applications, an emerging business theme, or personal relevance and interest to the student. Thus, economic duress, rather than the classic physical duress, is the focus of the duress discussion in contracts; business students are more likely to encounter economic duress, and courts appear to be more receptive to it than previously. Similarly, the California Supreme Court's contract-based *Marvin* v. *Marvin* "palimony" decision, which has potential personal economic significance for some students, is used to consider judicial flexibility in formulating contract remedies.

"White Collar Crime"

Legislation and shifting enforcement policy confront the businessperson with greater risk of criminal prosecution in the 1980s than in the 1970s. Material addressing this important development is sprinkled throughout the book as follows:

Criminal law procedure	Chapter 2, The Judicial Process
Criminal liability for other's conduct	Chapter 31, Corporate Directors and Officers
Fraud in financial statements	Chapter 33, Federal Securities Regulation
Foreign Corrupt Practices Act	Chapter 33, Federal Securities Regulation
Price fixing	Chapter 35, Antitrust

Glossary

A glossary of approximately 1,000 words and phrases is included. A special effort has been made to avoid the familiar problem of a chain reaction of legal terminology, i.e., the use of a new or unfamiliar technical term when defining another term.

Readability

Much legal writing is criticized as ponderous, cold, and redundant. For these reasons and because of our multiple authorship, we have given particular attention to readability. Frequent headings and subheadings are employed for focus and emphasis. We have sought to avoid the long, convoluted sentence and have aspired to a lively and lucid writing style. Each author made a conscientious effort in this direction, the lead author then reviewed all manuscript, a professional development editor took a third cut at the material, and finally normal copy editing was done.

Society, in speaking to business and businesspersons through the mechanism of the law, is articulating a rising set of expectations and demands. It is necessary and desirable that business education continues to become more interdisciplinary. In this interdisciplinary spirit we have aspired to make a worthwhile contribution to the education of tomorrow's leaders.

ACKNOWLEDGMENTS

A number of excellent research assistants have assisted us over the years. Making particularly noteworthy contributions were Michael C. Bellas; Michael Broderick, III; Ralph Coti; Vaiyapuri Jaikumar; Sanford W. Morhouse; Vincent Okoro; Christina R. Pfirrman; Mitchell P. Pines; Thomas Powell; James Snow; Nathan Szyszko; Grover T. Wickersham; Alan B. Winsor; and Michael DiIulio. We are indebted to each of them.

We wish to express our gratitude for the great interest and help given us by colleagues. Professor Ronald D. Greenberg of the Columbia Graduate School of Business prepared the first draft of Chapter 33 on federal securities law, his area of special interest. Professor Robert Whitman of the University of Connecticut Law School and W. Bruce Bassett of the Columbia Graduate School of Business were especially helpful at early stages of the project. Numerous thoughtful suggestions were also made by the following reviewers: Myron L. Erickson, University of Missouri; Gerard Halpern, University of Arkansas at Fayetteville; Charles T. Hartmann, Wright State University; Dugald W. Hudson, Georgia State University; Paul Lansing, University of Iowa; Arthur J. Marinelli, Ohio University; Daniel Reynolds, Middle Tennessee State University; and Arthur L. Wolfe, Michigan State University.

Producing a manuscript of this length is no mean feat. Mollie A. Lisberger's typing skills, alertness for inconsistencies, proofreading, and unflagging good spirit advanced the project enormously.

Columbia, Baruch, and Harvard have given generous and active support to our efforts. We thank them most warmly.

Short Contents

Contents

PART IV   Sale of Goods   245

I

INTRODUCTION

INTRODUCTION

In America, the law is a dynamic force, born out of society's need for order and change, with principles derived from the common law of England, and built on by all branches of government in the United States. The law is more than a body of rules, enacted by legislatures, imposing a duty of obedience on all citizens. While the law compels obedience by threat of sanction, it more often obtains support through the willing consent of the governed. Providing an understanding of these characteristics is the objective of this chapter.

An appreciation of the characteristics of our law is best accomplished by considering a few important views on the role of law in society and on the nature of law. This treatment is designed to give perspective on law and legal institutions by acquainting you with some of the ideas of legal philosophy, or *jurisprudence,* to use the name by which the general theory of law is more often referred to in the United States and Great Britain. In the long run, this initial discussion of philosophy or theory should facilitate an understanding of business law.

Oliver Wendell Holmes, Jr., has commented on the utility of theory in Holmes, "The Path of the Law," 10 Harv. L. Rev. 457, 477 (1897) thus:[1]

> Theory is the most important part of the dogma of the law, as the architect is the most important man who takes part in the building of a house. . . .
> It is not to be feared as unpractical, for, to the competent, it simply means going to the bottom of the subject. For the incompetent, it sometimes is true, as has been said, that an interest in general ideas means an absence of particular knowledge. I remember in army days reading of a youth who, being examined for the lowest grade and being asked a question about squadron drill, answered that he never had considered the evolutions of less than ten thousand men. But the weak and foolish must be left to their folly. The danger is that the able and practical minded should look with indifference or distrust upon ideas the connection of which with their business is remote.

1
OBJECTIVES AND NATURE OF LAW

The remoteness (or closeness) of this connection between jurisprudence and one's business which Holmes referred to warrants a brief word. The principles comprising the law often provide an outer parameter for business conduct, thereby restricting the businessperson's freedom to act. Frequently the businessperson will address a problem to an attorney, requesting a solution within the bounds of the law and consistent with the client's needs. The attorney is told that a certain contract result is desired or that assurance is needed that an agreement has been properly developed, and he is given the task of helping to shape a solution to the problem. As long as the solution is within the parameters defined by general principles of law, society permits those in business to make rules — small or transactional laws, so to speak — as they see fit. Thus, knowing the shape and location of these parameters becomes very important. Jurisprudence offers insight into the factors that influence these parameters.

A WORKABLE DEFINITION OF LAW

Holmes: Prediction Theory of the Law; Distinction Between Law and Morality

One of the most pragmatic and now generally accepted definitions of law was articulated by Mr. Justice Holmes in "The Path of the Law," *supra* page 3 at 457–61:[2]

> When we study law we are not studying a mystery but a well known profession. We are studying what we shall want in order to appear before judges, or to advise people in such a way as to keep them out of court. The reason why it is a profession, why people will pay lawyers to argue for them or to advise them, is that in societies like ours the command of the public force is intrusted to the judges in certain cases, and the whole power of the state will be put forth, if necessary, to carry out their judgements and decrees. People want to know under what circumstances and how far they will run the risk of coming against what is so much stronger than themselves, and hence it becomes a business to find out when this danger is to be feared. The object of our study, then, is prediction, the prediction of the incidence of the public force through the instrumentality of the courts.
>
> The means of the study are a body of reports, of treatises, and of statutes, in this country and in England, extending back for six hundred years, and now increasing annually by hundreds. In these sibylline leaves are gathered the scattered prophecies of the past upon the cases in which the axe will fall. These are what properly have been called the oracles of the law. Far the most important and pretty nearly the whole meaning of every new effort of legal thought is to make these prophecies more precise, and to generalize them into a thoroughly connected system. . . . It is to make the prophecies easier to be remembered and to be understood that the teachings of the decisions of the past are put into general propositions and gathered into textbooks, or that statutes are passed in a general form. . . .
>
> The first thing for a business-like understanding of the matter is to understand its limits, and therefore I think it desirable at once to point out and dispel a confusion between morality and law, which sometimes rises to the height of conscious theory,

---

2. Copyright © 1897 by the Harvard Law Review Association; reprinted by permission.

and more often and indeed constantly is making trouble in detail without reaching the point of consciousness. You can see very plainly that a bad man has as much reason as a good one for wishing to avoid an encounter with the public force, and therefore you can see the practical importance of the distinciton between morality and law. A man who cares nothing for an ethical rule which is believed and practiced by his neighbors is likely nevertheless to care a good deal to avoid being made to pay money, and will want to keep out of jail if he can.

I take it for granted that no hearer of mine will misinterpret what I have to say as the language of cynicism. The law is the witness and external deposit of our moral life. Its history is the history of the moral development of the race. The practice of it, in spite of popular jests, tends to make good citizens and good men. When I emphasize the difference between law and morals I do so with reference to a single end, that of learning and understanding the law. For that purpose you must definitely master its specific marks, and it is for that that I ask you for the moment to imagine yourselves indifferent to other and greater things. . . .

If you want to know the law and nothing else, you must look at it as a bad man, who cares only for the material consequences which such knowledge enables him to predict, not as a good one, who finds his reasons for conduct, whether inside the law or outside of it, in the vaguer sanctions of conscience. . . .

Take the fundamental question, What constitutes the law? You will find some text writers telling you that it is something different from what is decided by the courts of Massachusetts or England, that it is a system of reason, that it is a deduction from principles of ethics or admitted axioms or what not, which may or may not coincide with the decisions. But if we take the view of our friend the bad man we shall find that he does not care two straws for the axioms or deductions, but that he does want to know what the Massachusetts or English courts are likely to do in fact. I am much of his mind. The prophecies of what the courts will do in fact, and nothing more pretentious, are what I mean by the law.

OBJECTIVES OF LAW

The concept of justice underlies all objectives of law and the legal system. That is, it is expected that all law ought to be fair, evenhanded, and impartial. Of the many other objectives of law, predictability, adaptability to change, and universality are three of the most important.

Justice

Due Process and Fair Trials

At the core of the legal system is the expectation that the law contains an appreciation of the concept of justice. The moral philosopher John Rawls has spoken of the requirement in Rawls, *A Theory of Justice* 238–39 (1971) in the following way:

> Finally, there are those precepts defining the notion of natural justice. These are guidelines intended to preserve the integrity of the judicial process. If laws are directives addressed to rational persons for their guidance, courts must be concerned to apply and to enforce these rules in an appropriate way. A conscientious effort must be made to determine whether an infraction has taken place and to impose the correct penalty. Thus a legal system must make provisions for conducting orderly

trials and hearings; it must contain rules of evidence that guarantee rational procedures of inquiry. While there are variations in these procedures, the rule of law
requires some form of due process: that is, a process reasonably designed to ascertain
the truth, in ways consistent with the other ends of the legal system, as to whether
a violation has taken place and under what circumstances. For example, judges must
be independent and impartial, and no man may judge his own case. Trials must be
fair and open, but not prejudiced by public clamor. The precepts of natural justice
are to insure that the legal order will be impartially and regularly maintained.

People Through Legislation as Authors of Law

The law must seek to promote the general good, and it must obtain support
on the basis of that effort. As the philosopher Jean Jacques Rousseau notes
in Rousseau, *The Social Contract* (Tozer trans.) 40–41 (1967):

> Laws are properly only the conditions of civil associations. The people, being
> subjected to the laws, should be the authors of them; it concerns only the associates
> to determine the conditions of association. But how will they be determined? Will
> it be by a common agreement, by a sudden inspiration? Has the body politic an
> organ for expressing its will? Who will give it the foresight necessary to frame its
> acts and publish them at the outset? Or how shall it declare them in the hour of
> need? How would a blind multitude, which often knows not what it wishes
> because it rarely knows what is good for it, execute of itself an enterprise so great,
> so difficult, as a system of legislation? Of themselves, the people always desire
> what is good, but do not always discern it. The general will is always right, but
> the judgment which guides it is not always enlightened. It must be made to see
> objects as they are, sometimes as they ought to appear; it must be shown the
> good path that it is seeking, and guarded from the seduction of private interests;
> it must be made to observe closely times and places, and to balance the attraction
> of immediate and palpable advantages against the danger of remote and concealed
> evils. Individuals see the good which they reject; the public desire the good which
> they do not see. All alike have need of guides. The former must be compelled to
> conform their wills to their reason; the people must be taught to know what they
> require. Then from the public enlightenment results the union of the understand-
> ing and the will in the social body; and from that the close cooperation of the
> parts, and, lastly, the maximum power of the whole. Hence arises the need of
> a legislator.

Predictability Versus Evolution

Uncertainty and risk tend to go together, and when major decisions are being
made, the prudent person wants the risks to be as low as possible. For
example, a corporation making million dollar decisions wants to know what
the law is; that is, in terms of Holmes's prediction theory of the law, it would
like to predict or forecast with a high level of certainty what the outcome —
success or failure, and if failure, what range of sanction — would be if the
proposed corporate action became the subject of litigation. For similar reasons,
individuals whose personal wealth and liberty could be jeopardized also desire
a high level of predictability or certainty in the law. On the other hand, law
needs to change. The law should be able to evolve as the nation's technology,
demography, and economics change and as its political and social values

shift. This evolution can in some cases be purely additive, as by articulating a new principle to deal with a problem that did not previously exist. The process can also be substitutive, when a principle once viable must be discarded and a new one set in its place. But whether the process of change is the product of legislation or of judicial decree, tension necessarily exists between the dual objectives of predictability and evolution. Society, through its legislators, judges, and juries, must prudently reconcile these highly desirable but conflicting values.

Stare Decisis

Stare decisis is a judicial invention of our Anglo-American legal system that seems to reconcile the objectives of predictability and evolution. The doctrine holds that when a court has laid down a principle of law to govern a particular set of facts, that court and all inferior courts must apply the principle in future cases where the facts are substantially the same. "The doctrine is a salutary one, and should not ordinarily be departed from where the decision is of long standing and rights have been acquired under it, unless considerations of public policy demand it." *Colonial Trust Co.* v. *Flanagan*, 344 Pa. 566, 25 A.2d 728 (1942).

The legal realist Karl Llewellyn has written of stare decisis in Llewellyn, "Some Realism About Realism — Responding to Dean Pound," 44 Harv. L. Rev. 1222, 1252–53 (1931) as follows:[3]

> If (i) the possible inductions from one case or a series of cases — even if these cases really had each a single fixed meaning — are nonetheless not single, but many; and if (ii) the standard authoritative techniques of dealing with precedent range from limiting the case to its narrowest issue on facts and procedure, and even searching the record for a hidden distinguishing fact, all the way to giving it the widest meaning the rule expressed will allow, or even thrusting under it a principle which was not announced in the opinion at all — then the available leeway in interpretation of precedent is (relatively to what the older tradition has consciously conceived) nothing less than huge. And only policy considerations and the facing of policy considerations can justify "interpreting" (making, shaping, drawing conclusions from) the relevant body of precedent in one way or in another. And — the essence of all — stare decisis has in the past been, now is, and must continue to be, a norm of staying put, and a means of staying put. The growth of the past has been achieved by "standing on" the decided cases; rarely by overturning them. Let this be recognized, and that peculiar one of the ways of working with precedent which consists in blinding the eyes to policy loses the fictitious sanctity with which it is now enveloped some of the time: to sit, whenever judges for any reason do not wish to look at policy.

Change is achieved by relying on precedent, even when judicial decisions rest squarely upon stare decisis or the wording of a statute. A judge's latitude in interpreting the statute and in arrangement of the precedent is influenced by a perception of attendant advantages or disadvantages to society.

Considerations of Social Advantage Versus Logic

Once again quoting Holmes, "The Path of the Law," *supra* page 3 at 465–67:[4]

> The training of lawyers is a training in logic. The processes of analogy, discrim-
> ination, and deduction are those in which they are most at home. The language
> of judicial decision is mainly the language of logic. And the logical method and
> form flatter that longing for certainty and for repose which is in every human
> mind, but certainly generally is illusion, and repose is not the destiny of man.
> Behind the logical form lies a judgment as to the relative worth and importance
> of competing legislative grounds, often an inarticulate and unconscious judgment,
> it is true, and yet the very root and nerve of the whole proceeding. You can give
> any conclusion a logical form. You can always imply a condition in a contract.
> But why do you imply it? It is because of some belief as to the practice of the
> community or of a class, or because of some opinion as to policy, or, in short,
> because of some attitude of yours upon a matter not capable of exact quantitative
> measurement, and therefore not capable of founding exact logical conclusions.
> Such matters really are battle grounds where the means do not exist for deter-
> minations that shall be good for all time, and where the decision can do no more
> than embody the preference of a given body in a given time and place. We do
> not realize how large a part of our law is open to reconsideration upon a slight
> change in the habit of the public mind. . . .
>
> I think that the judges themselves have failed adequately to recognize their
> duty of weighing considerations of social advantage. The duty is inevitable, and
> the result of the often proclaimed judicial aversion to deal with such considerations
> is simply to leave the very ground and foundation of judgments inarticulate, and
> often unconscious.

Universality

Another objective of law is that it be universal, that is, that it be applicable
to everyone or to all cases. In regard to the universality of law, consider the
following passage from Boswell, *The Life of Samuel Johnson*, 500–501 (1953):

> I, therefore, return to my original position, that a law, to have its effects, must
> be permanent and stable. It may be said in the language of the schools, *Lex non
> recipit majus et minus*, — we may have a law, or we may have no law, but we
> cannot have half a law. We must either have a rule of action, or be permitted to
> act by discretion and by chance. Deviations from the law must be uniformly
> punished, or no man can be certain . . . he shall be safe.

SCHOOLS OF LEGAL THOUGHT

There is greater agreement among philosophers on the objectives or characteristics of a legal system than there is on its basic nature. There are several
schools of thought regarding the nature of law. The four schools of legal
thought presented here are not mutually exclusive. Rather, they differ in the
aspect of law discussed and the stress or weight given to that aspect in contrast

---

4. Copyright © 1897 by the Harvard Law Review Association; reprinted by permission.

to others. In reading the extracts, it may be useful to recall the Hindu fable of the blind philosophers describing the elephant.[5] Each touched one part of the beast — tusk, trunk, leg, side, and tail — and based his description on what he felt. Their analogies to spears, snakes, trees, walls, and ropes reflected their particular perspectives. No one was clearly wrong, but neither was anyone completely correct. Certainly no one correctly described the totality.

Natural Law

Natural law recognizes the intrinsic relationship that exists between law and justice. Although thought of by many as relevant only in the past, natural law has been resorted to as authority by many recent critics of society. The theory of natural law provides a critical norm external to society against which the desirability of a proposed law or the validity of a law already promulgated can be measured. St. Thomas Aquinas, one of the greatest natural law theorists, defined law as "an ordinance of reason for the common good, made by him who has the care of the community, and promulgated." Aquinas, *Summa Theologica* (Fathers of the Dominican Prov. trans., 2nd ed.) Part II, 8 (1927). The natural law, he continues, "is promulgated by the very fact that God instilled it into man's mind so as to be known by him naturally." *supra.* He continues:

> Since the law is chiefly ordained to the common good, any other precept in regard to some individual work must be devoid of the nature of law, save in so far as it regards the common good. Therefore every law is ordained to the common good. *supra* at 69.

St. Thomas sees that lawmakers in society necessarily have much discretion. Laws can differ from state to state, as rational people often disagree on the most desirable course of action. For the most part, St. Thomas believed that individuals should operate within the legal structure and in conformity with the laws enacted by government. Still, there are times when this law will conflict with a higher law. In such circumstances, according to St. Thomas, *supra* at 69–70:[6]

> Laws framed by man are either just or unjust. If they be just, they have the power of binding in conscience, from the eternal law whence they are derived. . . . Now laws are said to be just, both from the end, when, to wit, they are ordained to the common good — and from their author, that is to say, when the law that is made does not exceed the power of the lawgiver, — and from their form, when, to wit, burdens are laid on the subjects, according to an equality of proportion and with a view to the common good. For, since one man is a part of the community, each man, in all that he is and has, belongs to the community; just as a part, in all that it is, belongs to the whole; wherefore nature inflicts a loss on

---

5. Saxe, "The Blind Men and the Elephant," *J. G. Saxe's Poems* 259 (1876); Rumi, "The Elephant in a Dark Room," *The Spiritual Couplets of Maulana Jalalu-L-Din Muhammad i Rumi* (Whinfield trans.) Book III, Story V, 122 (1887).
6. Reprinted by permission of Burns & Oates Ltd., London.

the part, in order to save the whole; so that on this account, such laws as these, which impose proportionate burdens, are just and binding in conscience, and are legal laws.

On the other hand laws may be unjust in two ways: first, by being contrary to human good, through being opposed to the things mentioned above: — either in respect of the end, as when an authority imposes on his subjects burdensome laws, conducive, not to the common good, but rather to his own cupidity or vainglory; — or in respect of the author, as when a man makes a law that goes beyond the power committed to him; — or in respect of the form, as when burdens are imposed unequally on the community, although with a view to the common good. The like are acts of violence rather than laws; because, as Augustine says a law that is not just, seems to be no law at all. Wherefore such laws do not bind in conscience, except perhaps in order to avoid scandal or disturbance, for which cause a man should even yield his right. . . .

Secondly, laws may be unjust through being opposed to the Divine good: such are the laws of tyrants inducing to idolatry, or to anything else contrary to the Divine law: and laws of this kind must nowise be observed.

The courts and modern jurisprudential thinking had during the nineteenth century almost come to ignore the applicability of the teachings of the great natural law theorists. In more recent times, however, natural law influences have become more apparent. The extermination of the Jews in Nazi Germany under the color of law, compelled many social critics to reappraise their faith in a system of laws based solely on acts of government. In the United States, oppression of minority groups, also under the color of state law, resulted in a call by critics to respond to a higher system of values. Finally, United States involvement in the Vietnam War resulted in a period of civil unrest based on principles of justice and in direct conflict with the laws of the national government. It is not surprising that the concept of natural law has had a prominent position in the philosophy of many recent American leaders, including the Reverend Martin Luther King, Jr., who declared in "Letter from a Birmingham Jail" (April 16, 1963), reprinted in King, *Why We Can't Wait*, 86 (1964):

One may well ask: "How can you advocate breaking some laws and obeying others?" The answer lies in the fact that there are two types of laws: just and unjust. I would be the first to advocate obeying just laws. One has not only a legal but a moral responsibility to disobey unjust laws. I would agree with St. Augustine that "an unjust law is no law at all." . . .

One who breaks an unjust law must do so openly, lovingly . . . and with a willingness to accept the penalty. I submit that an individual who breaks a law that conscience tells him is unjust, and who willingly accepts the penalty of imprisonment in order to arouse the conscience of the community over its injustice, is in reality expressing the highest respect for law.

Positive Law

Another body of legal philosophers, rejecting the applicability of natural law principles, sees law as entirely governed by the rules of a sovereign government. These philosophers, called legal positivists, believe it is the legislature or the judiciary to which the law-making task is fundamentally entrusted. They contend that to follow the idea of natural law would often lead to conflict within society and in some cases render governmental action subject to rejection on individualistic, perhaps arbitrary grounds. A leading exponent of this notion of *nicht positivisches Recht* or "positive law" is Hans Kelsen. He reasoned in Kelsen, *The General Theory of Law and State* (A. Wedberg trans.), 113–15 (1945):[7]

> The system of norms we call a legal order is a system of the dynamic kind. Legal norms are not valid because they themselves or the basic norm have a content the binding force of which is self-evident. They are not valid because of their inherent appeal. Legal norms may have any kind of content. There is no kind of human behavior that, because of its nature, could not be made into a legal duty corresponding to a legal right. The validity of a legal norm cannot be questioned on the ground that its contents are incompatible with some moral or political value. A norm is a valid legal norm by virtue of the fact that it has been created according to a definite rule and by virtue thereof only. The basic norm of a legal order is the postulated ultimate rule according to which the norms of this order are established and annulled, receive and lose their validity. The statement "any man who manufactures or sells alcoholic liquors as beverages shall be punished" is a valid legal norm if it belongs to a certain legal order. This it does if this norm has been created in a definite way ultimately determined by the basic norm of that legal order, and if it has not again been nullified in a definite way, ultimately determined by the same basic norm. . . .
>
> Law is always positive law, and its positivity lies in the fact that it is created and annulled by acts of human beings, thus being independent of morality and similar norm systems. This constitutes the difference between positive law and natural law, which, like morality, is deduced from a presumably self-evident basic norm which is considered to be the expression of the "will of nature" or of "pure reason." The basic norm of a positive legal order is nothing but the fundamental rule according to which the various norms of the order are to be created. It qualifies a certain event as the initial event in the creation of the various legal norms. It is the starting point of a norm-creating process and, thus, has an entirely dynamic character. The particular norms of the legal order cannot be logically deduced from this basic norm, as can the norm "help your neighbor when he needs your help" from the norm "Love your neighbor." They are to be created by a special act of will, not concluded from a premise by an intellectual operation. . . .
>
> The derivation of the norms of a legal order from the basic norm of that order is performed by showing that the particular norms have been created in accordance with the basic norm. To the question why a certain act of coercion — e.g., the fact that one individual deprives another individual of his freedom by putting him in jail — is a legal act, the answer is: because it has been created in conformity with a criminal statute. This statute, finally, receives its validity from the constitution, since it has been established by the competent organ in the way the constitution prescribes.

According to Kelsen then, all law is positive law, for in order to be effective, it must be created and annulled by human acts. A legal norm receives its validity "by virtue of the fact that it has been created according to a definite rule and by virtue thereof only." Its validity, he contends, cannot be questioned on the ground that its contents are incompatible with some moral or political value. Those of a like mind to Kelsen's would severely constrict a judge's ability to interpret what legislative acts and judicial precedent have

---

7. Hans Kelsen, *The General Theory of Law and State*, translated by Anders Wedberg. Copyright 1945 by the President and Fellows of Harvard College, copyright renewed 1973 by Hans Kelsen. (New York: Russell & Russell, 1961). Reprinted by permission.

said. They would clearly proscribe appeal to any authority beyond the Constitution.

Realism

The debate between natural law and positive law has been joined by other schools of legal philosophy. Some legal philosophers, called realists, have placed great emphasis on the process by which legal rules have been applied and developed. The realists contend that the law is no more than what the judge says it is in the case at hand. They argue that judicial precedents do not constitute law, but are mere sources of law that the judges can use, ignore, twist, or even overrule in deciding the case at hand. So also, statutes become law only when and as applied by courts. The realists refrain from considering what judges say they do and focus on the actions themselves.

The Law as Judge-Made Rules

The realists' point of view was put forth in the opening years of this century by the American legal philosopher John Chipman Gray in *The Nature and Sources of Law* 82 (1916):[8]

> The Law of the State or of any organized body of men is composed of the rules which the courts, that is, the judicial organs of that body, lay down for the determination of legal rights and duties. The difference in this matter between contending schools of Jurisprudence arises largely from not distinguishing between the Law and the Sources of the Law. On the one hand, to affirm the existence of *nicht positivisches Recht,* that is declared to be an absurdity; and on the other hand, it is declared to be an absurdity to say that the Law of a great nation means the opinions of half-a-dozen old gentlemen, some of them, conceivably, of very limited intelligence.
>
> The truth is, each party is looking at but one side of the shield. If those half-a-dozen old gentlemen form the highest judicial tribunal of a country, then no rule or principle which they refuse to follow is Law in that country. However desirable, for instance, it may be that a man should be obliged to make gifts which he has promised to make, yet if the courts of a country will not compel him to keep his promise, it is not the Law of the country that promises to make a gift are binding.

Sources of Law

Legal realists do not contend that courts will act in a purely arbitrary manner or without resort to judicial authority. Rather, it is to be expected that courts will observe the authority of sources of law. Again, according to Gray *supra* at 118:[9]

---

8. Reprinted by permission of Peter Smith Publishers, Lexington, MA.
9. Reprinted by permission of Peter Smith Publishers, Lexington, MA.

The power of the rulers of the State or other community in reference to its judicial organs or courts is exercised in a twofold way, — first, by creating them, and secondly, in laying down limits for their action, or, in other words, indicating the sources from which they are to derive the rules which make up the Law. From what *sources* does the State or other community direct its judges to obtain the Law: These sources are defined for the most part in a very vague and general way, but one rule is clear and precise. The State requires that the acts of its legislative organ shall bind the courts and, so far as they go, shall be paramount to all other sources. This may be said to be a necessary consequence from the very conception of an organized community of men.

The other sources from which courts may draw their general rules are four-fold, — judicial precedents, opinions of experts, customs, and principles of morality (using morality as including public policy). Whether there is any precedent, expert opinion, custom, or principle from which a rule can be drawn, and whether a rule shall be drawn accordingly, are questions which, in most communities, are left to the courts themselves; and yet there are probably in every community limits within or beyond which courts may, or, on the other hand, cannot, seek for rules from the sources mentioned, although the limits are not precisely defined.

Gray contends that legislative acts and judicial precedents, often referred to as the law, are merely sources of the law, along with "opinions of experts, customs, and principles of morality (using morality as including public policy)." According to the realists, since law is no more than what the judge says it is in the case at hand, students of the law are advised to study the process by which judges reach their decisions.

Sociological Jurisprudence

Experts who have reported on the process of judicial review say that a judge will probably attempt to balance the often conflicting interests of members of society in reaching a determination. Those who view the function of the law as the balancing of varied interests in society adhere to a school of philosophy entitled sociological jurisprudence. A leading American exponent of this school of thought is the late Judge Learned Hand, who summarized much of his philosophy in Hand, "The Speech of Justice," 29 Harv. L. Rev. 617 (1916).

Judicial Restraint

Much of the law is indeed written in formal shape, the authoritative emanation of the state through agencies to which the judge is confessedly inferior. Beyond the limits of such ambiguity as the words may honestly carry, the judge surely has no duty but to understand, and to bring to his understanding good faith and dutiful acquiescence. For the results he may not justly be held accountable; to hold him is to disregard the social will, which has imposed upon him that very quiescence that prevents the effectuation of his personal notions. There is a hierarchy of power in which the judge stands low; he has no right to divinations of public opinion which run counter to its last formal expressions. *supra* at 617.[10]

---

10. Copyright © 1916 by the Harvard Law Review Association; reprinted by permission.

Law Must Lag Behind the Best Inspiration of Its Time

Two conditions are essential to the realization of justice according to law. The law must have an authority supreme over the will of the individual, and such an authority can arise only from a background of social acquiescence, which gives it the voice of indefinitely greater numbers than those of its expositors. Thus, the law surpasses the deliverances of even the most exalted of its prophets; the momentum of its composite will alone make it effective to coerce the individual and reconcile him to his subservience. The pious traditionalism of the law has its roots in a sound conviction of this necessity; it must be content to lag behind the best inspiration of its time until it feels behind it the weight of such general acceptance as will give sanction to its pretension to unquestioned dictation. Yet with this piety must go a taste for courageous experiment, by which alone the law has been built as we have it, an indubitable structure, organic and living. . . . Only as an articulate organ of the half-understood aspirations of living men, constantly recasting and adapting existing forms, bringing to the high light of expression the dumb impulses of the present, can [the living successors of past lawmakers] continue in the course of the ancestors whom they revere. *supra* page 13 at 618–19.[11]

The Legal Profession as a Mediator

[T]he profession [law] is still drawn, and so far as we can see, will always be drawn, from the propertied class, but other classes have awakened to conscious control of their fate, their demands are vocal which before were dumb, and they will no longer be disregarded. If justice be passable accommodation between the vital and self-conscious interests of society, it has taken on a meaning not known before. But the profession has not yet learned to adapt itself to the change; that most difficult of adjustments has not been made, an understanding of and sympathy with the purposes and ideals of those parts of the common society whose interests are discordant with its own. Yet nothing can be more certain than that its authority as interpreter of customary law must in the end depend upon its power to learn precisely that adaptation. As mediator it must grasp from within the meaning of each phase of social will; it must divine the form of what lies confused and unexpressed and must bring to light the substance of what is half surmised. To adjust and to compromise, to balance and to value, one must first of all learn to know, not from the outside, but as the will knows. This is the condition of the continued high position of the lawyer; without this he must degenerate to a mere rational automation, expounding a barren scholasticism which his society will quickly learn to value at its true worth. *supra* page 13 at 619–20.[12]

While these four contending theories of law are often in conflict, they are not mutually exclusive. For example, some positivists would argue that moral values have a role in legislative, as opposed to judicial, decision making and would not rule out arguments based on natural law in the legislative process of creating positive law. Similarly, while realists are critical of the restrictions positivists attempt to place on the judiciary, they certainly would agree that the written law, as one *source* of law, is essentially positive. Finally, the legal realists and sociological jurisprudents would agree in allowing judges substantial flexibility in their decisions. Thus, the four contending schools of jurisprudence act in a dynamic way. Each has persuasive adherents and each brings a different viewpoint to the law.

PROBLEMS AND QUESTIONS

1. What is Holmes's definition of law?

2. The distinction between law and morality is very important to Holmes. Is he contending that law is not the repository of morality? If not, why does he draw the distinction?

3. Holmes criticizes the tendency of lawyers and judges of his and earlier times to place too heavy a reliance on logic at the expense of "considerations of social advantage." In weighing considerations of social advantage, what types of topics should a judge think about? Are any of Gray's "sources" of the law sensible considerations?

4. Llewellyn contends that respect for precedent should be clearly seen as a way of change as well as a way of refusing to change. For Llewellyn to be correct must decisions be taken literally or must the judge explore their underlying policy?

5. Does judicial restraint include the idea that courts should not overturn constitutional acts of legislatures even if the judge thinks the legislation represents unwise policy?

6. A woman living in Germany in 1942 wished to be rid of her husband. He was a member of a group which aided Jewish families in avoiding the concentration camps. In accordance with then current law, she reported him to the authorities for anti-Nazi activities, knowing it was likely that he would be shot. After the war and the overthrow of the Nazi government, the woman was charged and convicted of the murder of her husband. The problem contains three interrelated questions. First, was it legal to send Jews to concentration camps? Second, was death a legal sanction for thwarting the concentration camp ordinance? Third, is a law valid if it requires one spouse to report another to authorities? How would natural law theorists analyze the issue of whether it was legal to send Jewish families to concentration camps? How would positivists analyze the same issue?

7. How would the role of the judiciary differ under a natural law system and under Kelsen's positive law system? Would a natural law approach by judges necessarily result in flexibility at the expense of all predictability?

8. Mr. Justice Marshall once stated that "this is a constitution we are interpreting." This implies that special considerations are operative when one interprets a constitution. Why should a constitution be interpreted in a manner different from all other laws? Is it because the Constitution is the ultimate norm under which all lesser laws are enacted?

9. Judge Hand stated that the law must lag behind the forces of change in society. Is it necessary then that society place the risk of serious punishment in the path of those, such as the civil rights workers of the 1960s, who refuse to obey laws they feel are immoral or unjust? Does it make any difference whether or not their position is ultimately vindicated?

10. John Chipman Gray states that "no rule or principle which . . . [judges] refuse to follow is law." What, if any, power does a legislature have to keep judges from disregarding rules or principles it thinks should be enforced?

2

THE JUDICIAL PROCESS

THE PROBLEM

The word *law* as it is most commonly used means the rules that define our legal rights and obligations to one another. The bulk of this book will be devoted to discussing this type of law — *substantive law*. For example, we will study the rights and duties of parties to a contract, the obligations of a person who injures another negligently, and the rules governing corporations.

When a transaction sours or parties disagree for other reasons on their rights and duties to each other, they may resort to the courts to settle their substantive rights. A distinct body of law governs the mechanics, or procedure, for settling their dispute. Since the basic principles of *procedural law* are so crucial to understanding how substantive rights are determined, we will devote all of this chapter to them.

Procedural law regulates such questions as where the lawsuit must be brought (jurisdiction and venue); how to compel the defendant to appear in court (service of process); how to notify your opponent and the court of your claims (pleadings); how to prepare for the trial discovery and pretrial conferences; how to choose the members of the jury, present evidence, and persuade the jurors (trial practice); how to appeal a verdict and judgment to a higher court (appellate practice); and how to compel the defendant to submit to the judgment of the court (execution).

We often hear the complaint that a particular case has been decided unjustly due to a legal technicality. Ordinarily, this is intended to mean that the party who should have won on the basis of substantive law has lost the suit because of an error in procedure. Actually, such a result is not as unjust as it seems. Substantive law is intended to ensure justice in each separate litigation, but it presumes the presence of a workable system. Procedural law is designed to make the system operate smoothly and establish a scheme of uniform rules to ensure fair play. Besides encouraging a just resolution of disputes, procedural law also seeks to ensure that disputes are settled speedily, efficiently, inexpensively, and in an orderly manner. These values are almost as important as the merits of a case, since an expensive litigation or one that drags on without end may be just as unfortunate as a ruling that goes against the merits of the case. Order, then, is no mere technicality.

In short, many rules of procedure are designed to promote the ends of efficiency, economy, and dispatch in the litigation process and to achieve a proper balance among the numerous demands made upon the courts by their multiplying case loads. A perpetual dilemma for procedural rulemakers is to devise functioning rules that will be at once general, knowable, efficient, and enforceable and that will at the same time ensure substantive justice in individual cases. These are enormously ambitious objectives, and they frequently fail of attainment.

COURT SYSTEMS

The Federal System

Constitutional Bases

Article III of the United States Constitution provides that the federal judicial power be vested in the *Supreme Court* and such lower courts as Congress establishes. The judicial power extends to all cases arising under the Constitution, the laws, and the treaties of the United States, and the courts have jurisdiction, among other things, over controversies between states and over disputes between citizens of different states.[1] The Supreme Court has *original jurisdiction* — that is, it may conduct trials and other initial proceedings — in specified cases, and this power cannot be removed by Congress.[2] In all other cases, the Supreme Court has jurisdiction to hear appeals, with such exceptions as Congress makes.

Under its constitutional mandate, Congress has instituted several inferior courts, the most important of which are the district courts and the courts of appeals.[3] (See Figure 1 on page 18.)

---

1. Article 1, section 2 provides: "The judicial power shall extend to all cases, in law and equity, arising under this Constitution, the laws of the United States, and Treaties made, or which shall be made, under their Authority; — to all cases affecting Ambassadors, other public ministers and consuls; — to all cases of admiralty and maritime Jurisdiction; — to Controversies between two or more states; — between a State and citizens of another State; between Citizens of different states; — between citizens of the same State claiming lands under grants of different states, and between a State or the Citizens thereof, and foreign states, Citizens or Subjects."

2. Original jurisdiction has two subdivisions, *exclusive* and *nonexclusive*. Instances of exclusive original jurisdiction arise infrequently (e.g., an ambassador is a defendant). Instances of nonexclusive original jurisdiction are numerous but as a policy matter, the Supreme Court refrains from exercising it, requiring the parties to go first to some other court.

3. Congress has also established some courts of specialized jurisdiction, such as the United States Customs Court, which makes determinations under the federal laws relating to customs duties, and the United States Court of Claims, which hears and determines certain claims against the United States. In addition, certain of the federal administrative agencies, such as the Interstate Commerce Commission, perform quasijudicial functions, in that they hear and determine controversies within their particular jurisdiction, subject to review by the courts of appeals.

Figure 1   Federal Judicial System

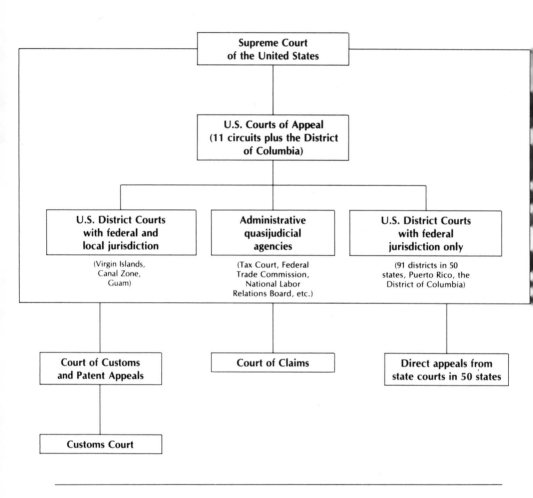

District Courts

Federal district courts have original jurisdiction in cases in which a federal question is involved — that is, where the case is a controversy about and arises under the Constitution, laws, or treaties of the United States. An example is a suit alleging an infringement of a U.S. patent or a violation of federal antitrust laws. District courts also have original jurisdiction in so-called diversity of citizenship cases. These are civil suits (noncriminal actions between private parties) where the matter in controversy exceeds $10,000, exclusive of interest and costs *and* the suit is between either:

1.   Citizens of different states

2.   Citizens of a state and a foreign state (or citizens or subjects of a foreign state)
3.   Citizens of different states, where foreign states or citizens or subjects thereof are additional parties.[4]

Suits must be brought in the proper *venue,* i.e., the district court in the appropriate geographic location. The United States (and the territories) are geographically divided into judicial districts, with each district containing a district court. There is at least one federal district court in each state.

Courts of Appeals

As of October 1, 1981, there were eleven judicial circuits in the United States, each containing a court of appeals. In addition, there is a court of appeals for the District of Columbia. A court of appeals can decide appeals from decisions of the district courts in its circuit and from decisions of the various federal administrative agencies. The losing party in a federal court has an absolute right to appeal decisions to the court of appeals. There is no similar broad right of appeal to the Supreme Court. Therefore, in most federal cases, the courts of appeals are the highest courts reached and make the final determination.

The Supreme Court

The membership of the Supreme Court consists of a chief justice and eight associate justices. Although the Court has some original jurisdiction conferred upon it by the Constitution, the bulk of its cases come up from inferior courts for review. Cases may come to the Supreme Court from the highest state courts as well as from lower federal courts. The Supreme Court retains a large degree of discretion about which appeals it will hear.

By way of summary, the district courts are trial courts where most federal cases originate; the courts of appeals are the appellate courts to which cases may be appealed from the district courts. The Supreme Court is a court of both original and appellate jurisdiction. Its jurisdiction is specified in part by the Constitution and added to by Congress, while the jurisdiction of the other federal courts is established entirely by Congress. The judges of the major federal courts are appointed by the executive branch with the advice and consent of the Senate and serve for life, contingent on good behavior.

---

4. It should be noted that this jurisdiction of the district courts is not exclusive. In other words, the state courts also can take jurisdiction over the controversy, and it is initially up to the plaintiff (the person commencing the suit) to choose the court. If he chooses a state court, the defendant may, within a prescribed time, ask that the suit be removed to the proper federal district court if the case meets the jurisdictional requirements of the federal court. The request is automatically granted.

State Courts

Each state has its own court system, with the complexity of the system depending, in large part, on the size of the state. Every state has separate courts of original jurisdiction for civil and criminal matters. Most states also have courts of limited, specialized jurisdiction, such as probate or surrogate's courts, justice of the peace courts, and family courts. And, of course, all states have higher appellate courts.

By relying on several specialized courts, states are better able to handle the huge volume of varied cases in an orderly manner than they would be using general courts. Also, specialized judges are better able to handle particular types of cases. Figure 2 is perhaps the easiest way to describe a typical state system. Each state's judicial system varies as to the number, name, jurisdiction, and powers of its various courts. Just as in the federal system, the number of the courts at each level increases as one goes down the judicial hierarchy. Fewer appellate courts than trial courts are required since not all cases are appealed and since appeals are less time consuming than trials. Thus there is only one Supreme Court, but many magistrate's courts.

Generally, state courts of original jurisdiction are roughly equivalent to the federal district courts, except that they usually have no monetary or citizenship limitations so long as the controversy has some relation to the state, i.e., one of the parties resides there, or it is the place where important events dealt with in the suit occurred. These general courts might exercise an appellate jurisdiction over some specialized courts of limited jurisdiction, but they are primarily trial courts.

Courts of limited jurisdiction are an extremely important segment of the judiciary because they transact so much of its legal business; these are the courts with which most people come in contact. Examples are the *probate* or *surrogate's* courts, which handle all wills and estates of decedents and cases dealing with guardianship, incompetency, and insanity; and the *small claims* courts, which handle the relatively uncomplicated but numerous cases involving small amounts of money, with limits of, say, $750.

Most state judicial systems include specialized agencies with limited jurisdictional powers. Agencies provide a speedy and efficient method of conflict resolution because of their specialized expertise and informal procedures. The relationship of the state and local agencies to the court system varies widely with the agency purpose and function. A decision of a local zoning board may be reviewed by a low level trial court, while a decision of a state tax board of appeals may go directly to an intermediate appellate court (defined in next paragraph). Finally, in some instances, as with a human rights violation claim, an individual may have the option of filing his claim with the agency or with a court.

In states with a particularly heavy case load, the appellate system might be comparable to the federal appellate system; that is, there may be intermediate appellate courts that serve to reduce the appellate load of the highest court of the state. Usually, appeals from the courts of original jurisdiction to the intermediate appellate courts are a matter of right; as in the federal system,

Figure 2　State Judicial System

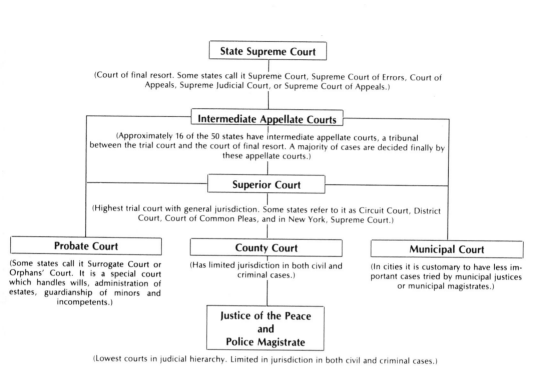

```
                    ┌─────────────────────────┐
                    │   State Supreme Court   │
                    └─────────────────────────┘
```
(Court of final resort. Some states call it Supreme Court, Supreme Court of Errors, Court of Appeals, Supreme Judicial Court, or Supreme Court of Appeals.)

```
              ┌────────────────────────────────────┐
              │    Intermediate Appellate Courts   │
              └────────────────────────────────────┘
```
(Approximately 16 of the 50 states have intermediate appellate courts, a tribunal between the trial court and the court of final resort. A majority of cases are decided finally by these appellate courts.)

```
                    ┌─────────────────────────┐
                    │      Superior Court     │
                    └─────────────────────────┘
```
(Highest trial court with general jurisdiction. Some states refer to it as Circuit Court, District Court, Court of Common Pleas, and in New York, Supreme Court.)

Probate Court	**County Court**	**Municipal Court**
(Some states call it Surrogate Court or Orphans' Court. It is a special court which handles wills, administration of estates, guardianship of minors and incompetents.)	(Has limited jurisdiction in both civil and criminal cases.)	(In cities it is customary to have less important cases tried by municipal justices or municipal magistrates.)

```
                    ┌─────────────────────────┐
                    │  Justice of the Peace   │
                    │          and            │
                    │    Police Magistrate    │
                    └─────────────────────────┘
```
(Lowest courts in judicial hierarchy. Limited in jurisdiction in both civil and criminal cases.)

most appeals terminate at that level. Often, the highest appellate court will have some discretion as to the cases it will accept on appeal, and this power to pick and choose lightens its burden. Its decisions are final, except in those few instances when, because of questions concerning the federal law, review by the United States Supreme Court is possible.

Thus we have two broad systems of courts that function side by side. Although this structure may seem unduly complex, it does break the court system into nearly manageable units. The ideal system for administration has not yet been devised, and many of the courts are badly overworked. Improving court administration continues to be a lively topic of discussion and studies are continually being made to devise new methods for easing delays and improving the quality of justice.

COMMON LAW AND EQUITY

Historical foundations are enormously important in explaining the shape of the judicial process. A good example is the development of the common law.

The Norman conquest of England in 1066 brought a centralization of government, but the Norman political system had not yet developed the concept of law enacted by a legislative body (legislative or statutory law). Centralization of justice was gradually achieved by expanding the jurisdiction and authority of the King's Court. The judges' central court was at Westminster. At the onset, in the twelfth century, there were an insufficient number of cases to justify other permanent court locations. The judges took law to the outlying areas by traveling "on circuit" to various locations throughout the country; cases would accumulate and await the arrival of the King's Court. In deciding the cases, the Court formulated legal principles that were basically founded on the customs and mores of the people. These principles became known as the *common law*. By the thirteenth century a body of common law rules had evolved from these judge-made decisions. Common law is thus judge made and should express the sense of justice of the people as expressed in their customs.

Common law is often contrasted with *statutory law,* a code or body of rules passed by some legislative body of the government. A body of legislative laws covering a particular area may be called a *code,* e.g., the criminal code or the commerical code. The code enacts rules of conduct that are thought by the legislature to be in the public interest.

Another area where history is particularly helpful is in understanding the distinction between common law and *equity,* which still has vitality today. Consider the following excerpt from Berman, *The Nature and Functions of Law,* 70–74 (1958):[5]

> In the majority of civil [as contrasted with criminal] cases, the plaintiff seeks "damages," that is, a money award. . . . However, the plaintiff [might] not [seek] damages but [rather] an injunction, which is a court order directing the person to whom it is addressed to do or . . . to refrain from doing certain acts. A suit for an injunction is called a "suit in equity," as contrasted with an "action at law." To understand what equity is, and in what kinds of cases an injunction is a proper remedy, requires a brief excursion into legal history.
>
> "Equity," derived from the Latin *aequitas,* has a general meaning of equality or justice. In Roman law, especially under the influence of the Christian emperors of Byzantium, equity came also to have the meaning of mercy or fairness, and it was invoked to mitigate the rigors of a strict application of the law. It was in this general sense, also, that the word equity was first used in English law.
>
> In the course of time, however, the word equity came to have a technical meaning in English law different from that which it has in other legal systems, due to the emergence in England of special courts which sat as "courts of equity," whose system of procedure and remedies came to be called "equity," in contradistinction to the system of procedure and remedies of the so-called "common law" courts. In English law and in its offspring, American law, equity came in the course of time to be just as "strict" in many respects as common law.
>
> . . . .
>
> Special "courts of equity" no longer exist in England, and continue to exist in the United States only in a few states. The body of law called equity continues to exist, however, and is administered by the same courts which administer the

---

5. Reprinted by permission of Foundation Press, Inc., publisher.

common law. Thus we have the interesting phenomenon that a judge can do certain things when sitting "in equity" that he cannot properly do when sitting "at common law."

. . . .

The following are some of the more important distinguishing features of the practice of the High Court of Chancery [the special court of equity] which were developed in the 14th and 15th centuries and which continue to distinguish "equity" from "law":

1. The procedure for starting a case in Chancery was more flexible than it was in the royal courts [the common law courts]. To get a case before the royal courts it was necessary to obtain a writ which specified the exact nature of the alleged wrong and to stick to the words of the writ once it was obtained. In Chancery, on the other hand, the action could be originated by a petition in the petitioner's own words, without any requirement of a set definition of the cause of action, and the "bill," as it was called, could easily be amended on trial. Today, under the influence of equity procedure, important reforms have been made in common law procedure, relaxing its earlier rigidity; it remains true, however, that the procedure for obtaining equitable remedies — an injunction, for example — is apt to be more flexible than the usual common law procedure.

2. The system of pleadings in the royal courts was directed toward the formulation by the parties, prior to trial, of a specific issue or a set of specific issues. At the trial the defendant could not be compelled, and was rarely allowed, to testify, and every question of fact was submitted to a jury. In Chancery there was no formal system of pleadings and no jury trial. Issues did not have to be so sharply defined in advance of trial. The trial itself could cover more ground. The parties questioned each other under oath and submitted to questions under oath by the Chancellor. Although both equity and common law procedures have undergone drastic change in 500 years, it remains true in this country that there is no right of trial by jury in equity.

3. The writs issued in cases heard in the royal courts were directed to the sheriff, ordering him to have the defendant in court or to seize the defendant's property in satisfaction of a judgment. The Chancellor's orders and "decrees," on the other hand, were addressed directly to the parties and were backed by his subpoena [sub poena — "under penalty"]. Disobedience to a decree of the Chancellor was treated as contempt of the King, making the contemner a rebel. The contempt power of the Chancellor was especially important. In a time when sheriffs were apt to be too corrupt or too weak to bring into court the wealthy and lawless men who, in the words of the House of Commons in 1382, "are like kings in the country, so that justice can be done to none." The power of the equity court to order the defendent to do or not to do certain acts, under penalty of contempt of court, remains its principal distinguishing feature.

4. The Chancellor's Court, because it could compel obedience directly from the parties, had available a wide range of remedies which the royal courts could not administer. Chancery could adjust its decrees to all the circumstances of the case, and could extend its supervision of a matter over a period of time. For example, it could order a trustee to spend money entrusted to him in a particular way and to report periodically to the Chancellor, whereas the royal courts could not issue an "injunction" but could only award damages. Similarly, equity could order a recalcitrant seller of land or goods to deliver them to the buyer, and could, in general, in proper cases, command "specific performance" of a contract, whereas the royal courts would only award damages.

. . . .

Many other examples could be given of how the Chancellor would take jurisdiction in cases in which the royal courts would not give the kind of relief which in conscience the plaintiff should have. Thus equity became a supplementary system of Justice. The chancery court did not have a general jurisdiction over all kinds of disputes; it acted — and equity continues to act — in those cases where "the legal remedy is inadequate."

   . . . .

   In the 19th century the existence of a dual system of national courts was subjected to sharp criticism as hindering justice; also many felt that the advantages of equity procedure ought to be available not only in "suits in equity" but also in "actions at law." As a result there took place in all but a few states of the United States as well as in England a so-called "merger" of law and equity. The same judges administer both. Yet in the minds of lawyers and judges the two systems are kept distinct. An injunction, for example, is "an equitable remedy," and rules of equity — that is, rules first developed in the Court of Chancery before its abolition — are applied to it. It will be granted only if the petitioner shows that there is no adequate remedy at law available to him and that without injunctive relief he will suffer an irreparable injury. Furthermore, the petitioner must show that the granting of the injunction (or other equitable relief) will result in substantial justice.

The influence of the two separate systems has persisted also in regard to trial by jury. If a dispute brought today is one which would have been brought in equity, it will in all likelihood be heard by the judge alone, without a jury, whether in a federal or a state court.

PROCEDURES BEFORE THE TRIAL

Introduction

Having discussed in general terms the two court systems in the United States, and having looked quickly at the distinction between the common law and equity, we are now ready to consider the actual process of *litigating*, or conducting a case. The foregoing material was designed to give you a general background and understanding of certain legal terminology and the court systems. It will help you to understand the following discussion of how an individual case proceeds from beginning to end.

   Initially, of course, when legal problems arise, you contact a lawyer. The lawyer analyzes the factual situation and decides if you have a legal cause of action (or are facing one). In other words, the lawyer tells you whether you have a claim that might be enforced by the courts or whether someone might have a claim against you. Unless you have a legal basis to support your actions, there is no point in considering litigation.

   Even if your attorney indicates that you have a legal cause of action, there may still be compelling reasons for not going to court. A lawsuit is an imperfect remedy. American courts aim to restore the winner of a suit to the position held prior to the wrong, to make one whole, but they seldom succeed. If a person is hurt in an automobile accident and proves all the elements necessary to win the case, a sum of money is recovered that in theory should restore that person to the financial position occupied before the accident. Actually, however, the award will not include either the amount of the injured party's attorney fees (which may be up to a third of the award in negligence cases) or such other costs as the fees paid to expert witnesses who testified at the trial or the cost of printing the record of the trial for purposes of appeal. These expenses must be deducted from the damage award, and the remainder is the real amount recovered. In a suit to recover unpaid salary or commissions, a plaintiff will suffer a similar loss.

The theory in contract cases is that the injured party should be awarded a sum of money representing the value of the broken bargain, but, again, the award omits lawyer's fees, suit costs, and recompense for time lost in preparing and proving the case. Often this last factor is the most important, since litigation tends to be quite lengthy. Other factors which might dissuade a prospective plaintiff from litigating are emotional wear and tear, the burden of proving a case sufficiently to ensure victory, and the inconvenience caused by the time or location of an action.

After considering all the above factors, you and your attorney may still decide to go to court and begin the process of litigation. This does not mean that your case will immediately go to trial, however; several steps must be taken first. Procedural rules vary among court systems; we will be considering a representative model that may not correspond with any system in every detail, but that is fairly close to the federal one.

Service of Process

Establishing Jurisdiction

The first step in initiating legal proceedings is the *service of process.* Service of process means delivering a *summons* to the defendant, calling upon him to meet you in court. In many states the summons is prepared by the lawyer, merely by filling out a form purchased in blank from a legal stationer.[6] In the federal courts the clerk of the court issues the summons upon the filing of the complaint. (We will discuss the complaint below.) Figure 3 shows a sample summons. Note that it contains the name of the person who is suing (called the *plaintiff*) and the name of the person being sued (the *defendant*).

The purpose of the summons is to notify the defendant that a lawsuit has been started against him and by whom; this notice gives the court jurisdiction (power) over the person of the defendant. Jurisdiction is profoundly important. Unless the court obtains jurisdiction over the defendant, it has no power to try the case or to enter any judgment against the defendant. As we shall see shortly, there is more to jurisdiction than simply service of process, but proper service is essential.

In most cases, the summons must be delivered to the defendant personally. Meeting this requirement might involve considerable ingenuity, and service incognito is by no means rare. There are limits to what a court will permit in process serving, but generally if the defendant is not tricked into the geographical jurisdiction of a court, devious means of physically serving the process are upheld, so long as it is evident that the defendant was aware he was being served a summons.

---

6. Most states require that the pleadings be filed in the court prior to service.

Figure 3   Sample Summons

Court of the State of Colorado
Boulder County

A.B.,
     Plaintiff

    v.   summons

C.D.,
     Defendant

TO THE ABOVE-NAMED DEFENDANT:
  You are hereby summoned to answer the complaint in this action and to
serve a copy of your answer on the plaintiff's attorney within twenty days
after the service of this summons, exclusive of the day of service. In case of
your failure to answer, judgment will be taken against you by default for the
relief demanded in the complaint.

  Dated _____   X.Y.,
                                         Attorney for Plaintiff
                                         Address
                                         Boulder, Colorado

Gumperz v. Hofmann

Supreme Court of New York, Appellate Division, 1936. 245 App. Div. 622, 283 N.Y. Supp. 823 (1st Dep't 1935), aff'd, 271 N.Y. 544

[Defendant was a physician who lived in Buenos Aires. He was staying at a hotel
in New York City. Service was made upon him as follows: the process server
called defendant and claimed to be a doctor, with a letter from the president of
the New York County Medical Society which had to be personally delivered to
defendant. They arranged to meet in the lobby of the hotel. When defendant
arrived he was served with the summons. The trial court disallowed this service
upon the grounds that it was fraudulent. The appellate court reversed and said
service was valid.]

UNTERMYER, J.

We think that legal as well as practical considerations preponderate in favor of the
rule that service is not to be invalidated merely because secured by a deception
practiced on the defendant, which, in no true sense, was injurious to him. It
may fairly be said that there is a duty upon persons within the jurisdiction to
submit to the service of process. Although that duty is not legally enforceable, it
is, broadly speaking, nonetheless an obligation which ought not to be evaded by
a defendant upon whom service is attempted. The deception here was, therefore,
practiced for the purpose, and had only the effect, of inducing the defendant to
do that which in any event he should voluntarily have done.

  We cannot fail to be aware of the difficulties which beset the server of the
process on a defendant who is unwilling to be served, for it is evident that if he
discloses his intentions, such a defendant is likely to be even more inaccessible
than before. For that reason alone we should hesitate to surround the service of
process with unnecessary limitations. Needless to say, we do not approve of
misstatements made to procure service of process, but, except where the

defendant has been lured into the jurisdiction, we think the service is separable from these. Where real injury ensues, the person who is responsible may be held liable for damages in a civil suit. In a proper case he may even be prosecuted criminally. We do not need to go further by holding that service otherwise valid is vitiated on account of a misstatement by which it was procured.

Jurisdiction over Nonresidents

Proper service of process is a necessary but not a sufficient element to give the court jurisdiction over the person of the defendant. Not every person is subject to the jurisdiction of a particular court. If the prospective defendant lives outside the state in which the court sits, he must have some connection with the state in order for the court to have jurisdiction over him. Unless there are justifying circumstances, a state may not reach beyond its borders to impose its powers. It would be unfair to expose a defendant to a suit in a remote and inconvenient state unless that state had some strong connection with the parties or the subject of the litigation. Nevertheless, in the last few decades the trend of the law has been to allow state and federal courts more power to render judgments against nonresidents. This has come about by a continual expansion of the list of connections or contacts with a state that will serve as a basis for jurisdiction.[7]

An example of this trend is the so-called long-arm motor vehicle statute. Suppose that a Colorado man visiting in Nebraska is involved in an automobile accident with a pedestrian. Early in this century, the Nebraska pedestrian would not have been able to serve process in a Nebraska court once the Colorado man had returned home. But under the Nebraska long-arm statute he can now do so. Typically, the defendant will be notified of the action by registered letter and, if he fails to defend himself in the Nebraska court, the court may enter a judgment against him just as if he had been served personally in Nebraska and failed to respond. The Nebraska judgment will be sent to Colorado to be enforced against the motorist. The Supreme Court of the United States has upheld the constitutionality of these long-arm statutes by saying that if a state has "minimum contacts" with a nonresident person or corporation, it may subject him to personal judgments.

Conflict of Laws

Where a person of one state is involved in a legal dispute with a resident of another state, it is necessary to know which state's laws govern the suit because the laws are often different. For example, just because the case is being tried in a Nebraska court is not sufficient reason to use Nebraska law.

---

7. A corporation, even though chartered outside a state, may be served personally in a state if it has certain minimum contacts, such as soliciting and completing sales within the state.

Courts of one state often apply the law of another state in disputes before them. Determination of which law to apply depends on the facts of each case and on the principles of the body of law called *conflict of laws*, a complex and specialized set of legal principles beyond the scope of this book. (For limited additional discussion concerning contracts see page 241.) It is sufficient to note that care must be taken to know exactly what state's laws will apply to a transaction.

In Personam Jurisdiction

The question of jurisdiction over the person of the defendant is important, as we have said, because it allows the court to enter a judgment that will bind the defendant. This judgment can be enforced against the defendant or his property anywhere in the United States, since other state courts will generally give "full faith and credit" to a state court's determination and issue an order to enforce the judgment. Because it may be enforced against all assets of the defendant, it is known as a *judgment in personam*.

In Rem Jurisdiction

However, even though a court lacks jurisdiction to render a judgment over the defendant personally, either because he has had no contacts with the state or because he was not served properly, it may render a judgment affecting his property located within the state, exercising jurisdiction *in rem*. The way to obtain a valid judgment against the defendant's property located within the state is usually to bring it within the jurisdiction of the court by a sheriff serving a *writ of attachment* on the person who has physical possession of the property. Because it is assumed that the defendant will be aware of this attachment, personal service is generally not necessary. The defendant may be notified of the action by a published notice in a newspaper. This is known as *service by publication*. A judgment against the defendant in an attachment case may be enforced only against the particular property attached.

Jurisdiction: Trends and Implications

As business increasingly overruns state lines and firms have numerous contacts with many states, the basis of personal jurisdiction expands and the risks of suit away from the home office constantly increase. It becomes more difficult to estimate in which states the company could be susceptible to suit and hence which state laws must be complied with. Everyone concerned with the management of an enterprise must be alert to this problem of potential liability in various states. Keeping all the physical assets at home is not sufficient security. Vigilance and skilled legal counsel are essential if the laws of all the pertinent states are to be complied with and serious difficulties avoided.

Jurisdiction and the Relevant Law: Why the Complexity?

The existence of a federal system in the United States greatly complicates American law. Instead of a single law of corporations, or agency, or partnership, there are fifty sets of laws. Sometimes there are only two rules — majority and minority — but it is still necessary to find out which one your state follows.

Even the conflicts rules by which states decide whether to apply their own law or the law of another state vary between states. For example, if an accident occurred in state A between two citizens of state B (husband and wife) on vacation in state A, state A may apply A's law on whether a wife can sue her husband, while state B may apply B's law. The outcome of the suit would depend on the state where suit was brought.

The federal system adds complexity to obtaining jurisdiction over a defendant. Convenience and fairness to the defendant were not the major considerations under older rules. Long-arm statutes, discussed above, have made jurisdiction easier to obtain in some states, but state lines are still crucial to jurisdictional questions.

In an age when transactions are often nationwide and businesspeople generally behave as though state lines did not exist, why are we still confined by a federal system devised when communications moved no faster than post horses? What defenses of the federal system can you make? Consider Professor Hart's comments in Hart, "The Relations Between State and Federal Law," 54 Col. L. Rev. 489, 493, 539–40 (1954):[8]

> We could have, in principle, a perfect uniformity of law in the United States — at a price. . . . So Procrustean a solution of the problems of federalism is unlikely to find wide favor. Wholly apart from the natural inertia of institutions, one can discern two major reasons why this is so. The first is the workaday reason of administrative feasibility. . . . The second reason is more basic. Common sense and the instinct for freedom alike can be counted upon to tell the American people never to put all their eggs of hope from governmental problem-solving in one governmental basket. . . . The federal system has the immense advantage of providing forty-eight separate centers for experimentation. . . . [with] novel techniques of social control.

Pleadings

Pleadings are written documents that set forth the claims and contentions of each party as to the facts and the points of law in dispute. They serve the purpose of acquainting the court and the parties with the facts in dispute and giving reasonable notice to each disputant of the other's case.

The Complaint

The *complaint* informs the court and the defendant of the factual contentions upon which the plaintiff rests his claim. The lawyer states the facts to show

---

8. Reprinted by permission of the *Columbia Law Review*.

convincingly that the plaintiff is entitled to the relief he seeks. In most states, no special form is required, and the complaint need only include a short and plain statement of the claim and the prayer for relief. This last part of the complaint sets forth the remedy to which the plaintiff claims he is entitled. The most common remedy is money damage, but sometimes some form of equitable remedy, such as injunction, is demanded.

Figure 4 shows a sample complaint taken from the Federal Rules of Civil Procedure.

The Answer

Denials. We noted above that the plaintiff usually encloses a copy of the complaint with the summons served on the defendant. The defendant is then given a certain amount of time, usually twenty days, in which to respond to the complaint by means of an *answer*. He might deny each and every allegation of the complaint, called a *general denial*, or might attack only certain facts contained in specific allegations, in a *specific denial*. If the defendant fails to deny any particular allegation, the effect is the same as if he had expressly admitted it. He will not be allowed to contest the allegation during the course of the trial. The defendant may also state that he is in doubt as to whether a particular fact is true. This is equivalent to a denial.

Affirmative Defenses. Besides denying the specific allegations of the complaint, the answer may also contain affirmative defense. An *affirmative defense* consists of facts not indicated in the complaint that serve to defeat the plaintiff's claim.

Figure 4   Sample Complaint

COMPLAINT ON A PROMISSORY NOTE

1. Allegation of jurisdiction.
2. Defendant on or about June 1, 1981, executed and delivered to plaintiff a promissory note whereby defendant promised to pay to plaintiff or order on June 1, 1982, the sum of ten thousand dollars with interest thereon at the rate of eighteen percent per annum.
3. Defendant owes to plaintiff the amount of said note and interest.
4. Wherefore plaintiff demands judgment against defendant for the sum of ten thousand dollars, interest, and costs.

Signed: _____
        Attorney for Plaintiff

Address: _____

An example of an affirmative defense is the *statute of limitations*. Most legal actions must be brought into court within a specified period of time after the alleged offense occurred. For example, an action on a contract right might have to be brought within six years from the time the breach of contract occurred. If an action is brought after the time period set by law, a defendant could assert in his answer that the action did not meet the statute of limitations requirement. The plaintiff's cause of action would fail, and the action would be dismissed. The purpose of this statute is to protect persons from being brought into court after evidence has been lost, witnesses have died, or claims forgotten.

If the defense attorney fails to include an affirmative defense in the answer, the defendant may lose the right to use that defense even though it would have been good if raised. The defense is said to be *waived*. The possibility of inadvertent waiver reemphasizes the necessity of careful and thorough pleading.

The plaintiff need not respond to the affirmative defense. All affirmative defenses are treated as automatically denied by the plaintiff. At the trial, the plaintiff may introduce evidence to defeat the defense. For example, the plaintiff might show that the statute of limitations had not expired because defendant had been out of the state and was not accessible for a law suit.

Counterclaims. In his answer, the defendant may also introduce a *counterclaim*. This is an independent claim that could have been raised by the defendant in a suit of his own initiation against the plaintiff. Usually, a counterclaim is somehow related to the plaintiff's claim, but this is not necessary. The only real requirement is that it could have been the subject of an independent suit between the defendant and plaintiff. For example, suppose plaintiff sues defendant for breach of contract. Defendant may counterclaim for personal injury received by the defendant in an automobile accident caused by the plaintiff.

If the defendant raises a counterclaim, the plaintiff must respond with a *reply*, which serves the same function as the defendant's answer; it must admit or deny the allegations of the counterclaim or raise some affirmative defense. The defendant need not answer the reply; like the affirmative defense, it is considered denied.

The Demurrer or Motion to Dismiss

Instead of attempting to dispute the factual issues raised by the plaintiff, the defendant may wish to challenge the sufficiency of the complaint on a point of law. Although this could be done in the answer, the more direct way is in a *demurrer* or *motion to dismiss*. This is a motion asking the judge to dismiss the complaint.

The complaint might be legally deficient because the court lacks jurisdiction to hear the case. Lack of jurisdiction is such a fundamental defect in the plaintiff's case that it cannot be waived. Thus, even if the defense attorney neglects to move to dismiss or to raise the issue in the answer, the matter may be raised at any time during the trial or even on appeal.

The complaint can also be deficient because plaintiff has not stated a cause of action. Assume that the complaint alleges that defendant scowled at plaintiff. Even if this were proved conclusively, there is no legal remedy available to plaintiff. The defendant would demur or move to dismiss, and the judge would dismiss the action.

If the complaint is potentially good, the judge will overrule the motion to dismiss and give the defendant time to file an answer.

Amendments

In recent years, courts have become more lenient regarding pleading practice. Courts will allow amendments to pleadings in order to correct omissions and errors, such as failure to raise appropriate defenses. This attitude rests on the philosophy that courts should seek if at all possible to decide cases on their underlying merits, and on the principle that procedural errors should not bring disaster. In certain circumstances, because of prejudice to the other party, amendment will be forbidden. Thus, even though some pleading oversights can be repaired, a good lawyer will be very careful in drafting his pleadings.

Default Judgments

If the defendant fails to respond defensively to the plaintiff's complaint and he is within the jurisdiction of the court, the plaintiff is entitled to a *default judgment* because his case went uncontested. If the plaintiff had asked for a definite amount of money, the judgment against the defendant can simply be entered by the court clerk. If, however, the amount of the damage is not certain, a hearing is held before a judge and the extent of damage determined. In either case, a binding judgment will be entered, which can be enforced against the defendant.

Discovery

Although the pleadings and preliminary motions have all been filed and disposed of, we still are not ready to begin the trial. There are several other pretrial procedures that must be considered.

One rather important group of pretrial procedures is called *discovery*. Discovery is a method by which one litigant is able to obtain from his adversary information and evidence that will be useful in preparing for the trial. The purpose of discovery is to eliminate time-consuming proof of matters that are not really in dispute, to sharpen and define the issues framed by the pleadings, and to prevent surprise tactics that cause parties to be caught off guard. It is an attempt to ensure that the outcome of the case will depend on the merits of the issue and not upon the cleverness of counsel.

Depositions

One particularly important discovery device — in which you are quite likely to become involved at some time — is the *deposition* or *examination before trial.* With this device, either party may examine the adverse party or a witness under oath in advance of trial. The deposition of the adverse party serves the function of discovering new evidence and checking into the factual foundation of the opponent's case in order to eliminate surprise at the trial. Depositions of witnesses also serve this purpose, but their primary function is to preserve testimony, and they can be entered into the evidence if the witness is not available. All depositions may be used during the trial to show discrepancies between two versions of the witness's or party's story.

Interrogatories

Interrogatories, another discovery device, are written questions that one party presents to the adversary, who must then answer them in writing or explain his inability to do so. In theory, interrogatories enable a party to gather information essential to the preparation of his case but within the particular knowledge of his adversary. Naturally the parties frequently disagree as to whether the information requested is essential. Recipients of questions frequently suspect the askers of engaging in fishing expeditions and of attempting to inflict costly and time-consuming burdens. The courts are increasingly being called on to resolve such disputes.

Subpoenas

The examining party can compel the attendance of an individual at an examination before trial by service of a *subpoena,* a written order to appear and give testimony at a specified time and place. Documents and other important papers can also be inspected, either independently or concurrently with the taking of a deposition. Production of documents can be compelled by service of a *subpoena duces tecum.* Both the subpoena and the·subpoena duces tecum are court orders, enforceable by contempt of court penalties such as fine or imprisonment for failure to comply.

Other Mechanisms

A party may also examine physically or mentally the other party before trial in an action where such condition is in controversy. For example, the plaintiff in a personal injury action may be ordered to submit to a physical examination of his injuries if the defendant is not sure of their nature and extent.

Another device, the *notice to admit,* is used to eliminate the necessity of proving factual matters not truly in dispute. If the party upon whom such notice is served unreasonably refuses to admit the matter, he may be forced to bear the cost of proving it at the trial.

The Pretrial Conference

A relatively recent pretrial device is the *pretrial conference,* composed of the judge and the attorneys in the case. This is an informal get-together in which the lawyers and the judges discuss the facts in dispute and the points of law to be involved. Issues are clarified, and frequently the parties decide to settle the case before actually going to trial. Even when that is not the result, by achieving a greater understanding of the issues, the parties are better able to conduct the litigation effectively and quickly.

At the close of the pretrial conference, the judge dictates a statement consisting of facts admitted, any amendments to the pleadings, issues eliminated, and steps agreed on. This procedure is said to lead to shorter trials and often generates out-of-court settlements. However, the effectiveness of the pretrial conference depends entirely on the cooperation of the lawyers and the judge. No agreements can be compelled. There are no rules or requirements; thus there is a maximum degree of flexibility.

Summary Judgments

If there is no genuine issue of fact in dispute, there is no need to go through the time and expense of a trial. Therefore, either party may make a *motion for summary judgment* before the trial commences. He should submit any written proof he needs to support his contention that a trial is unnecessary. If the judge believes that no genuine issue of fact exists, he will grant the motion and award judgment to the party who has made the motion. The party against whom the motion is granted may appeal the motion. A judge is wary in granting this motion.

It is apparent that the pretrial period is much more complicated and involved than the average layman would suspect. The primary aim of all the various pleadings, discovery devices, motions, and conferences, is to clarify, simplify, and expedite the trial, or to avoid it entirely. This objective is both commendable and quite necessary in view of the overcrowded calendars of most courts today. The role of the attorney is not only to safeguard and advance the interests of his client but also to promote the efficient and unprejudiced administration of justice by cooperating with the judge and other lawyers.

THE TRIAL

Introduction

When we have finally completed all the pretrial procedures, our case is ready for trial. It is placed on the calendar of the court and called for trial as soon as preceding cases are disposed of. Unfortunately, most court calendars are so crowded that there is often a wait of several months. This long delay is another reason we may not want to go through the entire litigation process. When we do, however, we go through the following steps.

The purpose of the trial is to settle the issues of fact raised in the pretrial stage. In general, this is the function of the jury. The jury watches the proceedings, listens to testimony, scrutinizes material items of proof, and reaches its conclusions as to the truth of each side's allegations. However, in equity cases (see page 23), the judge hears the case without a jury, and he decides the issues of fact. In cases where the plaintiff seeks a money judgment or seeks to recover his property, he has a right to a jury trial on the issues of fact. However, if a plaintiff sues to enjoin the defendant from doing certain acts or to reform a contract, which are suits in equity, the issues of fact will be resolved by the judge alone. In any case, even where there is a right to trial by jury, both parties may agree to waive that right and have the case heard by the judge.

In all cases, issues of law are decided by the judge alone. *Issues of law* are questions of interpretation of legal rules rather than interpretation of evidence. For example, it is up to the judge to decide whether a particular item of proof is admissible as evidence.

Selecting a Jury

The list of prospective jurors, or the *jury panel,* is selected at random, usually from the voter registration list, in an effort to obtain an impartial cross-section of the community. It is from this list that the jury is chosen. At the beginning of the trial the court bailiff draws out twelve names by lot (some jurisdictions require only six jurors), and these people take their place in the jury box. Each lawyer (or, in some courts, the judge) then questions the individual jurors as to their qualifications to serve. This is known as the *voir dire* (to speak the truth) examination. If, for example, a juror is closely related to a party in the case, or is employed by him, or has his mind already made up, the opposing attorney can *challenge* the juror *for cause* and the juror will be excused by the judge. Another juror is called to fill his place, and she or he too is examined.

In addition to challenges for cause, each side is allowed a small number (usually three) of *peremptory challenges.* These require no justification. The attorney simply objects to the juror who is excused by the judge. Peremptory challenges are used when the attorney suspects subtle or hidden prejudices that might harm his case.

Once the twelve jurors are selected, the attorneys ready their opening statements.

Opening Statements

The purpose of the opening statements is to explain to the jury what the case is about. The plaintiff's lawyer goes first, stating the issues and what he expects to prove. The defendant's lawyer follows with a similar statement. Neither statement is intended to produce evidence; rather, the purpose is to assist the jury in understanding and evaluating the evidence later produced.

Introduction of Evidence

Each side must now produce its evidence to prove its contentions as to the truth. Because he has the burden of proving that the defendant has wronged him, the plaintiff introduces his case first. After the close of the plaintiff's case, the defendant must produce his evidence. Then, in most courts, the plaintiff has a chance to introduce evidence he did not bring in during his first presentation.

Each witness called may be questioned by both parties. Suppose the plaintiff calls a witness. He will question him first to bring out the witness's story in the *direct examination*. In order to discredit the witness and to bring out possible errors in his testimony, the defendant then *cross-examines* the witness. If the cross-examination has been damaging, the plaintiff will then question the witness once again to restore the believability of the testimony. This is known as the *re-direct examination*.

The most important thing to remember about the introduction of evidence is that not all items of evidence are admissible in a particular trial. The rules of evidence are too intricate and mechanical to go into in detail, but let us examine a few general principles.

Because a trial is an adversarial proceeding, it is up to the attorneys for each side to safeguard the interests of that side. The judge acts only as an impartial umpire. If an attorney believes that evidence being introduced by the other side should not be admitted, he must object to its presentation. The judge will then rule as to its admissibility. If he rules that the evidence may be admitted, it becomes part of the proof in the case and may be considered by the jury in their determination of the facts. If he declares that the evidence is inadmissible, then it is excluded from the case and the jury may not consider it. They are told not to allow it to have any bearing on their decision as to the facts. Of course, lawyers do not object to every bit of inadmissible evidence, partly to save time and partly to avoid making a bad impression on the jury.

Although we shall not examine any of the technical rules of evidence, we should mention the rule of *relevance*. We noted above that the pleadings set up the framework of the case. All evidence must pertain to the claims established in the pleadings. Evidence will be admitted only if it is relevant, that is, only if it has some bearing on the facts disputed in the case. Suppose that John Smith sues Tom Jones for defamation. John claims that Tom made false and malicious statements about him, calling him a coward. Tom contends that he never did so. At the trial, John seeks to introduce evidence showing that Tom had said similar things about other people in the past. This is probably relevant, since it goes to prove that Tom has a tendency to make defamatory statements. But suppose that John seeks to introduce evidence showing that Tom beats his wife. This is probably irrelevant and therefore inadmissible, because, even if true, it would not help prove John's case. Such irrelevant evidence would confuse the issues, unduly prejudice the jury, and waste the court's time. Therefore, it is irrelevant and inadmissible.

After the presentation of all the evidence and the completion of all proof by both sides, the attorneys for each side make a *closing argument* to the jury. This argument is designed to be persuasive, stressing the strong points of each side's case, but the attorneys must, of course, deal only with the evidence introduced in the case.

The Judge's Charge

After the closing arguments, the case goes to the jury for deliberation. In order to guide the jury in their consideration, the judge delivers an *instruction* or *charge* just before they begin deliberating.[9] The judge instructs the jury as to the legal principles they must apply to the facts as they construe them. He also instructs them as to the alternative verdicts they may reach.

The Verdict

The jury will retire after the judge's charge to deliberate the case and decide on which verdict, of those called for by the judge, they will bring in. The verdict may be general or special. With a *general verdict*, the most common, the jury simply determines the case in favor of one of the parties and, if for the plaintiff, assesses his damages. A *special verdict*, on the other hand, does not decide in favor of a party. When the judge asks for a special verdict, he presents the jury with a list of questions of fact for their determination. On the basis of the jury's responses to these questions, the judge then decides which party shall receive judgment. Even if the judge asks for a general verdict, he may ask the jury to answer specific questions of fact.

The verdict must be unanimous in criminal cases, but many states allow less than unanimous agreement in civil suits (e.g., a 5/6 rule). When the judge receives the jury's verdict, he pronounces judgment. The precise wording of

---

9. The opposing lawyers often draft the charges and the judge picks and chooses among these.

this judgment is usually prepared by the winning attorney and submitted to the court.

Motions During and After the Trial

Mistrial

During and after the trial, there are several motions either party may make asking for a particular outcome for the case. During the trial either party may make a *motion for a mistrial*. The moving party claims that some improper conduct has occurred during the trial and that therefore the trial has been unfair. Showing that a juror had been bribed or that improper evidence had been introduced which was so prejudicial that a jury could not disregard it even if instructed to do so (such as the fact that the defendant in an accident case was insured) will be grounds to dismiss the case then and there. A retrial, of course, may be scheduled.

Directed Verdict

A *directed verdict* can be asked by the defendant at the close of the plaintiff's case or by either party at the close of all the evidence. This motion asks that the court direct the jury to bring in a verdict in favor of the party making the motion. The judge then examines the evidence introduced. If it is so over-whelmingly in favor of the moving party that no reasonable jury could find otherwise, the judge may direct the verdict. In effect, there is nothing for the jury to decide — it must agree with the judge's opinion. If the motion is denied, the case will be submitted to the jury as usual; if the motion is granted, the losing party may, or course, appeal.

Nonsuit

In a case heard by the judge alone, the defendant may make a *motion of nonsuit* at the close of the plaintiff's evidence. This motion is similar to the one for directed verdict, except that there is no jury. It simply asks the judge to dismiss the case because the plaintiff's case is so very weak that it would be unreasonable to award him victory. The case may be dismissed with prejudice, meaning that the plaintiff cannot bring another suit. Of course, the dismissal may be appealed. Or the judge may feel that the deficiency in proof can be corrected and dismiss without prejudice, allowing the plaintiff to sue again on the same claim. If the nonsuit motion is denied, the trial continues.

Judgment Notwithstanding the Verdict

There are two motions available to the party against whom a verdict has been rendered: the *motion for judgment notwithstanding the verdict* and the *motion for a new trial*.

The motion for judgment notwithstanding the verdict (also called *judgment n.o.v.*) is similar to the motion for directed verdict. The moving party asks the judge to throw out the jury's verdict because it is wholly unreasonable in light of the evidence introduced in the case. In effect, he says that the jury's decision was unjustifiable. If the judge grants the motion, he will enter judgment for the moving party despite the fact that the jury has decided the other way. Since this is a final decision (with prejudice), it may be appealed.

Because of the similarity in grounds, it is quite likely that where a judgment n.o.v. is requested, a motion for directed verdict has already been denied. One might ask why the moving party is given another chance. Two reasons are given as a matter of practicality: first, the judge has had more time to consider the evidence, whereas he is quite rushed at the earlier stage of the trial; second, denying the motion for a directed verdict may save the time and expense of a retrial. If the judge had directed a verdict earlier and then been reversed on appeal, a new trial would be necessary in order for a jury to have an opportunity to consider the case. However, if he grants judgment n.o.v. and is reversed on appeal, all that is necessary is reinstatement of the original verdict of the jury. A cautious judge will therefore prefer to await a motion for judgment n.o.v.

New Trial

The motion for a new trial is used more frequently. The judge may grant a new trial (with another jury) if the verdict is against the weight of the evidence, rather than being completely unjustifiable. In this instance, reasonable men could disagree on the evidence, so the use of the directed verdict or judgment n.o.v. is improper, but the judge feels the jury reached the wrong result. The judge may also grant the motion for a new trial on other grounds: because the damages awarded are excessive or inadequate, or because errors were committed during the trial, or because newly discovered evidence appears, or simply in the interests of justice. In sum, the trial judge has very broad discretionary powers to grant a new trial.

Judgment

Assuming that there has been no mistrial and no new trial is granted, judgment is entered. The *judgment*, signed by the judge or his clerk, is simply a formal document prepared by the winning lawyer and stating the net result of the case. It grants or denies a remedy and also assigns the burden of *costs*, which are the procedural expenses of litigation. These do not include attorney's fees.

EXECUTION

The judgment grants or denies a remedy, but it does not carry the remedy into effect. As soon as the judgment is filed in the office of the clerk of the court, it becomes a *lien* on any real estate owned within the jurisdiction of the court. If the judgment is not otherwise satisfied, the sheriff can sell the land to satisfy it. The defendant might voluntarily obey the judgment. However, if he does not, the plaintiff must have the judgment executed or carried out. A *writ of execution* is a paper issued by the clerk of the court that directs the sheriff to seize and publicly sell the property of the defendant and turn the proceeds over to the plaintiff in order to satisfy the judgment. Also, the wages of the defendant may be *garnished* by the plaintiff, meaning that the defendant's employer is directed to pay over a certain percentage of the defendant's wages to plaintiff. The federal Wage Garnishment Act and most state laws impose a limit on the percentage of wages that may be garnished, but the reserved salary is modest.[10]

If the defendant conceals his property or tries to take it out of the state, the plaintiff may resort to *supplementary proceedings*. The court will order the defendant to appear and testify concerning his assets, liabilities, and any possible transfers of his property to friends or relatives. If the court decides that the defendant does have property, it will order him to pay. If he still refuses, he will be ruled in contempt of court and jailed until he complies.

Note that in every state certain kinds of property are exempt from execution. These usually are necessaries such as clothes, tools of trade, necessary articles of household furniture, and war pensions.

In many cases, the plaintiff will be justifiably concerned that the defendant may be considering concealing his property or removing it from the jurisdiction or otherwise evading execution. He then will apply to the court for a *provisional remedy*. These may be used at any time — before, during, or after the suit — to ensure that there will be property around to satisfy the judgment.

The *injunction* is an example of provisional remedy. It should not be confused with the decree of injunction at the end of an equity case. It is only temporary and does not have anything to do with the merits of the case. The plaintiff must present to the judge an affidavit showing that speed is imperative and the damage done without an injunction would otherwise be uncorrectable. The plaintiff must post a bond to compensate the defendant for any injuries he may suffer if the subsequent hearing shows the plaintiff was not actually entitled to the injunction.

Despite the availability of provisional remedies, there are still many instances of unsatisfied judgments. These result largely because the defendant has insufficient assets to cover the judgment. Such asset-poor defendants are termed *judgment proof* because no judgment can be satisfied by them. A de-

---

10. Until July 1, 1970, garnishment was governed exclusively by state law, which varied greatly. However, in 1970 the first federal law on wage garnishments became effective as a part of the Consumer-Creditor Protection Law, popularly known as the Truth-in-Lending Law. Pursuant to federal law, the amount of weekly wages subject to garnishment was limited to the lesser of 25 percent of the disposable earnings of the debtor or the amount by which the weekly disposable earnings exceeded 30 times the hourly wage. In the event state garnishment law is more favorable to the debtor or is substantially the same as federal law, the state can be exempted from coverage by the federal law.

fendant who is judgment proof at the time a judgment is declared, but later has sufficient assets, is subject to a later execution, since the judgment is usually good for a number of years. However, bankruptcy of the defendant will sometimes defeat all past judgment claims, and even if he later amasses a fortune, these will not be available for execution.

RES JUDICATA

Res judicata ("a matter adjudged") means, basically, that those issues already settled shall not be raised again. A judgment finally and conclusively settles the controversy between the parties. If the same cause of action is brought up in a second suit between the same parties, no new trial on the merits will be allowed. If the same parties are involved in a second suit concerning a *different* cause of action, the judgment in the first suit is binding for all issues decided in the first suit.

Suppose that, in suit one, A sues B for breach of contract and wins; the jury decides that there was a valid contract in existence and that B did not perform as he should have. Judgment is entered for A. B now sues A, claiming that there never was a contract. Because this issue was decided in the first case, it may not be raised anew in a new trial. Suppose, however, that the first case ended in a mistrial because of a serious procedural error. If so, no issues were decided on their merits. Therefore, every issue may be raised in a second suit. Res judicata will not apply unless the first suit, and the issues therein, were decided on the merits.

Generally speaking, the only way to challenge a judgment validly made by a court with jurisdiction is by *direct attack* — that is, either to appeal, to make a *motion to vacate* (set the judgment aside) addressed to the trial court itself, or to file a separate action in another court seeking to enjoin enforcement of the judgment on the ground that it was fraudulently obtained. As we have seen, commencement of a second suit will not work. Moreover, the judgment is binding on other states and the federal courts as well. Searching for a friendlier court will not work either.

APPEALS

After judgment has been entered, the losing party may, if he chooses, appeal the judgment to a higher court. The reasons for allowing appeals are two. First, they help achieve uniformity in the law. The decisions of the highest court in the state have a binding effect on all lower courts in that state and must be followed. On the other hand, lower court decisions need not be followed in other cases in other courts of the same level. Thus, one lower court judge may declare that the rule is A, while another may say it is B, another C, and so on. If decisions are made by the higher court, however, these will bind all lower courts and the rules of law will be uniform in all the courts of the state on matters decided by the highest court. The second reason to allow appeals is that greater skill and knowledge can be brought to bear on the case. Appellate courts have three or more judges, as opposed to the single trial court judge, and they are usually more experienced and often more qualified. Furthermore, they are less rushed than trial judges and have time to discuss among themselves how the case should be decided. Most legal innovations are made by appellate courts for these reasons; trial judges feel they have neither the time nor the overview to make major changes in the law.

Some of the more common grounds for appeal are: the admission of evidence that should have been barred or the rejection of evidence that should have been admitted; an improper charge to the jury; too large or too small an award of damages; a verdict that is not supported by the evidence. Two rules must be remembered. For an error of the trial court to be reversible on appeal, it must have prejudicial or harmful effects to the complaining party: it must have had some effect on the outcome of the case. Harmless errors are not grounds for overturning the decision. Secondly, the error, with few exceptions, must have been made by the judge. Appeals are not granted on the basis of mistakes by jury or counsel. Also, the error must have been called to the attention of the trial judge by an objection or by a motion, and the judge must have had an opportunity to consider the possible error.

Appeals are not new trials. They are oral arguments of law (old issues of fact are not reargued) before the appellate judges. The judges have before them copies of the pleadings, verdict, judgment, and trial testimony, as well as written briefs prepared by counsel. The decision of the appellate court will either affirm, reverse, or modify the judgment below. At times the appellate court will order a new trial.

CRIMINAL LAW PROCEDURE VERSUS CIVIL

Introduction

Criminal procedure is not the same as the civil processes we have been discussing. Although we will not study criminal law in this book, we should note some basic differences between civil and criminal procedures. First, a criminal action is always brought by the state against a criminal defendant and is started by an arrest. Even if there has been a victim of the crime, that person is not the plaintiff. At most, the victim brings the offense to the attention of the authorities and testifies at the trial. The action is brought only by the state because the offense is considered to be against society (represented by the state), rather than just against the victim. The victim may have a civil case for the same wrongful act.

The Grand Jury

For major crimes (felonies), prosecution is usually begun by an indictment issued by the grand jury. The district attorney brings complaints concerning crimes to the attention of the *grand jury* (to be distinguished from the jury, which actually tries cases), which, after hearing the evidence, may bring in an *indictment*. This does not decide whether the defendant is guilty or innocent. It merely indicates that the grand jury believes the evidence strong enough to warrant a trial. In states that do not have a grand jury procedure or require only an indictment for felonies, the prosecution is started by an *information*, a written accusation made by the public prosecutor, generally after a magistrate's examination of the defendant or a set of alleged facts.

The criminal trial proceeds in the same manner as a civil trial, except that the accused cannot be compelled to testify, although he may do so voluntarily. Since the state must prove guilt beyond a reasonable doubt, a much heavier burden than that in a civil suit, the jury's verdict must be unanimous in most cases.

Double Jeopardy

Instead of res judicata, criminal trials have the *double jeopardy* rule, meaning that a defendant cannot be tried twice for the same offense by the same state. Moreover, in the great majority of states, if a defendant is found not guilty by the jury, the state may not appeal this verdict. Only the defendant may appeal a criminal verdict.

Plea Bargaining

A controversial area of growing importance in the criminal law is *plea bargaining*. Here a person charged with a crime, not a major crime such as murder or rape, bargains with the district attorney either to reduce the charges to a lesser degree of wrong or to drop some of the charges in exchange for agreeing to plead guilty. Either the attorney for the accused or the district attorney may initiate the plea bargaining. From the standpoint of the accused, the risk of a greater penalty is avoided. As for the district attorney, whose office is probably swamped with cases, plea bargaining provides a method of quickly disposing of lesser cases in order to concentrate on the more important ones.

Let's consider an illustration. Mark Rudd, who was the leader of the 1968 student revolt at Columbia University, after spending seven years in hiding, surrendered himself in October 1977. Rudd had five misdemeanor charges outstanding against him. His attorney had plea bargained to have all but one dropped. When Rudd appeared in court the judge asked him if he understood that in pleading guilty he was giving up his right to a trial and the opportunity to confront witnesses against him. Mr. Rudd walked out of criminal court a free man after having pleaded guilty to just one charge on criminal trespassing. The sentence was suspended.

CRITICISM OF THE JURY SYSTEM

Our system of jury trials is not universally cherished. Several critics have declared that it should be discarded in civil cases. It is true that jury cases take more time than cases heard by a judge alone — sometimes three times as long. Time is consumed in selection of jurors, opening and closing statements, and antics intended to influence the jury. Also, jury trials are more expensive. Moreover, the process of reaching the verdict has been criticized. Juries are said to disregard the judge's instructions and make their own determinations as to the legal rules. Allegedly jurors on occasion decide the case on the basis of their partiality toward one lawyer and disfavor toward the other or on their own prejudices. On the other hand, the judge has prejudices, too. At least the jury contains a minimum of six and usually twelve people whose prejudices may counteract one another, while there is nobody to counteract the judge's. A recent discussion of several of these issues is found in the following case.

Memorex Corp. v. Int'l. Bus. Mach. Corp.
United States District Court, Northern District of California, 1978. 458 F. Supp. 423

[Memorex and ILC Peripherals sued IBM alleging the latter monopolized various markets in the computer industry. After five months of trial and after the jury reported itself deadlocked, the court declared a mistrial. The court granted IBM's motion for a directed verdict and ordered that, in the event of a remand for retrial, Memorex's jury demand be stricken. The court's discussion follows:]

The trial lasted for five months and consumed 96 trial days. The parties called 87 witnesses whose testimony filled more than 19,000 pages of transcript. More than 2,300 exhibits were admitted into evidence. After deliberating for 19 days, the jury reported itself hopelessly deadlocked, and the court declared a mistrial.
. . . .

The Seventh Amendment to the United States Constitution preserves the right of trial by jury "[i]n Suits at common law, where the value in controversy shall exceed twenty dollars." In England and in the federal courts in the United States until 1938, there was a clear division between law and equity. This situation changed with the adoption of the Federal Rules of Civil Procedure. In *Ross v. Bernard*, 395 U.S. 531, 539–40 (1970), the Supreme Court said:

> Under the Rules there is only one action — a "civil action" — in which all claims may be joined and all remedies are available. . . . Under the Rules, law and equity are procedurally combined; nothing turns now upon the form of the action or the procedural devices by which the parties happen to come before the court.

The Court indicated that "[t]he Seventh Amendment question depends on the nature of the issue to be tried rather than the character of the overall action." The Court continued in a footnote:

> As our cases indicate, the "legal" nature of an issue is determined by considering, first, the pre-merger custom with reference to such questions; second, the remedy sought; and third, the practical abilities and limitations of juries.

. . . The remedy sought by Memorex for IBM's alleged antitrust violations is damages which has traditionally been regarded as a legal remedy. It is the third factor of the equation, the practical abilities and limitations of jurors, that causes the court to conclude that the issues in this case must be considered to be equitable.
. . . .

Throughout the trial, the court felt that the jury was having trouble grasping the concepts that were being discussed by the expert witnesses, most of whom had doctorate degrees in their specialties. This perception was confirmed when the court questioned the jurors during the course of their deliberations and after they were discharged. When asked by the court whether a case of this type should be tried to a jury, the foreman of the jury said, "If you can find a jury that's both a computer technician, a lawyer, an economist, knows all about that stuff, yes, I think you could have a qualified jury, but we don't know anything about that." Several of the other jurors indicated that they thought that the major stumbling block was the requirement that the verdict be unanimous. When they were questioned after the trial, most of the jurors indicated that they thought a complex antitrust case like this one should be tried to the court.

The parties initially estimated that the trial of this case would last ten months. Because the hardship that such a long trial would impose on the jurors was obvious, a special pool of 175 prospective jurors was called in for this case. After excuses, there were only 29 candidates remaining from which to select 14 jurors. The 11 jurors to whom this case was submitted probably represented a random cross-section of people in the community who could afford to spend ten months serving on a jury, but it is open to question whether they were a true cross-section of the community. The six men and five women on the jury ranged in age from 32 years to 65 years, with the majority over 50. Several of the jurors were housewives, one was retired, and those who were employed worked at jobs where they could be replaced, but where neither their jobs nor their incomes were in jeopardy. Only one of the jurors had even limited technical education. While the court was appreciative of the effort they put into deciding the case, it is understandable that people with such backgrounds would have trouble applying concepts like cross-elasticity of supply and demand, market share and market power, reverse engineering, product interface manipulation, discriminatory pricing, barriers to entry, exclusionary leasing, entrepreneurial subsidiaries, subordinated debentures, stock options, modeling, and etc.

An additional consideration which the court feels warrants discussion is the burden that cases of this type impose upon the judicial system. The trial of this case occupied the time of the court and its staff almost exclusively for seven months. Because of the estimated length of the trial, the court went off the new case assignment wheel for its duration, thereby increasing the work load of the other courts and personnel of the Northern District. In addition, the jury expenses (borne by the government in this case) amounted to more than $32,000. All of this time and expense went for naught when the court was forced to declare a mistrial.

When a trial is by jury rather than to the court, there is the possibility that no decision will be made. In this case, a second trial by jury could very easily suffer the same fate as the first because the composition of the jury will not change significantly. . . .

For the reasons indicated above, the court hereby finds that the magnitude and complexity of the present lawsuit render it, as a whole, beyond the ability and competency of any jury to understand and decide rationally, and orders, in the event of a remand for retrial, that Memorex's jury demand be stricken. The jury was originally conceived as a protective shield between the litigants and the danger of an arbitrary decision by the sovereign. It would be a subversion of this ideal to insist upon submitting a case to a jury when there is a substantial risk that its decision will be arbitrary.

ARBITRATION

Arbitration is a voluntary process of resolving disputes. In some types of disagreements, it has replaced the use of the judicial process; in other areas, it presents an increasingly attractive alternative. Excluding personal injury cases, it is estimated that more than 70 percent of the legal disputes between private persons are now decided through arbitration rather than in court. It is the accepted procedure in labor-management disputes and is popular in the construction industry. About half the states have statutes making commercial agreements to submit an existing dispute to arbitration enforceable in court, and nearly a third more have laws that provide for agreements to arbitrate future disputes.

Arbitration is a relatively informal procedure. Generally, a contract will stipulate that the parties agree to submit disputes about certain matters to an arbitration board and outline who will do the arbitration and what general body of law they should follow. It is claimed that, compared with court proceedings, arbitration has the advantages of speed — there are no appeals — informality, convenience, economy, and privacy. It is also said to be preferred because it shuns technical rules of evidence and procedure and promotes sounder fact-finding, particularly in those complex issues where special expertise is required. It is thought by some to produce decisions more in accord with popular conceptions of justice. On the other hand, some observers see arbitration as a lawless and unreliable process, sacrificing fair and orderly adjudication for quick, informal decisions, often based on an unreasoned compromise. Undoubtedly, the truth lies somewhere between. Arbitration is quicker and cheaper, but it has neither the safeguards nor the predictability of judicial proceedings.

Generally, an agreement to submit a dispute arising under a contract to arbitration must be in writing. Often the writing will be found in the fine print on purchase orders, sale confirmations, and similar documents. Careful scrutiny of such papers is necessary in order to avoid committing oneself to unwanted arbitration. Failure to disavow the arbitration clause may result in the undesired consequence of having to submit disputes to a designated arbitration board.

Not all types of disputes are appropriate for settlement by arbitration. Many states restrict the procedure to controversies that might be the subject of court actions. This would bar arbitration of an agreement, for example, which provided that the sale price of the property in question would be in an amount set by a particular third person. In some industries, arbitration has become the standard method of settling disputes, and the industrial arbitration boards have developed their own body of predictable law. Usually, however, the decision to agree to arbitration will involve a tradeoff between the speed and economy of the technique against the greater predictability of a court of law. This is a business decision so closely intertwined with legal problems that legal advice may be advisable before an arbitration contract is signed.

PROBLEMS AND QUESTIONS

1. State courts are obligated to enforce federal rights — including constitutional rights — just as the federal courts do. Does this mean that Congress could fail to create any lower federal courts and rely on state courts for enforcement of federal rights? Do the federal courts have an additional function that only they can perform?

2. Is it true that any really big case, say, one that involves damages for $50 million, has a chance for final review by the United States Supreme Court?

3. The Supreme Court of the United States ruled in 1977 that lawyers could not be barred from advertising their services. Do you think that members of a profession should be allowed to advertise? Will this help you find an attorney when you need one? Will the least able attorneys, perhaps being the shortest of clients, place the largest ads? To what extent should the states regulate attorneys' advertising?

4. In what areas is uniformity in state laws important? Which is more important, uniformity in contract, divorce, or negligence law? Why? How can uniformity be achieved where needed? Do you think it feasible to persuade states to adopt uniform laws? Is federal legislation that preempts state law in certain areas a solution?

5. The plaintiff advertised in a Boston newspaper for a salesman to cover its New England territory. Defendant, a resident of Massachusetts, traveled to Albany, New York, at plaintiff's request and expense in response to the ad. There, they reached an agreement. Defendant worked in the New England area for four years, based from his home in Massachusetts. Upon termination of the relationship plaintiff sued defendant for alleged breaches of contract, seeking jurisdiction over defendant in New York State because the contract had been made in New York. Is there a basis for New York to have jurisdiction? Could Massachusetts have jurisdiction? What would be the grounds upon which any such jurisdiction would rest?

6. Chief Justice Burger has commented on the misuse of pretrial proceedings, which he has termed one of the great developments in the last forty years. Pretrial procedures may be used excessively and lengthen litigation; in effect a case must be tried twice, pretrial and again in the court room. Some attorneys file a suit and then take depositions just to determine whether there is a basis for the lawsuit. Excessive pretrial discovery procedures can be used as a weapon against a financially weak opponent. Consider these criticisms and discuss the benefits of pretrial procedures. Do the positives outweigh the negatives?

7. We rely on the adversary system for reaching the truth in most types of trials. We assume that having opposing lawyers present and develop the evidence that supports their respective contentions will give the factfinder — judge or jury — the fullest picture of what actually happened and provide the best basis for a correct decision. Is this a fair assumption if one advocate is far more skilled at presenting evidence or appealing to the jury's emotions than the other? If some or all of the jurors are unable to remember, understand, and evaluate the evidence or the law? What is the lawyer's role in the adversary system? Is he more correctly described as a partisan or an officer of the court?

8. Is it fair that a party is foreclosed from relitigating a cause of action? For example, if an accident victim sues and recovers $200 medical expenses and later discovers a bad whiplash, he cannot relitigate the issue of damages. In some cases the interest in having the dispute settled one way or the other can be very strong — for example, in determining who has title to a piece of land and can build on it. Is the interest in a negligence case that compelling? Is possible harassment of the defendant an explanation for res judicata? Judicial efficiency?

9. Do you think that the pressure on the district attorney from understaffing, short budget, and large backlog of cases, is a valid reason for quick disposal of cases by plea bargaining? What areas of potential abuse do you see? Obviously judges and district attorneys will differ in their views on plea bargaining and the leniency in applying it. Could you foresee some real jockeying by an attorney with a particular district attorney to have his accused client come before a judge who believes in compromise?

10. In many courts the bulk of trial work involves the auto accident, an action in alleged negligence. A jury trial generally at least doubles the time of trial compared to a trial without a jury. Great Britain has basically done away with the jury system for civil cases. Why should we not abolish the jury system in the United States for civil cases, or at least for negligence cases?

11. Can jurors forget damaging evidence just because they are told to do so? It is well known that juries may temper harsh laws in criminal cases by refusing to convict clearly guilty people; this is widely considered one of the benefits of the jury system. Does similar nullification have any place in civil cases? For example, juries tend to favor certain classes of plaintiffs, and will often give larger damage awards if they suspect the defendant has insurance. It is very difficult to challenge improper jury proceedings. What are the arguments in favor of the jury? Against?

12. The Federal judicial system is initiating an experiment in three federal district courts to encourage arbitration of civil disputes and to determine the benefits to the litigants. Do you feel that arbitration would deny you your right to trial? If the arbitrator was a specialist in the area in which he heard cases, might not such a procedure lead to more uniform and better decisions? Do you see any dangers in the arbitration proposal?

13. Law does not just regulate actual disputes. As Professor Llewellyn said:

> [Law] ceases to function merely as a last resort machine to take care of disputes that by no other

means work out to settlement, and becomes indirectly but potentially a factor in regulating what people *do, before* disputes, how people actually go about their ordinary business and, at times, even, where there are legal prohibitions, what business people go about. (Llewellyn, *Bramble Bush* 22 (1960).

Thus you will work with your lawyer in structuring transactions to accomplish what you want to do with minimal legal complications.

a.   Does criminal law have a similar structuring effect on conduct?

b.   Does law also structure behavior when a dispute has come up and an out-of-court settlement is being negotiated?

14.   Professor Llewellyn argues that when a lawyer seeks to predict what the courts will do when faced with a specific problem he should look at what courts do as well as what they say they do (*Id.* at 14).

a.   Is the uncertainty implicit in this description of the legal process more upsetting to the lawyer working out the tax aspects of a merger or to the citizen who is trying to avoid illegal conduct?

b.   Are the exact provisions of the law more influential on a citizen's activities in some situations than others?

15.   Based on your reading of Chapters 1 and 2 do you tentatively agree with all or any parts of the following quote from Alexis de Tocqueville, 1 *Democracy in America,* Ch. 16:

> In America there are no nobles or literary men, and the people are apt to mistrust the wealthy; lawyers consequently form the highest political class and the most cultivated portion of society. They have therefore nothing to gain by innovation, which adds a conservative interest to their natural taste for public order.
>
> If I were asked where I place the American aristocracy, I should reply without hesitation that it is not among the rich, who are united by no common tie, but that it occupies the judicial bench and the bar.
>
> The more we reflect upon all that occurs in the United States, the more we shall be persuaded that the lawyers, as a body, form the most powerful, if not the only, counterpoise to the democratic element. In that country we easily perceive how the legal profession is qualified by its attributes, and even by its faults, to neutralize the vices inherent in popular government. When the American people are intoxicated by passion or carried away by the impetuosity of their ideas, they are checked and stopped by the almost invisible influence of their legal counselors. These secretly oppose their aristocratic propensities to the nation's democratic instincts, their superstitious attachment to what is old to its love of novelty, their narrow views to its immense designs, and their habitual procrastination to its ardent impatience.

II

TORTS

3: Personal Injuries

INTRODUCTION

Nature and Complexity

Tort law is concerned with the array of injuries that are byproducts of a complex society. These include areas as different as motor vehicle collisions, industrial injuries, harm from defective products, fist fights, defamations, invasions of privacy, and regulation of business competition, among others.[1] In many of these situations, the victim claims that another member of the society should be forced to pay for losses the victim has sustained. These claims require the judicial system to determine whether to honor the victim's claim or to tell the victim that he or she must bear the losses alone with no help from the law. This group of decisions constitutes the *law of torts.* In each case the court must decide whether to thrust liability on a person who has not consented in advance to bear the victim's loss. This lack of consensual undertaking is what distinguishes tort law from contract law. Indeed, in most tort cases the parties have never met before the harm occurred and are not likely to meet again. The law is dealing with an unfortunate byproduct of our multiple daily interactions.

As you have observed, tort law goes beyond physical injuries and protects such other interests as reputation, privacy, and fair competition. Although these areas are all important in tort law, we are going to limit our discussion and consideration to the problems posed by physical injuries to persons, for several reasons. First, tort law is involved with a vast network of situations covering a great sweep of human life and experience. Any effort to cover all of it — even cursorily — would be difficult and would produce a very lengthy document. Focusing on one area permits

3

PERSONAL INJURIES

---

1. The same wrongful act may give rise to two actions at law. For example, the fist fight will constitute criminal assault and at the same time give rise to a civil assault action for damages. Many torts (by definition a civil wrong) are so antisocial as to constitute crimes, civil and criminal negligence. A crime, after all, is an action against some person or company that is so antisocial as to be deemed an offense against the state, such as theft.

in-depth coverage of at least one facet. Second, the chosen area is quantitatively the most significant current problem in tort law — as well as one of the most challenging intellectually. One word of warning is appropriate, however: each area of tort law has its own historical background, its own concepts and approaches. The exploration we are about to undertake suggests how tort problems are approached, but you should not assume that the law of defamation, for example, uses the same concepts or terms or analyses as physical injury cases.

Intentional Injury

Even the category we have called physical injuries is too broad for convenient handling. A line is often drawn between physical injuries intentionally caused and those unintentionally caused. The intentional aggressor is antisocial in spirit, as well as destructive in result. The attempt to control such conduct must have been one of the imperatives of the earliest legal systems. Thus, it should come as no surprise to learn that without some justification (such as self-defense), one who intentionally inflicts physical injury on another must pay for the harm he has done. (Virtually all murders and assaults create potential tort liability, but such cases are rarely brought because of the defendant's financial condition — though in some states public funds may be used to help victims of crime.) The question of what justifications are acceptable may sometimes present troublesome issues, as in the following case.

Katko v. Briney
Supreme Court of Iowa, 1971. 183 N.W.2d 657

[Defendants, husband and wife, had inherited a farmhouse. Since the couple already had a dwelling place, they left the farmhouse uninhabited. The farmhouse became the scene of several burglaries; antiques and glass jars were taken. Although the defendants reported these losses to the sheriff and posted "no trespassing" signs, the entries continued. Defendants finally decided to set a spring gun in the inner bedroom of the house. To be hit an intruder would have to break into some other room of the house and would then have to try to get into the bedroom. When the intruder opened that door, a spring on the gun would be released and it would fire at his legs. One night the plaintiff did break into the house and tried the bedroom door. The gun went off striking him in the leg and causing serious permanent injuries. The plaintiff pleaded guilty to a charge of larceny in the nighttime of property of less than $20 value. He was fined $50 and costs and paroled during good behavior from a 60-day jail sentence. Plaintiff then sued the defendants on the theory that they intentionally caused his injuries. The defendants argued that they were legally privileged to engage in their behavior. The jury awarded the plaintiff $20,000 for actual, or compensatory, damages and an additional $10,000 in punitive damages. The defendants appealed.]

MOORE, CHIEF JUSTICE.

. . . .

   The main thrust of defendants' defense in the trial court and on this appeal is that "the law permits use of a spring gun in a dwelling or warehouse for the purpose of preventing the unlawful entry of a burglar or thief." They repeated this contention in their exceptions to the trial court's instructions 2, 5 and 6. They took no exception to the trial court's statement of the issues or to other instructions.

In the statement of issues the trial court stated plaintiff and his companion committed a felony when they broke and entered defendants' house. In instruction 2 the court referred to the early case history of the use of spring guns and stated under the law their use was prohibited except to prevent the commission of felonies of violence where human life is in danger. The instruction included a statement that breaking and entering is not a felony of violence.

Instruction 5 stated: "You are hereby instructed that one may use reasonable force in the protection of his property, but such right is subject to the qualification that one may not use such means of force as will take human life or inflict great bodily injury. Such is the rule even though the injured party is a trespasser and is in violation of the law himself."

Instruction 6 stated: "An owner of premises is prohibited from willfully or intentionally injuring a trespasser by means of force that either takes life or inflicts great bodily injury; and therefore a person owning a premise is prohibited from setting out 'spring guns' and like dangerous devices which will likely take life or inflict great bodily injury, for the purpose of harming trespassers. The fact that the trespasser may be acting in violation of the law does not change the rule. The only time when such conduct of setting a 'spring gun' or a like dangerous device is justified would be when the trespasser was committing a felony of violence or a felony punishable by death, or where the trespasser was endangering human life by his act."

. . . .

The overwhelming weight of authority, both textbook and case law, supports the trial court's statement of the applicable principles of law.

Prosser on *Torts*, Third Edition, pages 116–118, states:

> . . . the law has always placed a higher value upon human safety than upon mere rights in property, it is the accepted rule that there is no privilege to use any force calculated to cause death or serious bodily injury to repel the threat to land or chattels, unless there is also such a threat to the defendant's personal safety as to justify a self-defense. . . . spring guns and other man-killing devices are not justifiable against a mere trespasser, or even a petty thief. They are privileged only against those upon whom the landowner, if he were present in person would be free to inflict injury of the same kind.

. . . .

In *Hooker* v. *Miller*, 37 Iowa 613, we held defendant vineyard owner liable for damages resulting from a spring gun shot although plaintiff was a trespasser and there to steal grapes. At pages 614, 615, this statement is made: "This court has held that a mere trespass against property other than a dwelling is not a sufficient justification to authorize the use of a deadly weapon by the owner in its defense; and that if death results in such a case it will be murder, though the killing be actually necessary to prevent the trespass. *The State* v. *Vance*, 17 Iowa 138." . . .

. . . .

The legal principles stated by the trial court in instruction 2, 5 and 6 are well established and supported by the authorities cited and quoted supra. . . .

. . . .

We express no opinion as to whether punitive damages are allowable in this type of case. If defendants' attorneys wanted that issue decided it was their duty to raise it in the trial court.

The rule is well established that we will not consider a contention not raised in the trial court. In other words we are a court of review and will not consider a contention raised for the first time in this court.

. . . .

. . . When malice is shown or when a defendant acted with wanton and reckless disregard of the rights of others, punitive damages may be allowed as punishment to the defendant and as a deterrent to others. Although not meant to compensate a plaintiff, the result is to increase his recovery. He is the fortuitous beneficiary of such an award simply because there is no one else to receive it.

The jury's findings of fact including a finding that defendants acted with malice and wanton and reckless disregard, as required for an allowance of punitive or exemplary damages, are supported by substantial evidence. We are bound thereby.

. . . .

Study and careful consideration of defendants' contentions on appeal reveal no reversible error.

Affirmed.

All Justices concur except LARSON, J., who dissents.

The complexity of tort law becomes apparent when we realize that in a single judgment the court is doing two distinct things: it is taking money from a defendant and giving that money to a plaintiff. When both results are justifiable, tort law functions smoothly. But if only one of the two results is thought warranted, tensions develop. Does this help your analysis of *Katko*? Does this dual analysis help you with a case in which an innocent plaintiff is hurt by a defendant who reasonably, but mistakenly, believed that the plaintiff was about to injure the defendant and hit the plaintiff in what he thought was self-defense?

Our focus shifts now to unintentional physical injuries. Tort law, of course, provides no redress to a person hurt in a situation in which no one else had anything to do with the injury — for example, where he falls asleep at the wheel or is struck by lightning. The injured person must bear these losses himself, unless he anticipated such misfortune by shifting the risk to an insurer or is eligible for aid under a government program. The question of who should bear a loss caused by an unintentional injury has engaged much of the thought and effort of judges through the years.

Historical Development of Unintentional Injury

In the early days, the judges had developed the doctrine of *strict liability* to cover unintentional injuries. It mattered not whether the defendant was careless in permitting harm to fall on the plaintiff or was innocent of blame. In all cases, the defendant who caused the harm had to pay damages to the plaintiff. This approach prevailed until the late 1700s in England, when the courts began evolving a pattern requiring that the defendant be shown to be at fault before becoming obligated to pay. Apart from some instances of strict liability, today's judges still generally apply rules of *fault liability*.

Why did the law shift from strict liability to fault liability? This is not only a question of historical interest; it also may help us to appreciate changes now occurring. What events occurred in England toward the end of the eighteenth century to influence judges to reject strict liability? Several bits of history may combine to provide an answer, though it must be remembered that judges rarely articulate such basic reasons for their decisions even when they themselves are aware of them.

First, on the economic scene, the Industrial Revolution was transforming England. Infant industries were developing, and with them came an increase in industrial injuries. The courts recognized, at least implicitly, that the doctrine of strict liability might well stunt the growth of many of these industries, a socially undesirable result. And no liability insurance was available (it did not develop until the late nineteenth century) to help these industries absorb damages costs. The second reason was a philosophical one. At this time, the laissez-faire philosophy of individual freedom in the economic sphere was becoming popular. This emphasis paralleled political theory in England and, later, that arising out of the French Revolution, with its stress on individual rights and freedom. In the legal domain, the rise in England of the courts of equity, with their emphasis on ethical behavior, provided impetus to a system based on considerations of fault — a system in which a person could act as he chose so long as he did not act unreasonably in injuring another. As a result, fault became the predominant basis of liability in England by the early nineteenth century, as it did later in the United States, with the development of this country's Industrial Revolution.

In considering fault as the basis of liability, we will first examine the anatomy of negligence and then turn to alternative bases of compensation.

ANATOMY OF NEGLIGENCE

The Reasonable Person Concept

The presence of fault on the part of the defendant has come to be called *negligence* in legal parlance. The traditional test of negligence has been phrased in terms of a very important figure in the world of torts — *the reasonable man*, or, more recently, *the reasonable person*. This reasonable person of ordinary prudence is not a living person, but a hypothetical human being with certain imputed attributes. He has normal intelligence, mental capacity, perception, and memory, and a minimum amount of knowledge common to those in the community. He has the actual physical attributes of the actor. Finally, he has such superior skills and knowledge as he actually possesses or claims to possess. Notice the asymmetry of requiring the hypothetical person to have at least normal mental capacity but then using a higher level if he has that higher level. Special variations of these attributes are developed for children.

But if the basis of liability is fault, why is negligence not judged in the personal terms of the specific defendant rather than the impersonal objective terms of the reasonable person? The answer is a practical one. Although subjective determination of fault would be more in keeping with the ethical basis of the doctrine, it is impractical to investigate the strengths, weaknesses, and idiosyncrasies of each and every defendant. Although potentially unfair to those defendants who do not have the qualities of the reasonable person, the objective approach has the merit of uniformity and ease of application.

Using the reasonable person analysis does not avoid all difficulties. Sometimes the facts clearly indicate whether the defendant acted reasonably. Thus, if the only question in the case is whether the defendant drove past a clearly visible stop sign without stopping, the answer to that fact question will go far toward determining whether the defendant was negligent. But sometimes it is difficult to determine whether in a given situation the defendant has acted as a reasonable person.

Adams v. Bullock
Court of Appeals of New York, 1919. 227 N.Y. 208, 125 N.E. 93

CARDOZO, J.

The defendant runs a trolley line in the city of Dunkirk, employing the overhead wire system. At one point, the road is crossed by a bridge or culvert which carries the tracks of the Nickle Plate and Pennsylvania railroads. Pedestrians often use the bridge as a short cut between streets, and children play on it. On April 21, 1916, the plaintiff, a boy of twelve years, came across the bridge, swinging a wire about eight feet long. In swinging it, he brought it in contact with the defendant's trolley wire, which ran beneath the structure. The side of the bridge was protected by a parapet eighteen inches wide. Four feet seven and three-fourths inches below the top of the parapet, the trolley wire was strung. The plaintiff was shocked and burned when the wires came together. He had a verdict at Trial Term, which has been affirmed at the Appellate Division by a divided court.

We think the verdict cannot stand. The defendant in using an overhead trolley was in the lawful exercise of its franchise. Negligence, therefore, cannot be imputed to it because it used that system and not another. There was, of course, a duty to adopt all reasonable precautions to minimize the resulting perils. We think there is no evidence that this duty was ignored. The trolley wire was so placed that no one standing on the bridge or even bending over the parapet could reach it. Only some extraordinary casualty, not fairly within the area of ordinary prevision, could make it a thing of danger. Reasonable care in the use of a destructive agency imports a high degree of vigilance. . . . But no vigilance, however alert, unless fortified by the gift of prophecy, could have predicted the point upon the route where such an accident would occur. It might with equal reason have been expected anywhere else. At any point upon the route, a mischievous or thoughtless boy might touch the wire with a metal pole, or fling another wire across it. If unable to reach it from the walk, he might stand upon a wagon or climb upon a tree. No special danger at this bridge warned the defendant that there was need of special measures of precaution. No like accident had occurred before. No custom had been disregarded. We think that ordinary caution did not involve forethought of this extraordinary peril. It has been so ruled in like circumstances by courts in other jurisdictions. Nothing to the contrary was held in *Braun v. Buffalo Gen. El. Co.*, 200 N.Y. 484. . . . There is, we may add, a distinction, not to be ignored, between electric light and trolley wires. The distinction is that the former may be insulated. Chance of harm, though remote, may betoken negligence, if needless. Facility of protection may impose a duty to protect. With trolley wires, the case is different. Insulation is impossible. Guards here and there are of little value. To avert the possibility of this accident and others like it at one point or another on the route, the defendant must have abandoned the overhead system, and put the wires underground. Neither its power nor its duty to make the change is shown. To hold it liable upon the facts exhibited in this record would be to charge it as an insurer.

The judgment should be reversed. . . .

In the *Braun* case cited by Judge Cardozo, defendant had strung electric wires over a vacant lot. The wires had been strung sometime around 1890 with insulation that was expected to last three years. They were never inspected. Fifteen years later, during construction of a building on the lot, plaintiff's intestate, a carpenter, came in contact with the now-exposed wires and was electrocuted. The court speculated that in some circumstances reasonable care might include maintaining the insulation:

> Little need or can be said about the condition of the wires, for if the respondent owed any obligation whatever of making them safe it would scarcely have been more negligent if, instead of allowing them to remain uninspected and unrepaired as it did, it had strung and maintained absolutely naked wires. The only question which is at all close is whether the respondent in the exercise of reasonable care and foresight should have apprehended that the premises over which the wires were strung might be so used as to bring people in contact with them, and whether, therefore, it should have guarded against such a contingency. As indicated, I think this was fairly a question for the jury. Here was a vacant lot in the midst of a thickly built-up section of a large city. It was no remote or country lot where no buildings could be expected. The neighboring land was covered with buildings. It was the only vacant lot in the vicinity. It fronted on a street and there was plenty of space for a building. Now, what was reasonably to be anticipated — that this lot would be allowed indefinitely to lie unimproved and unproductive, or that it, like other surrounding lots, would be improved by additions to the old building or by the erection of new and independent ones? Was it to be anticipated that its use would be an exception to the rule prevailing in the entire neighborhood or that it would be in conformity therewith? It seems to me that the answer to these questions should have been made by the jury, and that the latter would be justified in saying that the respondent was bound to anticipate what was usual rather than that which was exceptional and act accordingly. It does not appear how much this neighborhood may have changed since the wires were first strung, but assuming that it had materially changed in respect of the use of lots for buildings, such a change in a neighborhood for aught that appears in this case requires some time, and as a basis for responsibility it is not too much to charge a company stringing such wires with notice of gradual changes in the locality through which the wires pass.

In *Blyth* v. *Birmingham Waterworks Co.*, 11 Exch. 781 (1856), the defendant's water main sprang a leak during a severe frost and the escaping water damaged plaintiff's house. On appeal from a jury verdict for the plaintiff, Baron Alderson's entire opinion stated:

> I am of the opinion that there was no evidence to be left to the jury. The case turns upon the question, whether the facts proved show that the defendants were guilty of negligence. Negligence is the omission to do something which a reasonable man, guided upon those considerations which ordinarily regulate the conduct of human affairs, would do, or doing something which a prudent and

reasonable man would not do. The defendants might have been liable for negligence if, unintentionally, they omitted to do that which a reasonable person would have done, or did that which a person taking reasonable precautions would not have done. A reasonable man would act with reference to the average circumstances of the temperature in ordinary years. The defendants had provided against such frosts as experience would have led men, acting prudently, to provide against; and they are not guilty of negligence, because their precautions proved insufficient against the effects of the extreme severity of the frost of 1855, which penetrated to a greater depth than any which ordinarily occurs south of the polar regions. Such a state of circumstances constitutes a contingency against which no reasonable man can provide. The result was an accident for which the defendants cannot be held liable.

Judge Learned Hand sought to analyze negligence with a formula. He contended that the amount of care "demanded of a person by an occasion is the resultant of three factors: the likelihood that his conduct will injure others, taken with the seriousness of the injury if it happens, and balanced against the interest which he must sacrifice to avoid that risk." Conway v. O'Brien, 111 F.2d 611 (2d Cir. 1940). The Supreme Court reversed, but on other grounds. 312 U.S. 492, 61 S.Ct. 634 (1941). Judge Hand later restated this in algebraic terms: "if the probability be called P; the injury L; and the burden B; liability depends upon whether B is less than L multiplied by P; i.e., whether $B < PL$." United States v. Carroll Towing Co., 159 F.2d 169 (2d Cir. 1947).

In another case, Judge Hand indicated that reliance on group behavior as a test of reasonableness is a general rule to which there are exceptions. Judge Hand was confronted by a situation in which cargo owners claimed that a tug company had been negligent in allowing its tugs to sail from Virginia to New York without having operating radios to receive weather forecasts. When the tugs left the weather was fine. Later forecasts indicated danger but the tugs had no way to learn of this. The tugs sank in a storm and the cargo was lost. The defendant argued that it had behaved reasonably and proved that only one tug line supplied its masters with radios. Judge Hand observed that receiving sets were inexpensive and could have avoided major losses. He also noted that

> . . . in most cases reasonable prudence is in fact common prudence; but strictly it is never its measure; a whole calling may have unduly lagged in the adoption of new and available devices. It never may set its own tests, however persuasive be its usages. Courts must in the end say what is required; there are precautions so imperative that even their universal disregard will not excuse their omission. T. J. Hooper, 60 F.2d 737 (2nd Cir. 1932).

Causation

In addition to proving that the defendant behaved unreasonably in the particular circumstances of the case, the plaintiff must show that the unreasonable conduct caused the harm for which plaintiff is suing. Some of the difficulties are suggested in the following case.

Wolf v. Kaufmann

Supreme Court of New York, Appellate Division, 1929. 227 App. Div. 281, 237 N.Y.S. 550

FINCH, J.

The defendants appeal from an order setting aside the verdict of a jury in their favor and granting a new trial. The order should be reversed in so far as it grants a new trial, and the complaint dismissed, upon the ground that, assuming the existence of all the facts claimed by the plaintiff upon the trial, no cause of action exists against the defendants.

The action is in negligence to recover damages for the death of plaintiff's intestate. The plaintiff's cause of action is based upon the fact that the deceased was found injured and unconscious at the foot of a flight of stairs in premises owned by the defendants, coupled with the fact that the hallway was unlighted in violation of section 76 of the Tenement House Law which provides: "Every light required by this section . . . shall be kept burning by the owner every night from sunset to sunrise throughout the year."

. . . .

A fatal defect exists, however, in the case of the plaintiff in that, assuming the accident to have occurred after sunset and the hallway to have been unlighted, there is a total absence of proof of any causal connection between the accident and the absence of light. The deceased was shown to have entered the premises and was heard by tenants upon the stairs and in the hallway. Following a thud, also heard by tenants, he was found at the foot of the stairs. No one saw him fall. Without further proof it would be solely a conjecture for a jury to draw the conclusion that the deceased fell down the stairs because of the absence of light. . . .

. . . .

In the case at bar there is nothing to show that the accident occurred in the use of the stairs in the ordinary manner. In the absence of such proof, there are many possible conjectures for the accident.

It follows that the order appealed from in so far as it grants a new trial should be reversed, with costs, and the complaint dismissed, with costs.

DOWLING, P.J., MCAVOY, MARTIN, and O'MALLEY, JJ., concur.

In the absence of further evidence, is one of these analyses superior to the other?

1. Although we know that individuals often fall down lighted stairways, falls occur more frequently on dark stairways, so that the proof is adequate.
2. Since we know that individuals often fall down lighted stairs, there is no reason to assume that the darkness had anything to do with this fall in the absence of some showing to that effect by the plaintiff.

The plaintiff must prove all elements of the cause of action by a preponderance of the evidence. This can sometimes cause serious difficulties, as suggested in the following summary of a case. The defendant, a physician, set the plaintiff's broken hip properly, but the two parts separated naturally. The defendant negligently failed to discover this until it was too late to attempt to reset the fracture and plaintiff sustained permanent injury. Expert witnesses at the trial testified that the likelihood the bones would unite the first time was in the range of 65–80 percent, but that the chances of success on a resetting would only have been one-fourth as high. The court ruled that at most the plaintiff could show that had the doctor attempted the resetting within the proper time, the likelihood of success would not have been more than 20 percent. From this the court concluded that the plaintiff could not establish that it was more likely than not that the defendant's negligence had caused her injury. Traditionally, courts in this situation will not award a percentage of the damages. Instead, they require that the plaintiff prove that the defendant's negligence caused the plaintiff's harm by "a fair preponderance of the evidence" or by a "more likely than not" standard. If the plaintiff can do this, she will be entitled to recover the full amount of her damages. But in this case she was entitled to no damages whatever. *Kuhn* v. *Banker* 133 Ohio St. 304, 13 N.E.2d 242 (1938).

Damages

We turn now to what it is that the negligence must be shown to cause — actual damages. In the following case, the damages consist of two parts: pecuniary loss by the person injured and the pain and suffering caused by the injury. It is the amount awarded for the latter that was under dispute.

Seffert v. Los Angeles Transit Lines
Supreme Court of California, 1961. 56 Cal.2d 498, 364 P.2d 337, 15 Cal.Rptr. 161
PETERS, J.

Defendants appeal from a judgment for plaintiff for $187,903.75 entered on a jury verdict. Their motion for a new trial for errors of law and excessiveness of damages was denied.

At the trial plaintiff contended that she was properly entering defendants' bus when the doors closed suddenly catching her right hand and left foot. The bus started, dragged her some distance, and then threw her to the pavement. Defendants contended that the injury resulted from plaintiff's own negligence, that she was late for work and either ran into the side of the bus after the doors had closed or ran after the bus and attempted to enter after the doors had nearly closed.

. . . .

These injuries were extremely painful. They have resulted in a permanently raised left heel, which is two inches above the floor level, caused by the contraction of the ankle joint capsule. Plaintiff is crippled and will suffer pain for life. Although this pain could, perhaps, be alleviated by an operative fusion of the ankle, the doctors considered and rejected this procedure because the area has been deprived of its normal blood supply. The foot is not only permanently deformed but has a persistent open ulcer on the heel, there being a continuous drainage from the entire area. Medical care of this foot and ankle is to be reasonably expected for the remainder of plaintiff's life.

. . . .

Although plaintiff has gone back to work, she testified that she has difficulty standing, walking or even sitting, and must lie down frequently; that the leg is still very painful; that she can, even on her best days, walk not over three blocks and that very slowly; that her back hurts from walking; that she is tired and weak; that her sleep is disturbed; that she has frequent spasms in which the leg shakes uncontrollably; that she feels depressed and unhappy, and suffers humiliation and embarrassment.

Plaintiff claims that there is evidence that her total pecuniary loss, past and future, amounts to $53,903.75. This was the figure used by plaintiff's counsel in his argument to the jury, in which he also claimed $134,000 for pain and suffering, past and future. Since the verdict was exactly the total of these two estimates, it is reasonable to assume that the jury accepted the amount proposed by counsel for each item.

The summary of plaintiff as to pecuniary loss, past and future, is as follows:

Doctor and hospital bills	$10,330.50	
Drugs and other medical expenses stipulated to in the amount of	2,273.25	
Loss of earnings from time of accident to time of trial	5,500.00	$18,103.75
Future medical expenses:		
$2,000 per year for next 10 years	20,000.00	
$200 per year for the 24 years thereafter	4,800.00	
Drugs for 34 years	1,000.00	25,800.00
		43,903.75
Possible future loss of earnings		10,000.00
Total pecuniary loss		$53,903.75

There is substantial evidence to support these estimates. . . .

This leaves the amount of $134,000 presumably allowed for the nonpecuniary items of damage, including pain and suffering, past and future. It is this allowance that defendants seriously attack as being excessive as a matter of law.

It must be remembered that the jury fixed these damages, and that the trial judge denied a motion for new trial, one ground of which was excessiveness of the award. These determinations are entitled to great weight. The amount of damages is a fact question, first committed to the discretion of the jury and next to the discretion of the trial judge on a motion for new trial. They see and hear the witnesses and frequently, as in this case, see the injury and the impairment that has resulted therefrom. As a result, all presumptions are in favor of the decision of the trial court. . . . An appellate court can interfere on the ground that the judgment is excessive only on the ground that the verdict is so large that, at first blush, it shocks the conscience and suggests passion, prejudice or corruption on the part of the jury. . . .

. . . .

. . . While the amount of the award is high, and may be more than we would have awarded were we the trier of the facts, considering the nature of the injury, the great pain and suffering, past and future, and the other items of damage, we cannot say, as a matter of law, that it is so high that it shocks the conscience and gives rise to the presumption that it was the result of passion or prejudice on the part of the jurors.

. . . .

The judgment appealed from is affirmed.

GIBSON, C.J., WHITE, J., and DOOLING, J., concurred.

TRAYNOR, J. — I dissent.

. . . [I]t is my opinion that the award of $134,000 for pain and suffering is so excessive as to indicate that it was prompted by passion, prejudice, whim, or caprice.

Before the accident plaintiff was employed as a file clerk at a salary of $375 a month. At the time of the trial she had returned to her job at the same salary and her foot had healed sufficiently for her to walk. . . .

. . . . [The plaintiff's counsel proposed and the jury awarded the following amounts:]

Total pecuniary loss		$ 53,903.75
Pain and suffering:		
From time of accident to time of trial (660 days) @ $100 a day	$66,000.00	
For the remainder of her life (34 years) @ $2,000 a year	68,000.00	134,000.00
Total proposed by counsel		$187,903.75

. . . .

The crucial question in this case, therefore, is whether the award of $134,000 for pain and suffering is so excessive it must have resulted from passion, prejudice, whim or caprice. "To say that a verdict has been influenced by passion or prejudice is but another way of saying that the verdict exceeds any amount justified by the evidence." . . .

. . . .

The excessive amount of the award in this case was undoubtedly the result of the improper argument of plaintiff's counsel to the jury.

. . . .

Counsel may argue all legitimate inferences from the evidence, but he may not employ arguments that tend primarily to mislead the jury. A specified sum for pain and suffering for any particular period is bound to be conjectural. Positing such a sum for a small period of time and then multiplying that sum by the number of days, minutes or seconds in plaintiff's life expectancy multiplies the hazards of conjecture. Counsel could arrive at any amount he wished by adjusting either the period of time to be taken as a measure or the amount surmised for the pain of that period.

. . . .

I would reverse the judgment and remand the cause for a new trial on the issue of damages.

SCHAUER, J., and MCCOMB, J., concurred.

So far as damages for medical expenses and economic loss are concerned, notice that two separate problems are raised. First, there is the fairly straightforward problem of measuring past losses under each heading. But future losses present much more serious problems. This prediction of the future is required by the common law tradition that the plaintiff must sue only once for all damages attributable to the defendant's behavior. Probably this was developed for administrative convenience and to allow both parties to know where they stood with finality. Arguably the requirement is less critical today where insurance companies provide virtually all funds used to satisfy tort judgments. The shift in emphasis from the single award to the continuing award will be seen in our discussions of workers' compensation and automobile no-fault in this chapter.

Other Hurdles for the Plaintiff

Until now we have assumed that if one's failure to use due care caused damages to another, there was legal liability. This is only part of the picture. We now explore other rules that have been developed by the courts to limit the liability of defendants in unintentional harm cases.

Duty

For a variety of reasons, the courts have developed a series of exceptions to the general requirement of the duty of due care. Some of these exceptions have been developed because it has been thought too burdensome on the defendant to impose the due care obligation. For example, until quite recently those who own and occupy real property have not owed a general duty of due care for the safety of those who come on the land. The extent of the obligation was said to depend upon who came on the land and the reasons for that entry.

At another level, however, the courts have been reluctant to impose affirmative obligations on individuals who have played no part in causing risk to the particular plaintiff. The nature of this problem is suggested in the following case.

Kline v. 1500 Massachusetts Ave. Apartment Corp.
United States Court of Appeals, District of Columbia Circuit, 1970. 439 F.2d 477
[Plaintiff had been a tenant in defendant's building for several years. During that period the incidence of crime in the immediate area and through the city had increased markedly. There had been several thefts and at least one assault in the building. Defendant had taken no steps to secure the building, with its 585 apartments and business offices, against the intrusion by criminals. At shortly after 10:00 p.m. one night, plaintiff was assaulted and robbed just outside her apartment on the first floor above the street level. After hearing the evidence, the trial judge entered a judgment for the landlord on the ground that it had violated no duty of due care that was owed to the tenant. The tenant appealed.]

WILKEY, CIRCUIT JUDGE.
. . . .

As a general rule, a private person does not have a duty to protect another from a criminal attack by a third person. We recognize that this rule has sometimes in the past been applied in landlord-tenant law, even by this court. Among the reasons for the application of this rule to landlords are: judicial reluctance to tamper with the traditional common law concept of the landlord-tenant relationship; the notion that the act of a third person in committing an intentional tort or crime is a superseding cause of the harm to another resulting therefrom; the oftentimes difficult problem of determining foreseeability of criminal acts; the vagueness of the standard which the landlord must meet; the economic consequences of the imposition of the duty; and conflict with the public policy allocating the duty of protecting citizens from criminal acts to the government rather than the private sector.

But the rationale of this very broad general rule falters when it is applied to the conditions of modern day urban apartment living, particularly in the circumstances of this case. The rationale of the general rule exonerating a third party from any duty to protect another from a criminal attack has no applicability to the landlord-tenant relationship in multiple dwelling houses. The landlord is no insurer of his tenants' safety, but he certainly is no bystander. And where, as here, the landlord has notice of repeated criminal assaults and robberies, has notice that these crimes occurred in the portion of the premises exclusively within his control, has every reason to expect like crimes to happen again, and has the exclusive power to take preventive action, it does not seem unfair to place upon the landlord a duty to take those steps which are within his power to minimize the predictable risk to his tenants.

This court has recently had occasion to review landlord-tenant law as applied to multiple family urban dwellings. In *Javins* v. *First National Realty Corporation,* . . . Judge Wright, in clearing away some of the legal underbrush from medieval common law obscuring the modern landlord-tenant relationship, referred to an innkeeper's liability in comparison with that of the landlord to his tenant. "Even the old common law courts responded with a different rule for a landlord-tenant relationship which did not conform to the model of the usual agrarian lease. Much more substantial obligations were placed upon the keepers of inns (the only multiple dwelling houses known to the common law)."

Specifically, innkeepers have been held liable for assaults which have been committed upon their guests by third parties, if they have breached a duty which is imposed by reason of the innkeeper-guest relationship. By this duty, the innkeeper is generally bound to exercise reasonable care to protect the guest from abuse or molestation from third parties, be they innkeeper's employees, fellow guests, or intruders, if the attack could, or in the exercise of reasonable care, should have been anticipated.

. . . .

Other relationships in which similar duties have been imposed include landowner-invitee, businessman-patron, employer-employee, school district-pupil, hospital-patient, and carrier-passenger. In all, the theory of liability is essentially the same: that since the ability of one of the parties to provide for his own protection has been limited in some way by his submission to the control of the other, a duty should be imposed upon the one possessing control (and thus the power to act) to take reasonable precautions to protect the other one from assaults by third parties which, at least, could reasonably have been anticipated. However, there is no liability normally imposed upon the one having the power to act if the violence is sudden and unexpected provided that the source of the violence is not an employee of the one in control.

. . . .

Upon consideration of all pertinent factors, we find that there is a duty of protection owed by the landlord to the tenant in an urban multiple unit apartment dwelling.

. . . .

As between tenant and landlord, the landlord is the only one in the position to take the necessary acts of protection required. He is not an insurer, but he is obligated to minimize the risk to his tenants. Not only as between landlord and tenant is the landlord best equipped to guard against the predictable risk of intruders, but even as between landlord and the police power of government, the landlord is in the best position to take the necessary protective measures. Municipal police cannot patrol the entryways and the hallways, the garages and the basements of private multiple unit apartment dwellings. They are neither equipped, manned, nor empowered to do so. In the area of the predictable risk which materialized in this case, only the landlord could have taken measures which might have prevented the injuries suffered by appellant.

. . . [E]very segment of society has obligations to aid in law enforcement and to minimize the opportunities for crime. The average citizen is ceaselessly warned to remove keys from automobiles and, in this jurisdiction, may be liable in tort for any injury caused in the operation of his car by a thief if he fails to do so, notwithstanding the intervening criminal act of the thief, a third party. . . . In addition, auto manufacturers are persuaded to install special locking devices and buzzer alarms, and real estate developers, residential communities, and industrial areas are asked to install especially bright lights to deter the criminally inclined. It is only just that the obligations of landlords in their sphere be acknowledged and enforced.

. . . .

Thirdly, if we reach back to seek the precedents of common law, on the question of whether there exists or does not exist a duty on the owner of the premises to provide protection against criminal acts by third parties, the most analogous relationship to that of the modern day urban apartment house dweller is not that of a landlord and tenant, but that of innkeeper and guest. We can also consider other relationships, cited above, in which an analogous duty has been found to exist.

IV

We now turn to the standard of care which should be applied in judging if the landlord has fulfilled his duty of protection to the tenant. Although in many cases the language speaks as if the standard of care itself varies, in the last analysis the standard of care is the same — reasonable care in all the circumstances. The specific measures to achieve this standard vary with the individual circumstances. It may be impossible to describe in detail for all situations of landlord-tenant relationships, and evidence of custom amongst landlords of the same class of building may play a significant role in determining if the standard has been met.

. . . .

Given this duty of protection, and the standard of care as defined, it is clear that the appellee landlord breached its duty toward the appellant tenant here. The risk of criminal assault and robbery on any tenant was clearly predictable, a risk of which the appellee landlord had specific notice, a risk which became reality with increasing frequency, and this risk materialized on the very premises peculiarly under the control, and therefore the protection, of the landlord to the injury of the appellant tenant. The question then for the District Court becomes one of damages only. To us the liability is clear.

. . . .

The landlord is entirely justified in passing on the cost of increased protective measures to his tenants, but the rationale of compelling the landlord to do it in the first place is that he is the only one who is in a position to take the necessary protective measures for overall protection of the premises, which he owns in whole and rents in part to individual tenants.

Reversed and remanded to the District Court for the determination of damages.

One judge dissented. He contended that since the building also contained several business offices, public access was essential, and the building could not reasonably be converted into a "fortress." Since this was not a luxury apartment building, the security reasonably to be expected was of a lower degree. He also thought that there was insufficient notice of the likelihood of assaults in this particular apartment building since virtually all of the previous criminal behavior involved thefts and only one was an assault. He concluded that:

> hysteria of apartment dwellers in an inner city plagued with crime is understandable but they are not any more exposed there than they are on the streets or in office buildings and they cannot expect the landlord to furnish the equivalent of police protection that is not available from the duly constituted government in the locality.

Aside from the specific exceptions noted by the majority, the common law has generally imposed no duty of due care to aid another person in peril from any cause. This view has usually been explained in terms of the society's reluctance to force people to engage in helping behavior where their own conduct did not lead to the danger in the first place. Others have pointed to administrative difficulties in deciding who might be sued if twenty people watch someone drown without helping.

What do the cited exceptions have in common? Do you agree with the majority in the case that the landlord comes within the spirit of these exceptions? How far beyond the landlord should this doctrine be extended? Should the tenant next door have any obligations if he steps out of his apartment to find Kline lying in the hallway? Courts have created no obligation in this situation. Only one state legislature has imposed a general obligation to help others — although this is common in legal systems in Europe and elsewhere. In 1967 Vermont enacted the following statute (12 Vt. Statutes Annotated section 519):

> (a) A person who knows that another is exposed to grave physical harm shall, to the extent that the same can be rendered without danger or peril to himself or without interference with important duties owed to others, give reasonable assistance to the exposed person unless that assistance or care is being provided by others.
>
> (b) A person who provides reasonable assistance in compliance with subsection (a) of this section shall not be liable in civil damages unless his acts constitute gross negligence or unless he will receive or expects to receive remuneration. Nothing contained in this subsection shall alter existing law with respect to tort liability of a practitioner of the healing arts for acts committed in the ordinary course of his practice.
>
> (c) A person who willfully violates subsection (a) of this section shall be fined not more than $100.00

Notice that Vermont has made this a criminal statute.

Proximate Cause

One is not liable unless one's breach of duty caused an injury. In legend, Mrs. O'Leary's cow kicked over a lantern and much of Chicago burned as a consequence. Should the careless act of placing the lantern within reach of the cow's hoof be viewed as the cause — the legal cause — of a homeowner's loss across town?

Johnson v. Kosmos Portland Cement Co.
United States Court of Appeals, Sixth Circuit, 1933. 64 F.2d 193
[Defendant carelessly allowed gas vapors to collect in the hold of a ship. A dangerous condition developed creating the risk of explosion. That explosion did occur and several people were killed. The trial court found that the explosion occurred as the result of a lightning bolt that struck the barge. The trial judge ruled that although the defendant was negligent, the explosion of the gas "was not such a natural and probable consequence of leaving the gases in the barge as should have reasonably been anticipated" by the defendant and that therefore the plaintiffs could not recover. Plaintiffs appealed.]

SIMONS, CIRCUIT JUDGE.
. . . .

. . . The wrongful act or omission consisted in permitting the gases to remain in the barge. It was the explosion of the gases which produced the injuries. We escape here the usual difficulty which is inherent whenever a succession of events is relied upon, and where the problem is to determine whether they are so linked and continuous as to form an unbroken chain of causation. But difficulty remains. The primary cause, negligence, was not self-operating. Had there been no lightning, conceivably there would have been no explosion. Was the secondary cause, the lightning, the sole proximate cause of the disaster? Certainly the lightning was not in any sense dependent upon the original wrong, nor a force put in motion by it, or in response to its stimulus. But while disconnected from the primary cause, it likewise was not self-operating. Had there been no accumulation of gases, whatever might have been the result of the lightning, the explosion would not have occurred. We have here, then, no intermediate or intervening efficient cause operating between the wrong and the injury, and so destroying the causal relation of the former to the latter, but rather two concurring causes, neither self-operating, yet together efficient in bringing about the catastrophe here described.

But the fact that injury is the natural consequence of negligence is not enough; it must also be its foreseeable consequence. There is no actionable liability for an alleged negligent act, unless injury resulting therefrom could reasonably have been foreseen in the light of the attending circumstances. Indeed it may be said that, in the absence of wanton wrong or failure to conform to some arbitrary or absolute standard of care, "foreseeability" is a necessary test of the existence of negligence, and, if no injury can reasonably be expected to result, there is no negligence. We need carry this inquiry no further than to note, for its bearing upon subsequent discussion, that danger in permitting explosive gases to remain in the barge was obvious to the court below, and that in a sense, at least, reasonable expectation of injury was implied in its finding of negligence.

Reasonable apprehension of the danger of injury constituting the criterion of liability, whether the question be one of negligence or causation, is it a prerequisite to liability that the respondent should have foreseen the precise manner in which the injurious result was brought about, or is it sufficient to impose liability upon it if a generally injurious result should have been foreseen as reasonably probable in the light of the attending circumstances? If the former, it is argued that the ignition of explosive gases in the hold of a barge by lightning is so extraordinary, and so unprecedented an event, as not to be reasonably anticipated as a probable consequence of the alleged wrongful act or omission. Even were the rule relied upon the true rule, we are not certain of the soundness of this conclusion. . . . Lightning is, at least at the time and place here involved, no extraordinary manifestation of natural force. Lightning strikes, and injury results.

This is within our ordinary experience and observation. We take many precautions to avoid its injurious effect, insure and are insured against it.

Nor is reasonable expectation of injurious consequences to be determined by the fact that no similar injurious result has been known to follow a like wrongful act under identical attending circumstances. If this were so, peculiar circumstances could be discovered in almost every accident, and relied upon to defeat liability. . . .

We think, however, that the doctrine of foreseeable results calls for no such narrow test to be applied to anticipation of injury as the one above discussed. We think the true rule to be that when the thing done produces immediate danger of injury, and is a substantial factor in bringing it about, it is not necessary that the author of it should have had in mind the particular means by which the potential force he has created might be vitalized into injury. . . .

If we are right in our understanding of the true doctrine, its application to the facts of the present case compels reversal. The fault of the respondent consisted in its failure to remove gases from the barge. Their explosiveness presented continuous menace to the men working thereon. Any one of a number of expectable circumstances might have brought about the precise injury which resulted; a lighted match, the flame of the acetylene torch, a heated rivet, a spark produced by friction of a tool or boot, and so on. The danger of the injurious result was ever present, even though the manner in which, or the means by which, such result was brought about may have had in it some aspect of unusualness.

. . . .

The decrees below are set aside. The causes are remanded for further proceedings consistent herewith, including findings of damages, and degrees in favor of libelants.

MOORMAN, CIRCUIT JUDGE (dissenting).

In my opinion the application of the correct rule of proximate result to this case requires an affirmance. Had the gas exploded spontaneously, there would be an unbroken chain between the negligence and the injury. Had it attracted the lightning, the chain of causation would still be complete. In either case the explosion would be direct or, as sometimes said, the natural consequence of the defendant's negligence, and thus the proximate result. But the factual case is different. The gas was inactive or dormant, and a new outside force intervened and caused the explosion. This seems to me to make the defendant's negligence remote unless it created a situation where there was foreseeable danger of the intervention of the new force. Beale, The Proximate Consequences of an Act, 33 Harvard Law Review 632. I think the danger was not foreseeable. Thunderstorms, it is true, do come, lightning does strike, and men do take out insurance against these risks. So do men run trains into open switches . . . and automobiles into railway cars standing on highways. . . . Many things happen that reasonable foresight cannot anticipate; and so it is that a foreseeable thing is not that which has happened or may happen again but which "could reasonably have been foreseen in the light of all the attending circumstances." I think a stroke of lightning is beyond the scope of this expectation.

The majority position of *Johnson* v. *Kosmos Portland Cement Co.* is generally followed today. But does even that analysis go far enough? For example, what should be the result in the case if lightning had never before been experienced in that area and this was a freakish storm?

Another variation on this problem is suggested by a case in which a tank car was derailed because of the railroad's negligent maintenance of its tracks. Gasoline spilled, and the railroad may also have been negligent in not cleaning it up more quickly. In any event, gasoline escaped down a gutter and into a sewer. Three hours later an explosion occurred when a man named Duerr threw a lighted match on the street. The court held that the railroad should be liable for the damage caused by the explosion if it could be shown that Duerr was unaware of the presence of the gas and gas vapor or that he had been aware and had momentarily forgotten when he took out a match to light a cigar. There was also evidence suggesting that Duerr had been discharged by the railroad earlier that day and might have thrown the match deliberately to cause trouble for the railroad. If that view of the facts was accepted by the jury, the court said the railroad would not be liable for the fire even though its negligence had created the risk of explosion and fire — precisely what occurred. Why should the reasons for Duerr's lighting of the match matter on the question of the railroad's liability? See *Watson v. Kentucky & Ind. Bridge & R.R. Co.*, 137 Ky. 619, 126 S.W. 146, modified, 129 S.W. 341 (1910).

These cases concerned a peril that might have occurred in several different ways and that finally did come about in an unexpected way. A more complex problem occurs when one's negligence foreseeably exposes the plaintiff to a risk of one type or amount of harm but a different type or amount of harm actually occurs. In one such situation the courts are unanimous. If a defendant acts in such a way as to create a risk of modest physical harm to another person but, because of plaintiff's unexpected physical sensitivity, the harm that occurs is much worse than could have been reasonably anticipated, the courts agree that the negligent defendant must "take his victim as he finds him" and is liable for the full extent of the plaintiff's harm. Thus, a defendant who knocked a plaintiff over through negligence and could reasonably have expected to be liable for bruises and scrapes may be liable for paralysis if some latent disease was triggered and led to a loss of function.

The problem of unexpected harm is most powerfully demonstrated in two famous British Commonwealth cases that involved property damage rather than personal injury. In the first, as stevedores were unloading the plaintiff's ship, one of them carelessly dropped a plank into the hold of the ship. This might reasonably have been expected to damage cargo or to damage slightly the ship's hull. In fact, however, due to the presence of gas vapors that could not reasonably have been anticipated by the stevedores, the dropped plank caused a spark that ignited the entire ship, causing a loss of $1 million. In that case, the court held for the plaintiff and emphasized that the consequences need not be foreseeable if they followed directly from the admitted negligence. See *In Re Polemis*, 3 K.B. 560 (Court of Appeal, 1921).

In the second case, the defendant negligently allowed bunkering oil to escape from its ship and to spread over a considerable portion of the bay in Sydney, Australia. Defendant made no effort to clean up the oil or to disperse it. It was generally understood that the risk of fire was virtually nonexistent because of the high flash point of bunkering oil. Plaintiff operated a dry dock in the harbor and instructed its employees to be very careful while the oil was around. Two days later a fire broke out at the plaintiff's drydock, apparently caused by a spark from a torch held by one of its employees catching on some cotton debris floating on the water, allowing a sufficient temperature to develop so that the oil in the area could be ignited. The drydock suffered severe fire damage. The defendant admitted negligence in the sense that it carelessly allowed the bunkering oil to escape and admitted that it would be liable for any cloggage or oil damage done to facilities in the bay. It argued, however, that although it had been negligent in this regard toward the drydock, it was not liable for the unexpected harm that the drydock suffered from fire damage. The plaintiff in turn relied on *Polemis*. The court rejected the philosophy of *Polemis* — there could be no liability for unforeseeable damage and the notion of direct consequences was irrelevant:

> Enough has been said to show that the authority of *Polemis* has been severely shaken though lip-service has from time to time been paid to it. . . . For it does not seem consonant with current ideas of justice or morality that for an act of negligence, however slight or venial, which results in some trivial foreseeable damage the actor should be liable for all consequences however unforeseeable and however grave, so long as they can be said to be "direct." It is a principle of civil liability, subject only to qualifications which have no present relevance, that a man must be considered to be responsible for the probable consequences of his act. To demand more of him is too harsh a rule, to demand less is to ignore that civilized order requires the observance of a minimum standard of behavior.
>
> This concept applied to the slowly developing law of negligence has led to a great variety of expressions which can, as it appears to their Lordships, be harmonized with little difficulty with the single exception of the so-called rule in *Polemis*. For, if it is asked why a man should be responsible for the natural or necessary or probable consequences of his act (or any other similar description of them) the answer is that it is not because they are natural or necessary or probable, but because, since they have this quality, it is judged by the standard of the reasonable man that he ought to have foreseen them. Thus it is that over and over again it has happened that in different judgments in the same case, and sometimes in a single judgment, liability for a consequence has been imposed on the ground that it was reasonably foreseeable or, alternatively, on the ground that it was natural or necessary or probable. The two grounds have been treated as coterminous, and so they largely are. But, where they are not, the question arises to which the wrong answer was given in *Polemis*. For, if some limitation must be imposed upon the consequences for which the negligent actor is to be held responsible — and all are agreed that some limitation there must be — why should that test (reasonable foreseeability) be rejected which, since he is judged by what the reasonable man ought to foresee, corresponds with the common conscience of mankind, and a test (the "direct" consequence) be substituted which leads to nowhere but the never-ending and insoluble problems of causation.

See *Overseas Tankship Ltd.* v. *Mort's Dock & Engineering Co. (The Wagon Mound)*, 1961 A.C. 388 (Judicial Committee of the Privy Council).

Another difficult question arises when the defendant's negligence creates an unreasonable risk of harm to a certain group of people but someone else suffers the harm. The most famous example involved a plaintiff who was standing on a railroad platform waiting for her train. As a different train came in, two men came running up the stairs to catch it. One of them got on safely, but the other was caught as the doors closed. Railroad attendants on the inside of the train and outside on the platform succeeded in pushing him into the train, but in the process a package he was carrying dropped between the train and the platform. As the train pulled out, an explosion occurred at the spot where the package fell, causing some scales used to weigh goods to fall on the plaintiff, who was some 30 feet from the scene of the explosion. She sued the railroad for negligence. The jury returned a verdict in her favor.

On appeal, the court ruled, 4 to 3, that there could be no liability to the plaintiff. Judge Cardozo's majority opinion said that the defendant could owe a duty only to persons who might foreseeably be hurt by the negligence of the servants. In this case, that might mean the man himself, others standing in the train near the door who might be hurt in the jostling, and people standing on the platform a few feet from the action. He denied that liability could extend to anyone who was not foreseeably endangered by whatever negligence the railroad's servants may have committed. The dissenters argued that the railroad agents had been negligent toward some people and that Judge Cardozo should not have flatly cut off the possibility of recovery by "unforeseeable plaintiffs," but should have allowed the possibility that such persons might recover in certain types of situations. See *Palsgraf* v. *Long Island R.R.*, 248 N.Y. 339, 162 N.E. 99 (1928).

In all these situations, the defendant argues that although his negligence played a part in the plaintiff's harm, it was not the *proximate cause* of the harm, either because someone else's conduct (the arsonist) was so outrageous or something so surprising and unusual occurred (*Wagon Mound* and *Polemis*) that it would be unfair to hold the negligent defendant liable.

Contributory Negligence

If the plaintiff himself has, through carelessness or ignorance, contributed to the circumstances that led to his own injury, does this invalidate his claim against the defendant? This is the question of *contributory negligence*, which is addressed in the following famous pair of cases.

Baltimore & Ohio R.R. Co. v. Goodman
Supreme Court of the United States, 1927. 275 U.S. 66, 48 S.Ct. 24
Mr. JUSTICE HOLMES.
This is a suit brought by the widow and administratrix of Nathan Goodman against the petitioner for causing his death by running him down at a grade crossing. The defence is that Goodman's own negligence caused the death. At the trial, the defendant asked the Court to direct a verdict for it, but the request, and others looking to the same direction, were refused, and the plaintiff got a verdict and a judgment which was affirmed by the Circuit Court of Appeals.

Goodman was driving an automobile truck in an easterly direction and was killed by a train running southwesterly across the road at a rate of not less than sixty miles an hour. The line was straight, but it is said by the respondent that Goodman 'had no practical view' beyond a section house two hundred and forty-three feet north of the crossing until he was about twenty feet from the first rail, or, as the respondent argues, twelve feet from danger, and that then the engine was still obscured by the section house. He had been driving at a rate of ten or twelve miles an hour, but had cut down his rate to five or six miles at about forty feet from the crossing. It is thought that there was an emergency in which, so far as appears, Goodman did all that he could.

We do not go into further details as to Goodman's precise situation, beyond mentioning that it was daylight and that he was familiar with the crossing, for it appears to us plain that nothing is suggested by the evidence to relieve Goodman from responsibility for his own death. When a man goes upon a railroad track he knows that he goes to a place where he will be killed if a train comes upon him before he is clear of the track. He knows that he must stop for the train, not the train stop for him. In such circumstances it seems to us that if a driver cannot be sure otherwise whether a train is dangerously near he must stop and get out of his vehicle, although obviously he will not often be required to do more than to stop and look. It seems to us that if he relies upon not hearing the train or any signal and takes no further precaution he does so at his own risk. If at the last moment Goodman found himself in an emergency it was his own fault that he did not reduce his speed earlier or come to a stop. It is true as said in *Flannelly* v. *Delaware & Hudson Co.*, 225 U.S. 597, that the question of due care very generally is left to the jury. But we are dealing with a standard of conduct, and when the standard is clear it should be laid down once for all by the Courts. . . .

Judgment reversed.

Seven years after *Goodman,* Mr. Justice Cardozo, one of our nation's greatest jurists, had to reconsider his illustrious predecessor's opinion. As you read *Pokora,* note that it is the standard of behavior regarding the use of vehicles at train crossings that is changing. There is no difference between Holmes and Cardozo as to the legal consequence of a finding of contributory negligence.

Pokora v. Wabash Railway Co.
Supreme Court of the United States, 1934. 292 U.S. 98, 54 S.Ct. 580
[Pokora drove his truck across a grade crossing that was partially obstructed to the north by a string of box cars on a side track. No bell or whistle was sounded. Pokora was struck by defendant's passenger train coming from the north at 25–30 miles per hour along the main track. Further facts are stated in the opinion. The trial judge directed a verdict for the defendant and the court of appeals affirmed on the basis of the *Goodman* ruling.]

MR. JUSTICE CARDOZO.
. . . .

In such circumstances the question, we think, was for the jury whether reasonable caution forbade his going forward in reliance on the sense of hearing, unaided by that of sight. No doubt it was his duty to look along the track from his seat, if looking would avail to warn him of the danger. This does not mean, however, that if vision was cut off by obstacles, there was negligence in going on, any more than there would have been in trusting to his ears if vision had been cut off by the darkness of the night. . . . Pokora made his crossing in the day time, but like the traveler by night he used the faculties available to one in his position. . . . A jury, but not the court, might say that with faculties thus limited, he should have found some other means of assuring himself of safety before venturing to cross. The crossing was a frequented highway in a populous city. Behind him was a line of other cars, making ready to follow him. To some extent, at least, there was assurance in the thought that the defendant would not run its train at such a time and place without sounding bell or whistle. . . .

. . . .

The argument is made, however, that our decision in *B. & O. R. Co.* v. *Goodman, supra,* is a barrier in the plaintiff's path, irrespective of the conclusion that might commend itself if the question were at large. There is no doubt that the opinion in that case is correct in its result. Goodman, the driver, traveling only five or six miles an hour, had, before reaching the track, a clear space of eighteen feet within which the train was plainly visible. With that opportunity, he fell short of the legal standard of duty established for a traveler when he failed to look and see. This was decisive of the case. But the court did not stop there. It added a remark, unnecessary upon the facts before it, which has been a fertile source of controversy. "In such circumstances it seems to us that if a driver cannot be sure otherwise whether a train is dangerously near he must stop and get out of his vehicle, although obviously he will not often be required to do more than to stop and look."

There is need at this stage to clear the ground of brushwood that may obscure the point at issue. We do not now inquire into the existence of a duty to stop, disconnected from a duty to get out and reconnoitre. The inquiry, if pursued, would lead us into the thickets of conflicting judgments. . . .

. . . .

Standards of prudent conduct are declared at times by courts, but they are taken over from the facts of life. To get out of a vehicle and reconnoitre is an uncommon precaution, as everyday experience informs us. Besides being uncommon, it is very likely to be futile, and sometimes even dangerous. If the driver leaves his vehicle when he nears a cut or curve, he will learn nothing by getting out about the perils that lurk beyond. By the time he regains his seat and sets his car in motion, the hidden train may be upon him. . . . Often the added safeguard will be dubious though the track happens to be straight, as it seems that this one was, at all events as far as the station, about five blocks to the north. A train traveling at a speed of thirty miles an hour will cover a quarter of a mile in the space of thirty seconds. It may thus emerge out of obscurity as the driver turns his back to regain the waiting car, and may then descend upon him suddenly when his car is on the track. Instead of helping himself by getting out, he might do better to press forward with all his faculties alert. So a train at a neighboring station, apparently at rest and harmless, may be transformed in a few seconds into an instrument of destruction. At times the course of safety may be different. One can figure to oneself a roadbed so level and unbroken that getting out will be a gain. Even then the balance of advantage depends on many circumstances and can be easily disturbed. Where was Pokora to leave his truck after getting out to reconnoitre? If he was to leave it on the switch, there was the possibility that the box cars would be shunted down upon him before he could regain his seat. The defendant did not show whether there was a locomotive at the forward end, or whether the cars were so few that a locomotive could be seen. If he was to leave his vehicle near the curb, there was even stronger reason to believe that the space to be covered in going back and forth would make his observations worthless. One must remember that while the traveler turns his eyes in one direction, a train or a loose engine may be approaching from the other.

Illustrations such as these bear witness to the need for caution in framing standards of behavior that amount to rules of law. The need is the more urgent when there is no background of experience out of which the standards have emerged. They are then, not the natural flowerings of behavior in its customary forms, but rules artificially developed, and imposed from without. Extraordinary situations may not wisely or fairly be subjected to tests or regulations that are fitting for the common-place or normal. In default of the guide of customary conduct, what is suitable for the traveler caught in a mesh where the ordinary safeguards fail him is for the judgment of a jury. . . . The opinion in *Goodman's* case has been a source of confusion in the federal courts to the extent that it imposes a standard for application by the judge, and has had only a wavering support in the courts of the states. We limit it accordingly.

The judgment should be reversed and the cause remanded for further proceedings in accordance with this opinion.

Comparative Negligence

In recent years judges have become unhappy with the idea of barring completely a plaintiff who was a little bit contributorily negligent, and have developed some approaches to avoid the perceived harshness of the rule. Among these has been the practice of sending a maximum number of cases to the jury with the expectation that the jury will apply some less harsh rule. This became explicit in a remarkable case in which the trial was before a judge without a jury. *Alibrandi* v. *Helmsley*, 63 Misc. 2d 997, 314 N.Y.S.2d 95 (1970). The judge concluded that the defendant was negligent and that the plaintiff had been contributorily negligent, and then continued:

> Plaintiff's injuries were not trivial. I am as confident as one can be about these matters that, had the case been tried to a jury, the jury would have determined the sum of plaintiff's damages in a substantial amount, deducted a portion equivalent to the degree of his negligence, and returned a verdict for the difference. In short, as every trial lawyer knows, the jury would likely have ignored its instructions on contributory negligence and applied a standard of comparative negligence.
>
> It would be comfortable for me simply to guess what the jury's verdict would have been and then file a one-sentence decision holding defendants liable in that amount. Comfortable but false. My duty is to apply the law as I understand it, and I do not understand that, no matter what a jury might do, a Judge may pretend to make a decision on the basis of contributory negligence while actually deciding on comparative negligence.

The *comparative negligence* mentioned by the trial judge is a doctrine that provides that in certain situations the fact that a plaintiff has been contributorily negligent is not a complete bar, but does serve to reduce the amount of the plaintiff's recovery. Until 1969, only seven states had adopted this type of statute. The other states had to struggle within the traditional bounds of the common law. As of 1981, at least thirty-two states had adopted some version of comparative negligence, thus making it available in a majority of states. The most common version provides that if the plaintiff's negligence was less serious than the defendant's (or, in some states, no more serious than the defendant's), the plaintiff's recovery is to be reduced by the proportion of his negligence. Thus, if the plaintiff's negligence amounted to 25 percent of the culpability in an accident and the defendant's accounted for the remaining 75 percent, the plaintiff would recover 75 percent of the damages from the defendant. Some jurisdictions, such as New York, have pure comparative negligence statutes that permit the plaintiff to recover even if his culpable conduct is found to exceed the culpable conduct of the defendant: the plaintiff's negligence will simply diminish damages.

The first of three states to change its rule by judicial overruling of the common law rule of contributory negligence was Florida. In *Hoffman* v. *Jones*, 280 So.2d 431 (Fla. 1973), the court offered these views on reasons for change:

> One reason for the abandonment of the contributory negligence theory is that the initial justification for establishing the complete defense is no longer valid. It is generally accepted that, historically, contributory negligence was adopted "to protect the essential growth of industries, particularly transportation." Institute of Judicial Administration, Comparative Negligence — 1954 Supplement, at page 2. Modern economic and social customs, however, favor the individual, not industry.
>
> We find that none of the justifications for denying any recovery to a plaintiff, who has contributed to his own injuries to any extent, has any validity in this age.
>
> Perhaps the best argument in favor of the movement from contributory to comparative negligence is that the latter is simply a more equitable system of determining liability and a more socially desirable method of loss distribution. The injustice which occurs when a plaintiff suffers severe injuries as the result of an accident for which he is only slightly responsible, and is thereby denied any damages, is readily apparent. The rule of contributory negligence is a harsh one which either places the burden of a loss for which two are responsible upon only one party or relegates to Lady Luck the determination of the damages for which each of two negligent parties will be liable. When the negligence of more than one person contributes to the occurrence of an accident, each should pay the proportion of the total damages he has caused the other party.

The court was also influenced by the fact that virtually every other common law country and most civil law countries had adopted comparative negligence. As to the argument that juries did not follow the old rule anyway, the court approvingly quoted a discussion that thought this bred disrespect for the law by putting citizens in a position in which they felt it necessary to disregard the judge's instructions.

Exculpatory Agreements

Another possible defense against liability involves contract law. This is a so-called *exculpation clause* under which the plaintiff agrees in advance not to sue the defendant for certain acts — usually the negligence of defendant or its servant for which it would otherwise be liable.

Ciofalo v. Vic Tanney Gyms, Inc.
New York Court of Appeals, 1961. 10 N.Y. 2d 294, 177 N.E. 2d 925

FROESSEL, JUDGE.

This action by plaintiff wife for personal injuries, and by plaintiff husband for medical expenses and loss of services, stems from injuries which the wife sustained as the result of a fall at or near the edge of a swimming pool located on defendant's premises. Plaintiff claimed that because of excessive slipperiness and lack of sufficient and competent personnel she was caused to fall and fractured her left wrist.

At the time of the injury, plaintiff wife was a "member" or patron of the gymnasium operated by defendant, and in her membership contract she had agreed to assume full responsibility for any injuries which might occur to her in or about defendant's premises, "including but without limitation, any claims for personal injuries resulting from or arising out of the negligence of" the defendant.

In addition to denying the material allegations of the complaint, defendant's answer set forth as an affirmative defense the provision of the contract above referred to. Defendant moved for summary judgment, and plaintiffs, by cross motion, moved to strike said defense, their attorney contending in an affidavit that the exculpatory clause is void as against public policy. Summary judgment was granted in favor of defendant, and the Appellate Division has affirmed.

Although exculpatory clauses in a contract, intended to insulate one of the parties from liability resulting from his own negligence, are closely scrutinized, they are enforced, but with a number of qualifications. Whether or not such provisions, when properly expressed, will be given effect depends upon the legal relationship between the contracting parties and the interest of the public therein. Thus such a provision has been held void when contained in the contract of carriage of a common carrier (*Conklin* v. *Canadian-Colonial Airways*, 266 N.Y. 244, 194 N.E. 692) unless a reduced fare was charged. . . ; or in the contract of a public utility under a duty to furnish telephone service. . . ; or when imposed by the employer as a condition of employment. . . .

On the other hand, where the intention of the parties is expressed in sufficiently clear and unequivocal language. . . , and it does not come within any of the aforesaid categories where the public interest is directly involved, a provision absolving a party from his own negligent acts will be given effect. . . .

Of course, contracts may not be construed to exempt parties from the consequences of their own negligence in the absence of express language to that effect. . . .

The wording of the contract in the instant case expresses as clearly as language can the intention of the parties to completely insulate the defendant from liability for injuries sustained by plaintiff by reason of defendant's own negligence, and, in the face of the allegation of the complaint charging merely ordinary negligence, such agreement is valid.

Here there is no special legal relationship and no overriding public interest which demand that this contract provision, voluntarily entered into by competent parties, should be rendered ineffectual. Defendant, a private corporation, was under no obligation or legal duty to accept plaintiff as a "member" or patron. Having consented to do so, it had the right to insist upon such terms as it deemed appropriate. Plaintiff, on the other hand, was not required to assent to unacceptable terms, or to give up a valuable legal right, as a condition precedent to obtaining employment or being able to make use of the services rendered by a public carrier or utility. She voluntarily applied for membership in a private organization, and agreed to the terms upon which this membership was bestowed. She may not repudiate them now.

The judgment appealed from should be affirmed, without costs.

Desmond, C.J., and Dye, Fuld, Van Voorhis, Burke and Foster, JJ., concur.

Judgment affirmed.

Proof of Negligence: The Res Ipsa Loquitur Exception

The plaintiff has the burden of proof in convincing the court that it should order the defendant to compensate the plaintiff. He may attempt to prove negligence by eyewitnesses, by physical evidence (e.g., tire skid marks), and by circumstantial evidence. But sometimes proof can be difficult. In *Byrne* v. *Boadle*, 2 H.&C. 722, 159 Eng. Rep. 299 (1863), the plaintiff, while walking on a public street, was struck and injured by a barrel that had fallen from the second floor window of the defendant flour dealer's premises. Because the plaintiff introduced no evidence to show how or why the barrel fell on him, the trial judge held that there was no proof that the defendant was negligent.

On appeal, the trial court was reversed. The appellate court states "There are certain cases of which it may be said, *res ipsa loquitur* [the thing speaks for itself], and this seems one of them. . . . A barrel could not roll out of a warehouse without some negligence, and to say that a plaintiff who is injured by it must call witnesses from the warehouse to prove negligence seems to be preposterous." Since the barrel was in the custody of the defendant, he must explain what happened.

STRICT LIABILITY

We turn now to the third major basis for imposing liability on those who have caused personal injury (first was intentionally inflicted harm and second was negligence, each having its own philosophical justification for imposing liability). The concept of *strict liability* is developing with no single rationale to support its imposition. Rather, we find a variety of arguments supporting such liability, which will emerge as we consider the material that follows.

Hazardous Activities

Exner v. Sherman Power Const. Co.
United States Court of Appeals, Second Circuit, 1931. 54 F.2d 510

[Defendant kept dynamite in a hut 935 feet from the dwelling house of plaintiff. Two servants of defendant were leaving the hut carrying boxes of dynamite when a series of explosions occurred that killed several people and caused physical injuries to plaintiff. The dynamite had been placed in the hut to keep it warm so that it might be used on a construction job nearby. Defendant proved that keeping dynamite in the hut was safer than bringing boxes from some remote storage to the construction site when needed. The trial court entered judgment for plaintiff without proof of negligence.]

AUGUSTUS N. HAND.

. . . .

The question remains whether there was an absolute liability for the damage caused by the explosion at common law. . . .

Dynamite is of the class of elements which one who stores or uses in such a locality, or under such circumstances as to cause likelihood of risk to others, stores or uses at his peril. He is an insurer, and is absolutely liable if damage results to third persons, either from the direct impact of rocks thrown out by the explosion (which would be a common-law trespass) or from concussion.

. . . .

We can see no reason for imposing a different liability for the results of an explosion, whether the dynamite explodes when stored or when employed in blasting. To be sure there is a greater likelihood of damage from blasting than from storage, but in each case the explosion arises from an act connected with a business conducted for profit and fraught with substantial risk and possibility of the gravest consequences. . . .

. . . .

. . . The extent to which one man in the lawful conduct of his business is liable for injuries to another involves an adjustment of conflicting interests. The solution of the problem in each particular case has never been dependent upon any universal criterion of liability (such as "fault") applicable to all situations. If damage is inflicted, there ordinarily is liability, in the absence of excuse. When, as here, the defendant, though without fault, has engaged in the perilous activity of storing large quantities of a dangerous explosive for use in his business, we think there is no justification for relieving it of liability, and that the owner of the business, rather than a third person who has no relation to the explosion, other than that of injury, should bear the loss. The blasting cases seem to afford ample analogies and to justify this conclusion.

[One judge concurred on another ground.]

A number of states adhere to the approach contained in the *Restatement of Torts*, Second, which is set forth below:

§519. (1) One who carries on an abnormally dangerous activity is subject to liability for harm to the person, land or chattels of another resulting from the activity, although he has exercised the utmost care to prevent such harm.

(2) Such strict liability is limited to the kind of harm, the risk of which makes the activity abnormally dangerous.

§520. In determining whether an activity is abnormally dangerous, the following factors are to be considered:

(a) whether the activity involves a high degree of risk of some harm to the person, land or chattels of others;

(b) whether the gravity of the harm which may result from it is likely to be great;

(c) whether the risk cannot be eliminated by the exercise of reasonable care;

(d) whether the activity is not a matter of common usage;

(e) whether the activity is inappropriate to the place where it is carried on; and

(f) the value of the activity to the community.

The *Exner* case alludes to one hybrid form of liability that partakes of both fault liability and strict liability. That is the rule of law known as *respondeat superior*. It holds a master liable for torts committed by his servant while acting for the master's benefit. This is fault liability to the extent that the plaintiff must prove that the servant was negligent; it is strict liability because the master is liable for such negligence no matter how carefully he picked his servant to perform a job within his capacity. Respondeat superior is an ancient rule of law, so commonplace that you may not have raised an eyebrow when noting that almost every case in this chapter is brought against corporate defendants for negligence of their servants. (Respondeat superior will be discussed further in Chapters 13–15, on Agency.)

Defective Products: Consumer Protection

Strict liability in tort is emerging as the dominant basis for liability in another area — injuries caused by defective products. This development, which provides increased protection for the consumer, was triggered by a series of important happenings involving guarantees in contracts for the sale of goods. These interrelated contract and tort concepts are addressed as a unit in Chapter 5.

Statutory Developments

Although the courts had original responsibility for developing the legal response to accidental injuries, the common law they developed was subject to statutory change whenever the legislature concluded that the courts were not reaching desirable results. This might occur for two main reasons: either the court voluntarily chooses a path that the legislature dislikes, or the courts realize that their decisions in an area are unsatisfactory but they are unable to reach desirable results because of the limitations on the judicial branch. For either reason, the legislature might conclude that it should enter the picture and adopt legislation to alter the direction that the law has taken. (Of course, legislatures may not do this if the judicial branch has based its decision on constitutional grounds.) On a narrow level we have already seen some examples of legislative activity, as in the development of comparative negligence statutes.

Massive legislative rejection of the judicial approach to accidents has occurred once in the past and is occurring again at this very moment. We turn first to the earlier episode.

Workers' Compensation

As the Industrial Revolution took hold, dangerous machinery became common and industrial injuries became both more numerous and more serious. The first cases brought by workers to recover for their injuries were based on fault and ran into a variety of defenses that suggested that courts doubted the wisdom of such claims. After some early ameliorative legislation received unsympathetic judicial treatment, the legislatures undertook a much more fundamental restructuring of the entire relationship between worker and employer. The details of that restructuring are discussed in the section on employer-employee relations (pages 611–13) in Chapter 34. Suffice it to say at this point that the essence of workers' compensation legislation is that the employee gives up the low probability of a substantial but (given the time absorbed in appeals) delayed recovery from his employer in return for the certainty of a timely but modest payment for injury and lost income from the insurance system.

It has not been easy to integrate workers' compensation into the basic tort system. In several situations a worker eligible for compensation from being hurt in the course of his employment may also, under traditional tort principles, have a claim against some other person. The initial bargain that led to workers' compensation forbids the employee from pursuing a tort action against his employer — at least where the accident is not attributable to some intentional or reckless behavior by the employer. Most states also extend this barrier to suits against fellow employees whose negligence may have caused the worker's injury. But the overwhelming view is that all other tort claims remain intact and are to be judged according to the usual rules.

If the worker succeeds in the tort action, the defendant must pay the plaintiff the full measure of damages without deduction for the workers' compensation benefits already received or available. This potential problem of double recovery is avoided by requiring the plaintiff to reimburse the workers' compensation carrier to the extent the tort award duplicates benefits already obtained from the workers' compensation fund.

Note that this potential for double recovery is present in all tort actions when the plaintiff receives some assistance from outside the tort system, such as from an insurance policy paying some medical expenses or protecting against loss of income through accident, or perhaps even some government benefit programs. The usual rule in such cases is that the defendant may not take advantage of any of these payments. This has the effect of forcing the defendant to pay for the full amount of the harm done and creates the possibility of double recovery by the plaintiff. In most cases, this danger is avoided by a requirement in the insurance contract that if any tort recovery duplicates an insurance payment, the amount of duplication is to be returned to the original insurer. In some situations, however, reimbursement is not called for, and there may be double recoveries. This problem has become increasingly important in recent years as more and more Americans are obtaining insurance against a variety of potential disasters.

There is another step to be considered, however. The defendant who has had to pay the plaintiff may not feel that justice has been done if this loss is left entirely, or even partially, upon him. He may believe that the liability is more appropriately placed on the shoulders of the employer of the injured worker, who was more at fault than was the defendant. Or, the plaintiff may be dissatisfied with the small compensation award and grasp at weak legal straws to establish tort liability on an outside defendant when in reality the most serious misbehavior was that of the employer, who is immunized from the worker's suit. The question is whether the employer is also immunized from having to share that judgment with the outside defendant, or perhaps reimburse that defendant entirely. In most ordinary tort cases, if a defendant is held liable to a plaintiff, that defendant may seek to share the judgment with someone who is equally liable with him (called a *contribution*) or try to place the full liability on others who have been more seriously at fault (called an *indemnity*). In workers' compensation cases, however, most courts have rejected these efforts on the ground that they seek to evade the initial bargain that led to workers' compensation — it is unfair to hold the employer liable for the compensation benefits and then for potential reimbursement of tort awards.

In most states, then, a worker may sue any outsider and recover a full judgment and return any duplication to the workers' compensation carrier. The party held liable in the tort action may seek contribution or indemnity from others, but not from the worker's employer.

Was there a better way to work all of this out? Should the worker's lawsuits be abolished against all defendants so that workers' compensation becomes the exclusive remedy for the worker?

Automobile No-Fault Legislation

Concern about using the fault system to adjudicate motor vehicle accidents has been voiced since the late 1920s. Extracts from one recent critique of the operation of tort law in this area follow.

The Present System in Theory. How fault law was applied to auto insurance is well summed up in Insurance Department of the State of New York, "Automobile Insurance . . . For Whose Benefit?" 7–9, 17–19 (1970):

> The cornerstone of the present way of handling the personal injury and property damage costs of automobile accidents is fault law, which, when combined with insurance indemnifying against liability for fault, becomes what we will call the fault insurance system.
>
> . . . .
>
> Fault law determines whether the fault insurance system pays or not. Fault law theory is based on the principle that these determinations should turn on the conduct at the moment of the accident of the individuals involved in the accident. It ignores insurance and other economic realities and frames its key questions as though what were being decided were whether the loss should rest with the victim or whether instead the loss should be shifted to another single individual and then should rest with him. In an automobile accident case today, what is really being decided is whether the loss of a particular victim should be taken out of the great pool of automobile insurance premiums paid by a multitude of people who had no connection with the accident at all. But the principles of fault law preclude us from thinking about it that way.

The Present System in Practice. The problems with applying fault law become clear in Insurance Department of the State of New York, "Automobile Insurance . . . For Whose Benefit?" 22–26, 30–31, 34–37, 47, 59–62 (1970):

> When fault law developed, there were no automobile accidents. In 1968, there were 14.6 million automobile accidents in the United States.
>
> It is not necessary to belabor the point that fault law, the courts and liability insurance were not designed to deal with the accident-causing propensity of the modern automobile. Nor is it necessary to belabor the point that the automobile has placed heavy burdens on all three institutions.
>
> Under these burdens, the fault insurance system might be expected to display in striking degree the defects — such as delay and inefficiency — that inhere in the system in theory. . . .
>
> . . . .
>
> UNCOMPENSATED VICTIMS
>
> We saw that, by its own theory, the fault insurance system is not supposed to pay benefits to everyone who suffers loss in an automobile accident.
>
> The practice quite lives up to the theory. One out of every four people suffering bodily injury in an automobile accident in this State receives nothing whatsoever from the fault insurance system.

DELAY

Even where the fault insurance system pays something, it pays slowly. Injured victims of automobile accidents face average delays in collecting under automobile liability insurance that are ten times as long as the delays in collecting under collision, homeowners or burglary insurance and forty times as long as delays under accident and health insurance. . . .

UNPREDICTABILITY

The fault insurance system operates through thousands of legal and extra-legal forms that apply its rules unevenly and unpredictably.

Because the legal rules of fault were laid down by appellate courts, it is easy to imagine the system is directed by those courts. But it is not. Only about 1% of automobile liability claims are decided by a court, and very few of these get to the appellate courts.

The litigated cases come up under circumstances which hardly permit accurate and uniform findings, and whose general surreality has been commented upon by many authorities.

The other 99% of the claims are settled in a proliferation of forums outside the judiciary — typically in unrecorded, private sessions between a claimant or his attorney and an insurance adjuster.

. . . .

MALAPPORTIONMENT OF BENEFITS

The award for "pain and suffering" is no longer ancillary to the award for economic loss. Quite the contrary. In the typical case today the award for "pain and suffering" is larger than the award for economic loss.

. . . .

LACK OF COORDINATION OF BENEFITS

Where and when and however much or little the fault insurance system pays, its benefits are not coordinated with those from other sources.

An accident victim often is entitled to payments from such sources as health insurance and income continuation plans. Today 91 percent of the workers in this State are covered by health insurance, and most are covered by income continuation plans as well.

These and other sources pay significant benefits to traffic victims. But under the "collateral source rule" of the fault insurance system, these other benefits are generally disregarded in setting the automobile liability insurance award.*

INEFFICIENCY

Because of its complex structure and the large number of individual acts and operations it involves, the fault insurance system is inherently expensive to operate. A significant part of the dollar that passes through the mechanism inevitably

---

*The "collateral source rule" of damages in negligence actions holds that the defendant should not benefit (by paying lower damages) by the happenstance that his victim, the plaintiff, received compensation from another source (e.g., the victim's own health insurance). The rule is understandable in the historical context in which it developed — when fault law had clear retributive overtones, liability insurance was unheard of, and litigations were seen as involving moral claims entirely based on comparing the conduct of the two individuals at bar.

sticks to the mechanism, burdening consumers and shortchanging victims. That we could see in the system in theory.

What happens in practice? What becomes of the personal injury liability insurance premium dollar?

First of all, insurance companies and agents use up 33 cents. Then lawyers and claims investigators take the next 23 cents.

Together these items make up the operating expenses, or frictional costs, of the fault insurance system — 56 cents out of every premium dollar or $384 million a year in this one State.

What happens to the 44 cents that get through to the accident victim?

. . . .

First, 8 cents of the 44 go to pay for economic losses that have already been reimbursed from another source. Subtracting these redundant benefits as having low priority leaves 36 cents of the premium dollar to pay net losses of victims.

But of those 36 cents, 21.5 cents go for something other than economic loss. The 21.5 cents are lumped together as "general damages" or "pain and suffering" which, in the typical case today, are simply by-products of the bargaining process of insurance adjustment. Once we look beyond the name which the operators of the fault insurance system have given this non-economic portion of liability payments and understand what it really is in the usual case, it assumes a low priority by any social or humane standard.

That leaves just 14.5 cents out of the premium dollar as compensation for the net economic loss of the accident victim — $100 million out of the $686 million which New Yorkers spend every year for automobile bodily injury liability insurance.

. . . .

RISING TENSIONS WITHIN THE SYSTEM

. . . .

Clearly all these developments are inconsistent with the theory of fault law and the theory of liability insurance. What has happened, and is continuing to happen, is that a new theory has taken hold — that victims should be compensated — and the fault insurance system is being distorted further and further to implement the new theory. More and more we are trying to run a compensation system in a fault liability framework.

Integration of Automobile No-Fault into the Tort System. One problem not mentioned in the excerpt is the increasing litigation that occurs between the insured and his liability insurer when the insurer rejects a settlement with the victim. If the case goes to trial and the victim recovers an amount not only in excess of the earlier settlement figure but also in excess of the limits of the insurance policy, the insured is liable for any excess. Insureds have been unhappy with this situation and have urged that insurers never be permitted to reject a settlement unless they are willing to pay the entire judgment that may follow. Courts have been unwilling to go that far, but they do insist that the insurer consider the interests of its insured in deciding whether to settle the case for a specific amount.

Some twenty states have now adopted no-fault legislation. About half the fifty states have adopted *add-on plans*, which provide that all victims of auto accidents are to receive some compensation for medical costs and loss of wages without having to prove anyone at fault in the accidents and even if they themselves were the only persons at fault. These benefits are generally provided by a first-party insurer, who pays directly to the victim. The operation of tort law is totally unaffected, but if the victim succeeds at tort law he will probably have to return his benefits to his insurer to avoid double recovery. Most advocates of no-fault plans deny that add-on statutes are really no-fault proposals because they do not alter the operation of the tort system.

The other half of the states have adopted plans that both provide no-fault benefits to victims, as do the add-on states, and also restrict the victim's right to bring a tort action. Some of these states impose relatively few limits on access to tort law, while others limit such access to those who are severely injured. Naturally, in the latter case, the no-fault benefits paid must be large enough to make the tradeoff a fair one.

The object of limiting tort law is to eliminate minor claims — those that were costly to process and were overcompensated in practice. As to the serious claims, the hope is that the periodic provision of no-fault benefits will reduce the desperate plight of the victim and give him more leverage in his tort claim. Since tort actions are not available against the employer in workers' compensation situations, why do all no-fault plans preserve tort actions for those severely hurt?

The actual operation of a no-fault plan depends on the details in each state's law. However, some useful generalizations can be made. Generally, the owner of every vehicle must procure an insurance policy that combines the conventional liability policy with a part that offers the required no-fault benefits. If the insured himself or a member of his family is hurt, he will seek recovery against his own insurance company for the statutory first party no-fault benefits. (In some states, passengers who are hurt claim against the car's insurer rather than against their own insurer. A pedestrian who does not have a policy may get benefits from any of the insurers whose cars were involved.)

The cost of this type of policy will vary with the type of no-fault plan the state has adopted. Thus, in an add-on system, the liability picture is unchanged and the policy covers additional no-fault benefits. One would expect this policy to be more expensive than current liability policies, unless there are hidden savings, because some victims who collect no-fault benefits decide not to sue anyone. In a state that bars minor law suits it is expected that there will be savings.

As with workers' compensation insurance, it is perfectly permissible for the victim to collect automobile no-fault benefits while at the same time pursuing whatever tort remedies are available to him. It should be emphasized that even the states that bar minor tort claims limit only cases against drivers and car owners. These states do not attempt to affect the law of defective products, for example, under which the victim might collect no-fault benefits but might then sue a car manufacturer for a defective part that caused the crash. If the victim recovers tort damages, either against another driver or against someone outside the system in most cases he will have to return the no-fault benefits that he has received from his insurer to avoid double recovery.

Some critics have been concerned that the states are moving too slowly and that these developments should be uniform. This has led to the introduction in Congress of a bill that would require states to adopt a no-fault statute that pays all medical bills and substantial economic loss but no pain and suffering and that limits recourse to tort law to those severely injured. If states do not voluntarily adopt such legislation they would come under an equally rigorous set of federal standards. In early 1974, the bill passed the Senate but died in the House. Similar efforts have been introduced in each session since 1974.

Future Developments

Are other no-fault plans on the horizon? If automobiles and job-related injuries are removed from the operation of the fault system, relatively few major activities remain. Perhaps the most significant is medical malpractice, under which physicians and surgeons are held liable for adverse results only if they are found to be at fault. Malpractice liability insurance premiums have increased greatly in recent years, partly because of more and larger recoveries by plaintiffs and partly because of the expense of defending malpractice cases, even if the defense is ultimately successful. For these and other reasons, there has recently been growing talk about no-fault medical harm compensation. There are several technical difficulties, such as defining the insurable event, but the effort has begun.

While the United States has been moving away from fault — and from the tort system — one step at a time, New Zealand has done it in one massive step. In 1974, after several years of discussion and planning, that country began operating under a system that abolished virtually all lawsuits for personal injury. In their stead is a governmentally operated social insurance scheme that pays full medical expenses, 80 percent of income loss, and in severe cases some compensation for loss of function and pain and suffering. There is no litigation even for severe injuries, and the government makes no attempt to recoup its expenses from negligent parties who cause the harm. There are three separate funds. One, covering all workers at all times, is financed by employers, much as their workers' compensation system was financed. The second plan covers motor vehicle injuries and is financed largely from costs on motorists. The third fund covers all other injuries and is financed from general funds. The philosophy behind the enactment was that injuries were a social responsibility and society should respond in a coherent, constructive way that emphasized rehabilitation and return to useful activity. Litigation was thought too haphazard to achieve those goals.

PROBLEMS AND QUESTIONS

1. A dissenting judge in *Katko* argued that *Hooker* could be distinguished from *Katko* because the plaintiff in *Katko* was doing something more serious and the defendant was protecting something more valuable than in *Hooker*. Do you agree? Since two cases can never be identical, the question more properly phrased is whether the essentials of the *Hooker* case cover *Katko*. What do you think? (Notice that the majority in referring to the *Hooker* case of ninety-eight years earlier says "we held . . ." — is this accurate?)

2. In protecting herself against what she believes to be assailants, defendant severely injures plaintiff, a

plainclothes policeman. Putting aside the question of criminal liability, is defendant liable for damages for plaintiff's injuries? For punitive damages?

3. If a man falls overboard from a ship that lacks life-saving equipment, how can we tell whether that lack of equipment was related to the man's drowning? What facts would help the plaintiff? What facts would help the defendant?

4. Plaintiff's eye was injured by a piece of metal. The doctor who treated her did not discover this and did not remove the metal immediately. However, the eye would have become infected even with timely treatment. Should the doctor be held liable?

5. Plaintiff, a member of defendant's track team, was overcome by heat. Despite his knowledge of this, defendant failed to render the required assistance, whereupon plaintiff died. Did defendant have a duty to care for the decedent?

6. Defendant left her automobile unattended and unlocked in the street with the key in the ignition, thereby violating a city ordinance. The car was promptly taken for a joy ride by some children: plaintiff was hit because the children could not find the brake. Should defendant be liable to plaintiff?

7. Is comparative negligence clearly an improvement over contributory negligence? Do you see any problems with comparative negligence?

8. Defendant, for the purpose of repairing her house, put a pole across a riding path. Plaintiff collided with the obstruction, was thrown from his horse, and was injured. There was evidence that plaintiff was riding very fast, and that it was light enough to see the pole one hundred yards away. Should plaintiff recover from defendant?

9. Would any of the court's analysis in *Ciofalo* change should the potential defendant offer customers a choice of retaining their negligence claims or relinquishing them in return for a reduced rate?

10. Does a sign indicating limitation of liability absolve a restaurant owner from the consequences of having hired a notorious pickpocket as a waiter?

11. In *Larson v. St. Francis Hotel*, 83 Cal.App.3d 210, 188 P.2d 513 (1948), plaintiff was struck by a chair thrown out of one of the defendant's rooms on V-J Day, August 14, 1945. Plaintiff proved the striking and her injuries and rested. The trial judge dismissed the case and the appellate court affirmed. How does this case differ from the barrel case?

12. Is the result in *Exner* consistent with sections 519 and 520 of the *Restatement of Torts*, Second?

13. Plaintiff is injured when his hand is caught in a machine which his fellow worker has accidentally turned on by merely touching the switch. Are plaintiff's recovery possibilities limited to workers' compensation?

14. Which is the most persuasive objection to the fault system in theory? In practice? Are the criticisms sufficient to lead you to reject the fault approach to dealing with automobile caused injuries?

15. Professor Keeton, a leader in the discussion of no-fault auto insurance, illuminates the nature of several of the important choices by setting out two competing plans, assumed to be roughly equivalent in cost:

a. Under the existing system, the package is $25,000 per person/$50,000 per accident liability insurance coverage, with the assurance (by uninsured motorist coverage) of the collectibility of one's valid claims against other drivers up to at least that same amount. This package would provide each person with the right to recover for both economic loss and general damages when there is a valid claim based on negligence, but no right to recover either kind of damages in other cases and no assurance of the financial responsibility of the negligent person above $25,000 per person and $50,000 per accident.

b. The other package is UMVARA, with guaranteed lifetime coverage, no overall limit and relatively liberal internal limits ($200 per week for wage loss and a semiprivate rather than a private room when hospitalization is needed). Subject to these internal limits, this package provides total coverage for economic losses sustained in automobile accidents regardless of negligence, but no chance of recovering general damages for noneconomic detriment (such as pain and suffering) unless the injury is severe.[2]

Which package would you choose? Why?

---

2. Keeton, "Compensation Systems and Utah's No-Fault Statute," 1973 Utah L. Rev. 383, 399 (1973).

III

CONTRACTS

SIGNIFICANCE OF CONTRACTS

The law of contracts is one of the most important subject areas of the American legal system. It provides the basis for practically all commercial transactions in this country and in international trade transactions as well. Moreover, the law of contracts provides the underlying rationale for a host of legal relationships that arise in virtually every area of civil law: the transfer of goods, securities, and real property are almost always affected through contractual agreements, and the law of business organizations is based on a host of contractual agreements.

As an indication of the contemporary significance of contract law consider that Westinghouse Electric Corporation spent two pages of its 1977 annual report discussing various litigation, principally suits by twenty public utilities alleging that Westinghouse is required to deliver to them 85 million pounds of uranium. At the January, 1978 market price of $40 to $45 per pound, potential damages for breach of contract represented $3.4 billion dollars. In contrast, the total net worth of Westinghouse was $167.7 million, and the market value of its stock — 87.3 million shares of stock multiplied by $19-⅙ per share, the common stock's average price in 1977 — was $1.7 billion. Thus, ownership of the company depends on the outcome of this breach of contract litigation.

DEFINITIONS

The *Restatement of Contracts* defines a *contract* as "a promise or a set of promises for the breach of which the law gives a remedy, or the performance of which the law in some way recognizes as a duty." *Restatement of Contracts,* section 1 (1932). Professor A. L. Corbin, an authority in the field of contracts law, endorses the *Restatement* definition in *Corbin on Contracts* (1952):

> A very common definition is that a contract is a promise enforceable at law directly or indirectly. This has the advantage of brevity, and it is perhaps

4

INTRO-DUCTION TO CONTRACTS

as useful a definition as any that has been thus far suggested. It places emphasis upon one of the operative acts, an expression of assent. This is restricted to an expression that is promissory in character. By restricting it further to a promise that is enforceable at law, it brings into the definition the element of legal operation and effect. Such a definition as this does not inform us as to what kind of facts will be operative to create legal rights and duties; it merely gives us a mode of describing such operative facts after we have found by other means that they do have legal operation.

Generally, then, contracts are enforceable agreements that bind two or more persons to a legal relationship involving a mutual exchange of rights and duties. In simple terms, the purchase of a daily newspaper at 25¢ and the purchase of an Alaskan oil lease at $50,000,000 are both contracts, governed by what has come to be known as the law of contracts. The agreements made by professors of universities to teach courses and by students to pay tuition are also contractual agreements. They involve some measure of enforceable legal rights, and they too are governed by the law of contracts.

As is obvious from what has been said, contractual obligations are many and varied and are found in numerous circumstances. They take place in the formal atmosphere of a corporate conference room and in the informal one of the corner grocery store. They may take the form of oral agreements, hastily done informal written agreements, or detailed and elaborately worded written drafts.

Not infrequently, the terms agreed on are embodied in already printed documents, or *form contracts,* where the names of the parties and the particular items involved are merely inserted. These form agreements are used in a variety of frequently occurring situations, including the purchase of a home or insurance, the lease of an apartment, and the granting of an installment loan or an installment purchase.

The purpose of this part is to indicate what contracts are, how they are formed, and to what extent and in what ways legal rights and duties arising under contracts will be protected and enforced. But this coverage will not exhaust the subject, for the law of contracts extends into other areas, often forming the basis of relationships among parties. Thus, although this section will consider contracts for the sale of goods, the treatment will not be detailed. This subject has become a highly specialized area of contract law and will be dealt with in more depth in Chapters 16–23. The same will be true for other areas of commercial law, such as negotiable instruments and secured transactions, which are based on contract law and are covered by the Uniform Commercial Code. Other areas of commercial law, such as insurance, real property, suretyship, agency, partnership, and corporate law are also heavily dependent on the law of contracts, although they are not covered by the Uniform Commercial Code. As the text surveys each of these areas, then, the law of contracts will be continually recalled.

It should also be borne in mind that the cases presented in these chapters are exceptional ones, dealt with and considered by appellate courts. They are exceptional in that most disputes — even those in which legal proceedings are instituted — never reach formal legal judgment. First, the vast majority of contracts are carried out to the satisfaction of all parties, without any dispute arising. Second, most disputes are settled between the parties or their attorneys, by negotiation, arbitration, or compromise of rights, without resort to the courts. And when proceedings are instituted, they are usually settled during the pleading, preparation, or trial stages. Thus, the cases that reach the appellate courts are unusual ones, involving a tiny fraction of 1 percent of all contracts that are made.

It should also be noted that the law of contracts cannot be considered as a system of rules to be relied on without a foundation in business judgment and without a sense of justice. Lawyers and businesspeople usually rely on the doctrines of contract law to guide them in conducting their affairs, but this cannot be exclusively so. For while contract law is based on the demand of society that promises be met and obligations be carried out in good faith in accordance with established patterns of behavior, the law will always be changing, developing its doctrines to meet new commercial and social needs. Thus, the wise student will learn the rules, but he will also learn of their rationale, and he will appreciate where changes may be taking place. He will, in short, be following the path of the law.

We will begin our discussion of contracts by defining the major concepts involved. As you read later chapters in this part, you may wish to refer back to these definitions.

Contracts and Their Formation

Express Contracts

An *express* contract is a written or oral ageement by the parties involved. The terms of the agreement are articulated by the parties and can be determined by referring to the actual contractual agreement.

Implied Contracts

An *implied* contract is an agreement that is not evidenced by an oral or written agreement as to terms, but by conduct that indicates an intention on the part of the parties to be contractually bound. For example, a customer in a restaurant does not specifically agree to pay the price of his meal as printed on the menu when he orders his dinner, but by ordering such a meal from the menu he shows that he intends to be bound by its price. Thus, the agreement is an enforceable one, for an implied contract is just as legally effective as an express contract.

Contracts Implied in Law

Also referred to as the *quasi-contract,* the *contract implied in law* is a legal obligation that is imposed in the absence of any specific agreement, express or implied. It is an obligation considered to be owed on account of considerations of justice or fairness. The quasi-contract is entirely lacking in the basic elements of agreement, but is imposed because of an assumed duty arising out of the transactions between the parties. Thus, when a physician renders necessary medical service to the unconscious victim of an automobile accident, the law implies an obligation on the part of the victim to pay the reasonable value of the services rendered. For while the victim did not, indeed could not, promise to pay for the services rendered, the law presumes a duty to pay based on an implied promise, as in the following case.

Chase v. Corcoran
Supreme Judicial Court of Massachusetts, 1871. 106 Mass. 286
GRAY, J.
The evidence introduced at the trial tended to prove the following facts: The plaintiff, while engaged with his own boats in the Mystic River, within the ebb and flow of the tide, found the defendant's boat adrift, with holes in the bottom and the keel nearly demolished, and in danger of sinking or being crushed between plaintiff's boats and the piles of a bridge unless the plaintiff had saved it. The plaintiff secured the boat, attached a rope to it, towed it ashore, fastened it to a post, and, after putting up notices in public places in the nearest town, and making other inquiries, and no owner appearing, took it to his own barn, stowed it there for two winters, and during the intervening summer made repairs (which were necessary to preserve the boat) and for its better preservation put it in the water, fastened it to a wharf, and directed the wharfinger to deliver it to any one who should prove ownership and pay the plaintiff's expenses about it. The defendant afterwards claimed the boat; the plaintiff refused to deliver it unless the defendant paid him the expenses of taking care of it; and the defendant then took the boat by a writ of replevin, without paying the plaintiff anything. This action is brought to recover money paid by the plaintiff for moving and repairing the boat, and compensation for his own care and trouble in keeping and repairing the same, amounting to twenty-six dollars in all. . . .

[Plaintiff testified that when found by him, the boat was worth five dollars. At the close of the evidence, the trial court directed a verdict for the defendant. Plaintiff appealed. After holding that no Massachusetts statutes were applicable, Gray, J., continued:]

The claim of the plaintiff is therefore to be regulated by the common law. It is not a claim for salvage for saving the boat when adrift and in danger on tidewater; and does not present the question whether the plaintiff had any lien upon the boat, or could recover for salvage services in an action at common law. His claim is for the reasonable expenses of keeping and repairing the boat after he had brought it to the shore; and the single question is whether a promise is to be implied by law from the owner of a boat, upon taking it from a person who has found it adrift on tide-water and brought it ashore, to pay him for the necessary expenses of preserving the boat while in his possession. We are of opinion that such a promise is to be implied. The plaintiff, as the finder of the boat, had the lawful possession of it, and the right to do what was necessary for its preservation. Whatever might have been the liability of the owner if he had chosen to let the finder retain the boat, by taking it from him he made himself liable to pay the reasonable expenses incurred in keeping and repairing it. . . .

Exceptions sustained.

Contracts and the Manner of Their Acceptance

Bilateral Contracts

A *bilateral contract* is a form of contract that occurs when an offer requires that an acceptance by the party to whom it is offered be made in the form of a promise to perform an act. Once that promise to perform has been made, both parties are contractually obligated to perform the agreement.

Unilateral Contracts

When an offer calls for the acceptance to occur by the performance of an act, rather than by the promise to perform, the contract is described as *unilateral*. It is termed unilateral because it only becomes effective — under traditional rules of offer and acceptance — upon the complete performance of the required act. The party's acceptance and his complete performance of the contract occur simultaneously. He is under no further obligation to perform, and since the obligations upon acceptance are only those owed by the other side, the contract is styled as unilateral.

Since contracts are enforceable agreements, the effectiveness of an attempted acceptance can be quite important. The difference between unilateral and bilateral contracts — which shall be dealt with in depth on pages 117–20 — is important and is illustrated in these two examples:

1. *Unilateral Contract.* The offer states: "I promise to give you $100 if you cross the Brooklyn Bridge." The party to whom the offer is made can only accept by actually crossing the bridge. His promises to do so are of no importance and are without legal effect. Until he actually crosses the bridge, his contractual rights are not determined; he cannot bind, nor can he be bound. And the offer can be withdrawn before acceptance.
2. *Bilateral Contract.* The offer states: "I promise to give you $100 if you promise to cross the Brooklyn Bridge." The party to whom the offer is made is able to promise first and then cross the bridge, knowing that a contractual undertaking, and obligation, has already been made. Both parties are bound to perform before actual performance begins, and both can hold the other to the required performance. This shows the greater certainty found in the bilateral than in the unilateral contract.

Contracts and Their Performance

Executory Contracts

An *executory* contract is one that has not yet been fully performed by either of the parties. Thus, an agreement to purchase an automobile, with delivery and payment to occur in ten days is, until performance, an executory contract. (This contract is bilateral.)

If one of the parties to the ageement has rendered his performance and the other has yet to do so, the contract is executory in part. Thus, if payment for the automobile had been made but delivery is still due, the agreement is executory in part. In a unilateral contract, only one side (the offeror's) will be executory.

Executed Contracts

The *executed* contract is the contract that has been fully performed by all parties to the agreement. When delivery and payment for the automobile have both been made, the contract has been executed.

Contracts and Their Effectiveness

Voidable Contracts

A *voidable* contract is an agreement that is initially binding and effective but may later be avoided by one of the parties. This rejection is perfectly proper, and the party who elects to avoid the contract — an act also called *disaffirmance* or *rescission* — usually does so on the basis of some bar to his proper assent to its terms or on account of a limitation on his contractual capacity to enter into that legal relationship. For example, one who has been the victim of a fraud by contracting to purchase goods the quality of which were intentionally misrepresented, may avoid the contract and be restored to the position he was in prior to the agreement.

Void Contracts

The *void* contract, unlike the voidable contract, has never been an effective agreement. It has no legal effect whatsoever, and none of the parties to the void contract are subject to it. In almost all states, gambling contracts are void, thus having no legal effect.

Unenforceable Contracts

An *unenforceable* contract is a valid contract, but one that cannot be enforced as valid in a court of law because it is defective in terms of one of its legal requirements. For instance, under the Statute of Frauds, unless certain kinds of contracts are in writing, evidence cannot be introduced in court to prove them as contracts. As a result, a party to a valid oral contract cannot recover in court for the breach of that agreement.

The unenforceable contract differs from the voidable contract in that the voidable contract confers a right upon the party avoiding the agreement to renounce his undertaking. No such right is given to the party against whom a contract is sought to be enforced when the contract is merely unenforceable. Rather, the unenforceable contract simply bars the party seeking to assert the agreement from effectively doing so. Of course, if the parties choose to honor the unenforceable agreement, they are free to do so.

THE REQUIREMENTS OF A CONTRACT

In order for an agreement to be recognized as a contract with legally enforceable rights, it must conform to certain fundamental requirements. These requirements will be briefly introduced below and elaborated on in the other chapters of this part.

Competent Parties

One important element is that of *competent parties*. Contracts made by ordinary individuals or organizations meet this requirement without difficulty. But there are many persons who are deemed by law to be incompetent parties to some significant degree. Little children — and not so little children — for example, as well as insane persons, among others, enter legal arrangements with different consequences on account of their incapacity. Thus, the competence of the parties will determine the effectiveness of certain contractual agreements, and in some situations the courts will find these contracts to be voidable.

Assent

Another element is that of assent by two or more parties. This assent reflects an understanding reached by the parties to the agreement. It is arrived at when one person makes an offer to another, which offer contains the power to bind the offeror through the acceptance of the offer. When acceptance has been made, there has been an *assent* between the parties.

Questions about assent turn on whether the assent manifested by the parties was a real assent. Such matters concern three possibilities: a mistake being made by one or both of the parties, misrepresentation of material facts by one or more of the parties, or duress or undue influence being used by one of the parties on the other. It may be that because of error or bad conduct, the assent on the part of the parties to the agreement will not be real and effective. It may be an assent that was improperly arrived at.

Proper Legal Form

Another element is that of *proper legal form*. The old adage "get it in writing" carries an important legal message: in certain situations, a writing is an indispensable requirement for an enforceable contract. Some types of agreements must be in writing or be evidenced by a writing; some contracts must contain signatures that are placed at the end of the agreement. As we shall see in more detail on pages 176–79, the rules are not universal from state to state.

Consideration

The contractual agreement must also contain *consideration*, a bargained for, mutually given element that usually — though not always — forms the substance of the agreement. Thus, when A sells his book to B for $5, the consideration given by A is the book, and that given by B is $5.

It is not necessary that consideration have a tangible form to be effective. Parties who give up legal rights to do certain things or who undertake to perform acts that they are not otherwise legally obliged to perform, also furnish consideration that is valid. The concept of consideration, it should be noted, is one that has been historically developed. Mastery of it seems elusive at first impression.

Valid and Lawful Purpose

Finally, the contract should serve a valid and lawful purpose. Contractual agreements must conform to the requirements of law, and must serve lawful ends. Legal disabilities will attach to contracts that call for the violation of the law, such as agreements requiring an antitrust violation or a contract to commit murder. Agreements that serve unlawful ends are often rendered void, and usually the courts will hesitate to intervene in disputes involving them.

PROBLEMS AND QUESTIONS

1. Implied in law contracts appear to be imposed on a party when that party would otherwise be unjustly enriched or benefitted at the expense of the other party. Is the foregoing statement true?

2. Can a bilateral contract be accepted with a promise rather than the performance of an act?

3. Are form contracts judged by the same general requirements as a drafted-to-order contract?

4. On Wednesday Mr. Bird promised his wife that he would take her to a football game the following Sunday.

a. Does Mrs. Bird have the right to sue for the value of a ticket to the football game if Mr. Bird fails to live up to his promise?

b. Is the promise given by Mr. Bird unenforceable under contract law principles because it was an oral promise? Would a written promise be enforceable under contract law principles in these circumstances?

5. Cynthia Fortune went to an auto dealer in her hometown and looked at a European sports car. The car was painted black. She told Harvey Jones, the salesman, that she really liked the car but would only buy a car that was silver. Jones ordered a silver car. A month later, after the silver car was delivered to the dealer, Fortune had no interest in buying the car.

a. May the dealer successfully institute an action against Fortune, based on an implied contract?

b. If Fortune had left no deposit with the dealer but had signed a written agreement to purchase the silver car, would the dealer have an action against her based on the written agreement?

Raymond Sanders purchased a television set from
V Sales, Inc., at a sale price of $400. The salesman
ssured him that the nineteen-inch model was avail-
ble at that price. A week later, when Sanders re-
urned from a business trip, he found that a fifteen-
nch model had been delivered to his home and had
een used by his family for a week. When Sanders
alled TV Sales, Inc., the manager of the store told
im that the salesman who had waited on him had
een fired and that only the fifteen-inch model tele-
ision had been on sale for $400. Assuming Sanders
an show he is entitled to some form of relief, is there
ny monetary award to which TV Sales is entitled?

Sam Watson bought a fifteen-inch television set
rom TV Sales, Inc., and agreed to pay for it on an
nstallment basis. The installment contract called for
n interest rate of 24 percent. The legal limit on in-
erest rates for an installment contract in the state was
8 percent. Can TV Sales legally enforce the 24 percent
rovision? Why?

Marx and Dunfey entered into a contract for the
ale of land which is unenforceable under local state
law. Marx performed her part of the contract and
deeded the land to Dunfey. Dunfey performed her
part of the contract by delivering a check to Marx. A
week after delivering her check, Dunfey decided that
she did not want the land and sought to revoke the
contract under the local state law provisions. Will she
be successful?

9. Reed sold his thriving leather goods shop to Ellis
for $25,000. Ellis also paid Reed $10,000 for his agreement not to open a competing shop in the same neighborhood during the next two years. Is this agreement
enforceable by Ellis? Has Ellis received any consideration for her $10,000 payment?

10. Gobel was employed by the owner of a building
to wash all its windows periodically. Herbert leased
a store in the building for his retail shoe business.
Herbert, unaware of the building owner's contract
with Gobel, agreed to pay Gobel $20 every time he
washed the windows of his store. Is this agreement
enforceable by Gobel? Has Herbert received any consideration for his promise to pay Gobel the $20?

5

MANIFES-TATION OF ASSENT

THE OFFER

A contract is typically formed when one party accepts the offer of another party to enter into a specified arrangement. The offer and acceptance are manifestations of the assent by each party and show the willingness of each to be bound to an agreement. Two key words must be highlighted: *offer* and *acceptance*. As "words of art" their meaning departs from ordinary language usage. In the language of law, the *offer* is a power-creating device; it gives the person to whom it is directed the ability — through acceptance — to link two or more persons contractually, establishing a legal contract relationship.

Professor Karl Llewellyn has defined an offer as "a remark which, if followed . . . by an acceptance will put a promisor where, unless he performs as promised, the court can be induced to kick him."

Definite and Certain Terms

The offer, an oral or written communication, must be more than a simple invitation to negotiate or to do business. It must be definite and certain and must reasonably indicate the offeror's willingness to be bound to certain fixed terms. For example, the question "Do you want to buy my car?" is never an offer when standing alone, nor is it made an offer by adding a price. In the absence of other circumstances, an answer of "yes" merely expresses the positive disposition of the party to whom the question was directed.

Definite and certain terms must be embodied in the effective offer because the court cannot ascertain the terms of agreement when they are uncertain and indefinite. This requirement of certainty is important, especially where transactions involve common law rules not modified by the Uniform Commercial Code. The following case illustrates the application of the rule of certainty.

Green v. Zaring
Supreme Court of Georgia, 1966. 222 Ga. 195, 149 S.E.2d 115

GRICE, JUSTICE.

Zaring is the owner of a described 43.3 acre tract of land, and Green is a general contractor engaged in the business of developing and improving real estate. They and Brown, who was instrumental in getting them together in this undertaking, desire to form a corporation through which this land would be developed and improved "with apartment buildings and related structures in accordance with the covenants and agreements" hereinafter set forth.

In consideration of the mutual covenants [promises] of the parties, they agree as follows:

A corporation shall be formed with specific powers to deal generally in all types of property, to acquire, develop, improve, mortgage, pledge, encumber and sell the same.

Green agrees to pay personally the legal expense involved in forming the corporation, and to advance for the corporation all monies required for architectural and engineering expenses necessary to obtain business permits. He shall be repaid by the corporation from "loans obtained to develop and improve" the land. Green also agrees to pay personally "all costs of construction in excess of the construction loan or loans."

Zaring, upon the formation and authorization of the corporation to do business, agrees to convey fee simple title to the above mentioned land to the corporation, which shall hold title for the purpose set forth in this agreement.

Green further agrees to serve as "general contractor in the developing and improving of said land with apartment buildings and related structures without salary from the corporation," and also "to use his ability to obtain the necessary loans" for the corporation "at the best obtainable rates in order for the corporation to develop and improve said land."

The corporation shall assume obligation for all costs and expenses required in developing and improving the land "with apartment buildings and related structures." Where required by any lender of monies to the corporation, Green and Zaring agree to personally endorse "any note evidencing any such loan."

The corporation shall develop and improve the land in three stages, as suggested by the architect to be employed to prepare the plans and specifications, with only the title to each divided tract to be pledged as security for "a loan or loans" for development and improvement of that particular tract.

. . . .

Count 1 of the petition alleged that Zaring is capable of complying with the terms of this agreement but has failed and refused to convey the property in accordance therewith and has repudiated the agreement in its entirety.

It is also alleged that Green, in compliance with the agreement, has performed as fully as possible its conditions . . . .

It is further alleged that the agreement is clear and unambiguous, was entered into for adequate consideration, and is subject to specific performance; that without specific performance Green will be irreparably damaged; and that he does not have an adequate remedy at law. This count prayed that Zaring be directed to specifically perform the contract.

Count 2 alleged that . . . except for Zaring's breach, "the corporation would have realized a total net profit on the 440 units . . . of $528,000"; and that Green, by virtue of his ownership of 49% of the stock, "would have realized a profit of $258,720," which he claims as his damage attributable to the breach of contract by Zaring. This count prayed for judgment against Zaring in the sum of $258,720.

1. We assess first the allegations of count 1.

It is axiomatic that the terms of a contract must be reasonably certain.

This requirement is especially applicable to agreements which are sought to be specifically performed. This court has held that: "A court of equity will not decree the specific performance of a contract for the sale of land unless there is a definite and specific statement of the terms of the contract. The requirement of certainty extends not only to the subject matter and purpose of the contract, but also to the parties, consideration, and even the time and place of performance, where these are essential. Its terms must be such that neither party can reasonably misunderstand them. It would be inequitable to carry a contract into effect where the court is left to ascertain the intention of the parties by mere guess or conjecture, because it might be guilty of erroneously decreeing what the parties never intended or contemplated." . . .

Measuring the agreement now before us by the rule just recited, we find it lacking in certainty.

. . . .

But nowhere in the document is there any statement with reasonable certainty as to what the parties were obligating themselves to do to effect what they envisioned, or as to what they envisioned. We refer to some of the deficiencies.

As to the improvements to be made, all that appears is "apartment buildings and related structures" and a reference to three stages of development. The number, size, design, or material content of the apartment buildings and related structures are not stated. Nor is their anticipated cost mentioned. The "related structures" are not identified in any manner.

As to financing for the improvements, the agreement says only "necessary loans," "at the best obtainable rates," with Green and Zaring agreeing to personally endorse "any note evidencing any such loan." Were the loans to amount to $5,000 or $5,000,000?

The foregoing deficiencies as to certainty are not alleged to have been cured by performance or conduct of the parties. Organization of the corporation by legal counsel procured by Green, to the apparent satisfaction of Zaring, is no remedy for those vital deficiencies.

Under these uncertain and indefinite provisions, the question arises as to what, then, Zaring would receive as consideration for conveying his land to the corporation? No accurate answer can be given.

With this uncertainty existing, equity will not grant specific performance.

. . . .

2. The lack of certainty, . . . , applies also to count 2, which seeks damages for breach of this alleged agreement.

. . . .

Accordingly, neither count 1 nor count 2, as we weigh them, was sufficient to withstand the general demurrers lodged against it. The judgment sustaining such demurrers is therefore affirmed.

While the courts require that contracts be definite and certain, as *Green v. Zaring* illustrates, it has also been held that the offer need not reflect every one of the terms of the agreement if it is possible that some certainty can be forthcoming out of the transaction itself. Where goods (tangible moveables — for a more extensive definition see Chapter 16) are involved — as opposed to services or real estate — the official comment on the Uniform Commercial Code (hereinafter referred to as the Code or UCC) provides a somewhat more tolerant approach to the issues of definiteness and certainty:

Subsection (3) states the principle as to "open terms" underlying later sections of the Article. If the parties intend to enter into a binding agreement, this subsection recognizes that agreement as valid in law, despite missing terms, if there is any reasonably certain basis for granting a remedy. The test is not certainty as to what the parties were to do nor as to the exact amount of damages due to the plaintiff. Nor is the fact that one or more terms are left to be agreed upon enough of itself to defeat an otherwise adequate agreement. Rather, commercial standards on the point of "indefiniteness" are intended to be applied, this Act making provision elsewhere for missing terms needed for performance, open price, remedies and the like.

The more terms the parties leave open, the less likely it is that they have intended to conclude a binding agreement, but their actions may be frequently conclusive on the matter despite the omissions.

The UCC's relaxed approach to contract formation reflects the fact that transactions in goods, especially between merchants, are numerous, often informal, and regulated by commercial practice. The facts in *Green* v. *Zaring* reflected a one-shot deal, a relatively infrequent transaction pattern. In such cases, the courts require more caution in the transaction than when the parties deal frequently with one another, or even with others. It is interesting to speculate whether, in a jurisdiction sharing the UCC's outlook for a broad host of commercial situations, the rule of *Green* v. *Zaring* would have been applied. In short, some jurisdictions may be more liberal than others on the question of the requisite definiteness and certainty. *Green* v. *Zaring*, then, should be read with a view toward understanding what terms could have been used when the contract was drafted to impart the requisite definiteness and certainty.

Advertisements and Price Quotations

Advertisements are usually presented as the most outstanding examples of the kind of language that does not constitute an offer. The courts, in considering the language of the usual advertisement, have almost invariably found a lack of definiteness and certainty. Advertisements are, in the language of the courts, *offers to deal* or *offers to negotiate*, and in effect, the customer must make the offer in the form of an offer to buy, which only becomes a contract with the seller's acceptance. Advertisements do not intend, nor is it reasonable to assume that they intend, that all persons reading them are capable of binding advertisors once they appear at the seller's place of business with purchase price in hand. The same rule applies to the more usual business catalogues and circulars, particularly as the limited quantity of goods available would appear to be sufficient to rebut any presumptions of a binding offer.

Craft v. Elder & Johnston Co.
Court of Appeals of Ohio, 1941. 34 Abs 603, 38 N.E.2d 416

[Action by Martha Craft against Elder & Johnston Co. for alleged breach of contract. From a judgment of dismissal plaintiff appeals.]

BARNES, JUDGE.

. . . On or about January 31, 1940, the defendant, the Elder & Johnston Company, carried an advertisement in the *Dayton Shopping News*, . . . of a certain all electric sewing machine for the sum of $26 as a "Thursday Only Special." Plaintiff in her petition, after certain formal allegations, sets out the substance of the above advertisement. . . . She further alleges that . . . on Thursday, February 1, 1940, she tendered to the defendant company $26 in payment for one of the machines offered in the advertisement, but that defendant refused to fulfill the offer and has continued to so refuse. The petition further alleges that the value of the machine offered was $175 and she asks damages in the sum of $149 plus interest from February 1, 1940. . . .

The trial court dismissed plaintiff's petition . . . .

It seems to us that this case may easily be determined on well-recognized elementary principles. The first question to be determined is the proper characterization to be given to defendant's advertisement in the *Shopping News.* . . .

"It is clear that in the absence of special circumstances an ordinary newspaper advertisement is not an offer, but is an offer to negotiate — an offer to receive offers — or, as it is sometimes called, an offer to chaffer." Restatement of Contracts section 25 (1932).

Under the above paragraph the following illustration is given,

" 'A,' a clothing merchant, advertises overcoats of a certain kind for sale at $50. This is not an offer but an invitation to the public to come and purchase."

"Thus, if goods are advertised for sale at a certain price, it is not an offer and no contract is formed by the statement of an intending purchaser that he will take a specified quantity of the goods at that price. The construction is rather favored that such an advertisement is a mere invitation to enter into a bargain rather than an offer. So a published price list is not an offer to sell the goods listed at the published price."

"The commonest example of offers meant to open negotiations and to call forth offers in the technical sense are advertisements, circulars and trade letters sent out by business houses. While it is possible that the offers made by such means may be in such form as to become contracts, they are often merely expressions of a willingness to negotiate."

We are constrained to the view that the trial court committed no prejudicial error in dismissing plaintiff's petition. . . .

This does not mean that an advertisement can never be an offer. There have been several instances where the manner of the advertisement and the reasonable impression created were such that the courts have decided that it was in fact an offer, and that it did in fact create an opportunity for acceptance by those to whom it was directed. The advertisements in question, however, were quite unlike the usual advertisements used in the ordinary course of business.

What would be the legal effect of the following advertisement?

Saturday April 7th 9 A.M.
1 R.C.A. Color T.V., Model 356
$150.00
First Come
First Served
Macy's Herald Square Store—6th Floor
34th St. and Broadway, New York City

Even in cases not involving advertisements, knowledge that a communication was simultaneously sent to several persons has been held by some courts to deny the effect of offer, even when the language was clearly the language of offer. Using analogies to advertisements, the courts contend that a reasonable man would know that an offer could not have been intended in view of the circumstance, since if more than one person would accept, it would be impossible to perform. Thus, it is implied that an offer inviting offers was reasonably intended.

"How much is it?" and its variants are probably some of the most frequently asked questions in business. An important question for the businessman is whether the answer carries with it an offer to sell. As indicated in *Craft* v. *Elder & Johnston*, the general rule is that a quotation of price is not an offer. It is possible, however, for businessmen to intentionally or carelessly come within an exception to this rule.

A prospective purchaser wrote: "Send me a quotation on one set of *Corpus Juris Secundum,* new." (*Corpus Juris Secundum* is a standard legal reference.) The prospective seller wrote: "Selling price for immediate acceptance is $1,500." What would be the effect of the prospective purchaser's reply, "Sold!" The prospective seller's statement was ambiguously worded. How would you, as the seller, have worded it?

Increased protection against false advertising has accompanied the advent of state consumer protection legislation. These protections, even when supported by criminal law sanctions, do not extend to converting a false statement into a valid offer. They do not create binding contracts between the parties.

Objective Intent

An offer is effective according to the terms manifested, not according to the meaning actually intended by the offeror. Otherwise, predictability, an important ingredient in social and commercial order, would be small, and the negative repercussions in cost, nuisance, delay, and chances of fraud would be great. An offer is measured by what is called *objective intent*. And the court must determine what a reasonable person would expect the offeror's language to mean. It is a maxim of our law that a contract does not arise until there has been a meeting of the minds. This meeting is measured by the manifested, or objectively assessed, intent of the parties.

Brant v. California Dairies
Supreme Court of California, 1935. 4 Cal.2d 128, 48 P.2d 13
Action by Brant against the California Dairies, Inc., and from a judgment for defendants, plaintiff appeals. [Reversed.]

LANGDON, JUSTICE.
This is an action for breach of contract to distribute milk.

Plaintiff is the owner of a dairy ranch in Los Angeles County, where he produces a high grade of milk from purebred Guernsey cows. In 1925, Crescent Creamery Company, defendant's predecessor, took over the marketing and distributing of plaintiff's milk, under an agreed schedule of price, subject to modification by mutual agreement, and without any fixed duration for the contract.

Some time prior to 1929 defendant California Dairies, Inc., succeeded to the business of Crescent Creamery Company, and proceeded with the distribution of plaintiff's milk on the same basis. In January of that year plaintiff informed K. L. Carver, vice-president in charge of sales of defendant company, that he was dissatisfied with their marketing agreement, which did not handle his entire output, and that he proposed to reduce his herd unless an arrangement to take the surplus could be made. A number of letters were written by plaintiff and Carver. It is plaintiff's contention that these letters resulted in a contract whereby defendant agreed to market a certain quantity of milk, 950 quarts per day, increasing this amount each month by 50 quarts, until a maximum of 1,500 quarts was reached; and that the contract was not terminable except upon one year's notice. It is defendant's contention . . . that . . . the contract actually entered into was a trial arrangement which could be terminated by defendant if the obligation became burdensome.

After some performance, defendant, on or about March 27, 1930, notified plaintiff that it would refuse to distribute his milk after April 10, 1930. Thereafter defendant refused plaintiff's tender of milk, and plaintiff disposed of his product elsewhere. The present action for damages followed. . . .

. . . .

On January 19, 1929, plaintiff wrote Carver that unless defendant was willing to take substantially his entire output at a fixed price, he was going to sell part of his herd and terminate the agency.

Carver did not at once reply, but on February 7th, he wrote plaintiff as follows:

"If we can keep our present pace of increasing Brant sales, we should be able to add at least an average of fifty quarts per day per month for a few months. My thought is that instead of accepting the proposition you offer, we should continue on the old basis, but with a commitment on our part to sell and pay for at our present price, until your present surplus production is absorbed, at least fifty quarts per day on the average more than we have sold during each preceding month.

"If, with this commitment hanging over our heads, it still becomes absolutely impossible for us to increase our sales this rapidly and the burden of paying the penalty that might result from our not being able to increase sales as outlined above, should become unbearable, then we will have to put our feet under the same table and talk it over — either admit that we have fallen down and release you to make some other connection, or work out whatever seems best at the time.

"Frankly, I hesitate to make the above commitment; nevertheless, I realize your position and I want to do everything reasonable to improve the situation so that you will be satisfied. I always have been enthusiastic about the marketing of your milk and I feel that it would be a very severe blow if we ever had to give it up."

On February 11, 1929 plaintiff replied to Carver's letter as follows:

". . . In foregoing this chance of making a sale of a good part or all of our cows, I think it only right that you agree to give us as much notice if you discontinue your agreement as you ask for building up our trade to the 1500 quart limit, so that we will have ample time to make other arrangements for the successful sale of our milk which will have fallen away under your management if you find it necessary to discontinue. This time period, as it works out under our plan, is one year.

"I will understand in accepting your commitment that you agree to the points above made, which are briefly 950 quarts as the starting point for January, 1000 daily for February and so on; one year's notice of discontinuance and approval in advance for our half of the advertising expenses which will be necessary to sell the milk.

"Unless I hear from you to the contrary, I will understand that the above is also your understanding. . . ."

Carver made no reply to this letter, and plaintiff wrote him again on March 4, 1929, requesting a reply to the letter of February 11, 1929.

On March 7, 1929, Carver made this reply:

"From the last paragraph of your recent letter, I assumed that it would not be necessary for me to answer your letter confirming the arrangement, unless I disagreed on some of the points. I believe our letters pretty well set forth what our understanding is, when coupled with our previous arrangements.

"When I get to it, I believe I should recap our various arrangements and letters into one condensed document, which would be concise and to the point.

"In the meantime, we will continue to operate as per our recent correspondence."

In reliance upon this understanding, plaintiff gave up the opportunity to sell any part of his herd, and installed additional equipment. . . .

There can be no doubt that the above correspondence resulted in a contract by the terms of which Carver undertook to bind defendant to market increasing quantities of plaintiff's milk each month; and that the agreement was made not subject to termination except upon one year's notice. Carver's indefinite counter-proposals were definitely rejected by plaintiff; the terms of plaintiff's proposal were stated clearly and explicitly, and Carver's letter of March 7, 1929, was undoubtedly an acceptance thereof.

The trial court, as stated above, found that the minds of the parties never met. This finding is based upon certain testimony of Carver, admitted over plaintiff's objection. Counsel for defendant read that portion of plaintiff's letter which specified one year's notice of discontinuance, and then asked Carver. . . .

"Q. Did you interpret that request for a year's notice as an agreement that if you could not sell it at the then price, and could not make an adjustment, that you would have to continue for a year? A. No, absolutely not. . . ."

Other statements of similar character were admitted. Together they amount to nothing more than a statement of what Carver personally believed the agreement of the parties to be. But it is now a settled principle of the law of contract that the undisclosed intentions of the parties are, in the absence of mistake, fraud, etc., immaterial; and that the outward manifestation or expression of assent is controlling. This is the "objective" standard, established by the modern decisions and approved by authoritative writers. . . . In construing a contract, the question whether an uncertainty or ambiguity exists is one of law, and the lower court's finding on this issue is not binding on appeal. . . . No showing of mistake is made here; and a fair reading of the correspondence discloses the terms of the agreement without uncertainty. The testimony of Carver as to his intention is in direct conflict with the plain meaning of the writings constituting the contract, and was therefore incompetent and inadmissible under the parol evidence rule. As the court said in *Payne* v. *Commercial National Bank*, ". . . no authority sustains the proposition that under the guise of construction or explanation, a meaning can be given to the instrument which is not to be found in the instrument itself, but is based entirely upon direct evidence of intention independent of the instrument." . . .

The judgment is reversed.

The Offer Made in Jest

No special words are necessary for an offer to be effective. All that is required is that the offeror communicate to the offeree words or acts from which a reasonable man would infer that the offeror intended to vest in the offeree the power to create a binding contract between them.

Offers made in jest may or may not be valid depending on several factors, which are extensions of the concept of objective intent. Thus, an offer that is obviously made in jest and appears so to a reasonable person may not be accepted, since such an offer was obviously not intended to create a power of acceptance in the offeree. Yet, the intention of the offeror does not alone control the determination, for it might be that what was intended as an offer in jest was not so understood, nor should have been so understood by a reasonable person. In such circumstances, the courts have determined such offers to be effective, and have permitted acceptances to bind the offerors to agreements. The moral to be learned from the above is that it is at best risky to make offers in jest: You may be subject to a lawsuit.

The Writing as Containing Terms of the Offer

Even where the offer is written, the complete terms of the offer may still be difficult to establish. This is true when one party has received a writing that arguably involves the acceptance of terms of agreement expressed in that writing, although there are other writings or other oral terms of the agreement expressed elsewhere. Thus, a receipt, a bill of lading, or an airplane ticket may include provisions which attempt to affect the contractual rights and duties of the parties and which are intended by the person giving the document as terms of the agreement. Frequently, however, the party who receives the writing may not realize that these additional terms have been presented and might have a very different sense of the scope of the agreement. The effectiveness of these clauses depends on the reasonableness of regarding them as terms of the agreement, as the following case demonstrates.

Miller v. Lykes Brothers Steamship Co., Inc.
United States Court of Appeals, Fifth Circuit, 1972. 467 F.2d 464

GODBOLD, CIRCUIT JUDGE.
The District Court entered summary judgment for Lykes Brothers in this removal case brought by Irene Miller and her husband, Albert, to recover for damages resulting from personal injuries to Mrs. Miller alleged to have been incurred on defendant's ship during a lifeboat drill supervised by the crew, and as a result of defendant's negligence and breach of warranty. Appellants alleged pain and suffering, physical handicap, and loss of employment by Mrs. Miller, and medical

expenses and loss of consortium by Mr. Miller. By answer appellee noted that suit was brought more than one year after Mrs. Miller's injury and pleaded affirmatively the limitation in the "Passenger Contract Ticket," which provides that "Carrier shall have no liability for loss of life or bodily injury unless . . . suit on such claim is begun not later than one year from the day when such death or injury shall have occurred." The District Court found this contractual provision binding on appellants. We affirm.

The "Passenger Contract Ticket" is a one page form with provisions on both front and reverse sides. The first half of the first page consists of spaces for notation of passengers' names, place of issuance, date of issuance, etc. Above the space for passengers' names the form provides, in bold face print, "This Passage is subject to terms printed, typed, stamped, or written below and on back hereof." The various contractual provisions, consisting of twenty-seven paragraphs of fine print, begin on the second half of the first page and continue on the reverse side. These contractual provisions are preceded by the following statement, in bold face print: "By acceptance of this Contract Ticket, whether or not signed by him or on his behalf, or of passage on the ship, the passenger named herein agrees that the following terms and conditions, which are incorporated herein as part hereof, shall govern the relations between and be binding upon the carrier and the passenger in every possible contingency." At the end of the contractual provisions, on the reverse side, are spaces for passengers' signatures, above which is the following statement, in bold face print: "Receipt of this Contract Ticket is acknowledged and terms and conditions hereof are accepted." The Millers signed the ticket at the designated space, but the record indicates that they did not retain a copy of it or examine closely its provisions.

A line of cases stemming from *The Majestic*, 166 U.S. 375, 17 S.Ct. 597, 41 L.Ed. 1039 (1897), establish the general rule that mere notices insufficient to bring the passenger's attention to restrictions set forth on the reverse side of tickets do not incorporate the restrictions into the contract of passage. . . . Were this a standard *Majestic*-type case, we would meticulously compare the ticket here with tickets at issue in prior cases to determine the sufficiency of the notices to effect incorporation by reference. This is not, however, a typical "notice-incorporation" case. The limitation provision, embodied within the general contractual provisions beginning on the first page of the ticket and culminating just prior to the space for signatures, was an integral part of the contract of passage. . . . As part of the contractual tissue the provision was binding on appellants irrespective of their failure to read it. "[P]rovisions that appear on the ticket as part of the contract of passage embodied in the ticket are binding regardless of whether they were read by the passenger, provided they are not unlawful in content."

    . . . .

The contractual bar to Mrs. Miller's claims operates equally to bar Mr. Miller's claims for loss of consortium and medical expenses, even though his losses, at least conceptually, may have occurred at a date substantially subsequent to the date of Mrs. Miller's injury. The contract unambiguously provides that claims for "bodily injury" shall be "begun not later than one year from the day when such death or injury shall have occurred." . . . We cannot hold that the contractual provision, and the statute after which it is patterned, countenance a limitation period for bodily injury different from the limitation period for such derivative claims as loss of consortium. Such a holding would burden the contract with a technical meaning at variance with its plain import. By a common-sense reading, the contract provides that claims for bodily injury, as well as claims derivative of that bodily injury, must be filed not later than one year from "such injury," and it is this effect that we give the provision.

. . . .

Affirmed.

Based upon *Miller* v. *Lykes*, what would be the effectiveness of a provision printed in small type on the reverse side of a parking ticket, presented when the car is taken from the driver by the parking lot attendant, if the provision says: "We are not liable for any damages to your automobile without regard to the cause of or reasons for such damage beyond $250"?

The problem is even more difficult when the written contract incorporates by reference other documents that one party has not read. In such cases the courts have divided. The effectiveness of the attempted incorporation will depend on the kind of clause that is sought to be incorporated and the relative experience and bargaining power of the respective parties to the agreement.

Knowledge of the Offer

From what has already been said, it is obvious that no special words are necessary for an offer to be effective. All that is required is that the offer be communicated to the offeree in words or acts from which a reasonable person would infer that the offeror intended to vest in the offeree the power to create a binding contract between them.

The courts have been insistent in holding that since the offer creates a power in the offeree, it must be communicated in order to be effective. Thus, until an offer is received by the offeree it is ineffective and can not be acted upon. When A sends a letter to B offering to buy B's car for $500, and B sends a letter to A offering to sell his car for $500, and the letters cross in the mail, there is no acceptance of any offer and there is no contract because the acceptance must respond to a power created in the offeree through a communicated offer, and no such power has been communicated in this example.

The Offeree

An offer must be directed to an offeree. It is not necessary that there be only one offeree, but the offer must be directed to at least one. Thus, offers made to a particular person, a particular class of persons, or persons performing certain acts are effective. Offers may be directed "to all persons reading this notice," or "to all persons who arrive at this store by 10 A.M.," or "to the first person who accepts this offer."

The fact that an offer has been made to many offerees, however, may have some effect on whether the court will construe the offer as legally effective. On more than one occasion, as noted previously, courts have held that since the writer indicated that similar offers were being sent to other persons, notwithstanding the language, he intended an invitation to offer, rather than an actual offer, and a reasonable person should have so understood.

The Time for Acceptance

An offer remains in effect for a period of time that may depend on the specific limitation contained in the offer itself. Such a limitation might read, "you have ten days from the date this letter was sent in which to accept."

If an offer merely states the essential terms of that offer without a time period for acceptance, the courts find that the offer is to remain open for a reasonable period of time unless it is withdrawn or rejected prior to that time. And what a reasonable time is becomes a function of the circumstances surrounding the offer. Thus, it is reasonable that an offer to purchase certain perishable goods, where price and supply varies considerably over time, implies a much more limited period for acceptance than does an offer to purchase certain nonperishable goods where the price is relatively stable and the supply rather constant. This is a circumstance of business and is readily understood by reasonable parties who might be engaged in such affairs.

In order to avoid the uncertainties that naturally occur when the period for acceptance is not provided for in the offer, cautious offerors will require notice of acceptance to be received by the offeror by a specific date. Thus, the offeror not only indicates when acceptance must be made, but requires that the acceptance be in hand. Thus, the cautious offeror might say: "Acceptance must be received by January 15." Saying: "Acceptance must be made by January 15" in no way alters the effectiveness of a properly posted acceptance that has become detained in the mails: the acceptance was made by January 15, although the offeror has not yet received it. The "received by" formulation enhances the position of the offeror by charging the offeree with the burden of communicating his acceptance by the stated date.

The Revocation

An ordinary offer may be revoked by the offeror at any time prior to its acceptance. The revocation becomes effective when it is communicated to the offeree. Since the offer represents a power given to the offeree that becomes effective when made known to him, the courts universally hold that the offeror can only revoke his offer when the revocation is communicated as well. Such communication need not come directly from the offeror or his agent, although that would be more prudent for the offeror. For example, suppose Jeffries offers to sell Ingels her Rembrandt painting. Ingels later sees that the painting is now owned by Beasley. Ingels may no longer accept Jeffries's offer. The offer was revoked when Ingels acquired knowledge of facts inconsistent with the offer's continued existence.

It is possible, however, for the rule requiring notification of revocation to be altered by the terms of the offer itself. This possibility demonstrates an essential aspect of business contracts: parties can alter the rules of law that act as substitutes for the intent of the parties. For example, an offeror can offer an item for sale to the offeree but indicate that the offer is made "subject to prior sale." If another offeree accepts the offer first, the offer immediately terminates without the requirement of communication. Such limitations imposed by offerors have tremendous power to condition the offers which they make.

Other situations exist where offers may be revoked without directly communicating revocation to the offeree, particularly when the offers are made in the public media and come before the eyes of many readers. The procedure for revoking such an offer is to communicate the notice of revocation in the same way that the offer was communicated. Thus, the offer of a reward made in the April 7 edition of a newspaper may be revoked by a similarly placed notice in the April 9 edition, even though every person reading the April 7 edition would not necessarily read the newspaper two days later.

The point to remember is that in the ordinary situations of offer and acceptance, the offeror is able to withdraw or revoke his offer at any time prior to the acceptance of that offer by the person to whom the offer is made.

Options and Firm Offers

There are circumstances, however, where the right of revocation is not permitted. This limitation is commercially necessary in many circumstances, for example, when an offeree incurs considerable expense in determining the feasibility of a project. When an offer is made to sell commercial real estate, the prospective buyer may have to invest considerable time, attention, skill, and expense in determining whether the investment might be profitable. He will try to determine the operating costs, whether there is tenant interest in the property, and whether financing can be arranged. Naturally, he will want to be protected from the offeror's power to revoke. He will want to restrict the ability of the offeror to find another purchaser at a higher price, or to simply decide not to complete the transaction. In most states, current law enables the prospective buyer to secure this right of acceptance without fear of revocation in one of two ways: through an option or through a firm offer. Both devices have the same effect in that they limit the right of revocation, but they arrive at that effect in different ways.

The *option* is a contract securing that right for the offeree through an agreement between the offeror and the offeree providing that the offer will not be revoked. It is best described as a contract within a contract. The offeror has bound himself contractually not to revoke the offer extended to the offeree. This is usually done through the payment by the offeree of a sum of money for the holding of an offer, which cannot be withdrawn for a period of time. In the usual course of such transactions, the sum of money is applied to the purchase price if the offeree accepts. If the option contract fails to state the period of time, it is held that the offer remains open for a reasonable period of time.

In the *firm offer*, the limitation of the right to revoke is self-imposed by the offeror and does not come about through an agreement. It is often established in a simple statement such as, "this offer will be held open for 30 days."

At one time, the firm offer was viewed as ineffective to limit the offeror's right to revoke without some form of payment by the offeree. The offeror could promise not to revoke his offer, but without payment he was still free to revoke. The law said that promises to hold the offer open, without being contractually agreed upon (as shown by payment), were without legal effect. This harsh rule has been limited in certain jurisdictions, which permit a writing to act as a substitute for the required consideration and make promises of firm offer effective.

The Code effected a similar revision of the basic common law rule when goods are involved. In section 2–205, the UCC provides that between merchants a signed, written offer to buy or sell goods is irrevocable for a reasonable time, but in no event may the period of irrevocability exceed three months. The comments of the UCC have indicated that, "[t]he primary purpose of this section is to give effect to the deliberate intention of a merchant to make a current firm offer binding."

There is no set formula to determine just precisely what words would be required to provide that a firm offer has been made. Saying "this is a firm offer" or "this offer is not revocable" clearly provides that the offer may not be withdrawn. But what about the phrase "you have until July 1st to accept"?

Destruction of the Subject Matter

Besides the passage of time or the offeror's revocation, other events may also terminate the offer. The most dramatic example involves destruction of the item before acceptance occurs. For example, suppose Neptune Shipping Company offers to sell Tankers, Inc., one of its ships. Tankers will not be permitted to accept that offer if, before acceptance, the ship sinks. The courts uniformly hold that destruction of the transaction's subject matter terminates the offer, even when the parties have no knowledge of the destruction.

Rejection of the Offer

An offer may also be terminated by the offeree's rejecting the offer. If Neptune offers to sell the ship to Tankers for $8 million and Tankers says "no," courts uniformly hold that a rejection has occurred and the offer has been terminated.

Of course not all transactions are so neatly terminated, and not all offers result in a termination through a directly communicated and clear rejection of the offer. Thus, there is no universal form of rejection that is necessary, and there are many situations where, because of an ambiguous rejection of the offer, the effectiveness remains in question. For example, if instead of saying "no," Tankers had said "would you accept $7.5 million instead of $8 million?" would the original offer of $8 million still stand? The usual rule of law would describe Tankers's statement as a *counteroffer* and hold that a counteroffer acts to terminate the original offer. However, courts could also describe the statement as a mere *inquiry*, which does not terminate the original offer. The facts in the example above are not altogether clear or complete. It is clear, however, that Tankers could have preserved its right to accept the original offer by adding the following phrase: "We are keeping your offer under advisement." It is also clear that they could have terminated the original offer by stating: "This is our final offer to you."

The rule of termination by the offeree is based on the perception that the offeror believes his offer of sale for $8 million has been rejected. This produces the offeror's related belief that he is free to find other offerees, since the original offeree is obviously no longer interested, at least on the offeror's present terms. For these reasons, and because the offeree could make his position clear, courts usually resolve doubtful language of rejection. Thus, the offeree, when making counteroffers or inquiries, should indicate his willingness to continue considering the original offer. Doing so shows the offeror that his original offer is still under consideration, that it has not been rejected, and that the power still resides in the offeree to accept the offer. Sometimes a counteroffer does not terminate the offer, since it is a reasonably understood part of the counteroffer that the original offer remains intact.

Minneapolis and St. Louis Ry. v. Columbus Rolling Mill
Supreme Court of the United States, 1886. 119 U.S. 149, 7 S.Ct. 168

This was an action by a railroad corporation established at Minneapolis in the State of Minnesota against a manufacturing corporation established at Columbus in the State of Ohio. The petition alleged that on December 19, 1879, the parties made a contract by which the plaintiff agreed to buy of the defendant, and the defendant sold to the plaintiff, two thousand tons of iron rails of the weight of fifty pounds per yard, at the price of fifty-four dollars per ton gross, to be delivered free on board cars at the defendant's rolling mill in the month of March, 1880, and to be paid for by the plaintiff in cash when so delivered. The answer denied the making of the contract. It was admitted at the trial that the following letters and telegrams were sent at their dates, and were received in due course, by the parties, through their agents:

December 5, 1879. Letter from plaintiff to defendant:

"Please quote me prices for 500 to 3000 tons 50 lb. steel rails, and for 2000 to 5000 tons 50 lb. iron rails, March 1880 delivery."

December 8, 1879. Letter from defendant to plaintiff:

"Your favor of the 5th inst. at hand. We do not make steel rails. For iron rails, we will sell 2000 to 5000 tons of 50 lbs. rails for fifty-four ($54.00) dollars per gross ton for spot cash, F.O.B. cars at our mill, March delivery, subject as follows: In case of strike among our workmen, destruction of or serious damage to our works by fire or the elements, or any causes of delay beyond our control, we shall not be held accountable in damages. If our offer is accepted, shall expect to be notified of same prior to Dec. 20th, 1879."

December 16, 1879. Telegram from plaintiff to defendant:

"Please enter our order for twelve hundred tons rails, March delivery, as per your favor of the eighth. Please reply."

December 16, 1879. Letter from plaintiff to defendant:

"Yours of the 8th came duly to hand. I telegraphed you today to enter our order for twelve hundred (1200) tons 50 lb. iron rails for next March delivery at fifty-four dollars ($54.00) F.O.B. cars at your mill. Please send contract. Also please send me templet of your 50 lb. rail. Do you make splices? If so, give me prices for splices for this lot of iron."

December 18, 1879. Telegram from defendant to plaintiff, received same day:

"We cannot book your order at present at that price."

December 19, 1879. Telegram from plaintiff to defendant:

"Please enter an order for two thousand tons rails, as per your letter of the sixth. Please forward written contract. Reply." [The word "sixth" was admitted to be a mistake for "eighth"—ed.]

December 22, 1879. Telegram from plaintiff to defendant:

"Did you enter my order for two thousand tons rails, as per my telegram of December nineteenth? Answer."

After repeated similar inquiries by the plaintiff, the defendant, on January 19, 1880, denied the existence of any contract between the parties.

The jury returned a verdict for the defendant, under instructions which need not be particularly stated; and the plaintiff alleged exceptions, and sued out this writ of error. . . .

Mr. Justice Gray, after making the foregoing statement of the case, delivered the opinion of the court.

The rules of law which govern this case are well settled. As no contract is complete without the mutual assent of the parties, an offer to sell imposes no obligation until it is accepted according to its terms. So long as the offer has been neither accepted nor rejected, the negotiation remains open, and imposes no obligation upon either party; the one may decline to accept, or the other may withdraw his offer; and either rejection or withdrawal leaves the matter as if no offer had ever been made. A proposal to accept, or an acceptance, upon terms varying from those offered, is a rejection of the offer, and puts an end to the negotiation, unless the party who made the original offer renews it, or assents to the modification suggested. The other party, having once rejected the offer, cannot afterwards revive it by tendering an acceptance of it. . . . If the offer does not limit the time for its acceptance, it must be accepted within a reasonable time. If it does, it may, at any time within the limit and so long as it remains open, be accepted or rejected by the party to whom, or be withdrawn by the party by whom, it was made. . . .

The defendant, by the letter of December 8, offered to sell to the plaintiff two thousand to five thousand tons of iron rails on certain terms specified, and added that if the offer was accepted the defendant would expect to be notified prior to December 20. This offer, while it remained open, without having been rejected by the plaintiff or revoked by the defendant, would authorize the plaintiff to take at his election any number of tons not less than two thousand nor more than five thousand, on the terms specified. The offer, while unrevoked, might be accepted or rejected by the plaintiff at any time before December 20. Instead of accepting the offer made, the plaintiff, on December 16, by telegram and letter, referring to the defendant's letter of December 8, directed the defendant to enter an order for twelve hundred tons on the same terms. The mention, in both telegram and letter, of the duty and terms of the defendant's original offer, shows that the plaintiff's order was not an independent proposal, but an answer to the defendant's offer, a qualified acceptance of that offer, varying the number of tons, and therefore in law a rejection of the offer. On December 18, the defendant by telegram declined to fulfill the plaintiff's order. The negotiation between the parties was thus closed, and the plaintiff could not afterwards fall back on the defendant's original offer. The plaintiff's attempt to do so, by telegram of December 19, was therefore ineffectual and created no rights against the defendant. . . .

Judgment affirmed.

The lesson to be learned from the practice of ordinary negotiations is that several offers can be made by each of the parties without their being accepted. In the hypothetical transaction involving the sale of the ship, both Neptune, the seller, and Tankers, the buyer, can be offerors and offerees of more than one offer. Neptune might offer to sell the vessel for $8 million, while Tankers offers to buy it for $7.5 million; Neptune might then offer to sell for $7.8 million, and Tankers offer to buy for $7.6 million; Neptune next offers to sell for $7.7 million, and so forth. There have been several offers, and there have been several counteroffers. In terms of the contract there will be one offeror of the successful agreement, whose identity is determined when agreement is reached. For purposes of analysis, remember that since offers can go back and forth between the parties, the identity of the offeror of the contract becomes known only when the final agreement has been reached.

Death or Insanity of the Offeror or Offeree

When the offeror or offeree dies or becomes insane, the offer terminates immediately and without the requirement of notice. This rule only operates, however, where the power to revoke has not been contracted away and thus remains with the offeror. If this power has been contracted away, most usually through an option contract (but not firm offer), the courts have held that the offer remains effective, and the death or insanity of the offeror is hence without legal effect on the acceptance so long as the offeror was sane at the time he contracted away his right to revoke. The death of a party may pose problems for the way in which the contract is performed, which will be dealt with on page 218.

Operation of Law

It is also possible for the offer to be terminated by operation of law. In such an instance, a statute might operate to make what was formerly legal now unlawful, and as a result, an offer to engage in the new illegal activity would be rendered incapable of acceptance.

THE ACCEPTANCE

Conforming to the Terms of the Offer

An acceptance, given in response to the offer, is the vehicle whereby the offeree manifests his assent to the agreement and enters into a contractual relationship with the offeror. At one time, in most transactions in most jurisdictions, it was absolutely indispensable that the acceptance conform totally and completely to the terms of the offer. Thus, if the offeree varied the terms of acceptance in any way, the acceptance was deemed ineffective and it instead operated as a rejection of the original offer. In some instances, the rejection was referred to as counteroffer if the offeror was given, in return, the right to accept the new terms.

This common law rule has been significantly modified by the UCC with regard to the sale of goods. In section 2–207 it is possible for an acceptance that varies or adds to the terms of the offer to actually become an acceptance of the offer notwithstanding that difference.

This particularly important code section provides:

(1) A definite and seasonable expression of acceptance or a written confirmation which is sent within a reasonable period of time operates as an acceptance even though it states terms additional to or different from those offered or agreed upon, unless acceptance is expressly made conditional on assent to the additional or different terms.

(2) The additional terms are to be construed as proposals for addition to the contract. Between merchants such terms become part of the contract unless:

(a) the offer expressly limits acceptance to the terms of the offer;

(b) they materially alter it; or

(c) notification of objection to them has already been given or is given within a reasonable time after notice of them is received.

(3) Conduct by both parties which recognizes the existence of a contract is sufficient to establish a contract for sale although the writings of the parties do not otherwise establish a contract. In such case the terms of the particular contract consist of those terms on which the writings of the parties agree, together with any supplementary terms incorporated under any other provisions of this Act.

The UCC provides different rules for merchants and nonmerchants. For merchants, the Code distinguishes between acceptances that materially and nonmaterially alter the terms of the offer. Between merchants, when a definite and seasonable acceptance occurs, a nonmaterial alteration becomes part of the agreement unless the offer has been limited to acceptances that completely accord to the offer or unless the offeror objects within a reasonable period of time.[1] In the case of material alterations between merchants, the UCC provides

---

1. It is possible for the offeror to restrict all acceptances to the terms of the offer only. It is also possible, using a form type of confirmation for convenience, for him to indicate his objection to any and all variations from the terms of the original offer without regard to their materiality. All variation — material or not — is barred in such circumstance.

that these become proposals for additions to the agreement and are without effect unless they are accepted by the offeror.

If one or more persons who are not merchants are involved, the Code does not distinguish between material and nonmaterial alterations in the acceptance. Where the expression of acceptance is definite, any alterations become proposals for additions to the agreement.

The UCC exceptions to the usual rules concerning acceptance are based on business practice, where buyers and sellers characteristically communicate with one another through the use of their own form documents. These form documents are replete with language that attempts to limit the liability of the persons using them. Sellers insist on buyers' objecting to nonconforming goods within a short time, insist on a narrow definition of defects, and want a severe limitation on their warranty obligations. Buyers insist on more time for objecting to nonconforming goods, want a broad definition of nonconformity, and want generous warranty coverage. If traditional rules regarding the conformity of offer and acceptance were to apply, there would rarely be a commercial contract binding in law, although in the overwhelming number of cases both parties would believe binding agreements exist. The comments to section 2-207 indicate that: "Under this Article, a proposed deal which in commercial understanding has in fact been closed is recognized as a contract." The Code has honored the expectations of businesspersons in this regard and attempted to keep the law in accord with the practices and the reasonable expectations of the parties involved.

In terms of practice, the Code comment indicates that the following are *nonmaterial alterations* (comment to the UCC § 2-207):

> [those which] involve no element of unreasonable surprise and which therefore are to be incorporated in the contract unless notice of objection is seasonably given . . . : a clause setting forth and perhaps enlarging slightly upon the seller's exemption due to supervening causes beyond his control . . . ; a clause fixing a reasonable time for complaints within customary limits . . . ; a clause providing for interest on overdue invoices or fixing the seller's standard credit terms where they are within the range of trade practice and do not limit any credit bargained for; a clause limiting the right of rejection for defects which fall within the customary trade tolerances for acceptance "with adjustment" or otherwise limiting remedy in a reasonable manner.

Manner and Means of Acceptance

The fact that the acceptance must conform to certain requirements is largely a function of a party's freedom to become obligated only on terms acceptable to him. Since the offeror sets out the basic terms of the transaction through the grant of a power to the offeree, the offeree is required to adhere to those terms if he wishes to accept the offer.

If the offer provides that acceptance is required in a specific manner, then only that form of acceptance is permitted. Thus, if an offer directs an acceptance by mail, only a mailed acceptance is effective. If an alternative is attempted, acceptance does not accord to the terms of the offer, and there is no acceptance, and hence, no contract.

Additionally, however, rules of law developed in the early days of common law that dealt also with acceptances when no manner of acceptance was directly provided for in the offer. If an offer was silent as to the manner of acceptance, common law courts held that acceptance was invited in the same manner as the offer. Mailed offers invited mailed acceptances, telegraphed offers invited telegraphed acceptances. And the rule of law provided that the acceptance was effective when transmitted, not when received. Thus, the offeror bore the risk of a lost acceptance when he invited acceptance in the manner just indicated.

If instead of accepting in the manner provided by the offer, the offeree chose to vary the manner, the acceptance only became effective upon receipt. Thus, if the offer was in a letter and an acceptance was telegraphed, the acceptance only became effective on receipt. The common law rule has been altered by the Code in section 2–206:

> (1) Unless otherwise unambiguously indicated by the language or circumstances
> (a) an offer to make a contract shall be construed as inviting acceptance in any manner and by any medium reasonable in the circumstances. . . .

The comment to section 2–206 indicates a change from the earlier rule of law in this regard. It provides:

> Any reasonable manner of acceptance is intended to be regarded as available unless the offeror has made quite clear that it will not be acceptable. Former technical rules as to acceptance, such as requiring that telegraphic offers be accepted by telegraphed acceptances, etc., are rejected and a criterion that the acceptance be "in any manner and by any medium reasonable under the circumstances" is substituted. This section is intended to remain flexible and its applicability to be enlarged as new media of communication develop or as the more time-saving present day media come into general use.

It is, of course, possible for the offeror to remove from himself the burden of a misdirected acceptance. As mentioned earlier, the intelligent offeror will do so by saying in the offer, "acceptance only upon receipt" or "acceptance is not effective until received." In such an instance he places the burden of communicating the acceptance on the offeree.

Unilateral Contracts

Thus far we have concentrated on the more usual form of acceptance — the spoken or written promise. But in a unilateral contract, the offer may request more than a promise; it may require acceptance through a completed act. In such a contract, the acceptance and the performance by the offeree occur simultaneously. A simple example of an offer to enter into a unilateral contract provides: "I will give you $100 if you run across the Golden Gate Bridge in less than ten minutes." When the offeree accepts, he accepts not by promising to cross the bridge, but by running across the bridge within ten minutes. The acceptance does not occur until the performance has been rendered.

Unlike the bilateral contract, where the acceptance occurs before performance, the unilateral contract leaves both parties in doubt as to the effectiveness of their undertakings until performance. The offeree's promises are without legal consequence, so the offeror never knows that an acceptance will be forthcoming until it actually occurs. He can anticipate acceptance, but generally without legal recourse if he is disappointed. Since without an option contract or a firm offer the offer may be terminated before acceptance, the offeree performing the required acts is never fully certain, until completion, that the offer will not be withdrawn. Thus, both the offeror and offeree are expecting an agreement to be forthcoming, but can never be certain that a legal undertaking will finally occur until the acts required of the offeree have been performed.

This is quite dramatically demonstrated in the following case. Despite the fact that the offeree is injured by the revocation of the offer, either of the parties could have been injured, for the offerer could have waited in vain for the offeree to make good on his promise to appear with the payment as requested by the offer.

Petterson v. Pattberg
Court of Appeals of New York, 1928. 248 N.Y. 86, 161 N.E. 428
KELLOGG, J.
The evidence given upon the trial sanctions the following statement of facts: John Petterson . . . was the owner of a parcel of real estate in Brooklyn, known as 5301 Sixth Avenue. The defendant was the owner of a bond executed by Petterson, which was secured by a third mortgage upon the parcel. On April 4th, 1924, there remained unpaid upon the principal the sum of $5,450. This amount was payable in installments of $250 on April 25, 1924, and upon a like monthly date every three months thereafter. Thus the bond and mortgage had more than five years to run before the entire sum became due. Under date of the 4th of April 1924, the defendant wrote Petterson as follows: "I hereby agree to accept cash for the mortgage which I hold against premises 5301 6th Av., Brooklyn, N.Y. It is understood and agreed as a consideration I will allow you $780 providing said mortgage is paid on or before May 31, 1924, and the regular quarterly payment due April 25, 1924, is paid when due." On April 25, 1924, Petterson paid the defendant the installment of principal due on that date. Subsequently, on a day in the latter part of May, 1924, Petterson presented himself at the defendant's home, and knocked at the door. The defendant demanded the name of his caller. Petterson replied: "It is Mr. Petterson. I have come to pay off the mortgage." The defendant answered that he had sold the mortgage. Petterson stated that he would like to talk with the defendant, so the defendant partly opened the door. Thereupon Petterson exhibited the cash and said he was ready to pay off the mortgage according to the agreement. The defendant refused to take the money. Prior to this conversation Petterson had made a contract to sell the land to a third person free and clear of the mortgage to the defendant. Meanwhile, also, the defendant had sold the bond and mortgage to a third party. It, therefore, became necessary for Petterson to pay to such person the full amount of the bond and mortgage. It is claimed that he thereby sustained a loss of $780, the sum which the defendant agreed to allow upon the bond and mortgage if payment in full of principal, less that sum, was made on or before May 31st, 1924. The plaintiff has had a recovery for the sum thus claimed, with interest.

Clearly the defendant's letter proposed to Petterson the making of a unilateral contract, the gift of a promise in exchange for the performance of an act. The thing conditionally promised by the defendant was the reduction of the mortgage debt. The act requested to be done, in consideration of the offered promise, was payment in full of the reduced principal of the debt prior to the due date thereof. "If an act is requested, that very act and no other must be given." "In case of offers for a consideration, the performance of the consideration is always deemed a condition." It is elementary that any offer to enter into a unilateral contract may be withdrawn before the act requested to be done has been performed. A bidder at a sheriff's sale may revoke his bid at any time before the property is struck down to him. The offer of a reward in consideration of an act to be performed is revocable before the very act requested has been done. So, also, an offer to pay a broker commissions, upon a sale of land for the offeror, is revocable at any time before the land is sold, although prior to revocation the broker performs services in an effort to effectuate a sale. An interesting question arises when, as here, the offeree approaches the offeror with the intention of proffering performance and, before actual tender is made, the offer is withdrawn. Of such a case Williston says: "The offeror may see the approach of the offeree and know that an acceptance is contemplated. If the offeror can say 'I revoke' before the offeree accepts, however brief the interval of time between the two acts, there is no escape from the conclusion that the offer is terminated."

In this instance Petterson, standing at the door of the defendant's house, stated to the defendant that he had come to pay off the mortgage. Before a tender of the necessary moneys had been made the defendant informed Petterson that he had sold the mortgage. That was a definite notice to Petterson that the defendant could not perform his offered promise and that a tender to the defendant, who was no longer the creditor, would be ineffective to satisfy the debt. "An offer to sell property may be withdrawn before acceptance without any formal notice to the person to whom the offer is made. It is sufficient if that person has actual knowledge that the person who made the offer has done some act inconsistent with the continuance of the offer, such as selling the property to a third person." Thus, it clearly appears that the defendant's offer was withdrawn before its acceptance had been tendered. It is unnecessary to determine, therefore, what the legal situation might have been had tender been made before withdrawal. It is the individual view of the writer that the same result would follow. This would be so, for the act requested to be performed was the completed act of payment, a thing incapable of performance unless assented to by the person to be paid. Clearly an offering party has the right to name the precise act performance of which would convert his offer into a binding promise. Whatever the act may be until it is performed the offer must be revocable. However, the supposed case is not before us for decision. We think that in this particular instance the offer of the defendant was withdrawn before it became a binding promise, and, therefore, that no contract was ever made for the breach of which the plaintiff may claim damages.

The judgment of the Appellate Division and that of the Trial Term should be reversed and the complaint dismissed, with costs in all courts.

LEHMAN, J. (dissenting).
Here the defendant requested no counter promise from the plaintiff. The consideration requested by the defendant for his promise to accept payment was, I agree, some act to be performed by the plaintiff. Until the act requested was performed, the defendant might undoubtedly revoke his offer. Our problem is to determine from the words of the letter read in the light of surrounding circumstances what act the defendant requested as consideration for his promise.

The defendant undoubtedly made his offer as an inducement to the plaintiff to "pay" the mortgage before it was due. Therefore, it is said, that "the act requested to be performed was the completed act of payment, a thing incapable of performance unless assented to by the person to be paid." In unmistakable terms the defendant agreed to accept payment, yet we are told that the defendant intended, and the plaintiff should have understood, that the act requested by the defendant, as consideration for his promise to accept payment, included performance by the defendant himself of the very promise for which the act was to be consideration. The defendant's promise was to become binding only when fully performed; and part of the consideration to be furnished by the plaintiff for the defendant's promise was to be the performance of that promise by the defendant. So construed, the defendant's promise or offer, though intended to induce action by the plaintiff, is but a snare and delusion. The plaintiff could not reasonably suppose that the defendant was asking him to procure the performance by the defendant of the very act which the defendant promised to do, yet we are told that even after the plaintiff had done all else which the defendant requested, the defendant's promise was still not binding because the defendant chose not to perform.

I cannot believe that a result so extraordinary could have been intended when the defendant wrote the letter. . . . If the defendant intended to induce payment by the plaintiff and yet reserve the right to refuse payment when offered he should have used a phrase better calculated to express his meaning than the words: "I agree to accept." A promise to accept payment, by its very terms, must necessarily become binding, if at all, not later than when a present offer to pay is made. . . .

We should not read into the language of the defendant's offer a meaning which would prevent enforcement of the defendant's promise after it had been accepted by the plaintiff in the very way which the defendant must have intended it should be accepted, if he acted in good faith.

The judgment should be affirmed.

CARDOZO, CH. J., POUND, CRANE and O'BRIEN, JJ., concur with KELLOGG, J.: LEHMAN, J., dissents in opinion, in which ANDREWS, J., concurs.

Judgments reversed, etc.

The dissent of Judge Lehman demonstrates the way some courts will try to avoid finding the offer and acceptance in the strict terms of the unilateral form. Usually, where the language lends itself to such an interpretation, the courts will attempt to read what might appear to be unilateral contracts as inviting responses by promises rather than acts. There is a tendency, then, not to regard the offer as suggesting a unilateral agreement, but rather a bilateral one.

The UCC, in fact, finds that without an unambiguous intention to the contrary, an offer that presumes a unilateral acceptance might invite a bilateral contract.

The comments to section 2–206 of the UCC state:

> Either shipment or a prompt promise to ship is made a proper means of acceptance of an offer looking to current shipment. In accordance with ordinary commercial understanding the section interprets an order looking to current shipment as actually allowing acceptance either by actual shipment or by a prompt promise

to ship and rejects the artificial theory that only a single mode of acceptance is normally envisaged by an offer. This is true even though the language of the offer happens to be 'ship at once' or the like. . . .

The beginning of performance by an offeree can be effective as acceptance so as to bind the offeror only if followed within a reasonable time by notice to the offeror. Such a beginning of performance must unambiguously express the offeree's intention to engage himself. For the protection of both parties it is essential that notice follow in due course to constitute acceptance. Nothing in this section however bars the possibility that under the common law performance begun may have an intermediate effect of temporarily barring the revocation of the offer, or at the offeror's option, final effect in constituting acceptance.

The acceptance problems presented by unilateral agreements lead one to conclude that unilateral contracts are best avoided and that the preferences of the courts and the commentators for bilateral contracts is reasonable and understandable.

Acceptance by Forbearance or Silence

It is also possible, although far from usual, for an agreement to provide for acceptance of an offer by forbearance or by silence on the part of the offeree. This is extremely rare, since it is infrequent that the posing of an offer to an offeree is accompanied by a duty to respond.

Hence an unsolicited letter that reads "We will send you a one-year subscription to *Business Review* and bill you $10.00 unless you direct us not to do so" does not establish an acceptance when the recipient fails to respond. He is not under a duty to refuse the offer, and his silence does not constitute acceptance. To avoid any ambiguity as to whether unsolicited material sent to recipients might bind them unknowingly, the Postal Reorganization Act of 1970 provides that "unordered merchandise sent by mail may be retained, used, discarded or disposed of in any manner deemed appropriate without obligation" (39 USCA Sec. 3009). There are, however, situations where silence does constitute acceptance, and the Section 72 of the *Restatement of Contracts* provides:

> (1) Where the offeree fails to reply to an offer, his silence and inaction operate as an acceptance in the following cases and in no others:
>   (a) Where the offeree with reasonable opportunity to reject offered services takes the benefit of them under circumstances which would indicate to a reasonable man that they were offered with the expectation of compensation.
>   (b) Where the offeror has stated or given the offeree reason to understand that assent may be manifested by silence or inaction, and the offeree in remaining silent and inactive intends to accept the offer.
>   (c) Where because of previous dealings or otherwise, the offeree has given the offeror reason to understand that the silence or inaction is intended by the offeree as a manifestation of assent, and the offeror does so understand.
>   (2) Where the offeree exercises dominion over things which are offered to him, such exercise of dominion in the absence of other circumstances showing a contrary intention is an acceptance. If circumstances indicate that the exercise of dominion is tortious the offeror may at his option treat it as an acceptance, though the offeree manifests an intention not to accept.

Requirements Contracts

Agreements to agree were determined by the common law to be ineffective since the terms of the offer were sufficiently indefinite so that an acceptance could not be certain enough to be binding (see pages 98–101).

The same deficiency was fatal to *requirements contracts* (also called *output contracts*), agreements whereby a purchaser undertook to purchase all his needs and the seller undertook to provide them. Since needs were indefinite and could not be ascertained at the time of the making of the agreement, many common law courts charged these agreements with being too indefinite and hence ineffective.

Recognizing the business merit of requirements contracts where goods are involved, the UCC is not nearly so hostile to them as was the common law. The Code comments to section 2–306 are quite clear in asserting that the indefiniteness as to quantity of requirements contracts is not important enough to invalidate the agreement:

> 2. Under this Article, a contract for output or requirements is not too indefinite since it is held to mean the actual good faith output or requirements of the particular party. Nor does such a contract lack mutuality of obligation since, under this section, the party who will determine quantity is required to operate his plant or conduct his business in good faith and according to commercial standards of fair dealing in the trade so that his output or requirements will approximate a reasonably foreseeable figure. Reasonable elasticity in the requirements is expressly envisaged by this section and good faith variations from prior requirements are permitted even when the variation may be such as to result in discontinuance. A shutdown by a requirements buyer for lack of orders may be permissible when a shutdown merely to curtail losses would not. The essential test is whether the party is acting in good faith. Similarly, a sudden expansion of the plant by which the requirements are to be measured would not be included within the scope of the contract made but normal expansion undertaken in good faith would be within the scope of this section. One of the factors in an expansion situation would be whether the market price has risen greatly in a case in which the requirements contract contained a fixed price.
>
> 3. If an estimate of output or requirements is included in the agreement, no quantity unreasonably disproportionate to it may be tendered or demanded. Any minimum or maximum set by the agreement shows a clear limit on the intended elasticity. In similar fashion, the agreed estimate is to be regarded as a center around which the parties intend the variation to occur.

Suppose a contract provided that the buyer would purchase only those supplies he might desire. Would such a contract also be effective? Is there any suggestion of such result from the comments just stated? A close rereading of the comments would indicate that such an agreement would not be effective; it would be regarded as illusory — giving the illusion of contract, but nothing else — and be lacking in what the comment describes as "mutuality of obligation."

Acceptance Followed by Formal Writing

When parties agree to formalize an oral or written agreement in a document, there may be some question concerning when the agreement has been entered into and what is the effect of the writing. The formal document could only recapitulate and be a memorial of the contract entered into previously, or it could be the agreement itself and the agreement may therefore not be effective until the document is executed. The difference is important. It may be possible to enforce a contract that has been orally made and not yet formalized. It will not be possible to enforce an agreement that has not yet been entered into.

The intention of the parties governs. The courts will inquire into what the parties themselves sought to do in the execution of the document, and will decide in accordance with the expressed or implied wishes of the parties.

PROBLEMS AND QUESTIONS

Why do courts tend to read unilateral contracts inviting promises rather than acts, thus converting em into bilateral contracts?

Abraham's Department Store placed an adversement in a New York City newspaper indicating at it would sell, deliver, and install "all the major ands of television sets, with popular models at disunts of up to 40% off the list price."

On December 3, Karen Wessel, who had read an Ivertisement, went to Abraham's and ordered a Sylnia Television, model 126C, listing at $249.95. braham's refused to permit any discount on this articular model, and when Wessel insisted upon a scount, she was informed that other models were le priced but that this one was not. Is Wessel entled to a discount? Explain.

During a student protest on campus, one of the niversity guards, Steven Crane, was injured by a rown object. Later at the hospital he told the police much as he knew about the incident, and gave a escription of his assailant. The university later pubshed a circular for distribution near the campus hich provided for a reward of $1,000 "for inforation leading to the arrest and conviction of the erson or persons assaulting Steven Crane (the uniersity guard)."

Following up on the information given by Crane ter he was assaulted, the police discovered a suspect ho was subsequently identified by Crane and concted of the assault. Crane now seeks to recover the ward. Will he be successful? Explain.

Martha Morris, who owned an expensive tapesy, was asked by Brandon, in a letter, if she would nsider selling the tapestry. Morris did not wish to ll the tapestry and did not think that Brandon had nough cash to purchase it. Merely wishing to imress Brandon, Morris replied in a letter: "I will sell ou the tapestry you speak of for $3,500, provided at you wire your acceptance immediately upon re

ceipt of this offer, and that you arrange payment within ten days." Brandon wired his acceptance and a money order for $3,500. Morris replied, "I was not serious and did not intend an offer, but merely intended further negotiations. I am returning your $3,500 and reject your offer." When Morris remained firm in her refusal, Brandon sued. Decision for whom? Explain.

5.   Jack Coppola deposited a parcel for safekeeping at the Garden City Hotel Luggage Room. He paid 50 cents for the service and received a card measuring 3 inches by 2 inches. The card contained a number and date, and on the reverse side bore the notation in fine but legible print: "The Garden City Hotel shall not be liable for loss or damage of any parcel beyond $15." Coppola did not read the reverse of his card, nor was his attention called to it by anyone. When he claimed his parcel he was told that it had been given to someone else. He sued for $150, the value of the parcel. May he recover? Explain.

6.   Jill Saxxe, a mail order baker, sent written notices to five of her best customers indicating that she would be selling "the following bakery products from our new spring catalogue." Among the items listed were "300 2 pound fruit cakes." The notices further provided that the orders had to be placed within two weeks "for this special invitation to be accepted."

Rob Lardner, one of the five customers, determining that he could not use the items specified, sent a copy of the letter along to Kraft, a friend, who was interested in making some purchases. Kraft, upon receipt of the notice, ordered 300 fruit cakes within the two week limit. Upon receipt of his order, however, Saxxe refused to deliver the goods. Is Saxxe correct in her refusal?

7.   On August 15th, Sinclair mailed a letter to Barnes, one of his customers, which said: "I hereby offer to sell you all of my supplies on hand, which cost me $45,000, for $22,500. I am going out of business and want to liquidate. This is a firm offer until August 25.

On August 20, before Barnes had an opportunity to reply to Sinclair's offer, she received another letter from Sinclair which read, "Please consider my previous offer withdrawn. I have changed my mind and would like to continue in business." On August 22 Barnes wired her acceptance of the offer despite the second letter of Sinclair. Is Barnes's acceptance effective? Explain.

8. Spencer offered to sell his cabin cruiser, *The Pistachio*, to Caldwell for $15,000. The cruiser was docked off the Florida coast, and unknown to Spencer was destroyed in a hurricane after the offer was made, but prior to its acceptance.

Caldwell, also unaware of the loss of the cruiser, sent an acceptance to Spencer. Two days after receipt of the acceptance, Spencer discovered that the ship had been completely destroyed and notified Caldwell of the loss. She insisted that Spencer replace the vessel and comply with the terms of the agreement. Spencer refused. Decision for whom?

9. Lushing offered to sell a painting to Skerrett for $600. Skerrett replied: "I will pay $500 for the painting." After Lushing refused to take $500, Skerrett decided to accept the offer for $600. May he do so? Explain. Suppose Skerrett had replied: "I am considering your offer but if you are willing to make a quick deal I will pay $500 immediately." Would your answer have been different? Explain. Suppose Skerrett had replied: "Would you consider $500?" Would your answer have been that the offer remained open? Explain.

10. On January 10, Carter mailed a letter to Billings indicating, "I hereby offer to sell you my painting *The House* by Hannah Grote for $1,000 C.O.D. Acceptance must be made by January 20." On January 15, Billings sent a letter of acceptance that did not arrive until January 21. Was there a valid acceptance? If the letter of the 10th had said, "Acceptance must be received by January 20," would your answer be different?

11. On July 10, Maxwell sent Taylor a letter offering to sell her color television set, which was giving her some difficulty, for $600. In each of the following circumstances, explain whether a contract was formed.

a. Taylor, deciding to purchase the television, asked his agent, Kennedy, to accept the offer on his behalf. Kennedy mailed an acceptance on July 15.

b. On July 12, Taylor mailed an acceptance at 1 P.M. On July 12, at 11:30 A.M., Maxwell telephoned a revocation to Taylor.

c. Maxwell died on July 11, and Taylor, knowing of the death of Maxwell, mailed an acceptance on July 12.

d. Maxwell's offer was responded to by a letter from Taylor that read "I'll accept the offer to buy your television set if you will accept $500."

e. Taylor's letter of acceptance, proper as to form and properly addressed, was sent, but never reached Maxwell.

12. Parsons of Paris, a designer of expensive dresses, sent a letter to Sullivan, a business promoter in the United States, which read: "You are hereby authorized to procure distributors for my dress line in the United States. If you are successful in obtaining them I will pay you 2 percent of the gross receipts."

Within ten days Sullivan replied "I accept your propositions as contained in your letter of last week."

After two months of devoting much of her energy to the effort of securing distributors, without success, Sullivan received the following letter from Parsons of Paris: "I have decided not to market my product in the United States; consider the agreement not to have been in effect." Sullivan is unsuccessful in convincing Parsons to permit her to continue her efforts, and sues for breach of contract. Decision for whom?

13. Silber, a purchaser, sent a letter to a distributor which said: "Ship 200 cases of X-15 Hair Spray, 24 oz. size, at $3.50 per case." The distributor replied by letter: "Your order has been received, and shipment will be made within 2 weeks."

Prior to shipment, the distributor received a letter from Silber which said: "Cancel my order. I miscalculated my stock and am oversupplied." Could Silber cancel the order without breaching the agreement? Explain.

14. Aaron subscribed to a newspaper for three years, paying the entire amount at the time he subscribed. After the three years, and without any action on his part, the newspaper continued to be delivered to his home. He continued to read the paper, but did not respond to the bills he received. Would he be liable to the newspaper for the cost of the newspaper for the time he has continued to receive and to use it?

15. In December of 1972, Sills and Baxter entered into an agreement whereby Sills agreed to manufacture and deliver small boats to Baxter as ordered over a three year period. Baxter also agreed to act as the sole distributor for Sills's boats in the eastern half of Pennsylvania.

After three months, with sales declining, Sills sought to cancel the agreement with Baxter, charging that the agreement was too indefinite as to the quantity of boats to be ordered by Baxter. Is Sills correct? Explain.

FORM VERSUS REALITY

Once a proper offer and a proper acceptance have been made, both parties to an agreement have manifested their assent to the contract terms. It is possible, however, for this manifested assent not to be real; the appearance of assent may mask a failure of the parties to obtain real assent. An effective contract requires not only the manifestation of assent through an offer and acceptance; it also requires real and actual assent.

Three general kinds of situations can deny the reality of assent. A mistake by one or more of the parties in special situations can mean that no assent took place. There are possibilities of fraud and misrepresentation, where the basis for agreement is an erroneous belief perpetrated by one party on the other. Finally, one party may use coercive physical or mental pressure — duress and undue influence — to compel assent to the contract terms. These categories are significant exceptions to the rule that an offer and an acceptance proper in form result in a binding agreement.

MISTAKE

A *mistake* is an erroneous belief, honestly made by the parties to the agreement, concerning a present or past fact. (It does not refer to mistakes caused by one of the parties' conduct, commonly called fraud or misrepresentation.) If a party, induced by mistake, enters an agreement, the mistake may undermine the effectiveness of that agreement.

The law does not provide a remedy for every mistake. Trivial or immaterial mistakes, mistakes as to value, or mistaken opinions are not redressable. The law remedies mistakes of a material nature, those that go to the "essence of the agreement." Defining the term *material mistakes*, however, is a difficult problem. Furthermore, the available remedies vary with the type of mistake made.

There are three basic types of mistake. The first, *mutual mistake,* is a mistake by both parties.

6

THE REALITY OF ASSENT

The other two types of mistake are both *unilateral mistakes*, made by only one party. In one form of unilateral mistake, the nonmistaken party knows, or should know, of the other party's mistake. In the other form, the nonmistaken party does not know, and could not know, of the other party's mistake.

Mutual Mistake

A mutual mistake occurs when both parties to an agreement are mistaken as to a material and fundamental element of the agreement. For example, Robertson agrees to sell his warehouse to Halliday, and Halliday agrees to purchase it. Neither party knows the warehouse has been destroyed by fire. A court would find the parties mutually mistaken as to the existence of the subject matter of their agreement and rule that no contract had been formed. The parties would be restored to the position they were in before they made the agreement.

It is not always easy to determine precisely when a redressable material mistake of fact has occurred. If Friedman agrees to sell to Gadomski a particular object resembling an ordinary stone "2 inches by 2 inches by 2 inches in size" and the object turns out to be a valuable diamond, then no mistake of fact was made. The particular object was sold, and neither party made its nature or quality an essential term of the agreement. However, if Friedman agrees to sell to Gadomski "an ordinary stone 2 inches by 2 inches by 2 inches in size" and it turns out to be not an ordinary stone but a valuable diamond, then a mistake of fact has been made and the parties would be restored to their positions before the agreement. The question of mistake depends on the basis of the agreement. The following famous case demonstrates the dilemma of determining whether or not the parties to the agreement have made a mistake. As you meet that darling of the bar, Rose 2d of Aberlone, try to determine whether the judges agree on the contract terms. Did the agreement call for the sale of this particular cow, or did it call for the sale of a cow that was barren and happened to be named Rose?

Sherwood v. Walker
Supreme Court of Michigan, 1887. 66 Mich. 568, 33 N.W. 919
MORSE, J.
Replevin [a proceeding to secure possession of an object] for a cow. Suit commenced in justice's court. Judgment for plaintiff. Appealed to circuit court of Wayne county, and verdict and judgment for plaintiff in that court. The defendants bring error, and set out 25 assignments of the same.

The main controversy depends upon the construction of a contract for the sale of the cow.

The plaintiff claims that the title passed, and bases his action upon such claim.

The defendants contend that the contract was executory, and by its terms no title to the animal was acquired by plaintiff.

The defendants reside at Detroit, but are in business at Walkerville, Ontario, and have a farm at Greenfield, in Wayne county, upon which were some blooded cattle supposed to be barren as breeders. The Walkers are importers and breeders of polled Angus cattle.

The plaintiff is a banker living at Plymouth, in Wayne county. He called upon the defendants at Walkerville for the purchase of some of their stock, but found none there that suited him. Meeting one of the defendants afterwards, he was informed that they had a few head upon this Greenfield farm. He was asked to go out and look at them, with the statement at the time that they were probably barren, and would not breed.

May 5, 1886, plaintiff went out to Greenfield and saw the cattle. A few days thereafter, he called upon one of the defendants with the view of purchasing a cow known as "Rose 2d of Aberlone." After considerable talk, . . . the terms of the sale were finally agreed upon. [Plaintiff] was to pay five and one-half cents per pound, live weight, fifty pounds shrinkage. . . . He requested defendants to confirm the sale in writing, which they did. . . .

On the twenty-first of the same month the plaintiff went to defendants' farm at Greenfield, and presented the order and letter to Graham, who informed him that the defendant had instructed him not to deliver the cow. Soon after, the plaintiff tendered to Hiram Walker, one of the defendants, $80, and demanded the cow. Walker refused to take the money or deliver the cow. The plaintiff then instituted this suit.

. . . .

It appears from the record that both parties supposed this cow was barren and would not breed, and she was sold by the pound for an insignificant sum as compared with her real value if a breeder. She was evidently sold and purchased on the relation of her value for beef, unless the plaintiff had learned of her true condition, and concealed such knowledge from the defendants. Before the plaintiff secured possession of the animal, the defendants learned that she was with calf, and therefore of great value, and undertook to rescind the sale by refusing to deliver her. The question arises whether they had a right to do so.

The circuit judge ruled that this fact did not avoid the sale, and it made no difference whether she was barren or not. I am of the opinion that the court erred in this holding. I know that this is a close question, and the dividing line between the adjudicated cases is not easily discerned. But it must be considered as well settled that a party who has given an apparent consent to a contract of sale may refuse to execute it, or he may avoid it after it has been completed, if the assent was founded, or the contract made, upon the mistake of a material fact — such as the subject-matter of the sale, the price, or some collateral fact materially inducing the agreement; and this can be done when the mistake is mutual. . . .

If there is a difference or misapprehension as to the substance of the thing bargained for, if the thing actually delivered or received is different in substance from the thing bargained for and intended to be sold, then there is no contract; but if it be only a difference in some quality or accident, even though the mistake may have been the actuating motive to the purchaser or seller, or both of them, yet the contract remains binding. "The difficulty in every case is to determine whether the mistake or misapprehension is as to the substance of the whole contract, going, as it were, to the root of the matter, or only to some point, even though a material point, an error as to which does not affect the substance of the whole consideration."

The mistake or misapprehension of the parties went to the whole substance of the agreement. If the cow was a breeder, she was worth at least $750; if barren, she was worth not over $80. The parties would not have made the contract of sale except upon the understanding and belief that she was incapable of breeding, and of no use as a cow. It is true she is now the identical animal that they thought her to be when the contract was made; there is no mistake as to the identity of the creature. Yet the mistake was not of the mere quality of the animal, but went to the very nature of the thing. A barren cow is substantially a different creature than a breeding one. . . .

The court should have instructed the jury that if they found that the cow was sold, or contracted to be sold, upon the understanding of both parties that she was barren, and useless for the purpose of breeding, and that in fact she was not barren, but capable, then the defendants had a right to rescind, and to refuse to deliver, and the verdict should be in their favor.

The judgment of the court below must be reversed, and a new trial granted, with costs of this court to defendants.

SHERWOOD, J. (dissenting)

. . . There is no question but that the defendants sold the cow representing her of the breed and quality they believed the cow to be, and that the purchaser so understood it. And the buyer purchased her believing her to be of the breed represented by the sellers, and possessing all the qualities stated, and even more. He believed she would breed. There is no pretense that the plaintiff bought the cow for beef, and there is nothing in the record indicating that he would have bought her at all only that he thought she might be made to breed. Under the foregoing facts — and these are all that are contained in the record material to the contract — it is held that because it turned out that the plaintiff was more correct in his judgment as to one quality of the cow than the defendants, and a quality, too, which could not by any possibility be positively known at the time by either party to exist, the contract may be annulled by the defendants at their pleasure. I know of no law, and have not been referred to any, which will justify any such holding, and I think the circuit judge was right in his construction of the contract between the parties. . . .

In *Sherwood* v. *Walker*, the distinction between a barren cow and a fertile cow was considered to go to the "substance of the thing bargained for; to the essence of the contract." The majority believed that a barren cow and a fertile cow were two distinct kinds of subject matter, and since the persons had contracted for one kind of subject matter (a barren cow), Rose, the fertile cow, was not the subject matter agreed upon. Both parties, it was felt, were mistaken in their belief that the proper type of cow was being transferred.

Unilateral Mistake

Most courts take a stricter approach if only one party is mistaken when the contract is executed. The requirement remains the same: the mistake must be a mistake of fact that goes to the substance of the thing bargained for. When the mistake is unilateral, the courts provide a remedy only if the nonmistaken party knew or should have known a mistake was made.

Rushlight Automatic Sprinkler Co. v. City of Portland
Supreme Court of Oregon, 1950. 189 Or. 195, 219 P.2d 732

[The plaintiff submitted a bid to the defendant City of Portland for a certain sewage and disposal project. It submitted a bid of $429,444.20 and issued a certified check of $21,472.21 to be retained by the city in event that it failed to enter into contract after notice that the bid had been accepted was received. Upon opening the bids, it was found that the next lowest bid was $671,000. Then the plaintiff discovered that it had omitted an item of $99,225.68 and requested that its bid be withdrawn. Instead, this was refused, the bid accepted, the check cashed when the plaintiff refused to proceed with the work. Plaintiff seeks to recover the amount of the check. The court found for plaintiff and defendant appealed.]

ROSSMAN, J.

. . . As we said, the City concedes the mistake concerning the steel item which the plaintiff's officers, to their manifest embarrassment, described. The plaintiff prays that its mistake be deemed excusable; the City insists that the error was a culpable one. . . .

So far as we can ascertain, the plaintiff's bid was compiled by an adequate staff of estimators. No one challenged the competence of the estimators nor questioned the methods they pursued. The record shows that one of the estimators, after having calculated the amount of earth that would have to be moved in one phase of the construction work, called upon a member of the City Board of Engineers for the purpose of comparing his estimate with that made by the board. He found that the two were virtually the same. That fact and an occasional other one mentioned in the record tend to show that the estimators were careful. . . .

We believe that it is manifest from the evidence that the difference between the plaintiff's bid and the next higher was so large that all of those concerned with the undertaking were rendered uneasy. The plaintiff's officers at once returned to their work sheets, fearing that they must have committed a mistake. The City Engineer, according to his own words, found the variation so great that it "scared us to death." A member of the Board of Engineers, who seemingly expressed himself in wary words, described the plaintiff's bid as "a very low" one and termed the difference between it and the City's estimate "a very decided difference." The bid aroused suspicion in all minds. We think that the difference apprised the City that a mistake had probably occurred.

It is true, as already indicated, that the steel item accounts for only $99,255.68 or 41 per cent of the total disparity of $242,155.80 between the plaintiff's and the next higher bid. Therefore, it alone did not provoke the misgivings. The $99,225.68 was a substantial part of the total difference. The variation between the second and third high bids was only $2,232.06. The difference between the second and the fourth high bids was $13,291.50. The material fact is that the omission of the steel was a substantial factor in reducing the bid to such a low amount that the city officials surmised that it was too good to be true. . . .

From Williston on Contracts, Rev. Ed., 1573, the following is taken.

"In two classes of cases mistake of one party only to a contract undoubtedly justifies affirmative relief as distinguished from a mere denial to enforce the contract specifically against him;

"(1) Where the mistake is known to the other party to the transaction. . . ."

Section 503, Restatement of the Law, Contracts says: "A mistake of only one party that forms the basis on which he enters into a transaction does not of itself render the transaction voidable; . . ."

The Reporters' Notes to that section cites many illustrative decisions and some treatises. From the notes, we take the following:

"Where one party knows or has reason to know that the other party has made a basic mistake (see Comment c) restitution is granted. This situation has frequently arisen where there has been an error in the price given. In this case rescission is ordinarily allowed. . . ."

We believe that in this State an offer and an acceptance are deemed to effect a meeting of the minds, even though the offeror made a material mistake in compiling his offer, provided the acceptor was not aware of the mistake and had no reason to suspect it. But if the offeree knew of the mistake, and if it was basic, or if the circumstances were such that he, as a reasonable man, should have inferred that a basic mistake was made, a meeting of the minds does not occur. The circumstances which should arouse the suspicions of a fairminded offeree are many as stated in 94 of Williston on Contracts, Rev. Ed.: " . . . And the same principle is applicable in any case where the offeree should know that the terms of the offer are unintended or misunderstood by the offeror. The offeree will not be permitted to snap up an offer that is too good to be true; no contract based on such an offer can then be enforced by the acceptor. . . ."

. . . [T]he proof in cases of this kind must possess a high degree of cogency. The bidder must prove, not only that he made a material mistake, but also that the offeree was aware of it. In this case, the facts which we have mentioned are unchallenged.

It is our belief that although the plaintiff alone made the mistake, the City was aware of it. When it accepted the plaintiff's bid, with knowledge of the mistake, it sought to take an unconscionable advantage of an inadvertent error. Equity is always prepared to grant relief from such situations.

The decree of the Circuit Court is affirmed.

Could not, and should not, the dispute in question have been resolved without costly litigation by the construction company and the city agreeing to accept a revised bid, which was still almost $150,000 less than the next lowest bid?

If the contract is still executory, a few states permit rescission for non-negligent unilateral mistakes, even if the other party neither knew nor had reason to know of the error. How does this rule affect the enforceability of contractual undertakings? Are reasonable contractual expectations significantly impaired? Does it open the door to innumerable false claims of mistake by parties seeking to avoid their obligations?

So far in this chapter, the courts have had to decide if an agreement not yet performed could be terminated. The matter of executory contracts, however, is not the only one facing the courts in the area of mistake. Frequently, the parties fully perform the contract, and the aggrieved party seeks a remedy other than simple rescission. These cases often involve the reformation of fully performed contracts.

Reformation: An Occasional Remedy

Reformation is a remedy whereby the court re-forms the terms of the agreement to the parties' actual understanding. For example, if an agreement erroneously describes the property sold, one of the parties will ask the court to conform the writing to their actual understanding. Usually, the reformation is of an executory contract where the court must strive to determine the meaning of the parties and bring that meaning into effect. In other, and more rare, situations, the courts will reform executed contracts, as the following case demonstrates.

Nash v. Kornblum
New York State Court of Appeals, 1962. 12 N.Y.2d 42, 186 N.E.2d 551

[Harkness, plaintiff's agent, gave a written estimate of how much 5 foot high wire fencing was needed to enclose defendant's tennis courts. The estimate followed considerable discussion by the parties concerning the specifications of the job to be done. Harkness mistakenly recorded a measurement that was one-half of the true measurement since he forgot that the height of the fence (10 feet) required double the amount of running footage. He gave a price and a measure based on the perimeter of the court rather than on the cost of the running length of the 5 foot fence. The error was reflected in the estimate of price which he gave defendant.]

FOSTER, JUDGE.

It clearly and convincingly appears from the record here that this is a case of a mistake on the part of the plaintiff's agent in typing the erroneous linear ground measurement, which plaintiff did not discover before submission to the defendant, and the latter, with knowledge of the mistake, trying to take advantage of the error. The writing itself did not represent the understanding of either party as to the area to be fenced which had been agreed upon previous to the writing, and thus did not embody the true agreement, as mutually intended, relating to the area.

This is not a case where the plaintiff unilaterally and mistakenly estimated the linear feet and defendant, without a duty to speak and absent fraud, agreed to the proposal. Should these circumstances have been present in the contract's reduction to writing, there would be no scrivener's mistake or mutual mistake of fact, the agreement would be the intended one by the parties, and equity would not "reform" the executed contract. This set of circumstances is not presented here by the record.

There is clear and convincing evidence that there was an agreement between the parties as to the area to be fenced before the formal written contract was executed, and *then* an error was made, albeit by plaintiff, in the reduction of the antecedent expression of the parties into the complete contract. The only question between the parties on the execution of the written contract was the type of fencing to be constructed and cost thereof, and admittedly these essential terms were not fixed until the formal contract was signed. These latter terms are not sought to be reformed.

The situation presented clearly calls for relief, and the only practicable method of achieving such a result is by the equitable remedy of reformation. The Trial Judge dismissed the complaint with the finding that the proof failed to show fraud on the part of the defendant. In our view of the case it was unnecessary for the plaintiff to establish fraud on the part of the defendant. Perhaps reformation could have been predicated upon a unilateral mistake on one side and deceptive conduct on the other side which tended to obscure the true agreement. However, the situation presented as a result of the scrivener's error was closely akin, if not precisely, to a mutual mistake of fact, and as such was sufficient to call for the application of the equitable doctrine of reformation. Therefore, the judgment should be reversed and the case remitted to Special Term for proceedings not inconsistent with this opinion.

DESMOND, C.J., and DYE, FROESSEL, VAN VOORHIS and BURKE, J.J., Concur with FOSTER, J.

FULD, J., concurs in result.

Judgment reversed, with costs in all courts, and matter remitted to Special Term for further proceedings not inconsistent with this opinion.

FRAUD AND MISREPRESENTATION

Definitions and Recent Developments

Reality of assent does not exist when one party asks another party to sign a receipt that turns out to be a document purporting to be a contract, or when one party misunderstands the terms of the agreement because of the other party's conduct. These situations are cases of *fraud* or *misrepresentation*; when they occur, the courts, perceiving that there was no real assent to the contract, protect the aggrieved party. In essence, fraud stems from the actions of one of the parties committed upon the other, convincing the other that what was true was not, or conversely, that what was not true was actually true. In some cases, however, even silence can operate as fraud.

This area of the law has been an expanding one. Traditional rules placed considerable responsibility on each party to safeguard himself. The doctrine of *caveat emptor* (let the buyer beware) permitted the party who could engineer a one-sided transaction to do so without legal sanction. Today, however, this doctrine is severely qualified by increasing concern for fairness in the bargaining process. Today's emerging consumerism is one manifestation of that trend.

Elements

Fraud may broadly be defined as the communication by one party to another of (1) a false representation of fact, that (2) is material to the transaction; (3) the first party knows it is false but communicates it (4) intending the other party to rely on it; (5) and the second party reasonably relies on it (6) to his injury. If the third element is missing — if there is no guilty knowledge, or *scienter* (from Latin for "knowingly") — there is no fraud, only misrepresentation. In short, the third element need not be proved in a contract action.

False Representation of Fact. The courts insist that fraud and misrepresentation involve a fact, and not an opinion or an intention. Thus, if a seller indicates that his product is of "great value," the seller's opinion would be considered mere business "puffing," exaggerated extolling of one's wares and not a false statement of fact. Even if the item sold was not of "great value," the false statement of value is a matter of opinion and not a misrepresentation of fact.

Another situation raising troublesome problems concerns the distinction between law and fact. The courts for a long time determined that statements concerning the law were statements of opinion that could neither be adjudged to be false statements of fact nor mistakes. A lawyer's assessment, for example, that a breach of contract provided a certain remedy was a determination about which the courts might disagree. Since a lawyer's prophecy is uncertain until resolved by a court, it resembles an opinion more than a fact. Because the parties must expect occasional erroneous observations concerning the state of the law, such an observation could not be the basis for an action alleging mistake, misrepresentation, or fraud. This position has been modified in some jurisdictions. One needs to check local law to determine where the individual jurisdiction stands on this question.

Materiality. A fradulent act must also involve a material fact. Insignificant misrepresentations cannot be the basis for a challenge to the reality of assent. The fact is generally considered material if the injured party would not have entered into the agreement had the truth been known. Of course, the injured party will always assert this to be the case. Since the test involves what might have happened under a hypothetical state of affairs, the application of this rule is often difficult for the jury or judge and risky for the litigants.

Guilty Knowledge or "Scienter." From an evidentiary standpoint, it is usually difficult to show one of the parties to a fraud had guilty knowledge. The plaintiff must show that the person making the misrepresentation had knowledge that the fact was misrepresented. Mere failure to determine whether a statement is true is not sufficient proof that the person intentionally misrepresented a material fact. Because proving fraud is difficult, it is probable that many situations of fraud are proved as simple misrepresentations. Misrepresentation as an actionable wrong does not require a finding of intent; it is fraud without guilty knowledge. In some states the difference between fraud and misrepresentation is important because some remedies available for fraud are not available for misrepresentation.

Intent to Deceive. The law also requires that the misrepresentation had been made to induce someone to rely on the statement and enter into the contract. In the ordinary case, this element of misrepresentation and fraud poses little problem to the plaintiff; difficulties arise when third parties become involved.

If a party makes a material misstatement of fact, and unbeknownst to him a third party overhears it and acts upon it, the element of intent is generally lacking. No one expected an eavesdropper to rely on the statement and contract because of it. If, on the other hand, the statement was made with the intention that it be relied upon by A, but was instead relied upon B (who was told of the statement by A), the courts generally hold that such an intention is sufficient to give a cause of action to B.

Reasonable Reliance. The false statement must actually induce the contract. The injured party must rely on the false statement and this reliance must be reasonable. However, the complaining party need not, and seldom does, rely *solely* on the alleged false statement. It is enough that the false statement was a substantial inducement for his entry into the contract. This idea of reliance or substantial inducement begins to sound a lot like the second element, materiality. As a practical matter of proof, the boundary line between reliance and materiality becomes blurred. Conceptually though, the element of reliance, inducement, or causation — like the element of materiality — must be proved. Without reliance, one cannot avoid a contract on the grounds of misrepresentation or fraud.

The reasonableness test for reliance also creates some confusion. If the defendant is otherwise guilty of misrepresentation or fraud, it is a bit curious that the law permits him to defend himself on the ground that the plaintiff should not have fallen for his lie. On the other hand, a more liberal rule would help an unscrupulous party to escape from a bargain on the pretext that he was misled when, in fact, he was dissatisfied for other reasons. The materiality requirement guards against such maneuvers. The same danger requires reasonable reliance.

Injury. Finally, there is the requirement of injury. In some jurisdictions, the defrauded person who seeks a remedy in money damages must show that he sustained a quantifiable injury. If, however, he seeks a remedy other than money damages, such as rescission, the requirement is relaxed. Generally, a showing of real dollar loss is not necessary. Permitting rescission without proof of a dollar loss is consistent with the rationale that fraud and misrepresentation in a contract are fundamentally problems of assent. If no real assent was given, the party denying the effectiveness of that assent ought to be able to assert his claim regardless of his loss or suffering.

The *Entron* case that follows is a good example of judicial analysis of misrepresentation. As you read it, ponder two questions: does the evidence discussed appear to establish guilty knowledge? And, did it make any difference to General Cablevision whether fraud or only misrepresentation was established?

Entron, Inc. v. General Cablevision of Palatka
United States Court of Appeals, Fifth Circuit, 1970. 435 F.2d 995
TUTTLE, CIRCUIT JUDGE.
This is an appeal from a verdict and judgment in favor of the defendant-appellee on its counterclaim when it was sued for the balance due on a construction contract wherein the plaintiff agreed to construct, and did construct, a cable television system for the defendant. . . .

We now look at the facts in this case, which are substantially undisputed so far as they deal with the element of actionable misrepresentation. The contract, entered into after repeated statements by Bernard Karlen, Vice President of General Cablevision, that his company was strictly limited to the requirement that it have the job completed within sixty days, contained an express promise that Entron would construct and turn over a system on a "turnkey" basis within sixty days after beginning construction: the contract was not only not turned over within sixty days but was not offered for final acceptance until approximately three times that long, some 175 days after the contract was signed. Even this tender was accepted by General Cablevision, because the system failed to operate properly, and it was not until nearly three months later that the system began operating completely satisfactorily; substantial damage accrued to General Cablevision as a result of this failure of Entron to live up to its promise of performance, since General Cablevision opened offices and started selling service to prospective customers on the assumption that the sixty day completion would be carried out: in response to questions asked by defendant of the president of Entron that he name several comparable jobs performed by Entron, several were named, including one in Laurinburg, North Carolina: the Laurinburg job required four or five calendar months for completion; the president of Entron testified that as far as he could recall this was the shortest time Entron had ever been required to build and install a CATV System of comparable type.

It has been said that "the state of a man's mind is as much a fact as the state of his digestion." If this be true, if at the time a seller makes a statement as to what he proposes to do for the future when the true state of his mind would disclose that he knows he cannot do so, this is a misrepresentation of a material fact. The same would be true if the seller represents what he proposes to do at a time when he is either without knowledge as to his ability to perform or if he represents what he proposes to do under circumstances in which he should have known, but may not have known, of his inability to carry out his promise. There is no contention made by the appellant that whatever representations were made as to the sixty-day performance were not made for the purpose of inducing General Cablevision to act on them. Moreover, it is clear that General Cablevision did rely on the representation and this reliance resulted in injury.

Although not expressly argued on behalf of the appellee, we consider the very gross failure to perform the contract, even if standing alone, as strong evidence of the inability of the plaintiff-appellant to do what it promised to do — that is to complete the system within sixty days. Assuming, as we should, that when parties enter into a solemn written obligation to perform a contract involving a reasonably complicated mechanism and system as to which the promisor is presumed to be an expert, this should of itself be taken to be a holding out of a belief that the undertaking could be carried out, the failure of the promisor to carry out his agreement fully and adequately within anything like the terms of the formal contract is some evidence that the party did not intend to do it in the first place. To this there is to be added the testimony of the president of the appellant that the company had never performed a job of comparable size in a period of even twice as many days as the sixty-day period contemplated in this contract. We think this is sufficient to permit the jury to find all of the essential elements for actionable misrepresentation.

To be sure, the appellant points to testimony by Mr. Karlen, who at one point testified that he had thought of undertaking to do the job on behalf of General Cablevision itself rather than contracting it out, that he believed he could have done it within sixty days and that "so did Entron." Appellant contends that this statement by Mr. Karlen that Entron believed it could construct the system in the time allotted negates any possibility of a jury's finding that the representation made by Entron that it would perform in sixty days amounts to actionable misrepresentation. We think that the jury could find that the language used by Mr. Karlen, since he could not possibly have known what Entron "felt," went only so far as to indicate that the job could be done in that time, but it did not go so far as to exclude the likelihood that the Entron representatives made the promise to do so without any real intention of doing it, rather following their own schedule and convenience, and knowing that this is what they would do from the beginning.

When we consider this fact, together with testimony of the president of Entron that although there were five of six "comparable" jobs performed by Entron, no one of them had been completed in less than five months, which it required at Laurinburg, North Carolina, we conclude that there was more than substantial evidence to submit to the jury on this issue.

*

Disclaimer of Representation

What would be the result if A committed a misrepresentation or fraud upon B, and got B to acknowledge in a signed writing that no statement or lack of statement had been relied upon? Would this be the perfect method of committing a wrong and escaping from its consequences? The following case deals with this particular issue. Conceptually this topic can be viewed as a refinement of the requirement of a false statement of fact.

Danann Realty Corp. v. Harris
New York State Court of Appeals, 1959. 5 N.Y.2d 317, 157 N.E.2d 597

[Plaintiff, buyer, seeks damages for fraud, charging defendant, seller, induced a contract through false oral representations as to the operating expenses and profits to be derived from the investment in the lease of a building.

The written contract, entered into after the oral representations were made, provided that the seller made no "representations as to the physical condition, rents, leases, expenses, operations . . . except as herein specifically set forth. . . ." The contract also provided that "it is understood and agreed that all undertakings and agreements heretofore had between the parties hereto are merged in this contract, which alone fully and completely expresses their agreement, and that the same is entered into after full investigation, neither party relying upon any statement or representation, not embodied in this contract, made by the other. . . ."]

BURKE, JUDGE.
. . . . The complaint here contains no allegations that the contract was not read by the purchaser. We can fairly conclude that plaintiff's officers read and understood the contract, and that they were aware of the provision by which they aver that plaintiff did not rely on such extra-contractual representations. It is not alleged that this provision was not understood, or that the provision itself was procured by fraud. . . . [W]here a person had read and understood the disclaimer of representation clause, he is bound by it. The court rejected, as a matter of law, the allegation of plaintiffs "that they relied upon an oral statement made to them in direct contradiction of this provision of the contract." The presence of such a disclaimer clause "is inconsistent with the contention that plaintiff relied upon the misrepresentation, and was led thereby to make the contract."

The general rule was enunciated by this court over a half a century ago that "if the facts represented are not matters peculiarly within the party's knowledge, and the other party has the means available to him of knowing, by the exercise of ordinary intelligence, the truth or the real quality of the subject of the representation, he must make use of those means, or he will not be heard to complain that he was induced to enter into the transaction by misrepresentations.

In this case, of course, the plaintiff made a representation in the contract that it was not relying on specific representations not embodied in the contract, while, it now asserts, it was in fact relying on such oral representations. Plaintiff admits then that it is guilty of deliberately misrepresenting to the seller its true intention. To condone this fraud would place the purchaser in a favored position. This is particularly so, where, as here, the purchaser confirms the contract, but seeks damages. If the plaintiff has made a bad bargain he cannot avoid it in this manner.

If the language here used is not sufficient to estop a party from claiming that he entered the contract because of fraudulent representations, then no language can accomplish that purpose. To hold otherwise would be to say that it is impossible for two businessmen dealing at arm's length to agree that the buyer is not buying in reliance on any representations of the seller as to a particular fact.

Accordingly, the order of the Appellate Division should be reversed and that of Special Term reinstated, without costs. The question certified should be answered in the negative.

FULD, JUDGE (dissenting).
If a party has actually induced another to enter into a contract by means of fraud — and so the complaint before us alleges — I conceive that language may not be devised to shield him from the consequences of such fraud. The law does not temporize with trickery or duplicity, and this court, after having weighed the advantages of certainty in contractual relations against the harm and injustice which result from fraud, long ago unequivocally declared that "a party who has perpetrated a fraud upon his neighbor may (not) . . . contract with him in the very instrument by means of which it was perpetrated, for immunity against its consequences, close his mouth from complaining of it and bind him never to seek redress. Public policy and morality are both ignored if such an agreement can be given effect in a court of justice. The maxim that fraud vitiates every transaction would no longer be the rule, but the exception." . . .
. . . .

It is said, however, that the provision in this contract differs from those heretofore considered in that it embodies a specific and deliberate exclusion of a particular subject. The quick answer is that the clause now before us is not of such a sort. On the contrary, instead of being limited, it is all-embracing, encompassing every representation that a seller could possibly make about the property being sold and, instead of representing a special term of bargain, is essentially "boiler plate." . . .

In any event, though, I cannot believe that the outcome of such a case as this, in which the defendant is charged with fraud, should turn on the particular language employed in the contract. As Judge Augustus Hand, writing for the Federal Court of Appeals, observed, "the ingenuity of draftsmen is sure to keep pace with the demands of wrongdoers, and if a deliberate fraud be shielded by a clause in a contract that the writing contains every representation made by way of inducement, or that utterances shown to be untrue were not an inducement to the agreement, a fraudulent seller would have a simple method of obtaining immunity for his misconduct. . . ."

The rule heretofore applied by this court presents no obstacle to honest business dealings, and dishonest transactions ought not to receive judicial protection. The clause in the contract before us may lend support to the defense and render the plaintiff's task of establishing its claim more difficult, but it should not be held to bar institution of an action for fraud. Whether the defendants made the statements attributed to them and, if they did, whether the plaintiff relied upon them, whether, in other words, the defendants were guilty of fraud, are questions of fact not capable of determination on the pleadings alone. The plaintiff is entitled to its day in court.

Judge Burke's opinion indicates that "to hold otherwise would be to say that it is impossible for two businessmen dealing at arm's length to agree that the buyer is not acting in reliance on any representations of the seller as to a particular fact." What rule do you surmise he would think appropriate for the nonbusinessperson? Does the court sanction fraud if "particular language [is] employed in the contract" as Judge Fuld charges? If so, what language is sufficient? How about the statement "there has been no fraud"?

Silence as a Fraudulent Act

Parties to an agreement are generally not under an obligation to disclose all they know about the subject matter of their contracts. A manufacturer need not disclose that he has fabrics that wear better, cost less, or are generally better bargains. The seller of a home need not disclose that she is dissatisfied with her neighbors. A butler need not reveal that he considers his experience barely adequate. Certainly we expect this to be the case. But what about the manufacturer who is asked directly which of his fabrics is the best for the money? What of the seller who is asked whether or not she is satisfied with her neighbors? And what of the butler who is asked for whom and how long he worked? Where there has been a failure to reveal these facts, are contracts vulnerable to a charge of no reality of assent? Where does the burden to speak begin, and what is the extent of that burden?

The law recognizes an obligation to disclose information in terms of a duty. Thus, when the law determines a *duty of disclosure* is owed, it finds silence a breach of that duty and declares it fraudulent. Actionable fraud involves more than misstatements; it also involves the obligation to speak the truth if a duty to do so has been found.

The *Restatement of Contracts* has, in its comments, indicated the duty to disclose as follows (Restatement Section 472):

> b. A party entering into a bargain is not bound to tell everything he knows to the other party, even if he is aware that the other party is ignorant of the facts; and unilateral mistake, of itself, does not make a transaction voidable (see 503).
>
> But if a fact known by one party and not the other is so vital that if the mistake were mutual the contract would be voidable, and the party knowing the fact also knows that the other does not know it, non-disclosure is not privileged and is fraudulent.
> . . . .
> d. The extent to which special rules of law deny immunity to one entering into a transaction to withhold facts with which he is acquainted is appropriately stated with reference to particular subjects, such as insurance, security and sales rather than in this Restatement.

Note that the second paragraph of the comment speaks of three of the elements previously discussed: materiality, scienter, and intent. Two other elements — false statement of fact and reasonable reliance — are not characteristics subjects in subpart d of the Comment leads one to conclude that in virtually every case of potential misrepresentation by withholding facts, the determination of what is proper conduct will be made in terms of the subject matter of the misrepresentation and the circumstance at hand. In general, the duty to provide information is found to exist only when a fiduciary relationship, a special relationship of trust, exists.

Remedy for Fraud and Misrepresentation

At one time, the courts paid special attention to the form of the misrepresentation when determining the remedy for it. Thus, if a misrepresentation occurred and the person upon whom it was committed did not realize he was manifesting assent to an agreement, the courts held that the agreement was void and without effect. This form of misrepresentation is called either *fraud in the procurement* or *fraud in the factum*. If Allison signed what appeared to be a receipt for Worthington and Worthington, through a sleight of hand, substituted a document in contract form to buy a farm, the courts held the agreement void; neither Allison nor Worthington was bound. A different rule applied if the fraud was contained in an instrument that both believed to be a contract, but which contained fraudulent statements of fact concerning, for example, the condition of the crops on the farm. In such situations, called *fraud in the inducement*, the person against whom the fraud was committed would have the option of enforcing the agreement or avoiding it through the defense of fraud.

In the first situation, the perpetrator of the fraud is also in the position of avoiding the agreement he induced. Some jurisdictions, in the interest of equity, have held the contract can be avoided only by the party against whom the fraud was committed.

Putting aside the question of whether the agreement was voidable or void, the remedies for misrepresentation and fraud go in two different directions. If the contract lacks reality of assent, the injured party may want the agreement set aside by seeking to avoid or rescind it. On the other hand, he may prefer to keep the contract in effect. Thus, his remedy is not rescission, but compensation for the loss he suffered. Finally, he may decide he wants the benefits of both remedies. He may want to rescind the agreement, restoring himself to where he was before the agreement, but he may also want compensation for damages he sustained while the contract remained in effect — the money he expended, for instance, in turning a sour project into a good one. How could the defrauded party claim there was no assent, and at the same time, claim damages from the contract, a relationship built upon assent? This problem perplexed the courts, and in many situations, the defrauded party was required to choose his remedy — either damages or rescission. To a considerable extent, this refusal to allow recovery on both grounds has been relaxed.

Full damages for fraud — or rescission for fraud and misrepresentation — are limited by several circumstances. First, the fraud perpetrated upon the victim may be knowingly ratified by the victim. The power to avoid a contract because of fraud or misrepresentation is lost when the injured party acquires knowledge of the fraud or misrepresentation and manifests an intent to affirm the agreement or accepts the contract's benefits. After knowingly ratifying the agreement, the victim may not later change his mind and avoid it.

The right of rescission may also be lost by the failure to make timely use of the remedy. Since rescission is an equitable remedy, the courts demand that the victim assert his rights without unreasonable delay. An unreasonable delay after discovering the fraud triggers the doctrine of *laches* (the equitable counterpart to the statute of limitations), which prevents rescission.

In many situations, part of an agreement may be desirable despite some fraud. For instance, a party may wish to affirm part of the agreement and to rescind a part. The conventional rule in this area is that a transaction that is voidable for fraud or misrepresentation cannot be avoided only in part. This holds true in virtually all situations except when an entire installment of a divisible contract has been performed. Then, the courts permit avoidance of the remaining portions of the contract.

Additionally, a person may seek through rescission the return of goods that were sold to a third person. If the third party innocently purchased the goods, he acquires good title that cannot be taken from him. The acquisition of goods by a bona fide purchaser who gives value for the goods converts the seller's voidable title to good title. Finally, the person seeking rescission must return the consideration he received from the other party.

As with the remedies available for mistake, the courts, where appropriate, will permit reformation of contracts to express the parties' real intent. For example, if Goodman fraudulently inserts a clause in a previously written agreement between herself and Benoit, Benoit may apply to a court for a reformation of the contract. This remedy is used if the fraud has not rendered the contract of little use and the defrauded party wishes to continue with the agreement on the terms that were agreed upon before the insertion of the fraud.

So far we have concentrated on the defrauded party's right to rescind the contract. He also has rights for money damages based upon fraud. Here the defrauded party elects to continue the contract but to sue for the injuries sustained.

Jurisdictions differ on how appropriately to quantify the money damages for fraud and misrepresentations. Should the victim receive his out-of-pocket losses (*indemnity*)? Or should the victim receive the benefits of the bargain promised to him? For example, an item fraudulently represented to Schilling as worth $1,000 is sold to her for $800. In truth, it is worth $600. The states that calculate loss in terms of indemnity will award $200 (the selling price minus the real value). Those states that support the benefit of bargain theory will award $400 (the value as represented minus the real value). Finally, in many states, there is no damage remedy for simple misrepresentation. The damage remedy is reserved for cases of fraud alone. In such cases, the only remedy is simple rescission or reformation, the former being the more frequently sought.

DURESS AND UNDUE INFLUENCE

In General

Acts of duress and undue influence also determine whether assent is real. *Duress* is the actual or threatened use of force on a person or one close to that person which compels him to enter into an agreement without the exercise of free will. It includes the threat of illegal imprisonment.

Traditionally, the right to assert duress did not exist unless the harm threatened was imminent, physical, and such as to overcome the will of a "man of ordinary firmness" — for example, if a very large, surly fellow with drawn fist threatens mayhem unless you sign an agreement. To a considerable extent this stringency has been relaxed so that the test of duress involves determining whether a party has caused an impediment of the free will of the victim. In making such a determination, the courts will consider the victim's state of health, experience, age, and intelligence. The courts have also extended the application of the doctrine in situations of harm being threatened to third persons. Thus, the traditional cases that found duress where the threat of force was to a parent or child or spouse have been complemented by those cases finding duress where there was a threat of force against brothers and sisters or grandparents.

The courts have been reluctant to find duress in situations where it was quite obvious that the person making the threat was without power to enforce it. In such situations the courts have determined that there could have been no impediment to the exercise of free will, and thus the cause of the acts complained of were other than the duress or undue influence.

The duress remedy places the one seeking to use it in a desirable position. When duress occurs, two options exist. One can sue for a rescission of the contract and restoration to the position occupied prior to the agreement coming into effect. Or one can actually permit the agreement to continue in effect and seek damage for any loss sustained.

Not every kind of intimidation will constitute duress. It is common for those negotiating the enforcement of already executed contracts to insist on modifications, under the threat of civil suit. The mere threat to exercise one's legal rights through the prosecution of a civil suit does not constitute actionable duress. In many jurisdictions, however, threats of criminal prosecution — without regard to the guilt or innocence of the party coerced — will constitute duress.

Economic Duress and Unconscionable Contracts

In recent years, some courts have come to recognize economic compulsion as a form of duress. This trend seems likely to continue. It is of particular interest to the student of business law, since the businessperson is far more likely to encounter economic, rather than physical, compulsion. It is clear that mere business pressure is insufficient to constitute duress. Yet, there are situations where injury to business reputation or refusal to perform certain required acts in order to compel the other to perform certain acts would constitute economic duress and would permit the party coerced to sue.

Austin Instrument, Inc. v. Loral Corp.
Court of Appeals of New York, 1971. 29 N.Y.2d 124

FULD, CHIEF JUDGE.

. . . .

In July of 1965, Loral was awarded a $6,000,000 contract by the Navy for the production of radar sets. . . . [It] thereupon solicited bids for some 40 precision gear components needed to produce the radar sets, and awarded Austin a sub-contract to supply 23 such parts. . . .

In May, 1966, Loral was awarded a second Navy contract for the production of more radar sets and again went about soliciting bids. Austin bid on all 40 gear components but, on July 15, a representative from Loral informed Austin's president, Mr. Krauss, that his company would be awarded the subcontract only for those items on which it was low bidder. The Austin officer refused to accept an order for less than all 40 of the gear parts and on the next day he told Loral that Austin would cease deliveries of the parts due under the existing subcontract unless Loral consented to substantial increases in the prices provided for by that agreement — both retroactively for parts already delivered and prospectively on those not yet shipped — and placed with Austin the order for all 40 parts needed under Loral's second Navy contract. Shortly thereafter, Austin did, indeed, stop delivery. After contacting 10 manufacturers of precision gears and finding none who could produce the parts in time to meet its commitments to the Navy, Loral acceded to Austin's demands. . . .

. . . .

On September 15, 1967, Austin instituted this action against Loral to recover an amount in excess of $17,750 which was still due on the second subcontract. On the same day, Loral commenced an action against Austin claiming damages of some $22,250 — the aggregate of the price increases under the first subcontract — on the ground of economic duress. The two actions were consolidated and, following a trial, Austin was awarded the sum it requested and Loral's complaint against Austin was dismissed on the ground that it was not shown that "it could not have obtained the items in question from other sources in time to meet its commitment to the Navy under the first contract." A closely divided Appellate Division affirmed. . . .

The applicable law is clear and, indeed, is not disputed by the parties. A contract is voidable on the ground of duress when it is established that the party making the claim was forced to agree to it by means of a wrongful threat precluding the exercise of his free will.

The existence of economic duress or business compulsion is demonstrated by proof that "immediate possession of needful goods is threatened" or, more particularly, in cases such as the one before us, by proof that one party to a contract has threatened to breach the agreement by withholding goods unless the other party agrees to some further demand. . . . It must also appear that the threatened party could not obtain the goods from another source of supply and that the ordinary remedy of an action for breach of contract would not be adequate.

We find . . . [that] the evidence makes out a classic case, as a matter of law, of such duress.

It is manifest that Austin's threat — to stop deliveries unless the prices were increased — deprived Loral of its free will. . . . Because of its production schedule, Loral was, in July, 1966, concerned with meeting its delivery requirements in September, October and November, and it was for the sets to be delivered in those months that the withheld gears were needed. Loral had to plan ahead, and the substantial liquidated damages for which it would be liable, plus the threat of default, were genuine possibilities. Moreover, Loral did a substantial portion of its business with the Government, and it feared that a failure to deliver as agreed upon would jeopardize its chances for future contracts. . . . It was perfectly reasonable for Loral, or any other party similarly placed, to consider itself in an emergency, duress situation.

Austin, however, claims that the fact that Loral extended its time to resume deliveries until September negates its alleged dire need for the parts. A Loral official testified on this point that Austin's president told him he could deliver some parts in August and that the extension of deliveries was a formality. In any event, the parts necessary for production of the radar sets to be delivered in September were delivered to Loral on September 1, and the parts needed for the October schedule were delivered in late August and early September. Even so, Loral had to "work . . . around the clock" to meet its commitments. Considering that the best offer Loral received from the other vendors it contacted was commencement of delivery sometime in October, which . . . would have made it late in its deliveries to the Navy in both September and October, Loral's claim that it had no choice but to accede to Austin's demands is conclusively demonstrated.

We find unconvincing Austin's contention that Loral, in order to meet its burden, should have contacted the Government and asked for an extension of its delivery dates so as to enable it to purchase the parts from another vendor. Aside from the consideration that Loral was anxious to perform well in the Government's eyes, it could not be sure when it would obtain enough parts from a substitute vendor to meet its commitments. The only promise which it received from the companies it contacted was for commencement of deliveries, not full supply, and, with vendor delay common in this field, it would have been nearly impossible to know the length of the extension it should request. Moreover, there is authority for Loral's position that nonperformance by a subcontractor is not an excuse for default in the main contract. . . .

Loral . . . also had the burden of demonstrating that it could not obtain the parts elsewhere within a reasonable time, and there can be no doubt that it met this burden. The manufacturers whom Loral contacted comprised its entire list of "approved vendors" for precision gears, and none was able to commence delivery soon enough. . . .

It is hardly necessary to add that Loral's normal legal remedy of accepting Austin's breach of the contract and then suing for damages would have been inadequate under the circumstances, as Loral would still have had to obtain the gears elsewhere with all the concomitant consequences mentioned above. . . .
          . . . .

In sum, the record before us demonstrates that Loral agreed to the price increases in consequence of the economic duress employed by Austin. Accordingly, the matter should be remanded to the trial court for a computation of its damages.

Where goods are involved, a statutory basis for evaluating duress is available. Section 2–302 of the UCC authorizes a court to refuse to enforce an unconscionable contract or an unconscionable portion of a contract. It may also limit the application of an unconscionable clause to avoid an unconscionable result. This provision is discussed more fully in Part V, on the sale of goods.

Undue Influence

Similar to duress is undue influence. This form of bar to reality of assent has been described as mental coercion or mental duress. It is also an attempt to influence the free will of the victim and renders a contract voidable. Undue influence falls short of actual fraud, but is said to be "a species of constructive fraud." Undue influence involves the taking of unfair advantage of another on account of the close relationship of the parties. As a practical matter, undue influence has much in common with silence as a fraudulent act. Both depend on the existence of any one of a number of special relationships between the parties. They differ in that one involves silence while the other involves self-interested assertion or recommendation short of assertions of fact. For example, undue influence may result from weakness of mind in the person who was taken advantage of, but it is nonetheless effective in that situation as a form of improper conduct which precludes assent. Since undue influence renders the contract voidable, the victim is permitted either to avoid and receive rescission or contract damages. And when the victim is sued to compel adherence to the agreement, he may assert the defense of undue influence, and his performance will be excused.

PROBLEMS AND QUESTIONS

1. What is the difference between fraud and misrepresentation?

2. Why is injury a necessary condition of fraud?

3. In *Danann Realty Corp.* v. *Harris*, do you agree with the majority opinion or the dissenting opinion? Why?

4. On June 1, 1973, Joseph Schmidt sold to Paula Keogh his power lawnmower, a Mattell Model 65J. Keogh had seen the mower work for Schmidt and was impressed with its performance and the price. Upon discovering that the mower did not work as well as she had anticipated, she sought to avoid the sale on the ground of mutual mistake, charging that the bill of sale incorrectly identified the mower as a Mattell Model 65K. May Keogh avoid the sale on the grounds that the bill of sale was incorrectly drawn? Explain.

5. Stanton was given a piece of antique furniture by his uncle. Stanton did not find the furniture appealing and so when his best friend, Benson, admired it, Stanton offered to sell it to him for $10. Benson accepted, paid the $10, and took the furniture. The furniture was clearly marked as Chippendale. Several weeks later, Benson gleefully informed Stanton that he had inquired about the furniture and had learned it was worth $25,000. Stanton thereupon tendered Benson $10 and demanded its return. Benson refused and Stanton brought suit to recover the furniture.

a. Judgment for whom?

b. Would your answer be the same if Benson had known, at the time he bought the furniture, that Chippendale was a famous furniture maker and that the furniture was far more valuable than Stanton realized?

6. Rita Collins made a contract to buy a 9-room house in Brooklyn, New York. At the time of making the contract she mistakenly believed that the dining room was painted a dark blue. In fact, she confused the color of the dining room with the color of the alcove. When the time for delivery of the deed was

at hand, however, Collins refused to accept title since she had discovered that the room was not painted the color she had believed it to be. The seller, not knowing that the purchaser was in error as to this belief, insisted that she accept the deed as tendered. Is she bound to accept it? Explain. Would your answer be different if the seller knew of her mistake? Explain.

7. Carter submitted a bid on the construction of a school building for $900,000. His bid was the low bid and it was accepted. The following day, discovering that he had omitted from his calculations a $5,000 item, he gave immediate notice of withdrawal of his bid. He was met with refusal, and he now brings action to have the contract rescinded on the ground of mistake. Should he succeed? Why?

8. A husband called on the president of a bank to intercede for his wife, who had borrowed heavily at the bank to finance stock speculation and whose security the bank was threatening to sell. The president of the bank was under the impression that the husband was a man of great wealth and induced the husband to promise in writing, in consideration of the bank extending his wife's time of payment on her loans for six months, to personally guarantee the payment thereof. The husband died shortly thereafter and his estate was found to be insolvent. The bank thereupon notified the wife that unless her loans were repaid at once, it would sell her securities. The wife now brings an action to enjoin the bank from making such sale until the expiration of the six-month extension period. May she have relief? Explain.

9. Henrietta Baker went to the Chevrolet dealer in her hometown with the intention of purchasing a new gas-saving economy car to replace her five-year-old Mercury station wagon. Baker explained to the car salesperson that she had just accepted a sales representative position that required her to drive four to five hundred miles each week and she wanted to purchase a car that would give her thirty miles per gallon on long distance trips. The salesperson assured Baker that a new Chevette would give her that mileage. Baker ordered a new Chevette, to be delivered in two months. The following week, Baker saw an advertisement for Chevette indicating that the highway mileage is 29.5 miles per gallon. Baker sought to cancel the contract, saying the salesperson misrepresented the mileage performance. What would a court decide?

10. Austin contracted with Brown to buy the latter's hunting dog, Sport, for $200, Brown telling Austin that Sport had recently won first prize in the dog show at the state fair. Sport was actually worth $200, but had not won any prize at the state fair, as Brown well knew. Austin was induced to contract on the

basis of the dog's alleged performance record, and when Austin discovered Brown's deception, he was angry and sought to return Sport and collect the purchase price. Does he have a right to the return of the purchase price? Would there be a cause of action for money damages?

11. Plaintiff was the owner of a plot of vacant land on Elmwood Avenue and an adjoining plot of land on Highland Avenue with several houses on it. Defendant sought to purchase a portion of the plot of vacant land, stating honestly that she desired to purchase it for residence purposes. The defendant's representations that she intended to build dwellings on the land were repeated during negotiations and the plaintiff, relying thereon, gave her a deed to a portion of the plot for $5,525. A closer examination of her property convinced her that the land was better suited to commercial purposes, so two days following the delivery of the deed, the defendant instructed her architect to prepare plans for a garage to occupy the entire lot. Less than two weeks later she entered into a contract for the construction of a garage. Plaintiff claims to have been deceived by the defendant's representations and demands a reconveyance of the property sold and offers to restore the defendant's price. Is plaintiff entitled to his remedy?

12. An agreement was entered into between Collier Publishing and Josephowitz in which Josephowitz sold his business to Cromwell-Collier for $3,000,000. Before the agreement was made, however, defendant-seller made false representations to plaintiff-buyer as to earning, profitability, and growth record of the business. When plaintiff brought suit, defendant introduced the following clause from the written contract to prevent plaintiff from complaining about the fraudulent representations:

> "The agreement constitutes the entire understanding between the parties, and was not induced by any representations, warranties or covenants not herein contained."

Is such language sufficient to prevent a claim for fraud? Explain.

13. Cook owned five acres of land on which were two springs of mineral water and machinery for bottling the water. He sold the land to Weigel for $5,000, representing that the natural mineral water could be bottled as it flowed and that the natural flow was 4,200 gallons per day.

Weigel took possession and purchased additional machinery for $4,500. Later she discovered that the water was not natural mineral water, but rather chemically treated fresh water, and that the flow was far less than the 4,200 gallons per day that had been represented. What remedies are available to her?

14. Sellers sold her restaurant to Carson. In the course of negotiations, Sellers knowingly made untrue statements concerning the net income of the restaurant. These statements formed the basis of Carson's agreement to purchase the restaurant. In the first year of operation Carson discovered the statements to be false, but also realized that the first year profits were actually consistent with the false statements and that the business was doing well. He decided to keep the restaurant. By the second year, however, profits fell

and Carson sought rescission on the grounds of fraud. Decision for whom? Explain.

15. Graves was the principal stockholder of the Robby Corporation and Carlos owned one share of its stock. Graves claims that Carlos threatened to delay the sale of the corporation to a third party unless Graves paid him $5,000 for his one share. Graves did in fact give him a note for $5,000, which Carlos now seeks to have satisfied. Graves claims the $5,000 was paid for the stock because of the threat of Carlos to delay the sale of the corporation. May Graves refuse to pay on the grounds of the duress?

DEFINITION, ORIGINS, AND SIGNIFICANCE

Consideration, an essential requirement of a contract, is generally understood as a mutual exchange of benefits and detriments between the parties to a contract. The benefit and detriment is generally in the form of goods, services, or legal rights given to the other party in exchange for money or something else of value. Thus, an agreement providing for the sale of a National Football League franchise for $20 million is a contract involving consideration on both sides: the $20 million is consideration furnished by the buyer, and the franchise is consideration furnished by the seller. Both parties have received a benefit in the form of what they bargained for, and both have sustained a detriment in terms of the costs they have furnished.

Consideration is generally understood as an act, or forbearance, or a promise thereof, which goes to the basis of the agreement between the offeror and offeree. It is generally that which is bargained for and accepted by the parties to the agreement.

It is a long-standing requirement of the common law that both parties to an agreement furnish some consideration. Without consideration, the agreement is without legal effect, and a promise made without consideration cannot be enforced, for an obvious reason. The contractual agreement was born in a bargain, and our commercial understanding is that no one gives up something for nothing. Thus, if the bargain was reflected in a contract, it would be reasonable to expect that each party would furnish something to the other.

It is not necessary that consideration have tangible properties. Consideration can consist of giving up a legal right or of accepting a legal restraint upon one's right to act. Thus, a promise not to engage in a competitive business enterprise in return for $5,000 is an agreement supported by consideration from both parties. A promise to refrain from smoking in return for $500 is an agreement that is also supported by consideration on both sides. This is so even though the person who refrains from smoking might also stand to benefit

7

CONSID-
ERATION

otherwise from his conduct. Giving up something is the essence of consideration. It is a legal undertaking or legal obligation that did not exist before the bargain that becomes a basis for determining whether an enforceable agreement exists. If the parties appear to furnish consideration, but the agreement does not secure a legal obligation, the courts will find the agreement unenforceable for lack of consideration. For example, a promise "to deliver the boat on April 10 if I decide I want to" lacks consideration.

IMPORTANT SUBSIDIARY CONCEPTS

The "Bargained for" Aspect

Several aspects of consideration are worth additional treatment. The first is its "bargained for" aspect. This does not mean the bargain must result from harsh and strict negotiations. Rather, it is a matter of appearance or form and not substance. As Mr. Justice Holmes said in *Wisconsin & M. Ry. Co.* v. *Powers* 191 U.S. 379, 24 S.Ct. 107 (1903):

> [T]he promise [allegedly made by the state] and the detriment [allegedly sustained by the railroad] . . . [must be] the conventional inducements each for the other. No matter what the actual motive may have been, by the express or implied terms of the supposed contract, the promise and the consideration must purport to be the motive each for the other, in whole or at least in part. It is not enough that the promise induces the detriment or that the detriment induces the promise if the other half is wanting. . . . [I]t is clear that we should require an adequate expression of an actual intent. . . . [T]he two things . . . [must be] set against each other in terms of bargain.

The following case demonstrates the importance of the bargain aspect of consideration.

Bard v. Kent
Supreme Court of California, 1948. 19 Cal.2d 449, 122 P.2d 8

[Action by Ben Bard, as special administrator, etc., against L. E. Kent, individually, and as director, etc., to cancel and set aside an option to extend a lease. From a judgment in favor of the plaintiff, the defendant appeals.

Judgment affirmed.]

TRAYNOR, JUSTICE.
The defendant in this action, L. E. Kent, administered the business affairs of Mrs. Ruth Roland Bard, hereinafter referred to as Miss Roland, under a general power of attorney for many years before her death. In 1933, Kent, acting as agent for Miss Roland, leased for five years a parcel of real property owned by her to Cliff Odums and Albert M. Berkson, who constructed a building on the property and installed equipment for the operation of a restaurant named the Cat and the Fiddle. The restaurant failed, and Odums and Berkson abandoned the venture. Thereupon Kent, acting in his personal capacity together with Howard Hastings and Don Carpenter, organized a corporation, known as the Cat and the Fiddle Company, which assumed the obligations of Odums and Berkson and took over the operation of the restau-

rant. When this venture likewise proved unprofitable, Kent bought the stock of Hastings and Carpenter in the Cat and the Fiddle Company and continued to pay off the obligations that the company had assumed. Various sublessees who thereafter tried to operate a restaurant on the premises were unsuccessful.

On August 21, 1935, Miss Roland executed a lease of the premises to the Cat and the Fiddle Company for a term of five years. The lessee subsequently obtained an extension of the lease and written authority to sublease the premises to M. A. McDonnell. On August 30, 1935, the premises were subleased to McDonnell for a term of five years ending August 31, 1940, with an option to renew the lease for one year. . . . The restaurant operated by McDonnell proved highly successful, and he made improvements costing approximately $30,000. Meanwhile Kent dissolved the corporation, distributed its assets to himself, and continued his business as an individual under the fictitious name of the Cat and the Fiddle Company. . . .

During 1936 McDonnell told Miss Roland and Kent that he would undertake additional improvements at a cost of about $10,000 if his lease were extended for another four years. Miss Roland in subsequent conversations with Kent expressed a willingness to grant the extension if the proposed improvements would cost approximately $10,000. She suggested that Kent check the figures and have an architect draw sketches for the purpose of making an estimate. On August 17, 1937, Miss Roland executed to the Cat and the Fiddle Company an option to extend its lease for an additional four years in order that it in turn could give McDonnell an extension of his lease. The option was signed for Miss Roland by Kent as her attorney in fact. It recited that "For consideration of Ten Dollars ($10.00) and other valuable consideration" the Cat and the Fiddle Company was granted an option to extend its lease for an additional period of four years. After the option was signed, Kent instructed Kenneth McDonald, an architect, to draw sketches of the proposed improvements. These sketches were billed to Kent and paid for by him subsequent to the deaths of the architect and Miss Roland.

On September 22, 1937, before the option was exercised, Miss Roland died. The special administrator of her estate brought this action against Kent to cancel and set aside the option on the grounds that it was not only given without consideration and therefore revoked by the death of the offeror, but that it was obtained by fraud. It was stipulated that the sum of $10 was not paid to Miss Roland and that none of the proposed improvements were made. The trial court found that defendant made a complete disclosure of all the transactions to Miss Roland and that he was not guilty of any fraud or wrongdoing in his dealings with her. The court also found, however, that there was no consideration given for the option and that it was therefore revoked by Miss Roland's death. Defendant has appealed from the judgment in favor of plaintiff.

An option is an offer and if it is without consideration, it is revoked by the death of the offeror prior to acceptance. If consideration is given, it is a contract binding upon the offeror and upon his successors in interest after his death. . . . Since the trial court found that no consideration was given for the option in question, the judgment must be upheld if the finding is supported by sufficient evidence.

Defendant contends that his payment of the architect's fee for sketches of the proposed improvements is a consideration sufficient to make the option irrevocable. There is no doubt that such payment would be consideration for an option if the offeror agreed to accept it as such. . . . No act of an offeree, however, can constitute consideration binding upon the offeror unless the latter agrees to be bound in return therefor. . . . In the words of the Restatement of Contracts (§ 75): "Consideration must actually be bargained for as the exchange for the promise. . . . The existence or non-existence of a bargain where something has been parted with by the promisee or received by the promisor depends upon the manifested intention of the parties. . . . The fact that the promisee relies on the promise to his injury, or the promisor gains some advantage therefrom, does not establish consideration without the element of bargain or agreed exchange."

In the present case the trial court was justified in concluding from the evidence that Miss Roland did not promise to grant the option in return for Kent's engaging the architect. Under this interpretation of the evidence Miss Roland merely stated the conditions under which she was willing to extend the lease. Although, according to Kent's testimony, she suggested engaging an architect to check the figures on the proposed improvements, this suggestion did not constitute a promise by her to grant the option if that were done. Kent employed the architect to convince her that the necessary conditions existed, but she made no promise to extend the lease in the event they did, and remained free to withdraw her offer at any time before acceptance. Kent could have exercised the option as soon as it was executed, but he chose instead to wait rather than to undertake immediately the obligations incident to leasing the property for another four years. The engagement of the architect was to actuate Miss Roland to keep her offer open, but it did not constitute consideration binding her to do so. At best the evidence created a conflict for the trial court to resolve.

. . . .

The judgment is affirmed.

Occasionally, cases arise where promises are made in return for consideration before the agreement. For example, a retiring employee might be promised a pension in return for his years of faithful service. Since it is impossible to bargain for what has already been given, courts traditionally hold this form of consideration, called *past consideration*, to be no consideration and hence without legal effect. Thus, the promise to provide the pension is unenforceable. Some jurisdictions have modified the common law by statutes that give legal effect to past consideration, particularly when the promise is in written form.

Adequacy Versus Sufficiency

An important aspect of consideration is the distinction between adequacy and sufficiency. The linguistic difference between these terms is small, but the legal one is significant. The nub of *sufficiency* is whether that which is given by each party can qualify as consideration in its basic nature and substance. The nub of *adequacy* is whether enough economic value has been given. Courts do inquire into sufficiency, asking whether that which is given is the kind of thing that can qualify as consideration. Courts do not inquire into adequacy, ignoring the question of whether the economic value given by one party is comparable to that given by the other.

Several justifications exist for avoiding inquiries into adequacy. One is that judgments of worth are very personal, and judges and juries are not well equipped to explore them. For example, a Civil War sword might not be worth $2,000 to most people, but the price might be cheap to the great grand-child of him who carried it or to a collector finally locating an excellent example of the one type of sword missing from his collection. Moreover, if courts entertained inquiries into adequacy, they could be inundated with suits by people who belatedly concluded they had contracted improvidently. Professor Edwin Patterson has succinctly summarized the arguments against inquiring into adequacy of consideration as follows in "An Apology for Consideration," 58 Colum. L. Rev. 929, 953 (1958):[1]

> (1) The efficient administration of the law of contracts requires that courts shall not be required to prescribe prices. (2) The test of enforceability should be certain and should not be beclouded by such vague terms as 'fair' or 'reasonable' as tests of validity. (3) There is still the somewhat old-fashioned theory that persons of maturity and sound mind should be free to contract imprudently as well as prudently.

Modifications

Need for Consideration

Just as consideration is required for an initial agreement, it is also required for any modifications, as the following example shows. A builder and an owner of land agree that the builder will construct a ski lodge for $50,000. Midway into the work, the builder discovers that completing the building at that price would cause a substantial loss. He confronts the owner with this situation, and they both agree the owner will pay an additional $20,000. In this situation, many courts will generally find the builder is entitled to only the original $50,000, notwithstanding the modification, because the agreement to provide the additional $20,000 was not supported by consideration. The builder was only doing what he was legally required to do under a contract already in effect. He parted with no consideration to deserve the additional $20,000. This failure to provide consideration defeats recovery of what was promised to him in the modification.

There are ways to avoid this result. Some jurisdictions avoid it by carving out special exceptions in building cases where the parties agree to price mod-ifications. In essence, they dispense with the need for consideration in these cases. Other nonjudicial methods of avoiding the requirement of new con-sideration are difficult. The parties might terminate the first contract, thereby terminating its legal obligation, and form a second contract. This approach, however, might allow either party to terminate all duties after the first agree-ment is terminated and before the second agreement is formed. Thus, tre-mendous uncertainty attaches to this procedure.

Another method might be to furnish additional consideration. Under this procedure, the builder might advance the date of completion by one day or

---

1. Reprinted by permission of the *Columbia Law Review*.

might add an extra feature to the building. Of course, the new consideration is not worth the $20,000 given by the owner, but the rules governing adequacy of consideration assure the builder that such an objection is not legally relevant. New consideration affords the parties the opportunity to continue under the first contract instead of risking the uncertainties of terminating that contract and forming another.

Finally, it might be possible to modify the previous agreement by a written modification without new consideration. This approach is possible and popular in many jurisdictions. The writing substitutes for the consideration that is lacking in the new agreement.

The UCC changes the common law rule in contracts for the sale of goods. The Code provides in section 2–209 that modifications of existing contracts are effective without consideration. This revision of the common law operates in many situations where prices are later readjusted, quantities changed, or the parties review the credit terms of transactions and decide upon alternative arrangements. The comments to this section of the Code suggest the reasons for this change:

> 1. This section seeks to protect and make effective all necessary and desirable modifications of sales contracts without regard to the technicalities which at present hamper such adjustments.
>
> 2. Subsection (1) provides that an agreement modifying a sales contract needs no consideration to be binding.
>
> However, modifications made thereunder must meet the test of good faith imposed by this Act. The effective use of bad faith to escape performance on the original contract terms is barred, and the extortion of a "modification" without legitimate commercial reason is ineffective as a violation of the duty of good faith. Nor can a mere technical consideration support a modification made in bad faith.
>
> The test of "good faith" between merchants or as against merchants includes "observance of reasonable commercial standards of fair dealing in the trade" (Section 2–103), and may in some situations require an objectively demonstrable reason for seeking a modification. But such matters as a market shift which makes performance come to involve a loss may provide such a reason even though there is no such unforeseen difficulty as would make out a legal excuse from performance under sections 2–615 and 2–616.

"Paid in Full"

Suppose a check is received in payment of a $500 obligation that is due. The check, for $300, bears the notation "paid in full" or "in full payment." A question arises as to the effect on the debt of cashing the check. The solution turns on the notion of liquidated claims and the notion of consideration.

If the debt is *liquidated* (one quantified with exactness in the agreement both as to the existence of a debt and the amount owed), and if the amount due is $500, the courts hold there is still an obligation for the remaining $200. No new consideration is given for the acceptance of less than the full amount due; therefore, the creditor may claim the remainder of the liquidated obligation. However, if the amount of the obligation is in dispute and if the party receiving the money knows or should know of the dispute, then a contrary result follows. The instrument, by its terms, states that $300 is offered in full satisfaction of a disputed debt; cashing the check means that amount is accepted. Consideration by the paying party is found because that party, in offering $300, is doing something he contends is not required under the terms of the original obligation. This situation is analogous to the earlier example where one gave consideration by giving up the legal right to smoke. In this case, the party cashing the check is giving up a right to assert a claim for an additional $200, while the sender of the check is giving up what he contends is a right to pay either nothing or a sum less than $300. Note that the presence of a dispute and notice thereof is imperative if the paying party is held to give consideration. Simply writing "paid in full" on a check, however, is not ordinarily sufficient to apprise the other party of the dispute and the proposed settlement.

The cases in this area have not been entirely clear and certain, and there has been considerable disagreement concerning the effectiveness of the notation "paid in full" on the check. This stems, in large measure, from the separate questions of whether the debt is certain or in dispute and the giving of notice.

Accord and Satisfaction

Frequently when a debt is due but cannot be paid, the parties will agree to a settlement of it. The settlement raises the question of consideration. Consideration should support this agreement, or *accord* (which in this instance is a modification of a prior accord), or there should be a writing if the state permits a writing to substitute for consideration. The *satisfaction* is the payment that will, when made, terminate the obligation made under the agreement. The following case discusses the requirements of accord and satisfaction.

Roberts v. Finger
Supreme Court of Mississippi, 1956. 227 Miss. 671, 86 So.2d 463

[Plaintiff, Insurance Company, sued defendant for additional premiums owed on two insurance policies. Under both policies the estimated premiums were computed and paid since the actual premiums could not be determined until the termination of the policies. Upon the sale of his business, the defendant cancelled the policies and sent a check for $361.09 as the payment due according to the estimated premium schedule.

The check bore the following notation: "By endorsement this check is accepted in full payment of the following account. Date 7/24 Acct. in full. Total of Invoices _____. Less discount _____. Total deductions _____. Amount of check $361.09. If incorrect please return. No receipt necessary."

This writing was in print in a form commonly seen on the left side of printed checks. The check was endorsed by the plaintiff and paid by defendant's bank.

Thereafter the auditors for the insurance company determined that the defendant had not paid enough of the premiums and requested an additional $659.17. Upon refusal to pay, plaintiff brought suit. The defendant pleaded an accord and satisfaction based upon the acceptance of the check. At the trial a judgment was entered for the defendant and the plaintiff appeals.]

Gillespie, J.

The question is whether the acceptance of the check was an accord and satisfaction of the entire earned premium on the two policies of insurance. Ordinarily the acceptance of a check which states that it is in full of a demand is an accord and satisfaction of the whole demand.

. . . .

One of the essential elements of an accord and satisfaction is an agreement, or a meeting of the minds of the parties. This agreement must have all the essentials of a contract and may be express, or implied from the circumstances. Accord, or the agreement, precedes satisfaction, which is the execution of the agreement, resulting in accord and satisfaction. Essential to accord is the identity of the claim, or claims, account, or accounts, to be satisfied by acceptance of the accord. An accord and satisfaction is not accomplished by the tender and acceptance of a check with the words "account in full" thereon, unless the circumstances are such that the payee knows or should know, what account is intended to be satisfied; and where the parties are so circumstanced, or the state of affairs between them is such, that the payee reasonably understands that a particular account is intended to be satisfied, there is no accord and satisfaction of another and different account or claim. Whether the payee knew, or should have known, what claim or account was intended to be satisfied is to be determined from all of the surrounding circumstances attending the parties and the transactions involved.

The amount of the check was the amount owing by appellee on the books of appellant, being a balance from several other insurance policies and the estimated premiums on the two policies here involved. The final determination of the total earned premium could not have been known to either party when the check was written and it was not then known which party owed the other, or the amount. There is no contention that there was to be a mutual accord and satisfaction, and it would not be reasonable to infer that appellee was intended to be released from all liability as to the results of the audits, and still allow appellee to make claim against appellant if the audit revealed the earned premium was less than the estimated premium.

We think there is no proof, directly or by reasonable inference, that there was an agreement that the check was tendered in satisfaction of the final earned premiums under the two policies of insurance.

The foregoing case addresses the situation where there is no accord, but two other possibilities exist. First, there is an accord and it is satisfied (performed). Second, there is an accord, but it is not satisfied. Where the accord has been satisfied, the modification will withstand a charge of no consideration, and it will be enforced. Where the accord has not been satisfied, a special situation arises. Say a debtor owes a creditor $500. They agree to reduce it to $300 and provide that payment must be made one day earlier than previously required. As we've seen, consideration and an enforceable contract appear to exist. But, suppose the debtor fails to pay the creditor under the new agreement, i.e., there is no satisfaction. Most courts permit the creditor to sue on either the original obligation ($500 due April 1) or the accord agreement ($300 due March 31). The theory is that the accord does not discharge, but only suspends, the initial contract pending performance

(satisfaction) under the accord. Failure to satisfy the accord permits the creditor to sue for breach of the accord or to restore the original agreement and
sue under it.

In most situations where the creditor has broken the accord, the debtor
has the obligation of performing under the old agreement, but is permitted
to sue for damages for breach of the accord, or in a proper situation, to obtain
specific performance of the accord.

Composition Agreements

Consideration is a topic of some importance in cases involving agreements
by a number of creditors to accept less than the full amounts due to them by
their debtor, called a *composition agreement*. In such circumstances, the simple
rules of consideration are enhanced by the notion of the creditors' mutual
obligation to respect the claims of other creditors. Consideration is not found
in the debtor's pledge to pay less than he is obligated to pay; it is found in
the creditors' mutual agreement to refrain from battling to obtain more funds
from the debtor.

In the early cases involving consideration and composition agreements,
courts were unwilling to find consideration because it did not run from the
debtor. Today, however, the notion that the agreement is binding and that
consideration has been furnished is securely imbedded in the law.

Mutuality of Obligation

In essence, *mutuality of obligation* means that both parties are bound by the
agreement, or neither party is bound. There are some exceptions to this
general rule in other areas of contracts, most noticeably where real assent is
lacking (for example, an infant or victim of fraud has the power to disaffirm
an agreement); however, where the doctrine of consideration is involved, the
requirement of mutuality of obligation is very strong.

Courts will often strain to find consideration if an intent to consummate
a contract is clear. In the following famous case, the court, relying on the
obvious intent of the parties, cures a defect in the drafting of an agreement
by making wise use of the requirement of mutuality of obligation.

Wood v. Lucy, Lady Duff-Gordon
Court of Appeals of New York, 1917. 222 N.Y. 88, 118 N.E. 214
Appeal from Supreme Court, Appellate Division, First Department. Action by Otis
F. Wood against Lucy, Lady Duff-Gordon. From a judgment of the Appellate Divi-
sion which reversed an order denying defendant's motion for judgment on the
pleading, and which dismissed the complaint, plaintiff appeals. Reversed.

CARDOZO, J.
The defendant styles herself "a creator of fashions." Her favor helps a sale. Manufacturers of dresses, millinery, and like articles are glad to pay for a certificate of

her approval. The things which she designs, fabrics, parasols, and what not, have a new value in the public mind when issued in her name. She employed the plaintiff to help her to turn this vogue into money. He was to have the exclusive right, subject always to her approval, to place her indorsements on the designs of others. He was also to have the exclusive right to place her own designs on sale, or to license others to market them. In return, she was to have one-half of "all profits and revenues" derived from any contracts he might make. The exclusive right was to last at least one year from April 1, 1915, and thereafter from year to year unless terminated by notice of 90 days. The plaintiff says that he kept the contract on his part, and that the defendant broke it. She placed her indorsement on fabrics, dresses, and millinery without his knowledge, and withheld the profits. He sues her for the damages and the case comes here on demurrer.

The agreement of employment is signed by both parties. It has a wealth of recitals. The defendant insists, however, that it lacks the elements of a contract. She says that the plaintiff does not bind himself to anything. It is true that he does not promise in so many words that he will use reasonable efforts to place the defendant's indorsements and market her designs. We think, however, that such a promise is fairly to be implied. The law has outgrown its primitive stage of formalism when the precise word was the sovereign talisman, and every slip was fatal. It takes a broader view today. A promise may be lacking, and yet the whole writing may be "instinct with an obligation," imperfectly expressed. . . . If that is so, there is a contract.

The implication of a promise here finds support in many circumstances. The defendant gave an *exclusive* privilege. She was to have no right for at least a year to place her own indorsements or market her own designs except through the agency of the plaintiff. The acceptance of the exclusive agency was an assumption of its duties. . . .

We are not to suppose that one party was to be placed at the mercy of the other. . . . Many other terms of the agreement point the same way. We are told at the outset by way of recital that: "The said Otis F. Wood possesses a business organization adapted to the placing of such indorsements as the said Lucy, Lady Duff-Gordon, has approved." The implication is that the plaintiff's business organization will be used for the purpose for which it is adapted. But the terms of the defendant's compensation are even more significant. Her sole compensation for the grant of an exclusive agency is to be one-half of all the profits resulting from the plaintiff's efforts. Unless he gave his efforts, she could never get anything. Without an implied promise, the transaction cannot have such business "efficacy as both parties must have intended that at all events it should have." . . . His promise to pay the defendant one-half of the profits and revenues resulting from the exclusive agency and to render accounts monthly was a promise to use reasonable efforts to bring profits and revenues into existence. For this conclusion the authorities are ample. . . .

The judgment of the Appellate Division should be reversed, and the order of the Special Term affirmed, with costs in the Appellate Division and in this court.

This principal case has been widely followed. If Wood had done nothing for her, could Lady Duff-Gordon have sued him for breach of contract?

The problem of mutuality of obligation arises most frequently in connection with escape clauses, termination clauses, and requirements contracts. The problem of mutuality of obligations in requirements contracts for the sale of goods was discussed on page 122.

Escape and Termination Clauses

An *escape clause* defines a circumstance or condition the occurrence or non-occurrence of which will prevent major contractual obligations from arising. Questions sometimes arise as to the size of the escape hatch — the degree of control one has over the event or the probability that the event permitting escape will occur. At one extreme is a very large escape hatch, which a party can go through at whim. Here there is no mutuality of obligation and the contract is unenforceable. Alternatively, a small exit that one can squeeze through only in a limited set of circumstances indicates one has commitments of substance and mutuality exists.

A *termination clause* describes circumstances under which obligations under a contract in a state of ongoing performance can be terminated. Time and performance differentiate escape and termination clauses. The former permits escape before the time for major performance occurs. The latter terminates a performance that has been occurring. The legal question a termination clause occasionally raises is essentially the same as that raised by an escape clause, whether one party so controls the circumstances of termination that immediate exercise would mean he in effect had not obligated himself to do anything. If this should be so, there is no mutuality of obligation and the contract is unenforceable. The termination clause in the following case withstands such an attack.

Linder v. Mid-Continent Petroleum Corp.
Supreme Court of Arkansas, 1952. 221 Ark. 241, 252 S.W.2d 631
[Mrs. Linder leased a filling station to Mid-Continent Petroleum under a contract which Mrs. Linder now argues is void. She argues that the contract is void for lack of mutuality since by its terms only Mid-Continent was able to terminate the agreement and termination required the giving of only 10 days notice of its intent to do so.]

SMITH, J.

. . . .

It was argued by the appellants that the lease from Mrs. Linder to Mid-Continent is lacking in mutuality in that the lessee can terminate the contract upon ten days notice, while no similar privilege is granted to the lessor. This contention is without merit. Williston has pointed out that the use of the term "mutuality" in this connection "is likely to cause confusion and however limited is at best an unnecessary way of stating that there must be a valid consideration." . . . As we held in *Johnson* v. *Johnson,* the requirement of mutuality does not mean that the promisor's obligation must be exactly coextensive with that of the promisee. It is enough that the duty unconditionally undertaken by each party be regarded by the law as a sufficient consideration for the other's promise. Of course a promise which is merely illusory, such as an agreement to buy only what the promisor may choose to buy, falls short of being a consideration for the promisee's undertaking, and neither is bound. . . . If, however, each party's binding duty of performance amounts to a valuable consideration the courts do not insist that the bargain be precisely as favorable to one side as to the other.

In this view it will be seen that Mid-Continent's option to cancel the lease upon ten days notice to Mrs. Linder is not fatal to the validity of the contract. This is not an option by which the lessee may terminate the lease at pleasure and without notice; at the very least the lessee bound itself to pay rent for ten days. Even lesser duties than this are held to be a sufficient consideration to support a contract. . . .

Affirmed.

What would the result have been if the lease provided that the lessee could terminate at will upon sending notice to the lessor? Would the notice requirement be enough to satisfy the mutuality requirement? Would such an obligation constitute a "legal detriment" to the promisee? Are the last two questions in substance the same? If giving notice is a legal detriment, was this what the lessor bargained for?

Gifts

It is almost a universal proposition that a promise to make a gift is unenforceable because it is without consideration. Persons promising gifts have no legal obligation to do so. However, once one goes beyond promise to performance, a different rule applies. Where the gift is unconditionally given and the performance executed, courts will not undo the transfers — the giver cannot get the gift back. (Examples of assignments by gift of contract rights will be found at pages 189–90.) A subtle example of the difference between conditional and unconditional performance is found in gifts *causa mortis*, that is, gifts given in anticipation of the owner's death. (A supplementary discussion of gifts *causa mortis* is contained on pages 695–97.) Gifts *causa mortis* are effective if given when the donor is faced with imminent death from a specific disorder, and death results from that disorder without any intervening recovery. The gift takes effect only upon the death of the donor. Actual delivery of the subject matter of the gift to the donee is required. Thus, if a woman in the hospital for heart surgery transfers her diamond ring to her daughter, then an effective gift *causa mortis* is made if the woman dies during the operation. Conversely, if the woman recovers, the condition, death, has not occurred and the daughter must return the ring.

This executed gift concept has some relationship to other areas of business law, for example, accord. A person may accept $500 in return for a liquidated debt of $1,000 and give a receipt for the full $1,000. In these circumstances, some courts have decided the creditor actually intended to make a gift of the $500 balance due and manifested his gift intent by giving a receipt for the full amount. This notion of the *executed gift*, then, can be another device for correcting some of the shortcomings that take place under strict rules of consideration.

SUBSTITUTES FOR CONSIDERATION

The Writing

We have seen that in most cases, enforceable contracts enforced must conform to certain consideration requirements. Yet, consideration is not absolutely indispensable. We have, for instance, seen the widespread use of a writing as a substitute for consideration. This has been very much the case in situations of firm offers and modifications of agreements; most jurisdictions permit a written firm offer and less frequently a written modification of an existing contract to be given effect notwithstanding the lack of consideration. The UCC goes one step further and does not even require a writing in the limited case where a contract for the sale of goods is modified (and the Statute of Frauds is not applicable).

Promissory Estoppel

The courts, once again seeking a mitigating device to avoid the harshness of the consideration requirement, have developed a substitute called *promissory estoppel*. *Estoppel* literally means stopped, or barred. The promissory estoppel doctrine provides that when a promisor makes a promise that he reasonably expects will induce action or forbearance of a definite and substantial nature on the part of the promissee, and the promise does induce such action, the courts will enforce the promise if injustice can be avoided only by enforcement. Consider this situation; Allport makes a promise to Kincaid that leads Kincaid to expend money, time, or effort. Allport then retracts his promise. There has been no contract, for Kincaid has given no consideration to Allport in return for the promise, but has merely been led to act in a certain way. Under the doctrine of promissory estoppel, however, courts may enforce Allport's promise if the lack of enforcement could cause injustice. Several of the most important aspects of the concept are discussed in the following case.

Hoffman v. Red Owl Stores
Supreme Court of Wisconsin, 1965. 26 Wis.2d 683, 133 N.W.2d 267

[The complaint alleged that Lukowitz, as agent for Red Owl Stores, represented to and agreed with plaintiff that Red Owl would build a store in Chilton and stock it with merchandise for Hoffman to operate in return for plaintiff's investment of $18,000; that in reliance of the above agreement and representations plaintiff sold a bakery business and building, a grocery store and business, purchased a site in Chilton, rented a residence for himself and family, and disrupted the personal and business life of himself and his family. Plaintiff charged that he lost substantial amounts of income and expended large amounts of money as expenses, and demanded recovery for his damages when Red Owl refused to provide the franchise.

The jury determined in answer to questions posed by the trial judge that Red Owl stores had made representations to Hoffman that if he fulfilled certain conditions that he would be established as a franchise owner, that he relied upon these representations, that he was induced to act, that he exercised reasonable care, that he fulfilled the conditions required and that he sustained injury as a result. A verdict was returned for plaintiff. The defendant appeals.]

CURRIE, CHIEF JUSTICE.
. . . .
Many courts of other jurisdictions have seen fit over the years to adopt the principle of promissory estoppel, and the tendency in that direction continues. As Mr. Justice McFaddin, speaking in behalf of the Arkansas court, well stated, that

the development of the law of promissory estoppel "is an attempt by the courts to keep remedies abreast of increased moral consciousness of honesty and fair representations in all business dealings."

Because we deem the doctrine of promissory estoppel, as stated in sec. 90 of Restatement, 1 Contracts, is one which supplies a needed tool which courts may employ in a proper case to prevent injustice, we endorse and adopt it.

The record here discloses a number of promises and assurances given to Hoffman by Lukowitz in behalf of Red Owl upon which plaintiffs relied and acted upon to their detriment.

. . . .

We determine that there was ample evidence to sustain the answers of the jury to the questions of the verdict with respect to the promissory representations made by Red Owl, Hoffman's reliance thereon in the exercise of ordinary care, and his fulfillment of the conditions required of him by the terms of the negotiations had with Red Owl.

There remains for consideration the question of law raised by defendants that agreement was never reached on essential factors necessary to establish a contract between Hoffman and Red Owl. Among these were the size, cost, design, and layout of the store building; and the terms of the lease with respect to rent, maintenance, renewal, and purchase options. This poses the question of whether the promise necessary to sustain a cause of action for promissory estoppel must embrace all essential details of a proposed transaction between promisor and promisee so as to be the equivalent of an offer that would result in a binding contract between the parties if the promisee were to accept the same.

Originally the doctrine of promissory estoppel was invoked as a substitute for consideration rendering a gratuitous promise enforceable as a contract. See Williston, Contracts (1st ed.) p. 307, sec. 139. In other words, the acts of reliance on the promisee to his detriment provided a substitute for consideration. If promissory estoppel were to be limited to only those situations where the promise giving rise to the cause of action must be so definite with respect to all details that a contract would result were the promise supported by consideration, then the defendants' instant promises to Hoffman would not meet this test. However, sec. 90 of Restatement, 1 Contracts, does not impose the requirement that the promise giving rise to the cause of action must be so comprehensive in scope as to meet the requirements of an offer that would ripen into a contract if accepted by the promisee. Rather the conditions imposed are:

(1) Was the promise one which the promisor should reasonably expect to induce action or forbearance of a definite and substantial character on the part of the promisee?

(2) Did the promise induce such action or forbearance?

(3) Can injustice be avoided only by enforcement of the promise?

We deem it would be a mistake to regard an action grounded on promissory estoppel as the equivalent of a breach of contract action.

We conclude that injustice would result here if plaintiffs were not granted some relief because of the failure of defendants to keep their promises which induced plaintiffs to act to their detriment.

Where damages are awarded in promissory estoppel instead of specifically enforcing the promisor's promise, they should be only such as in the opinion of the court are necessary to prevent injustice. Mechanical or rule of thumb approaches to the damage problem should be avoided. In discussing remedies to be applied by courts in promissory estoppel we quote the following views of writers on the subject:

"Enforcement of a promise does not necessarily mean Specific Performance. It does not necessarily mean Damages for breach. Moreover the amount allowed as Damages may be determined by the plaintiff's expenditures or change of position in reliance as well as by the value to him of the promised performance. . . . In determining what justice requires, the court must remember all of its powers, derived from equity, law merchant, and other sources, as well as the common law. Its decree should be molded accordingly." 1A Corbin, Contracts, p. 221, sec. 200.

"The wrong is not primarily in depriving the plaintiff of the promised reward but in causing the plaintiff to change position to his detriment. It would follow that the damages should not exceed the loss caused by the change of position, which would never be more in amount, but might be less, than the promised reward." Seavey, Reliance on Gratuitous Promises or Other Conduct, 64 Harvard Law Review (1951), 913, 926.

. . . .

Since the evidence does not sustain the large award of damages arising from the sale of the grocery business, the trial court properly ordered a new trial on this issue.

Order affirmed.

PROBLEMS AND QUESTIONS

1. Why must consideration be bargained for?

2. Berger, a buyer of shoes for retail sale, ordered one gross of shoes of assorted size for $2,000 from Morris, a manufacturer. Payment was to take place 30 days after delivery. After the order had been received and shipment made, Berger discovered that one day after she had purchased the shoes, Morris had allowed a 10 percent discount on all orders placed. Berger telephoned Morris and requested the same discount, and Morris agreed to give it.

When payment was due, however, Morris insisted on the full $2,000 payment and indicated that his oral promise to grant a 10 percent discount was not effective since it was without consideration. Decision for whom? Explain.

3. Jones agreed to sell to Mason his 1969 Ford for $350. After paying the agreed price and receiving possession of the car, Mason discovered that the car was not suitable to her needs and was not worth the $350. She sought to give back the car and secure return of the money. Jones refused to agree, and so Mason brought legal action, seeking her purchase price for the return of the car on the grounds that she did not obtain fair consideration in exchange for the $350. Decision for whom? Explain.

4. Eisen contracted to build a barn for Hower by July 25, at a cost of $4,565. Because of an increase in the cost of essential supplies, Eisen refused further performance after he had completed one-third of the work. Hower promised to pay an additional $235 if Eisen continued to work. Eisen continued building and completed the work by July 23. He seeks the $4,800, but Hower insists that he accept the original price of $4,565. How much is Eisen entitled to receive and what should he have done to ensure even further his right to full payment?

5. Jones, in writing, employed Smith as a secretary for one year at an annual salary of $7,800, payable monthly. After working six months, Smith was offered a $8,500 job by Crown. She told Jones of this offer and said she would accept Crown's offer and leave at once unless Jones paid her at the same rate. Jones, not being able to replace Smith, at once promised to pay the additional compensation in the form of a bonus at the end of the year if Smith would remain with her. Smith agreed and remained in Jones's employ. At the expiration of Smith's term of employment, Jones, having paid the $7,800, discharged her and refused to pay the additional $700. What are Smith's rights under the agreement?

6. Baker agreed with Cary to perform services as an accountant for payment according to the work performed at a rate "usual and normal for such services." At the end of the next billing period, Baker submitted her bill for $1,500, which Cary considered to be excessive. Cary enclosed a check for $1,000, noted on the check that it was tendered "in full satisfaction of any and all claims due for services performed," attached the check to the bill, and attached a lengthy explanation of his objections to the charge, and sent them all to Baker. Baker asks your advice as to the

legal consequences of cashing the check. What do you tell her?

7. Gloria Zoll owes Sid Carter $2,000 presently due and payable. Carter agrees to reduce the debt to $1,800 and extend the time of payment for three months, and in return, Zoll agrees to give Carter as collateral for the debt, two shares of IBM stock valued at $600. Zoll pays the $1,800 before the end of the three months, and demands the return of the stock. Carter refuses to return the stock and threatens to sell it in order to realize the additional $200. May Carter do so?

8. Hill owes Barnet $1,000 on a promissory note that will become due in three months. Barnet writes to Hill as follows: "I will allow you $100 on the note and accept $900 in full payment, if you agree to pay me the $900 before the end of the month." Hill agrees to pay the $900.

At the end of the next month, however, when Hill does not pay the $900 as agreed, Barnet decides to wait until the end of the third month and sue for the $1,000. May he do so?

9. Defendant, an owner of real property in Cape Canaveral, Florida, engaged plaintiff, a real estate broker, to find a purchaser for her property under the terms of an agreement, which provided: "I hereby grant and give you the exclusive right to sell my premises. In the event that you find a purchaser for it, or that said real estate is sold by or through you or otherwise, then in consideration of your services I hereby agree to pay you 4 percent of the selling price."

The owner decided to sell the house herself, did so, and when the broker requested payment, the owner refused to pay on the basis that the broker had promised to do nothing in return for the 4 percent. The broker sued for breach of contract. Decision for whom? Explain.

10. Debbie Anderson owes three creditors a total of $20,000 and has assets of $10,000. In a meeting with all three creditors she agrees to pay 50 percent of each debt if they agree to discharge her. They all agree to do so, and she pays each creditor half of the original debt.

A month later, she inherits $20,000 and her creditors seek the additional $10,000 due them. Will they be successful? Explain.

11. An accountant was retained by a corporation to make an internal audit at a fixed per diem rate. In the

course of making the audit, the accountant uncovered a mistake whereby the corporation saved $5,000. When the audit was finished, the president wrote to the accountant, "We are grateful that you discovered the error and I am pleased to advise you that in addition to your agreed-upon fee, we shall enclose a check for $500." The corporation failed to pay the additional $500, and the accountant sought to compel payment. Is she legally entitled to be paid? Explain.

12. Crest, intending to assist his niece, Starr, work her way through college, promised in a letter to give her $500 for each academic year she remained in college. Starr, who was able to complete college without financial assistance and who had intended to do so all along, was pleased with her uncle's promise. Unfortunately, after two years had passed since the promise was made, Crest faced some business setbacks and found himself unable to pay Starr as he had promised. When he so informed her, Starr was indignant, and insisted on immediate payment. When that was refused, Starr sued. Would she win? Explain.

13. The president of the Dravon Corporation wrote to the senior vice president, who was sixty-five years old and contemplating retirement, "If you retire as planned and do not take another job in the industry, we will pay you a pension of $20,000 a year for the remainder of your life." The vice president replied affirmatively by letter. After a year, the pension payments stopped and the vice president sought the money due under the agreement. The corporation defends on the basis of lack of consideration. Decision for whom? Explain.

Suppose the letter had read instead, "In view of your faithful service for thirty-five years, and your decision to stay with us despite lucrative offers from our competitors, we will pay you a pension of $20,000 a year for the remainder of your life." Would your answer be different? Explain.

14. Mrs. Olveta Hogan promised the pastor of the Church of the Morning Dew that she would donate $5,000 to the church to enable it to pay off a mortgage coming due on its store front operation. The church secured, in reliance on her promise, an additional loan to meet the balance of the mortgage obligation plus funds to repair the building. Mrs. Hogan then refused to honor her pledge. Would the Church have the right to compel her to do so? Suppose the funds had been pledged as part of the annual gift-giving campaign and that no debt had been assumed by the church, would your answer be different? Explain.

CAPACITY OF PARTIES

Origins and Consequences of the Concept

The law assumes what we all know to be true — some persons are unqualified to make certain business judgments. It does not, however, make legally relevant the subjective judgment that some individuals have better business judgment than others have. Rather, the law makes an objective determination for several generally recognized classes of people. Agreements made by these persons are not enforceable to the same extent as they would be for ordinary persons.

The fully competent are considered competent to the same extent — the brilliant businessperson and the mediocre one — and their agreements are enforceable to the same extent. The incompetent fall into categories that the courts generally measure in terms of status rather than in terms of actual abilities. For example, persons under a statutory age — usually twenty-one, but often eighteen — are all infants; thus, an infant, age twenty and brilliant, is the same before the law as an infant, age twelve and dumb.

The determination of just who has inadequate capacity has not been made with clear reason or logic. Over the years, the persons lacking capacity have been set forth in various places at various times using different standards; the list of persons lacking capacity once was much more extensive than it is today. Among others, it has at one time included infants, insane persons, drunks, corporations, married women, spendthrifts, aliens, and convicts.

The legal position has generally been that contracts cannot be enforced against persons lacking capacity; they have the right to release themselves from the obligations of their agreements. This right is called the right of *disaffirmance*. Disaffirmance brings the parties back to their positions before they made the contract.

The party lacking capacity is ordinarily not required to exercise this right of disaffirmance, but is given the option of doing so. Thus, the incapacitated party may disaffirm all contracts,

8
CAPACITY
AND
ILLEGALITY

but generally chooses to disaffirm only those that are not to his advantage. In other situations, persons lacking capacity are barred from enforcing contract rights against others who also choose to disaffirm. (Capacity is also discussed in the chapter on commercial paper on page 427.) Thus, the question of capacity operates in two distinct ways. First, it is a device for the incompetent party to avoid a contract that the other party seeks to enforce. Second, and less frequently, it is a device to allow either of the parties to avoid their agreements. One is cautioned to deal carefully with persons somehow lacking full capacity.

Especially Troublesome Categories

The Aged

As you consider the following case, think about what, if anything, the buyer could have done to acquire the property without risking litigation.

Krueger v. Zoch
Supreme Court of Minnesota, 1969. 285 Minn. 332, 173 N.W.2d 18
GALLAGHER, J.
Appeal from a judgment of the Ramsey County District Court.
    This is an action brought by plaintiff, Clarence C. Krueger, against defendants, Joseph Zoch and James Zoch as guardian of Joseph Zoch, to specifically enforce an earnest money contract for the purchase of land or, in the alternative, for money damages. The contract was dated November 30, 1966, and was between plaintiff as purchaser and defendant Joseph Zoch as seller.
    The case was tried before the court without a jury on January 16, 1968. The court found that Joseph was incompetent at the time he made the earnest money contract with plaintiff. It determined that this made the contract null and void and refused specific performance. Plaintiff makes this appeal.
    The questions for consideration are (1) whether there was sufficient evidence to sustain the finding that Joseph was incompetent, and (2) whether a contract of the incompetent may be avoided under the evidence presented.
    Joseph was over 80 years of age in 1966. He lived alone on a farm that he owned in Little Canada, Minnesota. Because of his advancing age, he decided to sell his place. In June 1966 he first met plaintiff, who expressed interest in buying the farm. . . . The parties conducted negotiations for the sale of the farm from June to November 30, 1966, when the earnest money contract involved here was signed.
    On December 22, 1966, guardianship proceedings were held in Ramsey County probate court and on January 9, 1967, Joseph was placed under guardianship, with his son, James, as guardian.
    The evidence in the instant case established that, dating from before June 1966, Joseph was hard of hearing; that he rambled in his conversations and had trouble keeping to the subject under consideration; that his house was messy; that he was unable to care for himself; that during the guardianship proceedings he spoke loudly at improper times; that he trusted strangers rather than his own family; that he sold valuable antiques for next to nothing when approached by various dealers; and that he listed his house with two realtors at the same time. His son, James, testified that from his observations his father had been incompe-

tent for the previous five years. A contractor who met Joseph a number of times and was also trying to buy his farm testified that he broke off negotiations because he thought Joseph was incapable of handling his own affairs. Plaintiff and his three witnesses all testified that they thought Joseph was competent to handle his own affairs, but none of them was well acquainted with him nor could they rebut the above-mentioned testimony. From the foregoing, the trial court concluded that defendant Joseph Zoch was incompetent at the time he negotiated and signed the contract with plaintiff.

1. In accordance with our well-settled rules we must review the evidence in the light most favorable to the prevailing party and, since the findings of the trial court are entitled to the same weight as a jury verdict, we will not reverse unless the findings are manifestly contrary to the evidence.

The standard for determining whether a person is mentally incapable is whether or not that person can fairly and reasonably understand the matter he is considering. A person is competent if he has the capacity or ability to understand to a reasonable extent the nature and effect of what he is doing. . . .

It is our opinion that there is ample evidence in the record before us from which the trial court could have concluded that Joseph was incompetent on the date of the transaction. We recognize that the mere fact that he is elderly does not in itself show lack of mental capacity. . . .

The finding of incompetence in this case is greatly strengthened by the fact that Joseph was placed under guardianship on January 9, 1967. The subsequent adjudication of incompetency in guardianship is relevant and probative on the issue of his competence at the time he signed the earnest money contract, November 30, 1966. The closer in time the adjudication of incompetency is to the transaction, the greater the weight that can and should be given it. We hold that the finding of incompetency is supported by the evidence.

2. There are cases where it is stated that a person may not use incompetency as an offensive weapon to avoid obligations which he discovers later to be burdensome. In both of these cases the alleged incompetence lasted only a short time and the party alleging the incompetence was attempting to avoid performance of a contract after he was no longer incompetent. In that situation the court held that where the other party had no knowledge of the incompetence and where he took an inequitable advantage, the contract was enforceable. In neither of those cases was the incompetent placed under guardianship subsequent to the making of the contract. The present case is distinguishable. Here there is evidence from which the trial court could conclude that plaintiff had knowledge of the incompetence. For example, he knew that Joseph was hard of hearing; that he rambled in his conversation; and that he was unable to care for himself.

Affirmed.

The Infant

The infant, as perceived by the common law, was anyone who had yet to reach the twenty-first birthday. When the infant entered into contractual agreements, the common law, sensing that advantage was taken, gave this youth the right to disaffirm the contract merely on the grounds of infancy. It mattered not that the facts at hand concerning who took advantage of whom might be entirely at odds with the understanding of the law. Mere infancy was enough to give the right of disaffirmance to that incapacitated and incompetent party. The common law gave no such right to the adult. The right of disaffirmance requires no formal exercise. Actions by the infant that are inconsistent with the contract, such as refusing to pay insurance policy premiums, serve as the requisite acts of disaffirmance.

Recent Developments. Although few doubt the basic merit of infant incapacity (a jewelry store should not be able to hold a six year old to a contract for a diamond bracelet), many think the combination of education, improved nutrition, television, and a generally wealthier society have produced a generation of young people who are maturing earlier socially, judgmentally, and physically. Problems arise at the margin: contracts by physically and socially precocious nineteen year olds. The common law has, in many instances, lagged far behind current social and business attitudes. Emphasizing this lag is the current movement toward greater responsibilities and rights for youths, such as the eighteen year old's constitutional right to vote.

As might be expected, then, the common law principle is being modified. Some jurisdictions have lowered the age of legal adulthood from twenty-one to eighteen, and others have carved out a variety of special exceptions to the general rule. In some states, infants who are above a certain age and are engaged in business may not disaffirm contracts that are reasonable and provident if made in furtherance of their business. In other jurisdictions, infants' agreements with insurance companies, banks, colleges, universities, and landlords are fully binding. These legislated exceptions, which have entered the law unevenly from state to state, still highlight the infants' preferred status at ordinary common law.

Timely Disaffirmance and Ratification. The infant's conduct may limit his right to disaffirm. Thus, the almost universal rule requires the infant to disaffirm in a timely manner either during infancy or within a reasonable time after attaining legal age. The definition of a reasonable time, of course, varies from case to case and from state to state. However, the basic idea of a timely disaffirmance is one way of putting an affirmative duty on the disaffirming infant and thereby limiting that right. The states also place an obligation on the infant not to accept the benefits of his contract after attaining majority. If the *emancipated infant* (one who lives alone but is not of age) accepts the contract's benefits after reaching adulthood, the courts rule he has ratified his previous agreement. Almost all states have adopted these limitations of timely disaffirmance and ratification.

Misrepresentation of Age. A minority of jurisdictions have placed an additional and far-reaching limitation upon infants' right to disaffirm contracts. In these states, the courts have declared an infant's fraudulent misrepresentation of adulthood denies him the right to disaffirm the contract.

Limiting the infant's right to disaffirm, a majority of states provide an additional right to the party who dealt with the infant that balances the infant's right. The other party acquires his own right to disaffirm the agreement on the basis of the infant's misrepresentation of age. However, the party charging misrepresentation may accept the agreement by ratifying the infant's misrepresentation and, thereby, lose his right to disaffirm.

How fraud and misrepresentation apply to infancy varies from jurisdiction to jurisdiction, as the following case indicates.

Sternlieb v. Normandie Nat. Sec. Corp.
New York State Court of Appeals, 1934. 263 N.Y. 245, 188 N.E. 726

[In 1929, plaintiff Sternlieb, who was less than twenty-one years old, purchased five shares of stock for $990 from defendant, Normandie. In 1932, after the stock had become worthless, plaintiff sought to disaffirm the contract on the grounds of infancy. The defendant claimed that the right to disaffirm was lost by plaintiff's misrepresentation as to age, and the defense was stricken by the court below, which awarded judgment for the plaintiff. Defendant appeals.]

CRANE, J.

. . . .

At common law a male infant attains his majority when he becomes twenty-one years of age, and all unexecuted contracts made by him before that date, except for necessaries, while not absolutely void, are voidable at his election. In an action upon a contract made by an infant he is not estopped from pleading his infancy by any representation as to his age made by him to induce another person to contract with him. Neither could the infant be sued for damages in tort by reason of any false representations made in inducing or procuring the contract. For his torts generally, where they have no basis in any contract relation, an infant is liable, just as any other person would be, but the doctrine is equally well settled that a matter arising *ex-contractu,* though infected with fraud, cannot be changed into a tort, in order to charge an infant, by a change of the remedy. The only difference between an executory and an executed contract appears to be, that in the former the infant may disaffirm at any time short of the period of the Statute of Limitations, unless by some act he has ratified the contract, whereas in the latter, he must disaffirm within a reasonable time after becoming of age, or his silence will be considered a ratification.

This case pertains to an executed contract for the purchase of stock which the plaintiff has disaffirmed within a reasonable time. . . . We do not see how the allegation of fraud justifies any distinction of principle. It is a mere element or feature of the case. The fundamental principle is the same, whether the infant be plaintiff or defendant. He may repudiate and rescind his contract upon becoming of age, whether he has made false representations regarding his years or not, and in any instance, the party with whom he had his dealings is entitled to recoup under certain circumstances.

That the false representation regarding age does not prevent rescission, even when the infant be the plaintiff, is the holding of the courts in the majority of our States.

Some of the State courts, however, have taken a different view, and find that fradulent representations regarding age estop an infant from maintaining an action for relief.

Like so many questions of policy, there is much to be said upon both sides, and the necessities of one period of time are not always those of another. The law, from time out of mind, has recognized that infants must be protected from their own folly and improvidence. It is not always flattering to our young men in college and in business, between the ages of eighteen and twenty-one, to refer to them as infants, and yet this is exactly what the law considers them in their mental capacities and abilities to protect themselves in ordinary transactions and business relationships. That many young people under twenty-one years of age are improvident and reckless is quite evident, but these defects in judgment are by no means confined to the young. There is another side to the question. As long as young men and women, under twenty-one years of age, having the semblance and appearance of adults, are forced to make a living and enter into business transactions, how are the persons dealing with them to be protected if the infant's word cannot be taken or recognized at law? Are businessmen to deal with young people at their peril? Well, the law is as it is, and the duty of this court is to give force and effect to the decisions as we find them.

We, therefore, conclude that the law of this State, in accordance with the trend of most of the authorities, is to the effect that the defense is insufficient and was properly stricken.

Return of the Subject Matter. Although the infant's right to disaffirm seems to confer a significant benefit on the infant, this is not always the situation. The right to disaffirm is coupled with an obligation to return to the other party what was received under the agreement. Thus, when the disaffirming infant receives what he parted with, he must return what he received or its value. This requirement tends to prevent the infant from disaffirming.

The states affording the greatest protection to infants permit them to disaffirm their agreements and return the consideration they received regardless of its condition. Thus, an infant may return an almost totally demolished automobile and still receive the entire purchase price paid. Other states, not so generous to the disaffirming infant, condition the infant's right to disaffirm by holding him responsible for the deterioration in objects returned. Thus, in this situation, instead of receiving the entire purchase price for the demolished automobile, the infant would receive that part of the purchase price that represents the value of the car. This represents a significant practical limitation on an infant's willingness to disaffirm.

The infant's right to receive what he parted with may also be qualified by the right of third parties who purchased the objects of the original transaction. For example, suppose an infant sells his automobile to a used car dealer, who in turn sells it to a third party customer. Although the infant could disaffirm the agreement with the used car dealer and receive the car back, he cannot recover the automobile from a third party purchaser for value. Thus, parties with whom the infant deals may pass complete and full title to the goods to third party purchasers for value. The infant may recover only the value of the car from the used car dealer; he has no rights against the third party purchaser. Some states, however, permit an infant to disaffirm, notwithstanding his inability to return what he squandered. Thus, the infant receives the value of his resold used car, but is not required to return the now squandered money paid him for it. This is obviously a harsh result for the party who dealt with the infant.

There are, of course, exceptions to the general pattern of protecting third-party purchasers. The principal exception in several jurisdictions prevents a party who acquired title to real property from an infant from passing clear title. The party who deals with the infant receives voidable title, and the third-party purchaser likewise receives only voidable title. The infant can disaffirm the agreement and recover the property for a reasonable time after attaining majority in most states. To a significant extent, the care taken in searching title to real property virtually ensures that innocent third parties will not be mistakenly induced to accept voidable title obtained from an infant.

Necessaries. Finally, where necessaries are involved, an infant's right to disaffirm is substantially constrained by quasi-contract and agency principles. *Necessaries* are those items that an infant requires to maintain his life or style of life. Unlike *necessities*, which are measured in terms of objective need, necessaries vary from person to person depending on social class and standing. Thus, necessaries may include not only food, shelter, and clothing, but also a summer home or a college education. An *emancipated infant* — one who maintains himself and is not living under custody or responsibility of his parents — is personally liable under the theory of quasi-contractual liability for the necessaries for which he contracts. The infant is liable, not because of the agreement, but because his needs are serviced and he is required to provide for them. As we shall see, quasi-contractual remedies vary from the remedies under ordinary contract principles.

If the infant is not emancipated and purchases are made for necessaries, then contractual liability may attach to the parents under agency law. The infant was securing what his parents were legally obliged to supply and, thus, was acting for them when he incurred a legal obligation to the third party. Hence, the liability for the agreement attaches to the parents through their infant agent.

Although liability for contracts involving necessaries generally attaches to infants or their parents, the law in most states grants a further right to the infant. If the necessary goods or services have not been delivered to the infant, the infant may disaffirm the contract and cancel his liability. This holds true even if the infant has already paid for the goods and services.

The Insane and Drunk

Incapacity problems most often involve infants, yet infants are not the only incompetent parties who enter agreements that are affected by their lack of capacity. Insane persons, for example, possess limited capacity. If these persons, as well as other mentally incompetent individuals, make agreements during the periods of their insanity, they generally may be either ratified or declared void during their lucid moments. Persons who have been judicially declared insane fall into a different category; as a general rule their contracts are void and without legal effect. This distinction is important: contracts of the mentally incompetent but not judicially declared insane are voidable at their option but not void; contracts of persons judicially declared insane are void *ab initio*. Of course, the determination of just who is insane may vary from jurisdiction to jurisdiction. A person considered insane for contract purposes is generally incapable of appreciating the nature and effect of the particular agreement under question. The impairment goes beyond simply being slow or dull. Also, insanity may be present or absent in the same persons from time to time, as they pass from lucid moments to moments of insanity.

Like the insane person, the drunk may make agreements that are voidable at his option because of his incapacity. He is subject to the same requirements of disaffirmance and subject to the same conditions of ratification. Where persons have been declared judicially incompetent by reason of their drunkenness, their contracts are void.

ILLEGALITY

Background

Agreements must have a valid and lawful purpose, and this raises fundamental questions concerning the enforceability of certain agreements. The courts disapprove contracts that are tainted with illegality either in their formation or in their execution. There are several bases for illegality. The agreement might violate a statutory enactment that sets a direct standard for lawful behavior. Or the illegal contract may run counter to the common law or judge-made rules that have been honored over time but do not have their basis in statutory rules. Finally, the contract may violate rules of public policy that have been administratively or otherwise articulated within the jurisdiction. The nature and multiplicity of these sources necessarily introduce some uncertainty, exacerbated by the different laws of various jurisdictions; illegal contracts in some jurisdictions are perfectly proper and lawful in others.

Some agreements are clearly and always unlawful, however: contracts to bribe public officials or agents and agreements to frustrate justice by concealing facts or obtaining perjured evidence for a courtroom trial are two examples. However, when agreements come close to those countenanced as lawful in certain circumstances but deemed unlawful in other circumstances, the standards and definitions of illegality are troublesome.

The most usual effect of an illegal contract is that a court will not affect the relationship of the contracting parties. It will regard the agreement as tainted, refuse to deal with the parties, and leave them as it found them. When an agreement is made to pay a bribe and the bribe is not paid, the court will not grant relief to the person seeking payment. On the other hand, if the bribe is paid, the courts will not entertain a cause of action seeking recovery of the money. The courts consider each party at fault and afford them no remedy.

There are several exceptions to the foregoing. Where a small portion of the agreement is illegal, but the bulk of the transaction is not, courts will often sever the illegal provisions and enforce the lawful ones. Similarly, many courts will reform agreements to eliminate an illegal excess. Interest above the legal maximum (*usury*) is an example. Finally, if the parties are not *in pari delicto* (equally guilty), the courts allow recovery for the less guilty party. Thus, courts occasionally have permitted casual bettors to recover their wagers from professional gamblers.

Troublesome Transactions

Gambling

Wagering contracts are perfectly legal and proper if conducted at a horse racetrack or an off-track betting parlor licensed by the state, but may be unlawful and improper if conducted with the local bookie. The states, either by statute or case law, usually treat unlawful gambling contracts as void.

Exculpatory Clauses

Although the exculpatory clause in *Ciofalo* v. *Vic Tanney Gyms, Inc.*, 10 N.Y.2d 294, 177 N.E.2d 925 (1961) was held to be enforceable, exculpatory clauses in general have frequently been found to violate public policy (see pages 75–76).

Usury

One of the most significant kinds of illegal contracts concerns loans at interest rates greater than the maximum permitted by state law. These contracts, called *usurious*, are almost invariably contrary to state law and are illegal agreements. The effects of usurious interest rates upon the entire agreement vary from state to state. In some states the agreement is entirely and thoroughly tainted, and no recovery is permitted; in others interest cannot be collected although the party extending the loan may collect the principal; in still others interest exceeding the lawful rate cannot be collected, but the contract is reformed and the principal and maximum rate of interest permissible at law is due.

Covenant Not to Compete

Another troublesome agreement is the covenant not to compete, a contract the common law sometimes held unenforceable as an unreasonable restraint upon trade. The *covenant not to compete* involves a promise by one party to refrain from competing against another. The covenant not to compete is used most frequently when an employee leaves an employer, a partner retires, or a business is sold. The covenant usually contains three limitations: the time period of the restraint, the territory within which the restraint operates, and the type of business activity the restraint covers. In most states the covenant must meet the test of reasonableness. Since the test is reasonableness, it will be applied variously from state to state and from court to court. The covenant's reasonableness will also vary depending on the business involved, the extent of business activities involved, and whether the restraint is complete or partial. The restraint cannot exceed what is necessary to protect the noncompeting party's former employer or business.

Those who draft covenants tend to overprotect their clients. The time period may be excessively long, or the area covered excessively large, or the prohibited scope of business activity so broad that it prohibits noncompeting activities. In these circumstances, jurisdictions differ in dealing with the covenant. Some restructure the agreement and give it a lawful effect as reduced; others invalidate the covenant entirely and afford no protection. The following case illustrates the approach of one jurisdiction.

Coffee System of Atlanta v. Fox
Supreme Court of Georgia, 1970. 226 Ga. 593, 176 S.E.2d 71

[Plaintiff appeals from an order dismissing its complaint for failure to state a claim upon which relief can be granted. Coffee System of Atlanta sued Fox seeking damages and injunctive relief against continued violation of a restrictive covenant entered into between Fox and the plaintiff as a part of an employment contract.]

HAWES, J.

Among those contracts which are against public policy and which cannot be enforced are contracts in general restraint of trade. [However], "[a] contract . . . in partial restraint of trade and reasonably limited as to time and territory, and otherwise reasonable, is not void."

. . . [T]his court has customarily considered three separate elements of such contracts in determining whether they are reasonable or not. These three elements may be categorized as (1) the restraint in the activity of the employee, or former employee, imposed by the contract; (2) the territorial or geographic restraint; and (3) the length of time during which the covenant seeks to impose the restraint. It has been said that no better test can be applied to the question of whether a restrictive covenant is reasonable or not than by considering whether the restraint "is such only as to afford a fair protection of the interest of the party in favor of whom it is given, and not so large as to interfere with the interest of the public. . . . There can be no doubt that an agreement that during the term of the service, and for a reasonable period thereafter, the employee shall not become interested in or engage in a rival business, is reasonable and valid. . . . This is the rule followed by a majority of the American Courts and is supported by reason. . . . This court seems to be committed to the rule that the contract must be limited both as to time and territory, and not otherwise unreasonable. If limited as to both time and territory, the contract is illegal if it be unreasonable in other respects. And with respect to restrictive agreements ancillary to a contract of employment, the mere fact that the contract is unlimited as to either time or territory is sufficient to condemn it as unreasonable."

. . . The proscription against competition by the defendant embodied in the restrictive covenant in this case extends to 13 named counties in the state of Georgia. Insofar as geographic area is concerned, this is undoubtedly a reasonable restriction to be upheld by the courts if the contract is otherwise reasonable and not oppressive. The limitation as to the time within which the defendant may not engage in a competitive employment or enterprise, being one year from the termination of his employment with the plaintiff, is reasonable and not such a restriction as would render the contract void.

We now turn to the question of the reasonableness of the restriction against the activities of the defendant as contained in the covenant. The defendant Fox was employed . . . as a sales representative to offer on behalf of the plaintiff its "Coffee System Service," and to sell its replacement kits. He agreed that he would not, directly or indirectly, in any capacity, solicit or accept orders of business located within the area assigned to him (that is, the 13 named counties) during his employment with the plaintiff, and that he would refrain from doing this with respect to any organization which, or individual who, had been a customer or had been solicited as a customer of the plaintiff during that term. It must be noted that the contract does not restrict . . . [Fox] from accepting employment with a competitor, so long as such employment does not involve the direct or indirect solicitation and acceptance of orders from customers or those solicited as customers of the plaintiff. Even if the enforcement of the broad language forbidding the use by the defendant of business methods and techniques acquired during his employment with the plaintiff should, if enforced, effectively prevent the defendant from accepting employment with any competitor of the plaintiff within the limited area and time of the operation of the contract, it would not render the contract void as a matter of law. . . . As a general rule, this court seems to have established the principle in cases of this kind that, where the restraint as to time and territory is reasonably limited, a general prohibition against soliciting customers and accounts of the employer will be upheld. We need hold no more than that in this case.

With respect to the definition or description of the business engaged in by the plaintiff and which the defendant was employed by the plaintiff to conduct, the contract only refers to it as a "Coffee System Service," but we think this is enough. This court has upheld restrictive covenants where the description of the business was no more specific. The restraint imposed by the contract in this case is no more than is reasonably necessary to afford fair protection to the interests of the employer and is not unduly oppressive of the employee. It is not void for any reason urged by the appellee.

It follows that the trial court erred in sustaining the motion to dismiss and in dismissing the complaint. . . . From the language of the order appealed from it is clear that the trial judge did not reach the question of whether to grant or deny a temporary injunction. Therefore, no question in that regard is presented for our decision on this appeal.

Judgment reversed.

PROBLEMS AND QUESTIONS

1. Why does the law declare anyone under a particular age, usually twenty-one, no matter how smart or wise, an infant? Do you feel that this could be changed? What are the advantages of the present system?

2. What are the main types of illegal contracts?

3. Kerner, 80 years old, entered into a contract to sell his farm for $35,000. The farm had a market value of $60,000; during the past year Kerner refused several offers of $60,000, and substantial evidence was introduced at trial as to Kerner's mental imbalance. In fact, two months after concluding the sale, Kerner was adjudged mentally incompetent. His court-appointed guardian now seeks to set the contract aside and prevent delivery to the purchaser on the grounds of Kerner's incapacity. Will he be able to do so? Explain.

4. On June 1, 1972, Frances P. Duggan, age twenty, and owning a plumbing business, made a written contract with Regan Supplies for $1,000 worth of pipe.

Upon receiving the pipe, Duggan found that she had been in error as to the wisdom of the transaction and that the pipe was really only worth $750. She sought to disaffirm the contract on the grounds of infancy. May she do so? Would your answer be the same if Duggan had misrepresented her age as twenty-four?

5.   Plaintiff, aged seventeen years, brought action on a contract for the purchase of a bicycle, seeking to disaffirm the contract, and to have his purchase price returned. The agreed price was $50, and payment was to be on a weekly basis. The infant purchased the bicycle in July and used it until August when he sought disaffirmance. The seller accepted the bicycle, but refused to refund payments that had been made. She claims that the deterioration on the bicycle has been greater than the amounts paid by the infant. Would she be correct?

6.   An infant sold her farm and some personal possessions to a dealer. The dealer in turn resold both the farm, to Smith, and the personal property, to Jones. Immediately upon attaining majority, the infant sought to disaffirm the contract with the dealer, and sought the return of the farm and the personal property. What are the rights of the infant in such action to disaffirm her contracts? Explain.

7.   Spencer, a twenty-year-old student at Columbia, negotiated a loan with the college permitting him to attend his last year. The loan was for $3,500, and provided for the repayment to commence on a monthly basis three years after completing his education. Upon attaining the age of twenty-one, Spencer wrote to the Dean of Columbia College and announced that the $3,500 had been spent and that he was exercising his right as an infant to disaffirm the loan agreement. Might he do so? Explain

8.   Sirkin, a seller of goods, agreed to pay McGuinness, a purchasing agent of the Fourteenth Street Store, a "commission" of 5 percent on goods ordered by McGuinness for the store. Goods worth $1,500 were ordered by the store and McGuinness was paid her commission.

After the goods were delivered and the Fourteenth Street Store discovered that such an arrangement had been made, it refused to pay for the goods. Sirkin sued to recover the $1,500. Decision for whom? Explain.

9.   Mrs. Brown was president of the Nottingham Civic Club. She discovered an "understanding" between certain gamblers and city officials, and accumulated much evidence to support it. Stack, the district attorney, heard of her efforts, and, being a candidate for mayor of Nottingham, desired to use it in his campaign. He persuaded Mrs. Brown to turn over to him all her evidence and let him make the disclosures public, promising her in return that he would make her commissioner of parks if he was elected. Mrs. Brown agreed, and, largely as a result of the disclosures made by Stack with Mrs. Brown's evidence, Stack was elected mayor. He failed to appoint Mrs. Brown to any office, and she sued for the value of her time and services in collecting the gambling information. Should she recover? Explain.

10.   Reiner booked passage on the Graf Zeppelin for a flight from Friedschafen, Germany, to Lakehurst, New Jersey, in October 1928. When she purchased the ticket, she was required, as were all other passengers, to sign a contract stating that as consideration for passage she would not, while en route and for eight days thereafter, give interviews or send reports of the flight to anyone. (The Graf Company had sold exclusive rights to the use of all such news to the New York Sun.) Reiner, with full knowledge of the contract between Graf and the Sun, in contravention of her agreement with Graf Zeppelin, sold rights to her exclusive story to defendant for $1,000. Defendant used the story in a first installment and refused to pay Reiner. Reiner brought suit for that payment, and also sought to enjoin subsequent installments of the story. Decision for whom? Explain.

11.   The Greater Hartwick Council of Camp Scouts of America admits boys to its summer camp program only if the boys and their parents sign an agreement releasing the camp of all liability for injury, even if camp officials are negligent. Discuss the effectiveness of such a clause. What would be the effectiveness of a clause excusing liability for all injury without regard to cause, including gross negligence and intentional wrongdoing? Explain.

12.   Caroline Kelley, in need of cash, approached George Wills, requesting a loan of $30,000. To circumvent the usury laws Wills suggested that Kelley pay the legal rate of interest and in addition sell him 500 shares of stock at its fair market value of $2 per share and agree to repurchase the stock at the end of the year for $5 per share. Kelley sold the shares to Wills, but when the time came for repurchasing the shares, she refused to do so, claiming that the agreement was illegal. Decision for whom? Explain.

9
PROPER LEGAL FORM

Perjury is an easy and popular crime, hard to prove and often profitable. Suppose, for example, Peoples sues Veudler for specific performance of Veudler's alleged oral promise to sell Blackacre for $5,000. Actually, Blackacre is worth $20,000 and no contract was ever made. But in the courtroom, isn't it Peoples's word against Veudler's? Suppose there had been an oral contract but Veudler, having received a better offer, now denies the contract with Peoples. Same problem. Or what if the oral contract provided for a purchase-money mortgage, but Veudler now claims it provided for cash? The fear of such practices and other frauds, as well as the fallibility of human memory, prompted the English Parliament in 1677 to enact the Statute of Frauds, an act that has been widely adopted, virtually without major change, by every state in this country.

The Statute of Frauds cannot prevent all forms of fraud. For instance, in the Blackacre example, it would have been possible to present a forged contract of sale, or it would have been possible to present evidence that the formal written agreement had been destroyed and, hence, was not available for the scrutiny of the judge and the jury. Nevertheless, by requiring certain contracts to be in proper written form, the courts and the legislatures hope to reduce the incidence of fraud and to compel persons engaged in business transactions to record the terms of their more serious contractual obligations. Even if the Statute of Frauds does not apply in a particular situation, doesn't it make good sense to put your contracts in writing?

The Statute of Frauds basically provides that certain contracts must be in writing or a court will not enforce them. The central questions posed by the Statute of Frauds are threefold:

1. What kinds of contracts must be in written form?
2. What kinds of writings are sufficient to meet the requirements of the Statute of Frauds?
3. What alternatives permit certain oral agreements to be effective notwithstanding the lack of a required writing?

Contracts Required to Be in Writing

The Statute of Frauds has been enacted in every state in the United States. These laws usually provide that certain agreements must be in written form to be enforceable, as here in the California Civil Code:

> The following contracts are invalid, unless the same, or some note or memorandum thereof, is in writing and subscribed by the party to be charged or by his agent:
>
> 1. An agreement that by its terms is not to be performed within a year from the making thereof;
>
> 2. A special promise to answer for the debt, default, or miscarriage of another . . .;
>
> 3. An agreement made upon consideration of marriage other than a mutual promise to marry;
>
> 4. An agreement for the leasing for a longer period than one year, or the sale of real property, or of an interest therein; and such agreement, if made by an agent of the party sought to be charged, is invalid, unless the authority of the agent is in writing, subscribed by the party sought to be charged;
>
> 5. An agreement authorizing or employing an agent or broker to purchase or sell real estate for compensation or a commission;
>
> 6. An agreement which by its terms is not to be performed during the lifetime of the promisor, or an agreement to devise or bequeath any property, or to make any provision for any person by will;
>
> 7. An agreement by a purchaser of real property to pay an indebtedness secured by a mortgage or deed of trust upon the property purchased, unless assumption of said indebtedness by the purchaser is specifically provided for in the conveyance of such property.

The following contracts are most often covered by a statute of frauds. Note that all are not in the California law; each state may differ.

Contracts for the Sale or Lease of Real Property

The most common application of the Statute of Frauds requires written contracts for the sale of real property. In most jurisdictions this provision has been supplemented by provisions requiring a writing for trusts and gifts or devises of real property. In addition, the *equal dignity* rule requires an agent's authority to sell real property for their principals to be evidenced in writing. Finally, most jurisdictions require that leases of more than one year be evidenced by some form of writing.

Contracts for the sale of articles affixed to the land are also considered contracts falling within the provisions of most Statute of Frauds laws. This provision does not apply, however, if the seller severs the articles from the land before the conveyance, or the purchaser agrees to sever the articles from the land promptly after the sale. The sale may come within the Statute of Frauds with respect to the sale of goods of $500 or more.

Contracts Not to Be Performed Within One Year from Their Making

Contracts that by their terms are not to be performed within a year from the making fall within the Statute of Frauds. Because of interpretive difficulty, problems frequently arise in deciding just precisely what contracts fall within this category. First is the problem of a contract made at one time with performance to begin at a later time. An example is an employment contract made on February 15 for a term of employment to begin on June 1 and to end on March 1 of the next year. The contract is for services of less than one year; yet it comes within the Statute of Frauds because the term of the agreement itself exceeds one year.

Second is the problem of indefinite time. An agreement providing for the performance of services for as long as the Golden Gate Bridge stands is an agreement that by its terms *can* be performed within a year since it is possible for the bridge to fall within a year, although quite unlikely. Should it fall, the contract will be completely performed, meaning that the terms of the agreement do not provide for a term of more than one year. The law in this area obviously emphasizes possibilities, not probabilities; the test is not what is likely to happen, but what could happen.

The same rationale holds for a contract that provides for work to be completed within fifteen months. If there is a possibility, no matter how remote, that the work could be completed within a year, the contract does not come within the Statute of Frauds and therefore does not have to be reduced to a writing to be enforced.

Third is the problem of a contract in which one or more of the parties is given the option of terminating the agreement before the expected term of the agreement. Courts disagree as to whether this agreement is covered by the Statute of Frauds. The majority of states hold the agreement to be covered by the statute, but a minority, regarding the ability to terminate the contract as an alternative method of full and complete performance, see it as not covered by the Statute of Frauds.

Fourth is a contract providing for one party's performance within a year but allowing the other side more than a year. The majority of jurisdictions and the *Restatement of Contracts* hold that these contracts are covered by the Statute of Frauds.

Contracts for the Sale of Goods

The provisions of the Statute of Frauds concerning the sale of goods usually require contracts for $500 or more to be evidenced by a writing. The UCC in section 2-201 relaxes the requirements as to what the writing must contain and provides that certain conduct by the buyer or seller can ease the requirements of a writing (see page 182).

Promise by an Executor or Administrator to Answer Obligations of the Deceased Out of His Own Funds

If the obligation that an executor or adminstrator promises to meet is an obligation of the deceased and the executor or administrator agrees to meet the obligation out of his own funds, it falls within the provisions of the Statute of Frauds and must be in written form to be enforced. The historic concern about fraud and the perception that administrators and executors derive no personal benefit and often act without compensation support this provision. As a result special care has been taken to guard them from their own gratuitous and perhaps casual statements.

Promise to Answer for the Debt or Default of Another

The laws usually state that if one party promises a second party to pay the debts of a third party, if the third party does not pay those debts, then this promise is unenforceable unless reduced to written form.

This is the so-called *contract of guaranty*, which is discussed more fully in Chapter 41, on suretyship. It is subject to several qualifications. First, the promise must be actually made; it cannot be implied from the circumstances. Second, the obligation to pay "debts, defaults or miscarriages" applies to all obligations without regard to whether they are derived from contracts, or any other form of liability. Third, the promise must be made to the creditor of the debtor and not to the debtor. Thus, if Simpson promises Deller to pay Zender's debts if Zender does not pay them, then the statute applies. It does not apply if the promise of Simpson runs directly to Zender. That promise is absolute and is not a contract of guaranty; therefore, it does not come within the coverage of the Statute of Frauds.

A contract is not covered by the Statute of Frauds if it results in the discharge of Zender, the original debtor. A promise that extinguishes Zender's obligation is not a guaranty contract, because Simpson assumed Zender's debt instead of guaranteeing it. With only Simpson liable, and not Zender, the Statute of Frauds does not apply, because otherwise a grave disservice to Deller would result: Deller was good enough to release Zender, thinking the obligation would be undertaken by Simpson. Thus, the Statute of Frauds applies to situations where one party guarantees the obligation of another and not where one party assumes another's debts. The surety relationship is tripartite.

The promise, if performed, should discharge the primary debtor and its main purpose should be to benefit the debtor. Thus, under the main purpose rule, if a guarantor promises to answer for another's debts to ensure the creditor's continued dealing with the debtor, and this ensures the debtor's continued business with the guarantor, the promise does not come within the Statute of Frauds.

Other Contracts Covered by the Statute of Frauds

The kinds of contracts just discussed are the most important ones covered by the Statute of Frauds, but not the only ones. Contracts made in consideration of marriage — not mutual promises to marry — also come within the coverage of the statute in many jurisdictions. These contracts usually involve property settlements. In some jurisdictions, contracts measured by a lifetime fall within the Statute of Frauds. A careful rereading of the section dealing with contracts which by their terms cannot be performed within a year shows that an agreement to perform services for one year and one day must be in writing, while an agreement to perform services for the remainder of one's life does not because it is possible that one might die within a year and thereby fully perform the contract. In response to this deficiency, some states require writings for agreements measured by a lifetime.

The UCC introduces additional Statute of Frauds requirements; they apply not only to the sale of goods (section 2-201), but to contracts for the sale of investment securities (section 8-319), and to security agreements for nonpossessory security interests (section 9-203).

The Form of the Writing

In many cases, the agreements are not reduced to writing, but nonetheless still comply with the Statute of Frauds. The Statute of Frauds does not require the contract itself to be in writing; it merely requires that the contract be evidenced by a writing. Thus, the concept of written form does not require a formal written contract. Memoranda, notes, or written evidence of an oral agreement will suffice if it is signed by the party against whom enforcement is sought. Moreover, writings that could meet the requirements of the Statute of Frauds for contracts involving the sale of goods would not necessarily show a contract for the sale of real property. A moment of thought should make this apparent. The formalities attached to the sale of real property are usually not present when goods are sold. Frequently, merchants buy and sell goods over the phone and sell to many customers in a short time. Real estate is usually transferred at the attorney's conference table; a closing invariably means the presence of several lawyers, a representative of a lending bank, and the parties in interest. One expects the writings that result from the different kinds of agreements to differ in form; the law makes the same assumption.

The law does not require all parties to sign a written agreement or memorandum. It merely requires the signature of the party to be charged, the party against whom enforcement of the agreement is sought. One cannot hold the party who failed to sign. Thus, we are faced with what might appear to be a rather strange outcome; a contract may bind one party, but not the other. Naturally, the cautious businessperson will obtain the signature of the party with whom he deals and will be cautious about signing agreements that have not been signed by the other party.

The required signature is not that with which the ordinary person is familiar. A signature includes any symbol adopted or executed with the present intention of authenticating a writing. This could include the letter X as well as a stationery letterhead or initials.

The Statute of Frauds usually demands the most detail in contracts for the sale or lease of real property. It usually requires the contract to state all the material terms of the agreement and the consideration exchanged. It also requires the lessor or seller to sign the contract. Some jurisdictions require a subscribed writing rather than one that is merely signed. A *subscription* is a signature that is affixed at the end of the contractual agreement.

Other contracts covered by the Statute of Frauds need not be subscribed, merely signed, and need not include all the material terms. Additionally, the writings may be included in several documents that are attached or that make reference to one another and hence are integrated as written evidence of the agreement. The following case exemplifies whether a writing satisfies the requirements of the Statute of Frauds.

Crabtree v. Elizabeth Arden Sales Corp.
New York Court of Appeals, 1953. 305 N.Y. 48, 110 N.E.2d 55

FULD, J.

In September of 1947, Nate Crabtree entered into preliminary negotiations with Elizabeth Arden Sales Corporation, manufacturers and sellers of cosmetics, looking toward his employment as a sales manager. Interviewed on September 26th, by Robert P. Johns, executive vice-president and general manager of the corporation, who had apprised him of the possible opening, Crabtree requested a three-year contract at $25,000 a year. Explaining that he would be giving up a secure well-paying job to take a position in an entirely new field of endeavor —which he believed would take him some years to master — he insisted upon an agreement for a definite term. And he repeated his desire for a contract for three years to Miss Elizabeth Arden, the corporation's president. When Miss Arden finally indicated that she was prepared to offer a two-year contract, based on an annual salary of $20,000 for the first six months, $25,000 for the second six months and $30,000 for the second year, plus expenses of $5,000 a year for each of those years, Crabtree replied that that offer was "interesting." Miss Arden thereupon had her personal secretary make this memorandum on a telephone order blank that happened to be at hand:

```
            "EMPLOYMENT AGREEMENT WITH
NATE CRABTREE              DATE SEPT. 26 — 1947
at 681 — 5th Ave.                6: PM
Begin                 20000.
6 months              25000.
6 months              30000.
    5000. — per year expense money
(2 years to make good)
Arrangement with
   Mr. Crabtree
   by Miss Arden
   Present: Miss Arden
           Mr. Johns
           Mr. Crabtree
           Miss O'Leary"
```

A few days later, Crabtree phoned Mr. Johns and telegraphed Miss Arden; he accepted the "invitation to join the Arden organization," and Miss Arden wired back her "welcome." When he reported for work, a "payroll change" card was made up and initialed by Mr. Johns, and then forwarded to the payroll department. Reciting that it was prepared on September 30, 1947, and was to be effective as of October 22d, it specified the names of the parties, Crabtree's "Job Classification" and, in addition, contained the notation that "This employee is to be paid as follows:

"First six months of employment	$20,000 per annum
Next six months of employment	25,000 per annum
After one year of employment	30,000 per annum

Approved by RPJ (initialed)"

After six months of employment, Crabtree received the scheduled increase from $20,000 to $25,000, but the further specified increase at the end of the year was not paid. Both Mr. Johns and the comptroller of the corporation, Mr. Carstens, told Crabtree that they would attempt to straighten out the matter with Miss Arden, and with that in mind, the comptroller prepared another "payroll change" card, to which his signature is appended, noting that there was to be a "Salary increase" from $25,000 to $30,000 a year, "per contractual arrangements with Miss Arden." The latter, however, refused to approve the increase and, after further fruitless discussion, plaintiff left defendant's employ and commenced this action for breach of contract.

At the ensuing trial, defendant denied the existence of any agreement to employ plaintiff for two years, and further contended that, even if one had been made, the statute of frauds barred its enforcement. The trial court found against defendant on both issues and awarded plaintiff damages of about $14,000, and the Appellate Division, two justices dissenting, affirmed. Since the contract relied upon was not to be performed within a year, the primary question for decision is whether there was a memorandum of its terms, subscribed by defendant, to satisfy the statute of frauds.

Each of the two payroll cards — the one initialed by defendant's general manager, the other signed by its comptroller — unquestionably constitutes a memorandum under the statute. That they were not prepared or signed with the intention of evidencing the contract, or that they came into existence subsequent to its execution, is of no consequence; it is enough, to meet the statute's demands, that they were signed with intent to authenticate the information contained therein and that such information does evidence the terms of the contract. . . . Those two writings contain all of the essential terms of the contract — the parties to it, the position that plaintiff was to assume, the salary that he was to receive — except that relating to the duration of plaintiff's employment. Accordingly, we must consider whether that item, the length of the contract, may be supplied by reference to the earlier unsigned office memorandum, and, if so, whether its notation, "2 years to make good," sufficiently designates a period of employment.

The Statute of Frauds does not require the "memorandum . . . to be in one document. It may be pieced together out of separate writings, connected with one another either expressly or by the internal evidence of subject matter and occasion." . . . Where each of the separate writings has been subscribed by the party to be charged, little if any difficulty is encountered. . . . Where, however, some writings have been signed, and others have not — as in the case before us — there is a basic disagreement as to what constitutes a sufficient connection permitting the unsigned papers to be considered as part of the statutory memorandum. The courts of some jurisdictions insist that there be a reference, of varying degrees of specificity, in the signed writing to that unsigned, . . . The other position — which has gained increasing support over the years — is that a sufficient connection between the papers is established simply by a reference in them to the same subject matter or transaction. . . . The statute is not pressed "to the extreme of a literal and rigid logic," and oral testimony is admitted to show the connection between the documents and to establish the acquiescence, of the party to be charged, to the contents of the one unsigned. . . .

The view last expressed impresses us as the more sound, . . . and we now definitively adopt it, permitting the signed and unsigned writings to be read together, provided that they clearly refer to the same subject matter or transaction. . . .

. . . Parol evidence — to portray the circumstances surrounding the making of the memorandum — serves only to connect the separate documents and to show that there was assent, by the party to be charged, to the contents of the one unsigned. . . .

Turning to the writings in the case before us — the unsigned office memo, the payroll change form initialed by the general manager Johns, and the paper signed by the comptroller Carstens — it is apparent, and most patently, that all three refer on their face to the same transaction. The parties, the position to be filled by plaintiff, the salary to be paid him, are all identically set forth; it is hardly possible that such detailed information could refer to another or a different agreement. . . .

. . . Having in mind the relations of the parties, the course of the negotiations and plaintiff's insistence upon security of employment, the purpose of the phrase — or so the trier of the fact was warranted in finding — was to grant plaintiff the tenure he desired.

The judgment should be affirmed, with costs.

Would a different holding result in a fraud? Even though Crabtree won, look at his legal expenses. What advice would you have given him at the time he made the contract?

The writing requirement is most difficult to satisfy for a sale of real estate and easiest to satisfy for a sale of goods under the UCC. For most other contracts, the courts usually require the name of the parties as buyer and seller, the subject matter of the contract, and the material terms of the agreement. The UCC does not require an identification of the parties as buyer and seller, the material terms of the agreement, or all the conditions of the contract. Instead, the Code requires only three things: evidence of the contract, a signature of the party to be bound, and the quantity of goods sold. By instituting these relaxed requirements for a contract, the Code recognizes the realities of the business world: busy buyers and sellers have neither the time nor the inclination to prepare detailed written contracts, but rather base their agreements on the often unstated conventions of their trade. For instance, a contract may be merely jotted down on a scratch pad, or it may even omit the price where its reasonable limits would be known by both parties.

Taking the Contract Out of the Statute of Frauds

Full performance of an agreement by the parties makes the question of the enforceability of the agreement moot and eliminates the need to satisfy the requirements of the Statute of Frauds. This is the simplest way of avoiding the requirement of a writing. Thus, where goods have been delivered and paid for, where a deed to real property has been delivered and paid for, and where services have been provided and compensation made, the contracts have been fully performed, and the question of the applicability of the Statute of Frauds is not relevant. Partial performance, however, raises important questions of enforceability under the Statute of Frauds.

In some instances, notwithstanding the lack of a writing, an agreement may be enforced, at least in part, if the parties have partly performed. Thus, if one party orally agrees to employ another for two years, but the other party serves only three months, then the courts will find the agreement unenforceable for the remainder of the term, but will compensate the party for the three months of service. Similarly, under the UCC, if some of the goods are delivered or part of the price is paid, that partial performance is sufficient to meet the Statute of Frauds on the part performed.

If one party cannot perform within a year, but the other party has fully performed, the courts of most states adopt the *Restatement of Contracts* rule and take the contract out of the Statute of Frauds. The following example, provided by the drafters of the *Restatement*, demonstrates the application of this section:

> A promises B to pay B $5,000 in one month, in return for which B promises orally to render a stated performance during the whole of the ensuing two years. A pays the $5,000 as agreed. B then refuses further performance. The contract is withdrawn from the operation of the Statute.

Partial performance can take certain real property contracts out of the Statute of Frauds. Thus, when a conveyance of land has been executed, as through a deed, the courts usually enforce the remaining portion of the agreement and, for example, compel the purchaser to make the remaining payment. If oral agreement for the sale or lease of real property has been made, and the purchaser, with the seller's permission, enters upon the land or makes substantial and permanent improvements to the land, most courts take the agreement out of the Statute of Frauds. Simple payment and possession are not enough; usually, the requirement of substantial and permanent improvement is added.

THE PAROL EVIDENCE RULE

The *parol evidence rule* protects written contracts that reflect the entire agreement from attack by contradictory evidence that predates the agreement. It is intended to ensure the effectiveness of the written contract. It is based on the common sense notion that it makes little sense to have a written agreement if that written agreement can be challenged by other kinds of contradictory evidence.

The parol evidence rule has many qualifications. It applies to prior or concurrent oral or written evidence. It does not affect modifications of written agreements that occur after the initial agreement. It applies only if the entire agreement is reduced to written form. Thus, if contract terms are omitted or reference is made to other communications or other agreements, the parol evidence rule does not exclude testimony enhancing the agreement. Moreover, the rule does not apply if the parties did not intend the writing to reflect the entire agreement. In this case, the parties' intent is determined from information adduced from sources other than the body of the contract itself. Additionally, the parol evidence rule does not bar evidence of fraud or misrepresentation in the formation of the agreement. The courts will not, however, hear evidence that varies from the written terms. Finally, the rule does not bar evidence or testimony that explains an ambiguous portion of the contract.

Operation of the parol evidence rule should be distinguished from similar results compelled by other rules. Suppose an agreement is one required to be in writing by the Statute of Frauds. Hence, its modification may also require a writing. An attempted subsequent oral modification may be ineffective because of the Statute of Frauds rather than the parol evidence rule. Similarly, a prior written agreement may bar subsequent oral modifications. Thus, although the parol evidence rule does not bar admission of the subsequent oral modification, the modification is ineffective under the terms of the original agreement.

The following case demonstrates the problem of determining what evidence the parol evidence rule bars in protecting the integrity of the written agreement.

Mitchill v. Lath
New York Court of Appeals, 1928. 247 N.Y. 377, 160 N.E. 646
ANDREWS, J.

In the fall of 1923 the Laths owned a farm. This they wished to sell. Across the road, on land belonging to Lieutenant-Governor Lunn, they had an ice house which they might remove. Mrs. Mitchill looked over the land with a view to its purchase. She found the ice house objectionable. Thereupon "the defendants orally promised and agreed, for and in consideration of the purchase of their farm by the plaintiff, to remove the said ice house in the spring of 1924." Relying upon this promise, she made a written contract to buy the property for $8,400, for cash and a mortgage and containing various provisions usual in such papers. Later receiving a deed, she entered into possession and has spent considerable sums in improving the property for use as a summer residence. The defendants have not fulfilled their promise as to the ice house, and do not intend to do so. We are not dealing, however, with their moral delinquencies. The question before us is whether their oral agreement may be enforced in a court of equity.

This requires a discussion of the parol evidence rule — a rule of law which defines the limits of the contract to be construed. It is more than a rule of evidence, and oral testimony, even if admitted, will not control the written contract, unless admitted without objection. It applies, however, to attempts to modify such a contract by parol. It does not affect a parol collateral contract distinct from and independent of the written agreement. It is, at times, troublesome to draw the line. Williston, in his work on Contracts points out the difficulty. "Two entirely distinct contracts," he says, "each for a separate consideration may be made at the same time and will be distinct legally. Where, however, one agreement is entered into wholly or partly in consideration of the simultaneous agreement to enter into another, the transactions are necessarily bound together. Then if one of the agreements is oral and the other is written, the problem arises whether the bond is sufficiently close to prevent proof of the oral agreement." That is the situation here. It is claimed that the defendants are called upon to do more than is required by their written contract in connection with the sale as to which it deals.

The principle may be clear, but it can be given effect by no mechanical rule. As so often happens, it is a matter of degree, for as Prof. Williston also says where a contract contains several promises on each side it is not difficult to put any one of them in the form of a collateral agreement. If this were enough written contracts might always be modified by parol. Not form, but substance is the test.

In applying this test the policy of our courts is to be considered. We have believed that the purpose behind the rule was a wise one not easily to be abandoned. Notwithstanding injustice here and there, on the whole it works for good. Old precedents and principles are not to be lightly cast aside unless it is certain that they are an obstruction under present conditions. . . .

Under our decisions before such an oral agreement as the present is received to vary the written contract at least three conditions must exist: (1) The agreement must in form be a collateral one; (2) it must not contradict express or implied provisions of the written contract; (3) it must be one that parties would not ordinarily be expected to embody in the writing, or put in another way, an inspection of the written contract, read in the light of surrounding circumstances must not indicate that the writing appears "to contain the engagements of the parties, and to define the object and measure the extent of such engagement." Or again, it must not be so clearly connected with the principal transaction as to be part and parcel of it. The respondent does not satisfy the third of these requirements. It may be, not the second. We have a written contract for the purchase and sale of land. The buyer is to pay $8,400 in the way described. She is also to pay her portion of any rents, interest on mortgages, insurance premiums and water meter charges. She may have a survey made of the premises. On their part the sellers are to give a full covenant deed of the premises as described, or as they may be described by the surveyor if the survey is had, executed and acknowledged at their own expense; they sell the personal property on the farm and represent they own it; they agree that all amounts paid them on the contract and the expense of examining the title shall be a lien on the property; they assume the risk of loss or damage by fire until the deed is delivered; and they agree to pay the broker his commissions. Are they to do more? Or is such a claim inconsistent with these precise provisions? It could not be shown that the plaintiff was to pay $500 additional. Is it also implied that the defendants are not to do anything unexpressed in the writing?

That we need not decide. At least, however, an inspection of this contract shows a full and complete agreement, setting forth in detail the obligations of each party. On reading it one would conclude that the reciprocal obligations of the parties were fully detailed. Nor would his opinion alter if he knew the surrounding circumstances. The presence of the ice house, even the knowledge that Mrs. Mitchill thought it objectionable would not lead to the belief that a separate agreement existed with regard to it. Were such an agreement made it would seem most natural that the inquirer should find it in the contract. Collateral in form it is found to be, but it is closely related to the subject dealt with in the written agreement — so closely that we hold it may not be proved. . . .

Our conclusion is that the judgment of the Appellate Division and that of the Special Term should be reversed and the complaint dismissed, with costs in all courts.

LEHMAN, J. (dissenting). . . .

If the parties had reached an oral agreement concerning the ice house ten minutes after signing the written contract, would the result in *Mitchill* v. *Lath* have been otherwise?

While a judge's mind may not work in stages, the cases involving the parol evidence problem are perhaps best described for our purposes as involving four steps. First, the court must determine whether a valid written contract exists. At this stage, the rule does not apply. Thus, parol evidence is admissible to prove fraud, mistake, or failure of consideration, etc. Many courts admit proof of orally agreed to conditions precedent because the failure of these conditions prevents the contract from coming into existence. Second, once the court finds a valid written contract was made, it must then interpret it to determine whether the parol agreement varies or contradicts the true meaning of the writing. At the interpretive stage, the rule is still inapplicable. Thus, parol evidence is admissible to clarify or to create ambiguities in the writing. Similarly, local customs and trade usages that bear on the interpretation of the agreement may be shown. Third, the court must determine whether the parties intended the writing as a complete integration of their agreement. This is determined from the appearance of the document itself; a receipt, even if marked "paid in full," is hardly intended as a complete integration. On the other hand, five pages of boilerplate was probably so intended. If such intent is found, the rule is finally applied: the court, in the absence of the jury, decides whether the oral agreement varies or contradicts the writing, or whether it is admissible as an independent second agreement. At this point, the judge asks himself, as a matter of objective probability in light of all the circumstances of the case, whether the parties would have made two agreements or only one. If the parol agreement deals with the same subject matter as the writing and the writing seems exhaustive, the proffer of proof will probably fail.

Would *Brant* v. *California Dairies* on pages 103–6 (note particularly the last paragraph of the case), have been decided otherwise if California did not have the parol evidence rule? Was the rule really applicable there?

One interesting problem has sharply divided the courts. Suppose a written agreement, otherwise exhaustive, fails to specify a time for performance. Should the court interpret the agreement to require performance within a reasonable time and bar evidence of an oral understanding that contradicts this interpretation, or should it hold the agreement so incomplete that the rule does not apply, thereby allowing the oral agreement to be proved? Is this agreement at least admissible to show how much time is reasonable? If admitted for this purpose, do we not reach the same result by a slightly different road? The *Restatement of Contracts* allows parol evidence to contradict implications of law but not implications of fact.

PROBLEMS AND QUESTIONS

1. What is the purpose of the Statute of Frauds? Why does it apply not only to sales over $500 and real estate agreements but also to certain agreements between people that may involve only small amounts of money?

2. Explain how the parol evidence rule is used. What is the rationale for the rule?

Carling, a customer with a charge account in a local department store, called the manager of the store and said, "I am sending my friend to the store. Let him choose a suit under $150, and charge my account." The friend selected a suit for $100 and took away with him. When Carling failed to pay for the suit, the department store brought legal action. Carling defended on the grounds that the promise to answer for the friend's debt was not in writing. Decision for whom?

Lawrence and Brennan, mining engineers in New York, in a telephone conversation with Steel, a metallurgical chemist who resided in Chicago, hired her to take charge of their refinery in Texas for one year at a compensation of $1,000 per week. It was agreed that they would reimburse her for her traveling expenses, but that her employment would not begin until she actually arrived at the plant. Three months after her arrival there, Steel was discharged without sufficient cause. She sued for breach of contract. Has the employer an adequate defense? Explain.

A contractor entered into an oral contract with an owner of a farm, whereby the contractor would build a barn on the farm, completing the job within thirteen months. Before the contractor began work, however, the owner cancelled the contract. The contractor sued for the profit that would have been made in erecting the barn, but the owner defends on the basis of the statute of Frauds. Decision for whom? Explain.

Crane, wishing to commence her own business, borrowed $5,000 from Ranhart. She agreed to repay in one payment in three years. The entire transaction was oral and when the time for payment took place, Crane refused to pay. Ranhart sued for breach of contract. Has Crane a valid defense to the suit? Explain.

A seller and buyer entered into an oral contract for eight television sets at $100 each, COD. Delivery was to occur within ten days at the buyer's place of business, but the buyer notified the seller that he would refuse to complete the sales. May he do so? Explain. Suppose delivery of four of the television sets had occurred and that the buyer refused to accept any others. To what extent would the contract be enforceable? Explain.

Cantor, a manufacturer of children's clothing, telephoned Green, a supplier of fabrics, and ordered $5,000 worth of cloth. Green telephoned Berle, the manufacturer of the fabric and requested the fabric ordered by Cantor. Berle confirmed Green's order by mail, and Green did likewise to Cantor.

Within a week Cantor wrote to Green to cancel her order, and Green did likewise to Berle. Berle, however, insisted on holding Green to his contract and Green, in response, insisted on holding Cantor. To what extent are the parties bound? Explain.

9. Bolton and Shelburne discussed the sale and purchase of a certain piece of land called Blackacre. They then signed the following contract:

March 22nd

Shelburne agrees to sell Blackacre to Bolton for $30,000, delivery of the deed to be made on July 1st. Bolton agrees to pay cash on delivery of the deed to him.

(Signed) Shelburne
(Signed) Bolton

Bolton refused to carry out the contract and Shelburne sued for damages. Would the court, on the trial, allow Bolton, over Shelburne's objection, to testify as to the following:

a. That during the negotiations Shelburne falsely informed Bolton that the tenants on the land paid $500 per month in rent.

b. That, during the negotiations, Shelburne had threatened to prosecute Bolton's son for the embezzlement of funds while his son was in Shelburne's employ.

c. That the parties had both discussed the sale of Whiteacre, but that neither had intended to make a contract dealing with Blackacre.

d. That, in the negotiations, Shelburne had promised that he would give Bolton 30 days after delivery of the deed to pay for Blackacre.

e. That, two weeks later, they had agreed in a letter to lower the selling price and to delay the time for delivery of the deed.

f. That, at the time of signing the contract, Bolton had told Shelburne that before the agreement became operative, he was going to arrange for title search and if he were not satisfied as to its freedom from encumbrances, the deal was to be delayed or called off, and that Shelburne had agreed to this.

10. Connors and McMahon entered into an oral contract to buy and sell a color television set. Connors, the seller, sent a written confirmation of the agreement to McMahon, naming the parties, describing the television by make and model, but omitting the price. The buyer did not respond to the confirmation and later sued Connors when Connors refused to deliver the television that the buyer was willing to accept. May the buyer recover?

Suppose instead that the buyer had refused to accept the television when the seller delivered it. Would the result be different if Connors sought damages?

11.   Rotello entered into an oral agreement with Bertram in which Rotello agreed to sell a house to Bertram for $22,500. At the time of agreeing to the contract, Bertram paid Rotello $500 down. Later Rotello refused to convey the property, offering to return the $500. Bertram refused the offer and sued for breach of contract. Judgment for whom?

Would your answer be the same if Bertram had paid all of the money due Rotello and Rotello had delivered a deed, and subsequently wanted his property back? Why?

12.   On September 15th, a tenant orally rented an apartment for $2,400, payable monthly in advance, for one year beginning October 1. The tenant took possession and paid his rent regularly but on December 30, he vacated the apartment. On January 3rd the landlord sued for the rent due on January 1. Would she be successful?

13.   Boeing Aircraft contracted with Pittsburgh Steel for the latter to construct a supersonic wind tunnel. Freitag sold material to York, a subcontractor, who had agreed to do part of the work in constructing the wind tunnel. In order to persuade Freitag to continue supplying materials to York on credit in accordance with the agreement between Freitag and York, Boeing and Pittsburgh both orally assured Freitag that in the event that York defaulted he would be paid by them. Freitag was not, in fact, paid by York, and he then sued Boeing and Pittsburgh on the promise that they had made. They defended on the grounds that the assurances given Freitag were not written. Decision for whom? Explain.

BACKGROUND

Third Party Rights

Frequently, a contract confers some rights upon third persons who are not parties to the agreement itself. A life insurance policy, for instance, confers rights upon someone other than the parties to the contract, the insurance company and the insured. This third person, the beneficiary, receives money upon the death of the insured even though he did not participate in the making of the agreement. He benefits because the parties intended that he possess certain legally enforceable rights. The third party can enforce his rights under the policy, notwithstanding his not having agreed to the contractual undertaking and notwithstanding his not having furnished consideration. This common occurrence underscores the fact that it is a generally accepted principle of law that third parties, who are not directly involved in a contractual undertaking, may be vested with certain rights to enforce benefits conferred upon them under the terms of the agreement.

Definitions

This section deals with the rights of third persons — strangers, in a sense, to the bargaining process — to assert claims under an agreement between the offeror and the offeree. These third parties can be classified as follows.

Third Party Beneficiaries

Third party beneficiaries are those who receive benefits from an agreement to which they were not a party. The most common form of third party beneficiary is a life insurance beneficiary.

Assignees

Assignees are those who receive contract benefits from one of the parties to the agreement after

10

THIRD PARTIES

the original contract is made. Where A owes B, and B owes C, B may assign to C his contract right to receive payment from A.

At the outset, it may appear quite reasonable and not surprising that third parties can enforce contract rights. Assignments of contract rights and third party beneficiary contracts have worked themselves into the customary practices of business. Yet, this was not always the situation. For a long time courts were reluctant to provide third parties with legally enforceable rights for which they did not bargain. The requirement of *privity* — being a party to the agreement — died slowly and unevenly. Today the general rule permits parties to an agreement to provide enforceable rights to third parties.

The beneficiary arrangement occurs in many other business situations. If A owes B $100, and B owes C $100, A and B could agree that A will pay $100 to C in satisfaction of A's debt to B and B's debt to C. On the other hand, B may wish to confer a benefit upon C, who might be his wife, child, or close friend. A and B could agree that A will pay C. In the first instance, where B and C stand in a debtor-creditor relationship, the law designates C as a *creditor beneficiary* of the contract. In the latter situation, where no legal obligation between B and C exists, B merely intends to benefit C; the law treats C as a *donee beneficiary* of the contract.

Enforceability

The law of the several states has been in a good deal of flux concerning the enforceable rights of third party donee and creditor beneficiaries. The majority of states and the *Restatement of Contracts* allow both creditor and donee third party beneficiaries to enforce their rights. However, several states deny donee beneficiaries rights of recovery regardless of the contracting parties' intent, although they generally provide exceptions to this rule for certain classes of donee beneficiaries.

Another category of beneficiaries, labeled *incidental beneficiaries*, have no enforceable interests under the agreement, although they stand to benefit as an indirect result of the agreement. Thus, if A and B enter into an agreement whereby A is to pay B $100, and B intends to use this money to purchase goods from C, then A's breach of the contract does not confer upon C the right to enforce the agreement. C would have realized his beneficial interest if the agreement had been performed, but A and B do not intend for C to have enforceable rights under their agreement; C is an incidental beneficiary. The following case explores the topic of incidental beneficiaries.

Jett v. Phillips & Associates
United States District Court, Colorado, 1969. 307 F. Supp. 432

CHILSON, DISTRICT JUDGE.

The plaintiff seeks judgment on a promissory note against the defendants, Phillips & Associates, an unincorporated association, Joseph J. Phillips, Jack R. Alexander, and Henry C. Roth, as the makers of the note, and against Henry Chapman, Richard A. Williams, and Leslie J. Gottwald, as guarantors of the note.

There is little dispute in the essential facts. Prior to August 16, 1967, Phillips told plaintiff that he had an agreement to lease a desirable location in California, for the construction of a Dutch Inn and that $16,000 was needed initially to acquire a franchise from Dutch Inns of America, Inc., and for other expenses. Phillips proposed that plaintiff loan the $16,000 and that a loan would later be obtained from a financial institution for construction of the inn and to repay the $16,000 to the plaintiff. In consideration for making the loan, plaintiff would receive a 15% interest in the enterprise.

On August 16, 1967, the plaintiff and the defendants Phillips, Roth, and Alexander, met at the office of plaintiff's attorney in Denver, Colorado, at which time plaintiff's attorney prepared the note which is the subject matter of this action and a memorandum agreement whereby the plaintiff, in consideration of making the loan, would receive a 15% interest in the enterprise.

Upon execution of the note and the agreement, plaintiff delivered to Phillips, Roth, and Alexander, a cashier's check drawn on the First National Bank of Springfield, Colorado, in the amount of $16,000, payable to Phillips & Associates, Phillips, Alexander, and Roth. The cashier's check was subsequently endorsed by these payees and cashed presumably by Phillips. Although the record is silent as to what happened to the $16,000, it was not used to acquire the franchise, and the enterprise never came to fruition.

Some days after the execution of the note and agreement, a second memorandum agreement was prepared, but backdated to August 16, 1967, the date of the first agreement. By the second agreement, Williams, Chapman, and Gottwald agreed to guarantee the payment of the note. This agreement was not executed by Williams, Chapman, and Gottwald until some considerable time after August 16, 1967. At the time of the execution of the promissory note and the first agreement, Williams, Chapman, and Gottwald had not agreed to participate in the enterprise.

The plaintiff, as the holder of the note, was not a party to the second agreement, and the Court finds that Williams, Chapman, and Gottwald executed the second agreement with the intent and purpose to share with Phillips, Alexander, and Roth, their liability on the note with no intent to benefit the holder of the note. Any benefits to the plaintiff, as the holder of the note, were incidental and without any consideration therefor.

Nevertheless, plaintiff asserts a right to recover from Williams, Chapman, and Gottwald as the third party beneficiary of the second agreement.

At the conclusion of the evidence and the argument of counsel, the Court was of the opinion that Section 136, subsection (1) (a) of Restatement of the Law of Contracts, stated the applicable Colorado rule. Subsection (1) (2) [sic] states:

"Except as stated in Sections 140, 143, a promise to discharge the promisee's duty creates a duty of the promisor to the creditor beneficiary to perform the promise."

The first illustration of Subsection (1) found at Page 161 of Restatement states:

"A owes C $100. For sufficient consideration B promises A to pay the debt. B breaks his contract. C may sue B, and A also may sue B. Both A and C may recover judgment."

Although the Colorado Supreme Court has followed this rule in several fact situations, after considering the briefs, the Court concludes that the Restatement rule does not state the Colorado rule applicable to the facts presently before the Court.

. . . .

In *M. E. Smith & Co.* v. *Wilson* the 8th Circuit Court of Appeals in reviewing the Colorado rule applicable to actions on contracts by third party beneficiaries stated:

> "Colorado follows the rule generally announced in American jurisdictions which is that where two parties contract for the direct benefit of a third person, that person may adopt and sue upon the contract; but that where the contracting parties intend no direct benefit to such third person, he acquires no legal rights thereunder merely because he might be benefited incidentally if the contract be performed."

> We conclude that the Colorado rule applicable to the facts of this case is that set forth in the . . . *Smith* case. Since we have found there was no intent on the part of the parties to the second memorandum agreement to directly benefit the plaintiff as the holder of the promissory note, and that any benefits to the plaintiff were incidental and without consideration, under the Colorado rule, plaintiff cannot recover from Williams, Chapman, and Gottwald on the second memorandum agreement.

In short, as the law has developed, it is possible for the contracting parties to confer, within their agreement, enforceable rights upon third parties in the form of a beneficial interest. This beneficial interest might be enforced by the beneficiary himself if the contracting parties intended to actually confer such a right upon him.

ASSIGNMENTS

Third parties can also receive benefits from contractual agreements as a result of separate transactions that confer those contract benefits upon them. In such situations, these persons receive contract rights by assignment and are called *assignees*. The persons assigning those rights are *assignors,* and the device for assigning the rights is called an *assignment.* The assignment is unlike the third party beneficiary contract because the rights given through it are generally given in a separate transaction that occurs after the original contract was made. Thus, the assignee at a later time takes his rights from one of the parties, and sometimes the other party to the transaction, who owes the underlying obligation, has no knowledge of the assignment.

The refinancing of accounts receivable by a department store represents one type of assignment. The store, generally without informing its customers, refinances these credit sales through a financial institution, that is, the department store sells the account receivable for cash. The lending institution acquires the department store's rights to the sums due from customers, although it never notifies the customers of its acquired rights. Each customer merely pays the department store, which transmits the money to the financial institution.

In simple assignment, A and B enter into an agreement whereby A is to pay B for certain services. A might then assign the right to receive these services to C; B might also assign his compensation rights to D. In both situations, a contractual right has been assigned to a third party. The assignments may be made to C or D for consideration, but that is not necessary; assignments may also be gifts.

Although consideration is not a prerequisite to a valid assignment, gratuitous assignments are revocable at will unless there is clear evidence of a completed gift. The rights of a gratuitous assignee can be terminated by the death of the assignor, by express revocation, or by conduct indicating the assignor's intent to revoke the assignment, such as an assignment to another. On the other hand, an assignment is irrevocable if supported by consideration, or in some states, if made in a signed writing. Gratuitous assignments are revocable unless a gift was clearly intended and the donor physically delivered either the donation itself or a tangible token thereof to the assignee. The delivery must transfer to the assignee all control and dominion over the thing. For example, delivery of a bankbook, a stock certificate, or the only key to a safe-deposit box would probably suffice to make a gift of the bank deposit, stock, or contents of the box irrevocable. Nothing requires a specific form for an assignment except that the Statute of Frauds may require a writing for a real estate conveyance.

The most important aspect of the assignment is that it cannot increase the duties owed by the *obligor*, the other party of the original contract. Thus, the assignor may convey to the assignee only those rights that he actually has. All defenses to the rights of the assignor that would be available against the assignor are available against the assignee. If A and B enter into an agreement whereby A will pay $100 for B's services, and B assigns the right to collect the $100 to C, C cannot collect the $100 if A has a valid defense against B. For instance, if B failed to perform the services, B could not collect from A; therefore, neither can C. All the defenses A has against B he also has against C, but only if B simply assigns his rights to C. It is possible for C to receive greater rights against A, but this grant of greater rights requires the active cooperation of A.

Assignments and Third Persons

The obligor's status and his responsibilities under an assignment must be considered. When the assignor assigns his rights to the assignee, he is left with no rights under the original contract. The obligor may pay the assignee and by doing so disposes of his obligations to the assignor.

Yet, there are situations where the assignee does not communicate the assignment to the obligor. In such instances, the obligor may continue to pay the assignor as if no assignment were made. As noted previously, this frequently occurs in the case of department stores assigning their rights to receive payments. The department store (as the assignor) gives rights to the assignee (the financial company), but the assignment is never disclosed to the obligor (credit customer), who pays the department store, believing the relationship between himself and the department store has not changed. The obligor never knew the department store was not relying upon its own cash reserves. The department store's reputation as a solid enterprise is preserved. The more ordinary occurrence in assignments, however, is for the assignee to notify the obligor of the assignment. This enables the assignee to collect the money directly from the obligor rather than indirectly through the assignor.

It is important to recall that in a simple assignment the assignee stands in the shoes of the assignor. He has all the rights and liabilities that emanate from the underlying transaction between the obligor and assignor.

A further wrinkle develops when the assignor attempts to assign the same contract rights to more than one person. This successive assignment of the same contract right is likely to be fraudulent. Each of the successive parties to the assignment may, of course, collect from the party doing the wrong. Yet, the question, as a practical matter, is which of the assignees takes superior rights because the fraud doer has typically disappeared. States vary on this question, but the prevailing rule gives the first assignee the greater rights, subject to qualification. Other states vary the general rule by favoring the assignee who first gives notice of the assignment to the obligor.

Whether the state accepts the first assignment position or the first notice position often depends on policy considerations made by the state legislatures. The larger, industrial states have tended to opt for the first assignment rule because nonnotification assignments — like the department store situation — are very common. If the state opted for a first notice rule, creditors would be more reluctant to refinance sales transactions where notification is typically not given.

Limitations on Assignability of Rights

Although the courts today are liberal in enforcing assignments of contract rights, some restrictions remain. First, the parties to a contract may, by appropriate language, bar the assignment of rights arising thereunder. But the courts have come full circle from a position that refused to enforce assignments to a view that looks upon them with great favor. Thus, a stipulation that "neither party shall assign his rights under this agreement" does not prevent an effective assignment but simply leaves the assignor open to suit for breach of contract. On the other hand, a clause providing "any attempted assignment of rights acquired under this agreement shall be void" will have the desired effect of barring an effective assignment by either party.

Second, contract rights cannot be assigned if the assignment would materially alter the duties or risks of the obligor. For example, the rights acquired under a prenuptial agreement are nonassignable. Similarly, the rights of the obligee under a requirements contract or a loan agreement are nonassignable. In the following case, the question is raised whether a certain right can be assigned.

Meyer v. Washington Times Co.
United States Court of Appeals, District of Columbia, 1935. 76 F.2d 988
[The contract was in substance an agreement by the *Chicago Tribune* to furnish certain comics and features exclusively to the *Washington Post* on credit. The right to receive these features was assigned by the receiver of the *Post* to a successor newspaper, which offered to pay cash so that credit would not be extended to it. The *Chicago Tribune* claimed the contract was nonassignable, wishing to sell the right to publish these features to another paper in the area. The court in holding the contract assignable noted:]

VAN ORSDEL, ASSOCIATE JUSTICE.

It is insisted, however, that this is not strictly a contract but in the nature of a license to use and publish copyright material. Whatever may be the effect of such a license between the Tribune Company and the artists producing the comics in question may be disregarded, since the contract involved is not with the artists but with the Tribune Company for the sale of merchandise to one of its customers. There is nothing in the terms of the contract to forbid its assignment, nor is the contract of such a personal character as to prevent it from passing under the circumstances and terms of the receivership sale. There is nothing in this contract requiring the exercise of skill or peculiar qualifications on the part of the Post Company. It was merely a contract in the form employed by the Tribune Company in furnishing these comics to a multitude of publishers throughout the country. It amounted merely to one instance of a general series of transactions, divesting the contract of every element of nonassignability.

Would the result have been otherwise if the *Post*'s successor had not offered to pay cash for the features?

Some courts will also refuse to enforce partial assignments if enforcement would work a substantial hardship on the obligor. Thus, for example, in *Orr Cotton Mills* v. *St. Mary's Hospital*, 205 S.C. 114, 26 S.E.2d 408 (1943), fifteen of the mill's employees sought to assign several dollars a month out of their future wages to the hospital. The court held the assignments ineffectual, since enforcement would have required the mill to make at least 1300 deductions from its payroll, costing it considerable time and bookkeeping expense.

In some states the assignment of future wages is barred or limited by statute. Do you see the policy reason behind this limitation?

THE DELEGATION OF DUTIES

Thus far we have considered the assignment of contract rights. We must now consider the assignment of duties. As a matter of convention, we use the term *delegation* when speaking of duties, and *assignment* when speaking of rights. The delegation of duties introduces two questions: first about the kinds of duties that may be delegated, and second about the obligation of the party to whom a duty is owed to accept the delegation.

Duties that are clearly ministerial in function, that is, can be performed by virtually anyone, can be delegated. Thus, a delivery person's obligation to a customer to deliver a daily newspaper can be delegated to a younger brother, and the obligation will be met when the paper arrives as required. The customer is required to accept the performance as offered. Other situations in which delegation is proper include a lawyer's hiring of a process server, or the decision of an accountant to hire a junior accountant to assist in performing basic computations. One does not breach a contractual obligation by permitting others to assist in this way.

Duties that call for peculiar and unique skills cannot be delegated. Thus, neither Larry Bird nor Magic Johnson could turn over his position on the Boston Celtics and Los Angeles Lakers to another and consider the agreement to play basketball fulfilled. The agreement, by its nature, is one that does not imply the right to delegate duties, and there is no obligation on the part of the person to whom the duty is owed to accept the performance of the substitute. The services are of a highly personal nature, and it would stretch the definition of delegable duties to countenance such a delegation as coming within the terms of the agreement.

Macke Co. v. Pizza of Gaithersburg, Inc.
Court of Appeals of Maryland, 1970. 259 Md. 479, 270 A.2d 645
SINGLEY, J.

The appellees and defendants below, Pizza of Gaithersburg, Inc., Pizzeria, Inc., The Pizza Pie Corp., Inc., and Pizza Oven, Inc., four corporations under common ownership . . . operated at six locations in Montgomery and Prince George's Counties. The appellees had arranged to have installed in each of their locations cold drink vending machines owned by Virginia Coffee Service, Inc., and on 30 December, 1966, this arrangement was formalized at five of the locations, by contracts for terms of one year, automatically renewable for a like term in the absence of 30 days written notice. . . .

On 30 December 1967, Virginia's assets were purchased by the Macke Company (Macke) and the . . . [five] contracts were assigned to Macke by Virginia. In January, 1968, the Pizza Shops attempted to terminate the contracts. . . .

Macke brought suit in the Circuit Court of Montgomery County against each of the Pizza Shops for damages for breach of contract. From judgments for the defendants, Macke has appealed.

The lower court based the result which it reached on [the] ground . . . that the Pizza Shops, when they contracted with Virginia, relied on its skill, judgment and reputation, which made impossible a delegation of Virginia's duties to Macke. . . .

In the absence of a contrary provision — and there was none here — rights and duties under an executory bilateral contract may be assigned and delegated, subject to the exception that duties under a contract to provide personal services may never be delegated, nor rights be assigned under a contract where delectus personae was an ingredient of the bargain.

We cannot regard the agreements as contracts for personal services. They were either a license or concession granted Virginia by the appellees, or a lease of a portion of the appelles' premises, with Virginia agreeing to pay a percentage of gross sales as a license or concession fee or as rent, and were assignable by Virginia unless they imposed on Virginia duties of a personal or unique character which could not be delegated.

The appellees earnestly argue that they had dealt with Macke before and had chosen Virginia because they preferred the way it conducted its business. Specifically, they say that service was more personalized, . . . that commissions were paid in cash, and that Virginia permitted them to keep keys to the machines so that minor adjustments could be made when needed. Even if we assume all this to be true, the agreements with Virginia were silent as to the details of the working arrangements and contained only a provision requiring Virginia to "install . . . the above listed equipment and . . . maintain the equipment in good operating order and stocked with merchandise." We think the Supreme Court of California put the problem of personal service in proper focus a century ago when it upheld the assignment of a contract to grade a San Francisco street:

"All painters do not paint portraits like Sir Joshua Reynolds, nor landscapes like Claude Lorraine, nor do all writers write dramas like Shakespeare or fiction like Dickens. Rare genius and extraordinary skill are not transferable, and contracts for their employment are therefore personal, and cannot be assigned. But rare genius and extraordinary skill are not indispensable to the workmanlike digging down of a sand hill or the filling up of a depression to a given level, or the construction of brick sewers with manholes and covers, and contracts for such work are not personal, and may be assigned."

Moreover, the difference between the service the Pizza Shops happened to be getting from Virginia and what they expected to get from Macke did not mount up to such a material change in the performance of obligations under the agreements as would justify the appellees' refusal to recognize the assignment.
. . . .
. . . . Modern authorities do not support this result, and hold that, absent provision to the contrary, a duty may be delegated, as distinguished from a right which can be assigned, and that the promisee cannot rescind, if the quality of the performance remains materially the same. [See] Restatement, *Contracts* § 160 (3) (1932).

In cases involving the sale of goods, the Restatement rule respecting delegation of duties has been amplified by Uniform Commercial Code § 2-210 (5), which permits a promisee to demand assurances from the party to whom duties have been delegated.

As we see it, the delegation of duty by Virginia to Macke was entirely permissible under the terms of the agreements. . . .

[We] conclude that the Pizza Shops had no right to rescind the agreements. . . .

Judgment reversed as to liability; case remanded for a new trial on the question of damages.

When the party to a contract agrees to accept performance by a third party, it is not uncommon for him to also agree to release the party delegating the duty from his obligations under the contract. Thus, when a client agrees to accept performance from Lawyer B rather than from Lawyer A, when he has a right to performance from Lawyer A, he may release Lawyer A from any obligations under the original agreement between Lawyer A and himself. This agreement to discharge one obligor and to accept another in his place is called a *novation*.

PROBLEMS AND QUESTIONS

1. Explain the difference between a creditor beneficiary and a donee beneficiary.

2. When may a duty be delegated?

3. The City University of Los Angeles and the College Teachers Union on December 1 entered into a collective bargaining contract whereby the university agreed to pay, for three years, salaries to all teaching faculty at a specified rate.

On January 1, when the first mandated salary increase was to go into effect, several faculty members who were not members of the union were denied the increases as called for in the agreement. Since they were not members of the union, the union refused to press their demands with the university.

These members of the faculty were unable to obtain their increases from the university and so brought suit against City University. The university defended on the ground that there was no agreement to which these teachers were party. On what theory did the teachers base their claim? Would they win? Explain.

4. Cleary, a contractor, entered into a contract with Trapani, the owner of a construction site, providing that Cleary would act as general contractor in the building of an apartment house. Cleary also entered into agreements with subcontractors, one of whom was the Cerp Construction Corporation.

In the course of the work being performed, Cleary was unable to pay Cerp for services performed on account of breach of contract by Trapani, who had failed to pay Cleary for the work done. The contract between Trapani and Cleary had provided for payment to Cleary at two month intervals of "all the costs of construction, including the costs of all subcontractors, plus a 10% commission thereon."

Cerp, unable to collect from Cleary, sued Trapani under the Cleary-Trapani contract for the monies due for its work. Decision for whom? Explain.

5. Ames decided to open her own interior decorating firm. Her funds were inadequate to open a showroom, but she did have friends in the interior decorating field. Office Builders, Inc., agreed to subcontract some of their work to Ames during the forthcoming year. The First Hometown Bank agreed to loan Ames $10,000 if Ames would get written contracts for decorating work, and pay the receipts to the bank to the extent of Ames's indebtedness as soon as she received payment from her customer. Ames received the contracts from Office Builders, Inc., and during the course of the year paid $6,000 on the loan due to the bank. She then stopped making payments. The bank notified Office Builders, Inc., that all future payments up to $4,000 should be made directly to the bank. Is Office Builders required to comply?

6. Clark, the owner of a retail grocery, sold the business to Torres. The assets of the business consisted of a two-year lease, merchandise, fixtures, accounts receivable, and goodwill valued at $25,000. Liabilities consisted of $2,000 owed to wholesalers.

At the time of the sale, Torres agreed to pay $23,000 and to assume Clark's liabilities to the wholesalers, and an agreement embodying those terms was drawn up and signed by Clark and Torres. Garcia, one of the wholesalers to whom Clark owed $1,000, called upon Clark and was told by Clark that Torres had agreed to make the payment as it came due. Against whom might Garcia collect?

7. DeZorzi and Pinto entered into a contract to purchase goods for the price of $500. DeZorzi delivered the goods to Pinto and assigned to Kelly the right to collect the price. Pinto refused to pay Kelly, however, on the ground that the goods delivered by DeZorzi were so defective in quality as to be worthless. Kelly contends that she is entitled to the price and that Pinto must resort to DeZorzi for any damages that might have occurred from the delivery of defective goods. Is Kelly correct? Explain.

8. Ryan and Porter rendered market analysis services to Big Time Stores, Inc., which was interested in opening several new stores in the area. After receiving the results of the market analyses, Big Time decided that the economic climate was unfavorable for expansion. Big Time also failed to pay Ryan and Porter the $1,000 fee for their work. Porter and Ryan accepted $600 from Arm Twisters Collection Agency and assigned their rights against Big Time to Arm Twisters. What is the obligation of Big Time to Arm Twisters?

9. Shea owns a successful fur salon on Madison Avenue in New York City. Her customers are all wealthy women who pay by cash or check. Shea believes that the increasing number of professional women living in New York City would also like to own high quality furs, but cannot afford to pay for the furs unless her salon can offer an installment credit plan. Shea's salon does not have the financial resources to finance an installment credit plan. How can Shea make installment credit available to this new group of potential customers given her salon's lack of resources to do the financing herself?

10. On January 1st, Daisy Wittsenburg, noted impresario, contracted to have Joseph A. Ellis, distinguished pianist and composer, give a recital of his original music at Carnegie Hall on March 22. Ellis was unable to perform as contracted, since he would be in Dallas performing on the same evening, under a different contract. Ellis assigned Henry G. Fried, his associate, to perform for him at Carnegie Hall. Mrs. Wittsenburg refused to accept Fried and sued Ellis for breach of contract. Decision for whom? Explain.

11. Preston, owner of a hotel, contracted with Barnett and Barse, experts in the hotel business, to operate and maintain the hotel for ten years at a compensation measured by a percentage of the gross receipts. Barnett and Barse then formed the Barnett and Barse Corporation and were assigned the contract. The corporation went into possession of the hotel and began to carry out the terms of the contract. Preston then brought action to cancel the contract on the ground that the contract was not assignable. He alleges that he entered into the contract in reliance on the financial responsibility and character of Barnett and Barse and especially on Barnett's experience in conducting hotels. Should the plaintiff succeed? Explain.

12. William Jones, a painter who had been in business painting houses for twenty-five years, contracted to paint Wilfred Smith's house during the last two weeks of August. At the end of July, Jones decided that he needed a vacation and hired Nathan Clark to do the painting of the Smith house. Clark had five years of experience painting houses. May Smith insist that Jones, rather than Clark, paint his house?

INTERPRETATION OF CONTRACTS

Rules of interpretation are intended to resolve ambiguities in agreements. Suppose a clause in a form lease for an apartment provides "absolutely no pets," but a clause was added allowing a particular tenant to keep his dog. Which clause controls? If we rely upon the strict wording of the agreement, we are left with a situation incapable of reconciliation. Contracts are not measured by the words of the agreement alone, but rather by the intention of the parties as evidenced in their words and by their actions. In the case above, a specific provision governing a particular pet is thrust against a printed, general exclusion of pets; it is reasonable to assume the clause that most reasonably represents the intention of the parties is the one permitting the pet, which would be given legal effect.

The courts have adopted several rules of interpretation to determine the intention of the parties. One rule is shown in this example; if the language of the agreement conflicts, the courts prefer specific language over general, written over typed, and typed over printed.

Where technical language or trade language is used, the technical words or the trade language is given its precise meaning unless it is reasonable to assume one party to the agreement does not or should not know the meaning of the terms. Where one party drafts the agreement, and the other party approves it, any ambiguities will be determined against the person drafting the contract. The theory is that the drafter had it within his power to cure any ambiguities by a clear expression of his intention. When only one party to an agreement is represented by counsel, the courts tend to determine ambiguities in favor of the party who was not armed with legal counsel.

The language of an agreement is interpreted in light of the entire agreement. The courts look to the contract provisions and the purposes or objectives sought by the parties in determining the intention of the parties. The parties' conduct after the contract is formed reflects upon the meaning of the contract.

11

INTERPRET-ATION AND CONDITIONS

If a sequence of words is used without a general, catch-all phrase, only those meanings mentioned will be included. To avoid this result, contract forms often include such clauses as "and all other forms of related business activity." Additionally, a builder's form contract might provide for countless ways of excusing his timely performance, and then he might add, "or for any other reason deemed proper." The following case indicates the problems involved in interpreting the meanings of the parties.

Perruccio v. Allen
Supreme Court of Connecticut, 1968. 156 Conn. 282, 240 A.2d 912

[Action to recover the cost of improvements due upon termination of a lease of real estate, brought before the Court of Common Pleas in Hartford County and tried to the court. Judgment for the plaintiff and appeal by the defendants. No error.]

HOUSE, J.

The facts in this case are not in dispute. The defendants were associated with a yachting club in East Hartford and wished to have a marina on the Connecticut River. In April, 1959, they leased land fronting on the river to the plaintiff for the purpose of erecting and maintaining boating docks and boating facilities. The lease was for a term of two years at a rental of $50 a year with an option for the plaintiff to renew the lease for an additional term of three years at a rental of $75 a year. Both parties were represented by counsel at the time of drafting and execution of the lease although both are now represented by other than their original counsel. The plaintiff, exercising his option, operated the leasehold premises during the full term of the lease until April, 1964. In building the marina, he expended moneys and contributed labor to the value of $2600. At the conclusion of the term of the lease in April, 1964, the plaintiff surrendered the premises and left the marina to the defendants.

A paragraph of the lease which the parties have referred to as paragraph 7 provided: "The Lessee agrees to build all necessary boating docks on the river and land located on the demised premises at his own expense. However, upon the termination of this lease for any reason, the Lessors herein agree to reimburse said Lessee for all the costs of erecting said docks. . . :" The decisive question is whether the words "upon termination of this lease for any reason" include the ending of the lease by expiration of the term of years provided therein.

Relying on this paragraph of the lease, the plaintiff brought this action for reimbursement from the defendants for the cost of constructing the docks. It is his contention that the words "termination" and "expiration" as used in the lease are synonymous and that the word "termination," as used in paragraph 7 of the lease, especially when it is coupled with the unqualified and unequivocal phrase "for any reason," encompasses any ending of the lease, including the end of the period of its duration.

It is the contention of the defendants that the parties intended a technical or special meaning for the word "termination" as used in paragraph 7 of the lease and that the plaintiff was entitled to reimbursement only if his leasehold term was ended prior to the expiration of the full five-year term of the lease.

The court concluded that the provision "upon the termination of this lease for any reason" applied to any termination or ending of the lease and, accordingly, rendered judgment for the plaintiff in the amount of $2600. From that judgment the defendants have taken this appeal.

On the basis of the facts which it found and from an examination of all of the provisions of the lease, the court, applying the proper rules for its construction, could reasonably and logically have reached the conclusion which it did. In *Ingalls* v. *Roger Smith Hotels Corporation,* we said: "A lease is a contract. . . . In construing it, three elementary principles must be kept constantly in mind: (1) The intention of the parties is controlling and must be gathered from the language of the lease in the light of the circumstance surrounding the parties at the execution of the instrument; (2) the language must be given its ordinary meaning unless a technical or special meaning is clearly intended; (3) the lease must be construed as a whole and in such a manner as to give effect to every provision, if reasonably possible. If the language is ambiguous, the construction which favors the lessee should be adopted. Furthermore, an unexpressed intent is of no significance. The controlling factor is the intent expressed in the lease, not the intent which the parties may have had or which the court believes they ought to have had." We later reaffirmed this general rule, noting that it was subject to the principle that "if the terms of an instrument are fairly susceptible of two or more interpretations, the one which is the most equitable, reasonable and rational is to be preferred."

The record affords no basis for any determination of equities between the parties, and we cannot say that the claimed interpretation of "termination" by either party is, under the circumstances, more reasonable or rational or that any technical or special meaning of the word was clearly intended. . . .

The trial court concluded [after quoting from two dictionaries] that, in the ordinary meaning of the word, "termination" is a synonym for "expiration" and that as used in paragraph 7 of the lease it included termination of the lease by expiration of its time or term. As the court also noted, precisely the same result is reached by applying the principle to which we have already referred, i.e., that if the language is ambiguous, the construction which favors the lessee should be adopted. This is a generally applied and well-settled rule of construction when the words of a lease are doubtful in meaning or susceptible of more than one construction.

The court could reasonably and logically and by the proper application of accepted rules for the construction of ambiguities in a lease have reached the conclusion which it did.

There is no error.

It is not necessary for the written form to include all definitions relevant to the agreement. The courts will supply those consistent with practice and general understanding. For example, an agreement to pay implies payment in legal tender, and if a contract provides for delivery within thirty days, it is understood (and in fact the Code so provides, in the case of goods) that delivery on a legal holiday is not required.

One final rule deserves brief mention. The rules of interpretation clearly favor a legal purpose if the document supports an implication of either legal or illegal behavior.

CONDITIONS

Conditions are events that begin or terminate legal obligations. For example, it is possible for two persons to condition their contract for the purchase and sale of land on the purchaser obtaining a mortgage from a bank for a stated term at the prevailing rate of interest. He does not promise to obtain the mortgage; this is merely a condition that produces a duty of performance under the terms of the agreement. If the purchaser obtains the mortgage, then the condition is met and the duty to perform the contract exists.

In some instances, conditions may not require any obligation. For example, a purchaser may agree to buy property on the condition that the adjacent property, owned by someone else, is also put up for sale within a specified time. Neither the purchaser nor the seller has an obligation to bring that condition into effect. But in the mortgage example mentioned first, although the situation is one of condition and the purchaser has no affirmative duty to obtain the mortgage, a court will imply an obligation; the purchaser must make a good faith effort to procure a mortgage. Obviously, the purchaser would be under no contractual obligation whatsoever unless he had some duty to seek a mortgage. Hence, the courts imply a promise to seek a mortgage, although nothing guarantees success. Of course, it is also proper for a contract to provide for a sale regardless of the purchaser's ability to obtain a mortgage. In other words, the purchaser can assume the risk that his credit rating and the quality of the property will be inadequate to get a mortgage.

Condition Precedent and Condition Subsequent

The law distinguishes between conditions that begin and terminate legal duties. Those which create the legal duties are called *conditions precedent*, and those which terminate legal duties are called *conditions subsequent*. These conditions work as follows.

On October 1 an insurance policy is issued protecting a homeowner from fire loss. Among other clauses, it provides coverage for loss occasioned by fire and requires the homeowner to notify the insurance company within 30 days of a fire that causes a loss. At the time the contract is made, the insurance company has no obligation to make payment, because there has been no fire. This condition, the occurrence of a fire, does not imply a promise, for the insurance company will not consider the insured to have breached his agreement if no fire occurs. A fire is the condition precedent that obligates the insurance company to compensate the homeowner. The insurance company's obligation does not continue indefinitely; a condition subsequent complements the condition precedent. The condition subsequent requires notice within 30 days of the fire, otherwise the insurance company's obligation to indemnify for loss is discharged. The condition subsequent is reasonable in view of the insurance company's need to determine the character and extent of the accidental loss.

Characteristically, many business transactions that have a condition precedent also have a condition subsequent. For example, the mortgage situation spoken of earlier would generally have a condition subsequent that requires timely notice if the purchaser cannot obtain the mortgage. If such notice is not given, the buyer waives his right to escape performance; that is, the failure to give notice means the obligation to perform the contract remains intact. In the following case, the parties disagree whether the language of their contract stipulates a condition precedent.

McCall v. Freedman
Court of Appeals of Michigan, 1971. 35 Mich. App. 243, 192 N.W.2d 275

McGregor, Judge.

On December 17, 1968, plaintiffs sued defendants for breach of contract and specific performance, on a contract for the purchase of a home. The case was tried on June 18, 1970, in the circuit court; judgment was entered in favor of the plaintiffs.

The Bradley Building Company, one of the defendants, is a Michican corporation, actively engaged in the building business in the city of Warren. The co-defendant, Burton Freedman, was an employee of that corporation. During December, 1965, the plaintiffs and the defendant corporation entered into a contractual agreement whereby the plaintiffs were to purchase a home to be built by the defendant corporation, for a price of $16,940, with a down payment of $640. Subsequently, on November 23, 1968, the plaintiffs, in the presence of their attorney, executed a new contract for the purchase of the same home which, in effect, superseded the first agreement, the latter contract being in the amount of $16,740 with the same down payment. The new home was completed in late 1968; the reason for the delay is not pertinent to the issue before us.

The purchase contract provided for the buyers to apply for an FHA mortgage in the amount of $16,100. It was defendant Freedman who actually forwarded the required data to Capitol Mortgage Corporation, an FHA-approved lending institution, on November 25, 1968. The Capitol Mortgage Corporation rejected the application, apparently because of the lack of an FHA inspection and insufficient down payment. On November 27, 1968, defendant Freedman received a letter from Capitol confirming the rejection. Freedman testified that he attempted without success to call plaintiffs and their attorney. Freedman then sent the letter aforementioned, by certified mail, in a plain envelope, return receipt requested with a cashier's check, returning to plaintiffs their deposit of the down payment funds. Plaintiffs acknowledged receipt of this letter. On December 17, 1968, plaintiffs commenced this action for breach of contract and specific performance. On December 21, 1968, defendants sold the property for allegedly $22,000, although the deed of conveyance showed $24,700, and the purchaser took possession subsequently.

On July 6, 1970, after a circuit court trial, judgment was entered in favor of plaintiffs for $6,705.71 including interest at six percent and costs. . . .

. . . .

On appeal, defendants contend that the contractual duty of plaintiffs to apply for an FHA mortgage under the contract was a condition precedent to the defendants' tender of the property, and that the plaintiffs, not having fulfilled this condition, were not entitled to seek or claim a breach of contract.

It is sometimes said that a condition precedent is a fact or event which the parties intend to exist or take place before there is a right to performance. Courts are disinclined to construe the stipulations of a contract as conditions precedent, unless compelled by the language of the contract plainly expressed. In the instant case, it cannot be said that defendants demonstrated that a condition precedent was intended by the parties, nor does the language indicate that this was intended.

There was testimony that defendant Freedman agreed to process the application for an FHA mortgage and the plaintiffs relied upon the sellers to make the application for the FHA mortgage. The plaintiffs executed the papers necessary for such an application, which papers were forwarded to the FHA-approved lending institution by the defendants. After the plaintiffs had furnished the credit statement and required records to the sellers for purposes of preparing the application for the FHA commitment, the next communication they received from the defendants was a copy of the mortgage rejection letter and the cashier's check refunding their down payment.

We find it somewhat anomalous that the defendants, who actually submitted the mortgage application papers to the lender, now claim that it was a condition precedent for the buyers to do this. The trial court found that the plaintiffs had done everything that was asked of them. We agree.

Since the findings of the trial court are not clearly erroneous, its judgment is affirmed.

Implied Conditions

Thus far we have spoken about contract conditions that are clearly expressed in the agreement. Difficulties arise when the parties did not define their intentions with precision, or, more often still, because they had not foreseen the exact dispute or problem that ultimately arose, and thus there was no real "intent of the parties" on the point in question. In this event, the court seeks to divine what the parties would have done *if* they had considered the point in question, and, taking public policy also into account, it rejects an inappropriate condition or perhaps constructs an appropriate one. In the *Koppelon* case, which follows, we explore the principles and reasoning that influence courts when they consider the question of whether a particular circumstance or event was an implied condition.

Koppelon v. W. M. Ritter Flooring Corp.
Court of Errors and Appeals of New Jersey, 1922. 97 N.J.L. 200, 116 A. 491

TRENCHARD, J.

This action was tried at the Essex Circuit and resulted in a verdict for the plaintiff, and the defendant appealed from the consequent judgment.

We are of the opinion that the judgment must be affirmed. . . .

We are come now to the question of the legal sufficiency of the "defense" which was stricken out [by the trial judge]. [Did the trial judge err?]

The complaint averred that the plaintiff was building an apartment-house in East Orange; that the defendant contracted to furnish the labor and materials necessary to lay, scrape, and finish the floors for a stated price to be paid in stated installments as the work progressed; that when the time arrived for the defendant to begin performance, the plaintiff requested performance, but the defendant stated to the plaintiff that it, the defendant, refused, and thereafter would refuse, to perform the contract; and that the defendant has wholly repudiated and refused to perform the contract.

The defendant's answer in the "second separate defense," averred that since the execution of the contract the credit of the plaintiff had become impaired, so he was no longer a good credit risk, and that by reason of the plaintiff's poor financial condition the defendant was warranted in not performing the terms of the contract.

We think the question must be answered in the negative.

The fact that the credit of a party to a building contract (to whom by the terms of the contract labor and material are to be furnished) has become impaired, so that he is no longer a good credit risk, and that he has failed to meet other independent obligations, does not relieve the other party from performance, and is no defense to an action for the breach of such contract, for it does not appear therefrom that he cannot and will not perform his part when his time for performance comes.

. . . It has been held that mere doubts of the solvency of a party to a contract, or mere belief that he will be unable to perform when the time for his performance comes, will not excuse performance by the other party. If contracts could be repudiated upon the mere allegation that the credit of the other party had become impaired, there would indeed be much consternation in the business world, for contracts are made in view of the fact that credit fluctuates, and it is common knowledge that contracts are frequently fully performed by those whose credit has become impaired.

But we think that the mere insolvency of a party to a building contract (to whom by the terms of the contract labor and materials are to be furnished) does not terminate the contract, in the absence of provisions to that effect therein, nor does it justify the other party in refusing altogether to perform, for it does not follow therefrom that the insolvent party could not and would not perform his part even though insolvent. It might be that the insolvent party might find it advantageous and possible to carry out his part of the contract, since insolvency does not necessarily mean total lack of assets. To hold that mere insolvency of a party puts an end to a contract, and excuses the solvent party from the obligation altogether, would be intolerable. . . .

The defendant, however, contends that it was relieved of its obligation to do the work and furnish the materials "upon credit" when the plaintiff had become insolvent and that it could "only be obliged to proceed with its contract in case payment is assured it in cash by some satisfactory indemnity," and refers us to cases said to support that proposition.

But that question is not presented in the case at bar and will not be considered. Neither the defendant's pleading, as originally stated, nor as amended, raises that question, because it does not assert that defendant's refusal to proceed was due either to plaintiff's failure to pay in advance or to plaintiff's refusal to give assurance of payment, the pleader merely attempting to justify defendant's failure to proceed because of plaintiff's alleged poor financial condition and insolvency when the time arrived for defendant to begin performance.

The judgment will be affirmed, with costs.

Suppose defendant has refused to do the work unless the plaintiff paid cash or posted security. The overwhelming majority of cases on this point hold that an insolvent's refusal to satisfy such a demand excuses the other party from further performance (i.e., from further extension of unsecured credit).

Concurrent Conditions

When a businessperson sells and does not stipulate a time for payment, when must payment be made: before, after, or at the time of tender? If payment is due *after* delivery, the buyer cannot be sued for failure to pay until after the delivery. The seller must perform even if the probability of payment is slight or else be liable to suit for breach of contract; failure to perform (even to a poor risk) is fatal to his cause. On the other hand, if payment is due *before* delivery, the purchaser may have many anxious moments awaiting delivery from an unreliable party he has already paid. If in the light of all this uncertainty, the purchaser refuses to prepay, he is left with the prospect of being sued for breach of contract. All in all, placing the condition of performance on each of the parties at different times presents many difficulties. As a result, when there is no contrary intent, the law presumes *concurrent conditions* in a sales transaction: the obligation to pay does not come until the delivery is made; the obligation to deliver does not come until payment is made. In essence, both parties stand with hands extended, each delivering up what the contract requires. Their claims for relief, moreover, are based upon their conforming to the duties imposed by the concurrent conditions.

The conditions are not only concurrent, but also *dependent*. The seller is obliged to deliver the goods on the buyer's tender of payment, and he is required to deliver only if the buyer tenders that payment. The same holds true for the buyer. He may not claim failure to deliver unless he also claims his willingness to pay for the goods.

Independent Conditions

When payment and delivery are at different times, as in a credit transaction, the courts hold that the first event is an *independent condition*, but the second is *dependent* upon the first. Thus, when a contract provides for delivery on credit, the delivery must be made at the appointed time, but the duty to pay depends upon prior delivery of the goods.

The subject of independent and dependent conditions has been confused by the tendency of some courts to refer to these conditions as *conditional* and *unconditional* rather than as dependent and independent. In any event, the matter is considerably important in terms of contractual rights and duties.

A particular contractual promise often embodies both a promise and a condition. In the example of a sale on credit, a promise to deliver the goods creates a condition that affects the buyer's duty to pay for them. When the goods are not forthcoming, the purchaser sues for breach of contract, that is, for failure to deliver the goods as promised. The purchaser, moreover, does not have to allege his tender of payment because the duty to deliver was independent of the condition of payment.

Conditions of Performance

Contracting parties are required to perform according to the terms of the agreement. Thus, a contract calling for the sale of a particular kind of cloth requires cloth conforming to the contractual designation of color, quality, or any other feature of the fabric. The seller's right to the agreed price is conditioned upon proper performance.

The jury usually decides whether a condition was satisfied if the issue arises in litigation. In many commercial cases, however, the parties agree to arbitrate any disputes concerning performance of the contract. Commercial parties often prefer arbitration to litigation because it is usually quicker and less expensive.

Often a contract is silent on what constitutes acceptable performance. Sometimes this matter can be simply decided by applying rules fully appreciated by a layman. At other times, however, certain trade practices or industry standards provide the measure against which performance is considered. Consequently, the conditions of performance — the manner and degree to which the parties have adhered to their duties under the contract — are frequently the stuff of legal controversy.

Fitzmaurice v. Van Vlaanderen Mach. Co.
Superior Court of New Jersey, Appellate Division, 1970. 110 N.J. Supr. 159, 264 A.2d 740

Per Curiam,

Defendant Van Vlaanderen Machine Company appeals from a judgment of the Law Division awarding damages of $37,000 to plaintiff under an employment contract.

Plaintiff was a business consultant specializing in marketing and sales. Defendant manufactured printing presses as well as other machinery. Sometime around November 1965 it entered into discussions which, eventually, led to its retention of plaintiff as a management consultant.

The terms of the agreement between the parties were set forth in a letter, dated February 15, 1966, addressed by plaintiff to Peter Van Vlaanderen, the company's vice-president. It recited:

"This letter is to confirm our understanding in which you have agreed to engage me to provide business diagnosis and interim management for one year at $52,000.00. Fee to be paid monthly in advance. Out of pocket expenses to be reimbursed monthly. Extraordinary expenses, *e.g.* travel, to be agreed upon in advance.

Apart from my normal practice, I have agreed to release you from this contract three months from this date *if at that time you do not find my work profitable.* If this should occur, it is agreed that my fee will be $15,000 plus expenses. Otherwise the contract is to continue for one year." (Emphasis by court.) It was accepted by Peter Van Vlaanderen on behalf of the company on March 7, 1966.

The parties worked under this agreement until May 16, 1966, when Peter Van Vlaanderen telephoned plaintiff and told him his work was of no benefit to the company, its officers were unsatisfied and "we want to call it off." By then defendant had already paid plaintiff $15,000 plus his expenses. Plaintiff thererafter commenced the present action.

Defendant urges that (1) the contract between the parties was one for personal satisfaction, and therefore defendant was not required to show a reasonable basis for its decision to terminate its relationship with plaintiff; (2) the court erred in charging the jury that the burden rested upon defendant to prove that the contract was not profitable. . . .

Defendant argues that the contract was one of personal satisfaction, which permitted it unilaterally to cancel. Not so. The contract created an employment relationship covering a one year period, but subject to termination, at defendant's option, three months after its date if defendant did not find plaintiff's services to be profitable. The right to dissolve the contractual relationship was thus a conditional one. A personal satisfaction contract, so called, generally involves a subject matter which concerns the personal taste, fancy or feeling of another, who is thus made the sole judge of the quality of the performance. However, contracts which promise performance in the form of results to the satisfaction of another are in a different category and as to them, the New Jersey rule is that the party claiming dissatisfaction must act honestly and in good faith. This comports with the majority rule.

The contract here evidenced an intent that the continuation of plaintiff's relationship with defendant was not to be subject to the sole and unbridled discretion of defendant's officers but was to be cancellable only if they found plaintiff's services not to be "profitable." Whether or not such services were profitable would appear to be measurable by commercial standards. Defendant's decision thereon was, of course, subject to the test of good faith and reasonableness. Such a construction gives due weight to the language employed by the parties, considered in the context of their dealings, imposes the least hardship upon either of the parties and cannot be said to be unfair or unreasonable. Thus the jury was properly instructed that the test was whether defendant's conclusion that plaintiff's services were not profitable, on which it based its termination of the agreement, could fairly and reasonably have been reached under the proofs adduced. . . .

Defendant argues that the court erred in charging that the burden of establishing facts justifying defendant's termination of the contract rested with defendant. Not so. Plaintiff did not obligate himself to the satisfaction of defendant, but rather agreed to render business diagnosis and management services for the term of one year. Only upon the establishment of a contingency, i.e., the failure of defendant to find his work to be profitable, did he agree to release defendant from its obligation. Where a party seeks to avoid a contractual obligation by reason of the happening of an event or condition stipulated in a contract, the burden of establishing the occurrence of the condition rests upon the party asserting it. . . . Inasmuch as defendant asserted, both in the pretrial order and in its opening to the jury, the unprofitability of retaining plaintiff by way of avoidance of its obligations under the contract, this amounted, in effect, to an affirmative defense as to which the burden of proof rested upon defendant. . . .

The judgment is affirmed.

Conditions of Personal Satisfaction

Frequently the contract designates that the buyer must be "personally satisfied" with the goods or services, or that performance must satisfy a third party. In this case, clearly the quality of performance is a condition, and clearly two distinct kinds of questions are raised: first, what is the standard of personal satisfaction, and second, has that standard been complied with?

Personal satisfaction as a condition does not ordinarily mean a party can determine absolutely whether or not he is satisfied. In most circumstances and in most jurisdictions, contracts conditioned by personal satisfaction tests are taken to mean reasonable standards of personal satisfaction. If the standards are not reasonable, or if the dissatisfied party's judgment is arbitrary, then the courts will use an objective test to determine whether the requirement of personal satisfaction was met. The courts ask whether a reasonable person in the circumstances would have been satisfied by the performance.

Objective satisfaction is not the test in all cases. Where matters of artistic taste or questions clearly involving aesthetics and unique performance, such as a portrait, are raised, the courts in some jurisdictions have held the test for satisfaction is not whether a reasonable party would be satisfied by the performance, but whether the designated party is actually satisfied. If the person is not actually satisfied with the performance, then the courts will hold the condition is not met regardless of any unreasonableness or lack of judgment. In such situations, courts generally find that the party furnishing the unsatisfactory performance did not guarantee satisfaction and is, therefore, not liable for breach. The courts usually find that satisfaction was a condition and that there was a promise to make a reasonable effort to meet that condition. Thus, the failure to satisfactorily perform the contract is merely a failure of condition.

Conditions and Third Parties

Contracts frequently provide for a standard of satisfaction determined by a third party. For example, a certificate of occupancy by a building inspector is required to make a building or structure habitable. Where the determination of contract performance is left to a third party, most jurisdictions read this condition in the following terms: whatever determination this third party in good faith reaches determines the question of performance.

It does not matter if the judgment is erroneous; the determination — if fairly arrived at — disposes of the issue. Of course, it is possible to show the third party did not exercise his judgment but rather acted arbitrarily, as by not examining the facts. In this situation, the party does not challenge the third party's judgment, but rather asserts that the party did not exercise the required judgment. The court would accept this evidence.

Failure of Condition

If a condition is not met, all duties dependent upon that condition are discharged. In simple terms, the failure to deliver goods discharges the other party's obligation to pay for those goods. Thus, when the terms of the contract require a satisfactory portrait, the artist painting an unsatisfactory one will not be paid until he is able to meet the terms of the agreement.

Substantial Performance

In some cases, the failure of a particular condition may be slight, but its consequences severe. For instance, a contract might require a builder to construct a fifteen-story building and to use a particular type of electrical wiring. The failure to conform to the exact specification by using a different type of wiring, even if equally serviceable, could arguably lead to a total discharge of the duty to pay. The nonconformity might be ever so slight, and the cost of curing the defect might be great, but a strict application of the rules governing performance and conditions denies recovery for the work performed.

The severity of this rule, particularly in unintentional deviations or in areas where the cost of curing the defects remains great, has led to the development of the doctrine of *substantial performance*. Although the party failed to adhere to the entire set of conditions, the condition was materially satisfied; therefore, the full measure of damages for the failure to perform fully is not permitted. However, to protect the injured party, the courts allow as damages the difference between the value received and the value of the conforming performance.

The doctrine of substantial performance applies only in limited circumstances. The courts consider the cost of correcting the defect and the difference between the performance rendered and the performance agreed upon. The courts also look to the intent of the breaching party. If the breaching party intentionally breached the contract, the doctrine of substantial performance does not apply. The following cases demonstrate the problems involved in dealing with substantial performance.

Jacob & Youngs v. Kent
New York Court of Appeals, 1921. 230 N.Y. 239, 129 N.E. 889

CARDOZO, J.

The plaintiff built a country residence for the defendant at a cost of upwards of $77,000, and now sues to recover a balance of $3,483.46, remaining unpaid. The work of construction ceased in June, 1914, and the defendant then began to occupy the dwelling. . . . One of the specifications for the plumbing work provides that "all wrought iron pipe must be well galvanized, lap welded pipe of the grade known as 'standard pipe' of Reading manufacture." The defendant learned in March, 1915, that some of the pipe, instead of being made in Reading, was the product of other factories. The plaintiff was accordingly directed by the architect to do the work anew. The plumbing was then encased within the walls except in a few places where it had to be exposed. Obedience to the order meant more than the substitution of other pipe. It meant the demolition at great expense of substantial parts of the completed structure. The plaintiff left the work untouched, and asked for a certificate that the final payment was due. Refusal of the certificate was followed by this suit.

The evidence sustains a finding that the omission of the prescribed brand of pipe was neither fraudulent nor willful. It was the result of the oversight and inattention of the plaintiff's subcontractor. Reading pipe is distinguished from Cohoes pipe and other brands only by the name of the manufacturer stamped upon it at intervals of between six and seven feet. Even the defendant's architect, though he inspected the pipe upon arrival, failed to notice the discrepancy. The plaintiff tried to show that the brands installed, though made by other manufacturers, were the same in quality, in appearance, in market value and in cost as the brand stated in the contract — that they were, indeed, the same thing, though manufactured in another place. The evidence was excluded, and a verdict directed for the defendant. The Appellate Division reversed, and granted a new trial.

We think the evidence, if admitted, would have supplied some basis for the inference that the defect was insignificant in its relation to the project. The courts never say that one who makes a contract fills the measure of his duty by less than full performance. They do say, however, that an omission, both trivial and innocent, will sometimes be atoned for by allowance of the resulting damage, and will not always be the breach of a condition to be followed by a forfeiture. The distinction is akin to that between dependent and independent promises, or between promises and conditions. Some promises are so plainly independent that they can never by fair construction be conditions of one another. Others are so plainly dependent that they must always be conditions. Others, though dependent and thus conditions when there is departure in point of substance, will be viewed as independent and collateral when the departure is insignificant. Considerations partly of justice and partly of presumable intention are to tell us whether this or that promise shall be placed in one class or in another. . . . The margin of departure within the range of normal expectation upon a sale of common chattels will vary from the margin to be expected upon a contract for the construction of a mansion or a "skyscraper." There will be harshness sometimes and oppression in the implication of a condition when the thing upon which labor has been expended is incapable of surrender because united to the land, and equity and reason in the implication of a like condition when the subject matter, if defective, is in shape to be returned. From the conclusion that promises may not be treated as dependent to the extent of their uttermost minutiae without a sacrifice of justice, the progress is a short one to the conclusion that they may not be so treated without a perversion of intention. Intention not otherwise revealed may be presumed to hold in contemplation the reasonable and probable. . . . There will be no assumption of a purpose to visit venial faults with oppressive retribution.

Those who think more of symmetry and logic in the development of legal rules than of practical adaptation to the attainment of a just result will be troubled by a classification where the lines of division are so wavering and blurred. . . . The decisions in this state commit us to the liberal view, which is making its way, nowadays, in jurisdictions slow to welcome it. Where the line is to be drawn between the important and the trivial cannot be settled by a formula. . . . The same omission may take on one aspect or another according to its setting. Substitution of equivalents may not have the same significance in fields of art on one side and in those of mere utility on the other. Nowhere will change be tolerated, however, if it is so dominant or pervasive as in any real or substantial measure to frustrate the purpose of the contract. There is no general license to install whatever, in the builder's judgment, may be regarded as "just as good." The question is one of degree, to be answered, if there is doubt, by the triers of the facts and, if the inferences are certain, by the judges of the law. We must weigh the purpose to be served, the desire to be gratified, the excuse for deviation from the letter, the cruelty of enforced adherence. Then only can we tell whether literal fulfillment is to be implied by law as a condition. This is not to say that the parties are not free by apt and certain words to effectuate a purpose that performance of every term shall be a condition of recovery. That question is not here. This is merely to say that the law will be slow to impute the purpose, in the silence of the parties, where the significance of the default is grievously out of proportion to the oppression of the forfeiture: The willful transgressor must accept the penalty of his transgression. For him there is no occasion to mitigate the rigor of implied conditions. The transgressor whose default is unintentional and trivial may hope for mercy if he will offer atonement for his wrong.

In the circumstances of this case, we think the measure of the allowance is not the cost of replacement, which would be great, but the difference in value, which would be either nominal or nothing. Some of the exposed sections might perhaps have been replaced at moderate expense. The defendant did not limit his demand to them, but treated the plumbing as a unit to be corrected from cellar to roof. In point of fact, the plaintiff never reached the stage at which evidence of the extent of the allowance became necessary. The trial court had excluded evidence that the defect was unsubstantial, and in view of the ruling there was no occasion for the plaintiff to go farther with an offer to proof. We think, however, that the offer, if it had been made, would not of necessity have been defective because directed to difference in value. It is true that in most cases the cost of replacement is the measure. The owner is entitled to the money which will permit him to complete, unless the cost of completion is grossly and unfairly out of proportion to the good to be attained. When that is true, the measure is the difference in value. . . . The rule that gives a remedy in cases of substantial performance with compensation for defects of trivial or inappreciable importance, has been developed by the courts as an instrument of justice. The measure of allowance must be shaped to the same end.

The order should be affirmed, and judgment absolute directed in favor of the plaintiff upon the stipulation, with costs in all courts.

Belizzi v. Huntley Estates, Inc.

New York Court of Appeals, 1957. 3 N.Y.2d 112, 143 N.E.2d 802

DYE, J.

The defendant-respondent, a real estate developer, on or about August 19, 1950, contracted to sell to the plaintiff-appellant a lot designated as No. 235 in its development and to build a house thereon in accordance with its demonstration model known as "The 1951 Kent" which, among other features, had an attached garage with an access driveway substantially at street level. When the construction work was commenced, the defendant encountered rock close to the surface, and instead of excavating same, as might have been done without too much trouble at the time, it placed the house thereon, with the result that from the entrance of the garage to the street, a distance of 43 feet, there was a difference in elevation of 9 feet and 8 inches. This amounted to a 22-½% grade, which is so steep that the driveway cannot be used safely and conveniently. As a matter of fact, the evidence shows that a grade of 12% is considered the permissive maximum. While the plans are silent as to the grade of the driveway, the defendant does not now claim that the grade of the existing driveway is reasonable or that plaintiff has no cause for complaint. It defends against plaintiff's claim for damages on the sole ground that the trial court erred when it excluded evidence offered by it as to the value of the property and should not have refused to charge that the measure of damages "is the difference between the value of the building as constructed and its value had it been constructed conformably to the contract or the cost of repairs, whichever is the lesser." Instead, the trial court charged in substance that the measure of damage is "the fair and reasonable cost to remedy the defect in this controversy or to get a reasonably usable driveway."

The Appellate Division adopted the defendant's contention largely in reliance on *Jacob & Youngs* v. *Kent*. In that case, we had applied the "difference in value" rule simply because the proof failed to show any substantial damage or loss in value since the wrought iron galvanized pipe, as furnished, was substantially the same in quality, weight, market price, service-ability and appearance as pipe of "Reading" manufacture called for in the contract specifications and that the cost of replacing same with the "Reading" pipe as specified "would be great, but the difference in value . . . would be either nominal or nothing;" in other words, re-placement of the pipe, under the circumstances in that case, would have consti-tuted economic waste.

However, this litigation poses an entirely different kind of breach, the conse-quence of which is to burden plaintiff with an unusable, unsafe and unsightly driveway. While it is unfortunate that the defendant elected to build the garage at an unsuitable elevation in order to avoid the cost of excavating unforeseen rock and that to correct the defect will now cost much more than initially, nonethe-less, that loss should not fall on the innocent owner whose protests made at the time were cut off by the president of the defendant corporation with assurances not to worry, that when finished the grade would not exceed 10% and that the plaintiff would be happy when he got into his home.

The "difference in value" rule in defective performance of construction con-tracts seems to be applied only when it would be unfair to apply the general rule (cf. *Jacob & Youngs* v. *Kent*). In a case such as the present when the variance is so substantial as to render the finished building partially unusable and unsafe, the measure of damage is "the market price of completing or correcting the perfor-mance." It is only "If the defect is not thus remediable, damages are based on the difference between the value of the defective structure and that of the struc-ture if properly completed." This rule we have long applied.

Here, there is uncontradicted evidence that the dangerous and unsatisfactory driveway can be corrected. When that is done, the plaintiff will have received no more than he was entitled to under his contract and the defendant will have given no more than it obligated itself to furnish.

The order appealed from should be reversed, and the judgment of the County Court reinstated, with costs in this court and in the Appellate Division.

Installment Contracts

Other conditions take place in installment contract situations. An agreement might provide for monthly deliveries over three years. If one delivery is not met, is the entire agreement discharged? In legal terms, is the purchaser's performance conditioned on the complete and full performance of the seller? Certainly without situations like the one discussed in substantial performance, a buyer has the right to the exact specifications of his contract. He may reject performance that does not conform to the contractual undertaking. In the installment contract, however, the courts apply an ameliorative device much like the one of substantial performance. Unless the requirement of uninter-rupted delivery goes to the heart of the agreement, the courts will not consider the breach total. The agreement remains in effect, although, of course, pay-ment is not due for the performance not tendered. In the area of sale of goods, which covers most installment purchases, the UCC is most instructive. The Code in section 2–612 covers installment contracts for the sale of goods re-quiring delivery of goods in separate lots to be separately accepted. A failure to deliver an installment or the tender of nonconforming goods is a breach of the entire contract only if it impairs the value of the whole contract. When that occurs, the buyer may reject or cancel the entire agreement.

Time of Performance

Finally, the matter of the time of performance also raises questions of conditions. Invariably, agreements provide for performance within a certain time. When no period is stated, the courts imply a reasonable time, and that, of course, depends upon the circumstances of the transaction. Yet, what is the effect of the failure of timely performance in most cases where there is no contrary intent, the courts do not strictly apply the time provisions. This is particularly so in cases involving construction of buildings, and less so in the case of a sale of goods or services. On the other hand, the courts hold that time is of the essence where the delivery date for the sale of perishable goods is expressed.

To ensure the binding effect of an exact time for performance, unambiguous language is required. Thus, contracts attempting to give importance to the condition of time, characteristically include the provision that "time is of the essence."

Waiver of Condition

The parties, by their conduct, can waive certain conditions expressed in the contract. For instance, a contract for installment purchases provides for delivery of goods to take place on a Monday. The deliveries, however, have been taking place on Tuesdays, and the buyer has been accepting them as delivered. If, on a particular Tuesday, the buyer finds they are unacceptable because the contract calls for Monday delivery, the courts would find the prior conduct in accepting the goods on Tuesdays waived the conditon. Affirmative conduct is not the sole device for waiver; a party may also waive conditions by silence.

A waived condition may be reinstated if the other party has not materially changed his position in reliance upon that waiver. Usually, a waived condition is reinstated by giving notice of the intent to restore the condition. Of course, reinstatement will not affect the earlier waiver of condition with respect to performance already tendered.

PROBLEMS AND QUESTIONS

1. What guidelines do courts use in interpreting contracts?

2. Describe the difference between "the cost of replacement" and "the difference in value," as discussed in *Jacob & Youngs* v. *Kent* and *Belizzi* v. *Huntley*

Estates, Inc. When is each to be used as a measure of damages?

3. Plaintiff sued to recover a balance due for plastering work done for the defendant on his house. The written contract provided in part as follows:

We hereby agree to do the plastering work in the house now being built by George Bailey on Main Street, at the following prices: For one coat, 25 cents per square yard; For two coat work with hard finish, 33 cents per square yard; Plastering with cement-like surface, 45 cents per square yard.

Plaintiff claims that in determining the number of square yards for which payment is due they may include window and door openings, and that spaces behind cornices and baseboards are to be measured as though plastered with two coats, though only one coat is used. The two-coat formula and the rule regarding the measuring of spaces is a trade usage among plasterers and the court allowed proof of such usage at trial.

Defendant sought to testify as to ignorance of such usage but the court excluded such testimony stating that usage, when reasonable, uniform, well settled, and not in contradiction to the terms of the contract, is deemed to be part of the contract and enter into the intention of the parties. Did the court properly exclude defendant's testimony as to his ignorance of the usage? Explain.

4. Carson, a manufacturer of radios, and Cavett, a wholesale distributor, signed an instrument that provided as follows:

"Cavett agrees to sell, on behalf of Carson, over the next 5 years, radios as set forth in the schedule below. Carson agrees to pay Cavett a commission of 2% on the sales price of the radios which are sold to retailers. This agreement was entered into on March 17, 1972, and is agreed to by both parties.
(Signed) Cavett.
(Signed) Carson."

In September of 1972, Carson contended that he was free to terminate the contract at will and Cavett insisted that the contract had a definite duration and that Carson was obligated to supply radios as needed over the five-year period of the agreement.

What is the effect upon the interpretation of the written instrument of each of the following:

a. There was no provision binding Carson to fill orders placed by Cavett.

b. There was no provision binding Cavett to place orders with Carson.

c. The document had been prepared by Carson's attorney and presented to Cavett for his signature.

d. The document had been prepared by Carson and presented to Cavett for his signature.

e. The word *contract* was affixed to the top of the instrument.

5. On March 19, 1968, Jewel School, a select academy for girls, agreed in writing with Terrence, a teacher with a Ph.D. and the author of a widely acclaimed textbook on ethics, that Terrence should teach that subject for the school year beginning September 1, 1968 at the salary of $15,000. On July 16, 1968, the authorities of the school discovered that Terrence had been convicted of rape in Ohio in 1966 and had served a one-year prison sentence, during which time he had completed his work on ethics. At no time had anyone connected with Jewel School asked Terrence anything about his past life other than his scholastic attainments. On July 17, 1968, the Jewel School wrote to Terrence that by reason of his criminal record, he did not meet the fitness requirements necessary for employment as a teacher of ethics at their school. Is Jewel School in breach of the agreement?

6. Hannah Washington made a contract with Anne Lebow, whereby she agreed to purchase Lebow's home for $35,000. The contract of sale contained the provision that, "the contract is and shall be contingent upon purchaser obtaining a conventional mortgage in the sum of $20,000 for a period of 25 years at the prevailing rate of interest." After signing the contract, Washington decided that she did not want the Lebow home and did not make any effort to secure the mortgage from a lending institution. When the time came for passing title, Washington notified Lebow that she did not have the mortgage and was therefore not required to perform. If Lebow sues, who should win?

7. James, a contractor, entered into an agreement with Skytop Construction to do plumbing work at a construction site of Skytop. He also entered into a contract with Black, a subcontractor, who agreed to do the plumbing work "as provided in the contract between James and Skytop." The contract also provided that "James shall make payment to Black as James receives payment from Skytop." Black performed his tasks, as agreed, but received no payment from James, since James had received no payment from Skytop. Black sues James to recover the agreed price and James defends on the basis of the failure of Skytop to make payments under the agreement he had with the construction company. Decision for whom? Explain.

8. Mann entered into a written contract with Blake to sell 30 tons of casein. The agreement provided for "shipment to be made in June from Europe with notice of shipment to be sent by cable immediately as the goods are dispatched." In late June, Mann shipped the casein but did not cable notice of shipment to Blake. She did, however, send a letter by boat stating

that upon the arrival of the ship the thirty tons would be delivered as per the contract. Upon arrival of the casein, Mann tendered delivery but the buyer rejected the goods. The seller now sues for breach of contract, and the buyer defends on the basis of the seller's failure to send notice of shipment by cable. Judgment for whom? Explain.

9. The *Jersey Gazette* employed Pantano as an editor of the women's page under a two-year contract at $30,000 per year. It was also agreed that the *Gazette* could discharge Pantano if it was not satisfied with her services. After six months Pantano was discharged, and the *Gazette*, while expressing dissatisfaction with her services, refused to specify the reasons for its dissatisfaction. Pantano sues the *Gazette* for breach of contract. Decision for whom? Explain.

10. James Avco, a prominent dress designer of expensive fashions, ordered a quantity of fabrics from the Cellers Company, which were shipped upon receipt of Avco's order. The order form expressly provided that if the fabrics were not to Avco's personal satisfaction, Avco retained the right to return the goods within thirty days of receipt. When the goods arrived, Avco inspected them and found them not to his personal satisfaction, although conforming in all respects to the specifications as provided in his order. He seeks to return the goods, claiming that they do not meet his requirement of personal satisfaction. Cellers insists that he retain the goods since, by his own admission, the goods conform to the specifications contained in his order. Is Avco correct? Explain. Would your answer be the same if Avco manufactured low-budget dresses?

11. Thomas, a tobacco farmer, entered into a contract with the National Tobacco Company to sell a quantity of tobacco. The agreement provided that: "The quality of all tobacco delivered under this contract shall be subject to the approval of Theodora Blaise, an expert in the grading of tobacco."

Blaise inspected the tobacco and declared that it was not fit for the use intended by National Tobacco and the tobacco company refused to accept delivery of the goods. Under which of the following circumstances could Thomas claim breach of contract by National: (1) that Blaise's evaluation is not correct; (2) that Blaise and National agreed in advance to reject the Thomas goods, and that Blaise rejected them as a result of that agreement?

12. Fresh Fisheries, a wholesale seafood supplier, has a contract to deliver one hundred fresh lobsters to Supreme Seafoods, a retail fish outlet, early each Thursday morning. Thursday and Friday are the busy days at Supreme Seafoods. Most weeks the greater portion of the lobsters are sold by the time Supreme Seafoods closes on Friday evening at 7 P.M. This week Fresh Fisheries does not deliver the lobsters until Saturday morning. Is Supreme Seafoods required to accept delivery?

13. Barbara's Boutique, a women's clothing shop, ordered leather boots, belts, and handbags from Quality Manufacturing and requested delivery on August 31, so the shop would have these accessories available for the start of the fall selling season, September 2. Delivery was not made until September 7. May the store refuse to accept delivery because the contract was not timely performed?

DISCHARGE OF CONTRACTS

Forms of Discharge

The responsibilities under a contractual agreement may be discharged in several ways. We have already seen how conditions may operate to terminate an agreement. It is also clear that performance of the agreement according to its terms discharges it: deliveries are made, services are performed, payment is made, all parties are satisfied, and the contractual relationship is brought to a happy end. We will later see how a breach of the contract may also bring the legal relationship to an end, this time an unhappy one, calling for resort to various legal remedies.

There are several other ways to terminate a contract. The parties, for instance, may agree to terminate or modify the agreement. The contract may also be terminated by operation of law, as by a statute enacted by Congress prohibiting contracts from providing for the sale of goods at a price above a government ceiling. Additionally, as shall be noted in greater depth later, the contract may be discharged by the impossibility of performing the agreement. In such situations the contracts are deemed terminated.

12

DISCHARGE, BREACH, AND REMEDIES

Consumer Protection

In recent years, state and federal legislation has attempted to protect consumers against high-pressure sales tactics and improvident purchases by allowing consumers to terminate agreements without penalty provided they act within prescribed time limits. For example, the federal Consumer Credit Protection Act (CCPA) gives a debtor the right to rescind transactions within three days of the making of the contract when the credit transaction would impose a lien upon his home. Similarly, the Uniform Consumer Credit Code (UCCC) gives customers three days to avoid any contract for goods or services made in their homes through personal solicitation of the seller. Moreover, the seller has the obligation to inform the purchaser of his right to cancel; failure to do so results in the right to cancel continuing beyond three days. The seller's remedy under the UCCC permits him to retain a cancellation fee of 5 percent of the cash price, but in no case can it exceed the cash down payment (UCCC-502).

Impossibility of Performance

Impossibility of performance represents another circumstance for discharge. Essentially, the doctrine relieves a party of his responsibilities under the agreement when an event the parties did not contemplate makes it impossible to perform. For example, suppose a wholesale grocer contracts to buy a farmer's entire crop of apples for the next year. Before the harvest, a freak storm destroys the entire crop, leaving no apples to deliver. The impossibility of performing the contract results in a discharge of the obligation to deliver. Similarly, in a famous English case (*Taylor* v. *Caldwell,* King's Bench, 1863) fire destroyed a music hall shortly before a scheduled performance. The hall's owner was discharged from his contract to rent the hall for the performance since both parties had assumed the hall would be in existence for the performance. Note, however, that either party can assume the risk of an unlikely occurrence such as destruction by fire. Discharge for impossibility of performance only occurs where neither party assumed the risk. Essentially, then, impossibility of performance because of destruction is a variation on the implied conditions discussed in the preceding chapter: the implied condition is the continued existence of something.

Discharge by the impossibility of performance might also occur if one of the necessary parties dies or becomes incapacitated. A corporate officer's agreement to perform personal services as president for two years is subject to a condition of good health and continued capacity. The failure of such conditions renders his performance impossible and the doctrine discharges the parties' obligations. Discharge by death or incapacity occurs only if that party is indispensable to the contract. A seller dying before conveying title will not discharge an agreement for the purchase of a home. The deceased's estate is capable of conveying the property. The test for impossibility is whether the agreement can be performed at all, not whether the event poses an inconvenience or a difficulty.

Events less extreme than destruction or death may also activate the doctrine. For example, an agreement that provides for delivery of goods by a specific carrier and by a specific date may be rendered impossible by a labor strike. However, because of the frequency of strikes and other potential interruptions of delivery the parties may not have addressed in their contract, the UCC in section 2-164 specifically authorizes a commercially reasonable substitute performance and, thereby, minimizes the use of the impossibility doctrine.

A variety of other instances have also raised questions concerning the impossibility doctrine. If danger to the life or safety of the promisor will ensue from fulfilling the contract and the danger was not contemplated at the time the contract was made, the circumstance is held to justify discharge. And contracts to perform acts that were lawful when the contract was made but which have been rendered unlawful by legislation are discharged by impossibility.

The discharge renders the contract ineffective. Parties are relieved of their duties but they are not relieved of all obligations under the agreement; any party receiving benefits must pay for those benefits. In a situation where A agrees to work for B for one year and the contract is discharged midway by B's death, the courts permit A to recover for the services he performed up to B's death.

The law distinguishes between performance that is impossible and performance that is merely difficult, time consuming, or expensive. Consider again the farmer who contracted to sell his apples to the wholesale grocer. An agreement may or may not be discharged depending upon the way it is drafted. If the farmer agreed to sell the apples from his orchard, but the apples were destroyed, then it would be impossible to perform the contract. But if the farmer agreed to sell a certain quantity of apples — expecting them to come from his orchard but not so providing in the agreement — then it would be possible for the farmer to obtain apples elsewhere for sale to the grocer.

The *Restatement of Contracts,* as the following case illustrates, does not demand a scientifically exact meaning for impossibility.

City of Littleton v. Employers Fire Ins. Co.
Supreme Court of Colorado, 1969. 169 Colo. 104, 453 P.2d 810

The City of Littleton . . . brought an action against Latimer and Gaunt Contractors, Inc. . . . to recover damages resulting from the alleged breach of a contract. . . . The contractor's bonding company [was] The Employers Fire Insurance Company. . . .

. . . [On] May 8, 1961, Littleton and the contractor entered into a contract which required the contractor to build two pre-cast and pre-stressed concrete water tanks pursuant to plans and specifications supplied by Littleton. . . . During the course of construction, both tanks collapsed.

Thereafter, Littleton and the contractor entered into a Supplemental Agreement which . . . required reconstruction of the tanks pursuant to specifications and plans already in existence, and in accordance with instructions to be supplied by Littleton's consulting engineer. No work was done pursuant to the Supplemental Agreement. . . . [T]he contractor requested but was refused additional written details regarding reconstruction. . . .

Littleton brought the present suit, alleging that the contractor had breached its obligations under the Supplemental Agreement. After a trial to the court, the court found that performance under the terms of the Supplemental Agreement was impossible as a practical matter.

 . . . .

According to the Restatement, impossibility means not only strict impossibility but impracticability because of extreme and unreasonable difficulty, expense, injury or loss involved. As elaborated in the comment, "impossible" must be given a practical rather than a scientifically exact meaning. Impracticability rather than absolute impossibility is enough.

Commenting on the *Restatement* § 454, Williston has stated that:

> "[t]he true distinction is not between difficulty and impossibility. A man may contract to do what is impossible. . . . The important question is whether an unanticipated circumstance has made performance of the promise vitally different from what should reasonably have been within the contemplation of both parties when they entered into the contract. If so, the risk should not fairly be thrown upon the promisor."

. . . [W]e hereby adopt the definition of impossibility contained in the Restatement § 454 as interpreted by Williston.

II

The principal question remaining in this case is whether we must conclude as a matter of law that the evidence is insufficient to support the finding of the trial court that, within the framework of the Restatement definition of impossibility, the tanks contemplated by the Supplemental Agreement were impossible to build. . . .

. . . .

Nine engineers and contractors testified on the issue of impossibility of performance. . . . Even Jorgensen, the consulting engineer for Littleton, admitted that he was "scared of these tanks," according to the testimony of Latimer. On cross-examination, Jorgensen admitted that the specifications on one tank would have had to be changed to facilitate reconstruction. . . .

Without detailing the other testimony, suffice it to say that the consensus was that the tanks could not be reconstructed as contemplated under the Supplemental Agreement consistent with sound engineering practice. We conclude that there was substantial evidence in the record to support the trial court's finding. . . .

III

According to Littleton's argument, when the contractor entered into the Supplemental Agreement, it knew or had reason to know of the facts which later furnished the basis for the trial court's finding of impossibility of performance. If the evidence supports this assertion, then impossibility of performance would be no defense to Littleton's claim.

. . . .

Apart from expressly providing that construction should proceed in accordance with instructions from Jorgensen, the agreement outlined the scope of the work, "subject to modifications as the work progresses." . . . The record clearly supports the observation that after the collapse of the tanks both parties to the contract knew that some modifications of the original specifications would become necessary. But the evidence above also supports the further inference that on November 11, 1961, both parties to the contract expected that construction could proceed. We cannot, therefore, say that as a matter of law the trial court was required to find that the contractor undertook what it knew was impossible to accomplish when it signed the Supplemental Agreement.

Among other reasons which the trial court assigned for its finding of impossibility was a specific finding that performance was impossible due to the insufficient and defective plans, specifications and directions for reconstruction. . . .

The record is replete with evidence to support the proposition that conclusions as to the cause of the collapse were not reached until well after the Supplemental Agreement was signed. . . .

Jorgenson, the consulting engineer for Littleton, . . . testified that he had not reached a conclusion as to the cause of the collapse until March of 1962, over a year after the Supplemental Agreement was signed.

Twice in April of 1962, as the trial court found, the contractor requested additional instructions, and was told that the instructions already given were sufficient. Only after Littleton once more demanded that reconstruction begin, without supplying additional instructions, did the contractor terminate the agreement.

. . . .

IV

We turn now to the suggestion of Littleton that the parties to the agreement expressed an intention that impossibility of performance should not be a defense to an action for breach of contract. The Supplemental Agreement provides that the contractor "is not responsible for the engineering or design of the said tanks." . . . Thus Littleton argues that the contractor should have tried to erect two water tanks which . . . either could not be erected or could not stand once erected. Having failed to try, Littleton contends, the contractor cannot claim that his obligation was discharged by impossibility.

As Littleton argues, the defense of impossibility is inapplicable where a contrary intention has been manifested. The exception to the defense of impossibility is applicable where, on an interpretation of the contract in the light of accompanying circumstances and usages, the risk of impossibility due to presently unknown facts is clearly assumed by the promisor. In view of the contractor's express disclaimer of responsibility for defects in the design in the Supplemental Agreement, there can be no serious contention here that the promisor, i.e., the contractor, intended to assume the risk. . . .

There is no merit in Littleton's argument that defective specifications cannot provide the basis for the contractor's claim that performance was impossible. When the Supplemental Agreement was executed, both parties contemplated the necessity for additional instructions from Jorgensen. In this case, Littleton's insistence that the instructions were adequate, and its corresponding refusal to issue the additional instructions requested by the contractor, later provided the basis for the defense of impossibility of performance. . . .

The judgment is affirmed.

Mr. Justice DAY, Mr. Justice KELLEY and Mr. Justice GROVES concur.

The following case illustrates that the defense of impossibility may not be available if the contingency should have been foreseen and provided for in the contract.

Nebaco, Inc. v. Riverview Realty Co.
Supreme Court of Nevada, 1971. 87 Nev. 55, 482 P.2d 305

ZENOFF, CHIEF JUSTICE.

Nebaco, together with its parent organization, Nevada National Bank, seeks to set aside its obligations under a lease executed with Riverview Realty on the ground that performance on its part became impossible.

Without specific provision in the contract concerning the restraints and inhibitions to which the bank is bound under the federal laws the expectation is that it would build only what it could build with or without governmental permission. The administrator's consent is a factor with which only the lessee has to contend, not the lessor. One who contracts to render a performance for which government approval is required assumes the duty of obtaining such approval and risk of its refusal is on him.

Therefore, the central question here is not whether Nebaco exercised reasonable diligence to obtain financing, rather, it is the failure to obtain the Regional Administrator's permission which is relied upon as creating the defense of impossibility. This case is thus analogous to those in which a lease is restricted to a use legal in itself but with respect to which the law requires a license or permit. In such cases it is generally held that it will be presumed that the parties anticipated that a license would be obtained and if in fact a license is refused, the lessee is held to have executed the lease with an awareness of the existing law and to have assumed the risk of refusal.

The termination of the lease rested upon Nebaco's inability to obtain the required permission of the Regional Administrator, not upon its failure to obtain financing. In such a situation, the doctrine of impossibility is unavailable because the contingency which arose is one which should have been foreseen and provided for in the contract.

Affirmed.

BATJER, MOWBRAY, THOMPSON and GUNDERSON, JJ., concur.

The foregoing discussion of impossibility should alert you to the importance of drafting an agreement that accurately reflects the intention of the parties; arguably, the farmer intended to supply his apples and did not intend to become a broker for another farmer. It should also alert you to the possibility of providing in the agreement what forms of impossibility will discharge either the entire agreement or perhaps discharge one particular obligation, such as its timely performance.

It is possible then to frame the contract so that discharge occurs if there is difficulty in obtaining supplies from the usual suppliers. This agreement might be worded as follows:

Impossibility Clause

This Agreement is made the 10th day of May 1982 between John Doe, Strawberry grower, and James Roe, Union Official.

It is hereby agreed that James Roe, in consideration of a recruiting fee of $15 per laborer, will supply John Doe with 150 laborers for the harvest season starting June 1, 1972.

It is further hereby agreed that James Doe will exercise due care in providing the said laborers; however, should unforeseen circumstances, such as the unavailability of union labor in the county on June 1st, prevent effective recruitment by James Roe, it is hereby agreed that James Roe will be relieved of his responsibility to supply said workers and no liability for the failure to so provide the labor shall attach.

                                        Signed: John Doe
    Witness: _____   Signed: James Roe

Commercial Impracticability

Where goods are sold, the UCC provides another method for discharging contractual obligations that is closely related to impossibility of performance.

Section 2–615 of the Code allows the seller of goods to shift the loss to the buyer given: (1) a contingency, the nonoccurrence of which was a basic assumption of the contract, (2) the nonallocation of the risk, and (3) impracticability. A dictionary definition of the words "impracticability" and "impossibility" creates the impression that the former could be more frequently and easily satisfied than the latter. However, few cases have thus far been brought under section 2–615, and in those few, the courts have set high standards for satisfying the three requirements. The following case discusses the requirements and is indicative of the judicial attitude.

Eastern Air Lines, Inc. v. Gulf Oil Corporation
United States District Court, (S. D. Fla.), 1975. 415 F. Supp. 429

[Subsequent to the Arab oil embargo of 1973 and substantial price increases for imported crude oil, Gulf Oil Corporation threatened to shut off Eastern Air Lines jet fuel supply if Eastern did not agree to a fuel price increase. Eastern responded by filing an action for breach of contract.

The court discusses the historical business relationship between Eastern and Gulf, the two-tiered oil pricing system in the United States and the contract itself. The contract permitted Gulf to raise the price of jet fuel to Eastern if an industry-wide indicator price increased. The indicator price was the listed price of West Texas Crude, a type of domestic crude oil. The court also found Gulf's defense that Eastern was "fuel freighting" (varying the requirements of the contract widely by having an airplane tank up where the fuel price was lowest) to be without merit, since the practice was an established industry practice, well known to Gulf.]

KING, D. J.
Gulf's commercial impracticability defenses are premised on two sections of the Uniform Commercial Code specifically §§ 2–614 (F.S. 672.614) and 2–615 (F.S. 672.615). . . . [The Official Comments to section 2-615 provide:]

"4. Increased cost alone does not excuse performance unless the rise in cost is due to some unforeseen contingency which alters the essential nature of the performance. Neither is a rise or a collapse in the market in itself a justification, for that is exactly the type of business risk which business contracts made at fixed prices are intended to cover. But a severe shortage of raw materials or of supplies due to a contingency such as war, embargo, local crop failure, unforeseen shutdown of major sources of supply or the like, which either causes a marked increase in cost or altogether prevents the seller from securing supplies necessary to his performance, is within the contemplation of this section. . . ."

"8. The provisions of this section are made subject to assumption of greater liability by agreement and such agreement is to be found not only in the expressed terms of the contract but in the circumstances surrounding the contracting, in trade usage and the like. Thus the exemptions of this section do not apply when the contingency in question is sufficiently foreshadowed at the time of contracting to be included among the business risks which are fairly to be regarded as part of the dickered terms, either consciously or as a matter of reasonable, commercial interpretation from the circumstances. . . ."

In short, for U.C.C. § 2–615 to apply there must be a failure of a presupposed condition, which was an underlying assumption of the contract, which failure was unforeseeable, and the risk of which was not specifically allocated to the complaining party. The burden of proving each element of claimed commercial impracticability is on the party claiming excuse. . . .

The modern U.C.C. § 2–615 doctrine of commercial impracticability has its roots in the common law doctrine of frustration or impossibility and finds its most recognized illustrations in the so-called "Suez Cases," arising out of the various closings of the Suez Canal and the consequent increases in shipping costs around the Cape of Good Hope. Those cases offered little encouragement to those who would wield the sword of commercial impracticability. As a leading British case arising out the 1957 Suez closure declared, the unforeseen cost increase that would excuse performance "must be more than merely onerous or expensive. It must be positively unjust to hold the parties bound." . . .

Other recent American cases similarly strictly construe the doctrine of commercial impracticability. . . .

. . . .

Gulf's argument on commercial impracticability has two strings to its bow. First, Gulf contends that the escalator indicator does not work as intended by the parties by reason of the advent of so-called "two-tier" pricing under Phase IV government price controls. Second, Gulf alleges that crude oil prices have risen substantially without a concomitant rise in the escalation indicator, and, as a result, that performance of the contract has become commercially impracticable.

The short and dispositive answer to Gulf's first argument under U.C.C. § 2–615, that the price escalation indicator (posting in *Platt's Oilgram Crude Oil Supplement*) no longer reflects the intent of the parties by reason of the so-called "two-tier" pricing structure, is that the language of the contract is clear and unambiguous. The contract does not require interpretation and requires no excursion into the subjective intention of the parties. The intent of the parties is clear from the four corners of the contract; they intended to be bound by the specified entries in *Platt's*, which has been published at all times material here, which is published today, and which prints the contract reference prices. Prices under the contract can be and still are calculated by reference to Platt's publication.

It should be noted that *Platt's Oilgram Crude Oil Supplement* states on its face that its postings since the advent of "two-tier" are basically comparable to the postings historically quoted in *Platt's*, and that postings listed in *Platt's* were price controlled at the time of negotiation and execution of the contract, just as they are today and have been at all times in between. . . .

. . . .

With regard to Gulf's contention that the contract has become "commercially impracticable" within the meaning of U.C.C. § 2–615, because of the increase in market price of foreign crude oil and certain domestic crude oils, the court finds that the tendered defense has not been proved.

. . . .

No such hardship has been established. On the contrary, the record clearly establishes that 1973, the year in which the energy crises began, was Gulf's best year ever, in which it recorded some $800 million in net profits after taxes. Gulf's 1974 year was more than 25% better than 1973's record; $1,065,000,000 profits were booked by Gulf in 1974 after paying all taxes.

[Gulf stipulated in the parties' pretrial stipulation that it had the capability to perform the contract.]

. . . .

For the foregoing reasons, Gulf's claim of hardship giving rise to "commercial impracticability" fails.

But even if Gulf had established great hardship under U.C.C. § 2–615, which it has not, Gulf would not prevail because the events associated with the so-called energy crises were reasonably foreseeable at the time the contract was executed.

If a contingency is foreseeable, it and its consequences are taken outside the scope of U.C.C. § 2–615, because the party disadvantaged by fruition of the contingency might have protected himself in his contract.

Frustration of Purpose

The infrequently applied doctrine of *frustration of purpose* supports a discharge even if performance is technically possible. In the few cases where it has been upheld, the purpose of the agreement was well known to the contracting parties and was of dominant importance. For example, a man rented a room in a private residence for three hours on a particular day expecting to see the King of England pass by in his royal coach on the way to his coronation. When the coronation was postponed, the lessee sought the return of the prepaid rent; the landlord insisted the lessee could still use the room for three hours on the chosen day and that there was no impossibility of performance. The court awarded judgment to the lessee because the purpose of the agreement, known to the parties, was frustrated by the failure to crown the King on the chosen date. These stringent requirements of frustration have been relaxed to a minor extent in several jurisdictions over the past several years. On balance, this concept is interesting conceptually but of limited utility practically.

Failure to Pursue Remedies: Statute of Limitations

A party having a breach of contract claim may permit the claim to lie dormant for a long time, expecting the matter to take care of itself or expecting the breaching party to rectify his wrongdoing. In such situations, the aggrieved party permits time to work against his interests; if a cause of action is not brought within the time fixed by statute, the breaching party may assert, in his own defense, that his contractual obligations are discharged through operations of the statute of limitations. (The policy underlying the statute of limitations and the procedure for asserting it were discussed in Chapter 2.)

It should be noted that where several payments or debts are involved, the statute of limitations does not necessarily bar all recovery. When some but not all debts are beyond the statutory period and there is no special designation of payments, the creditor may apply the amount paid to that part of the debt barred by the statute.

Characteristically, the time period within which action must be brought begins at the time of breach. Thus, in a suit for nonpayment of goods, the statute starts running at the time payment is due.

Waiver of Breach

A party may, by behavior or contract, bar himself from otherwise available contract remedies. For example, a party who sues another for breach of contract but is himself in substantial breach, is barred from recovery until his breach is cured. Additionally, a party may, by words or conduct, waive his rights to recover, either by releasing another from his contract obligations or by contractually promising to refrain from suing for breach of a previous contract. By discharging another, the party prevents himself from recovering damages for breach of contract. Discharge, as was discussed earlier, short circuits the availability of remedies.

BREACH OF CONTRACT

We have seen how the contract provides the offeror and offeree with affirmative duties and how the party failing to adhere to these duties commits a breach. In simple terms, A and B contract for A to sell goods to B. When B arrives at the designated place, A refuses to sell him the goods. If A does so without legal cause, he breaches the contract; B has a remedy at law to satisfy any injury he sustains. It goes without saying that most contracts do not reach this stage. In most commercial arrangements, the parties conform to the expectations of one another and fulfill the contract's provisions. Yet, breaches do occur, and therefore a legal remedy is required.

Partial Breach

The breach may be total or partial depending upon the circumstances of the case. Where a *partial breach* occurs, the injured party may seek compensation for his injury, but cannot stop his own performance or regard the breach as total. In the sections dealt with earlier, we noted how the breach of one installment in an installment contract does not terminate the entire transaction. Only the duty to pay for the undelivered goods is terminated by the partial breach.

Total Breach

A material, or *total breach*, is required before the aggrieved party can terminate the agreement; this breach involves a contractual duty that is so important that it justifies a refusal to continue the agreement. Material breaches occur in numerous circumstances, such as the failure to perform a substantial obligation, the prevention of a party from rendering a substantial obligation, or a repudiation of the agreement by one of the parties. Several breach of contract categories are discussed below.

Repudiation

The easiest form of breach to conceptualize is simple *repudiation* of the agreement, in which a party refuses to conform to the requirements of his contract.

Repudiation can be direct or indirect. For instance, if C agrees to sell his automobile to A but conveys it to B, he has repudiated his agreement with A and has breached his agreement. It was not necessary for him to do so explicitly — his action of selling the automobile to B when he was under a contractual duty to sell it to A constitutes a repudiation of the agreement. The party injured receives two rights as a result of the repudiation: he is discharged from his contractual obligations and can sue for breach of the agreement.

Anticipatory Breach

In some situations, particularly in commercial settings, repudiation occurs before the time of performance. Until early in this century, the courts held that this type of early repudiation, called *anticipatory breach* of contract, did not give the offended party an immediate cause of action. To put it simply, if goods were due on March 1 and the seller notified the buyer before March 1 of his plan not to deliver, the courts were concerned that if the buyer were permitted to assert the breach on, say, February 1, he would obtain greater rights than he bargained for. The logic in this position is virtually unassailable, and yet its reasonableness is not altogether certain. Both the seller and buyer benefit if the buyer is able to accept the breach and seek performance from a third party for the original date. The buyer meets his needs, and the seller's liability is lessened. In many situations, the buyer might avoid loss altogether and thereby eliminate the necessity of a suit. In short, the early doctrine of anticipatory breach — not recognizing the injured party's rights until the date performance was due — made little sense. Emphasizing the desire to minimize economic waste, the courts have gradually modified their attitude. In many situations, notably the UCC's treatment of the sale of goods, a more practical attitude to remedies has resulted in a reduction in the loss suffered by the contracting parties.

Under present law, most courts permit an anticipatory breach to create an immediate cause of action. The party injured by an anticipatory breach can accept the breach immediately by bringing legal action or by attempting to remedy the situation by covering his loss. The breaching party may withdraw the anticipatory breach (cure the breach), however, if the aggrieved party has not relied upon the breach.

Failure to Conform to the Contract

Thus far we have discussed breach of contract by repudiation. A substantial number of breaches occur, however, through wrongful performance of an agreement. Here a party may ship nonconforming goods or may construct a house that cannot be certified as suitable for occupancy or may perform services that do not accord with the provisions of the contract. The aggrieved persons have a cause of action for breach of contract. Again, the requirements for a breach of contract require wrongs that go to the substance of the agreement, and the party committing the breach must default on an obligation that has come due.

Not all nonconforming tenders involve breach of contract. If the seller delivers nonconforming goods before the time peformance is due and the buyer rejects the goods, then the seller still has the opportunity to cure the defect and deliver conforming goods in accordance with the requirements of the agreement.

REMEDIES

The Function of Contract Remedies

The usual remedies in the law of contracts restore the aggrieved party to the position he occupied before the breach. Damages compensate the victim for actual loss; they do not provide a windfall. They are usually designated as *compensatory damages*, and they form the bulk of judicially awarded damage remedies. And when the parties provide for arbitration, as they frequently do, the damages stipulated in the arbitration agreement are also considered compensatory damages. Computing the actual loss is sometimes difficult, however, as the following case illustrates.

J. M. Rodriques & Co., Inc. v. Moore-McCormack Lines
New York State Supreme Court, Appellate Division, 1972. 38 App. Div.2d 341
MURPHY, J.

The sole issue involved on this submission of controversy pursuant to CPLR 3222 is the correct measure of damages to be applied in connection with plaintiff's conceded loss.

Plaintiff is the bona-fide purchaser of a clean "on board" bill of lading for 200 sacks of cloves received by defendant, a common carrier, for shipment to plaintiff at New York.

Defendant's vessel, the SS. Mormacpenn, which received the goods on Oct. 30, 1968, docked at New York on or about Dec. 20, 1968, but was unable to discharge any of its cargo because of an east-coast longshoremen's strike. The strike ended on or about Feb. 15, 1969; defendant's vessel discharged its cargo between said date and Feb. 21, 1969; but the goods in issue could not be located and defendant failed to make delivery.

It is conceded that the sound market value of the shipment of cloves at New York was $19,980 on Dec. 19, 1968, and $41,070 on the date the strike ended. Accordingly, plaintiff is entitled to judgment for one or the other of these amounts.

The general rule of damages for failure to deliver cargo has been stated to be their market value as of the date when it should have been delivered and as of the date it should have arrived. It would appear, however, that no distinction was intended since "(n)ormally, goods are delivered within a reasonable time after the ship docks."

. . . .

In order to complete its contract, by effecting delivery, the carrier was required to discharge its cargo to a fit and safe place on a pier or wharf, furnish notice to the consignee of its availability and afford the consignee a reasonable opportunity to take the goods away.

Since plaintiff's cause of action accrued, and the period of limitation began to run, from the date the goods should have been delivered, it follows that the measure of damages must also be applied as of that date. Moreover, it is only by computing the damages as of such later date, when the loss was apparently first discovered, that the plaintiff-consignee can be made whole.

Accordingly, unless the interposition of the strike mandates a different result, the measure of damages must be computed as of Feb. 15, 1969, the date the strike ended and the goods should have been delivered.

In such connection, the Carriage of Goods by Sea Act (46 U.S. C. sec. 1304) provides in pertinent part:

"(2) Neither the carrier nor the ship shall be responsible for loss, or damage arising or resulting from — . . .

"(j) Strikes or lockouts or stoppage or restraint of labor from whatever cause, whether partial or general. . . ."

We read the statute, however, as merely suspending the carrier's obligation to perform its contract. Defendant was required to deliver the goods when it was able to and the strike merely extended such delivery date for both parties. The ship, in effect, arrived at the dock when the strike was over. Plaintiff's damage, however, resulted from defendant's unexplained non-delivery and not because delivery was prevented by the strike.

In the light of the foregoing, we direct that judgment be entered for plaintiff in the sum of $41,070, with interest, costs and disbursements.

Settle order.

All concur except Capozzoli, J., who dissents in a dissenting opinion.

Capozzoli, J. (dissenting memo).

The threshold question which must be answered, in deciding the damage to be awarded herein, is when did the breach of the carriage contract take place? It is as of that time that the damages should be fixed. The proper measure of damages is the market value of the cloves at destination on the date when they should have arrived. Whether the cloves were lost before the ship arrived, or thereafter, is immaterial. The fact is that, in the absence of a strike, the truth would have been known and, if there was failure to deliver the cloves to the consignee, then the carrier would have been responsible in damages for the value thereof, as of that time.

Accordingly, damages should be fixed at $19,980.

Nominal Damages

Nominal damages are awarded when a party sustains an injury, but the injury carries no dollar loss. For example, A and B enter into an agreement for the sale of a used car for $400; when A refuses to accept the car as required by the contract, B sells it to C for $500 and suffers no other loss. In such a circumstance, B's recovery of additional money from A would not compensate him but would reward him. Historically, at common law, B would recover nothing. Today the only damages possibly payable to B would be some nominal amount specified by statute.

In commercial cases suits for nominal damages are infrequent. Parties do not usually litigate for limited economic gain. The breaching party, however, may have made a down payment on the transaction, and the nominal damages accruing to the seller may permit him to retain all or a portion of this payment. In this situation the reward of nominal damages can be important. The UCC (§ 2-718) obligates a breaching buyer for either the liquidated damages (see page 237) or the smaller of $500 or 20 percent of the value of total performance.

Punitive Damages

Another damage remedy, again not usual to commercial situations, is *punitive damages*. These damages are awarded for malicious, wanton, or wrongful conduct intentionally performed by the breaching party, for which a court awards damages as a form of punishment. Since the amount of the award should be such as to pursuade the breaching party not to commit similar acts in the future, the award for an identical breach could be larger against a wealthy defendant than against a poor defendant. Although punitive damages are unusual in commercial and contract cases, the amounts involved can occasionally be stunning. In a February 1978 decision where the safety of fuel tanks on Ford Pintos were at issue, a Southern California jury awarded $127.8 million in total damages, of which $125 million were punitive. The trial judge reduced the total award to $6.6 million, of which $3.5 million were punitive. The decision was affirmed on appeal. *Grimshaw* v. *Ford Motor Co.*, 174 Cal. Rep. 348 (Ct. App., 1981).

Compensatory Damages

As noted before, compensatory damages form the bulk of the damage remedies available under the law of contracts. Their objective is to make the party whole with a cash award. However, not all actual losses are recoverable. The courts long ago tied contract damages to the reasonable expectations of the parties.

Incidental or Direct Damages

Incidental or *direct damages*, also sometimes called *general damages*, constitute one of the two subdivisions of compensatory damages. They are such as follow immediately, normally, or necessarily from the act done.

Special or Consequential Damages: The Reasonably Foreseeable Test

If the breaching party knows, or should have known, that his breach would cause greater damage than the damage ordinarily expected in similar situations, the courts then hold him liable for a particular kind of compensatory damage usually referred to as *special* or *consequential damages*. Nevertheless, these damages are recoverable only where they were reasonably foreseeable by the breaching party.

Traylor v. Henkels & McCoy, Inc.
Supreme Court of Idaho, 1978. 99 Id. 560, 585 P.2d 970

[This is an appeal from a judgment in favor of Traylor in the amount of $103,171.14. The original suit sought damages for nonpayment of construction work performed by Traylor and for consequential damages to his business caused by that nonpayment. Traylor performed excavating work for Henkels & McCoy under a contract which contained a "rock clause" providing that the contract did not include the cost of moving any hard rock. When rock was encountered during the excavation, Traylor agreed to remove it at a price to be agreed upon later. After the excavation, including the hard rock, but before the cleanup work was completed, Henkels & McCoy removed Traylor from the job. Traylor sought damages of $39,963.22, equal to amounts due for the rock work, other extras and the unpaid balance on the original contract. He also sought additional damages due to the subsequent forced liquidation of his business. On appeal Henkels & McCoy contends the verdict is excessive to the extent it exceeds $39,963.22.]

SHEPARD, CHIEF JUSTICE.

Idaho is in accord with the orthodox rule that contract damages are recoverable only for the direct consequence of a breach in absence of a special agreement to the contrary. The rule was stated in Hadley v. Baxendale in the following manner:

"Where two parties have made a contract which one of them has broken, the damages which the other party ought to receive in respect of such breach of contract should be such as may fairly and reasonably be considered either arising naturally, i. e., according to the usual course of things, from such breach of contract itself, or such as may reasonably be supposed to have been in the contemplation of both parties, at the time they made the contract, as the probable result of the breach of it. Now, if the special circumstances under which the contract was actually made were communicated by the plaintiffs to the defendants, and thus known to both parties, the damages resulting from the breach of such a contract, which they would reasonably contemplate, would be the amount of injury which would ordinarily follow from a breach of contract under these special circumstances so known and communicated. But, on the other hand, if these special circumstances were wholly unknown to the party breaking the contract, he, at the most, could only be supposed to have had in his contemplation the amount of injury which would arise generally, and in the great multitude of cases not affected by any special circumstances, from such a breach of contract. For, had the special circumstances been known, the parties might have specially provided for the breach of contract by special terms as to the damages in that case, and of this advantage it would be very unjust to deprive them. . . ."

It is clear in the instant case that the damages sought by Traylor in excess of $39,963.22 are not such as may be expected to ordinarily result from the breach of a contract to excavate a trench. Henkels & McCoy might, however, be liable if, according to the second principle set forth in *Hadley* v. *Baxendale,* those damages were "in the contemplation of both parties, at the time they made the contract, as the probable result of the breach of it." Traylor does not seriously contend that those damages were in contemplation of the parties at the time they made the basic contract and we deem it to be a somewhat remote possibility that Henkels & McCoy would enter a contract conditioned upon its acceptance of liability for the liquidation of Traylor's business in the event of breach by Henkels & McCoy. Traylor also concedes that no contract arose from the agreement that Traylor would do the rock work. The parties at the time of the agreement to do the rock work left to later negotiations the question of compensation due to Traylor for the work. Such an agreement was never reached. In the absence of an agreement between the parties regarding the amount to be paid to Traylor, there was failure to agree on an essential term of the contract. Such an agreement is too indefinite to enforce. Traylor is not, however, without a remedy since he is entitled to recover the reasonable value of the work he performed at Henkels & McCoy's request.

Traylor rests his claim for consequential damages on the assertion that Henkels & McCoy had agreed to take responsibility for the financial stability of the business at the time of the modification of the basic contract. The parties are, of course, free to modify a contract. If the parties contemplated liability for special damages (for allegedly forcing the liquidation of Traylor's business) at the time the contract was modified, then the defaulting party must accept the consequences of that agreement. Traylor contends that there was a series of contract modifications regarding extras and that at some point Henkels & McCoy agreed with him for the performance of the extras, knowing full well that Traylor was depending upon the payment therefor in order to remain in business. The record does not sustain that contention.

We hold that the jury was not sufficiently instructed on the damages issue. If the jury were to allow Traylor's claim for damages to his business, the jury had to find that at the time Traylor agreed with Henkels & McCoy for the performance of extra work it was in the contemplation of *both* parties that if Henkels & McCoy breached its obligation to pay, it was foreseeable that Traylor would lose his business and have to sell his equipment. This is in accord with the general rule in contract cases that an award of damages for injury to the business can only be sustained if the jury finds that such harm was contemplated at the time the contract was formed as a foreseeable result of its breach. While one instruction of the court did state that recoverable damages must have been in the contemplation of the parties at the time the contract was formed, two previous instructions did not suggest that such a finding was necessary as to Traylor's claim for damages caused to his business. We conclude that the trial court improperly instructed the jury on the damages recoverable for injury to business.

It appears clear that the jury could have awarded damages due for the rock work, the extras and on the basic contract for $39,963.22, but that amount is exceeded in the jury's verdict by some $63,207.92. That amount could only have been awarded to compensate Traylor for the injury to and loss of his business and loss of future profits. The cause must therefore be reversed. The cause is reversed and remanded to the trial court for the entry of a remittitur reducing the judgment to the sum of $39,963.22, and if said remittitur is not accepted by the plaintiff-respondent J. B. Traylor, dba Traylor Construction Co., that a new trial be granted on the question of damages. Costs to appellant.

The Reasonable Certainty Test

In the following case the rule of reasonable certainty as applied to the determination of damages is discussed and applied.

Macke Co. v. Pizza of Gaithersburg, Inc.

Court of Appeals of Maryland, 1970. 259 Md. 479, 270 A.2d 675

[The earlier portion of this opinion is found in the material on third party rights in Chapter 10, pages 196–97.]

The assessment of damages for loss of profits following the breach of an executory contract has been a relatively recent development. Under the concept of "foreseeability" enunciated by *Hadley* v. *Baxendale,* which was followed in *United States Telegraph Co.* v. *Gildersleeve* (1868), in order to recover unrealized profits a plaintiff had to show that the breach of contract caused the loss and that the loss of profits was in the contemplation of the parties and the probable result of a breach. Some of the early American cases superimposed a test of certainty on the concept of foreseeability.

In the last hundred years, however, courts have modified the rule that anticipated profits were not an element of damages because of their inherent uncertainty, and have turned from the requirement of "certainty" to a more flexible test of "reasonably certainty."

This court, . . . said

"Courts have modified the 'certainty' rule into a more flexible one of 'reasonable certainty.' In such circumstances, recovery may often be based on opinion evidence, in the legal sense of that term, from which liberal inferences may be drawn. Generally, proof of actual or even estimated costs is all that is required with certainty.

"Some of the modifications which have been aimed at avoiding the harsh requirements of the 'certainty' rule include: (a) if the fact of damage is proven with certainty, the extent or the amount thereof may be left to reasonable inference; (b) where a defendant's wrong has caused the difficulty of proving damage, he cannot complain of the resulting uncertainty; (c) mere difficulty in ascertaining the amount of damage is not fatal; (d) mathematical precision in fixing the exact amount is not required; (e) it is sufficient if the best evidence of the damage which is available is produced; and (f) the plaintiff is entitled to recover the value of his contract as measured by the value of his profits."

To recover direct profits in a case such as this, the measure of damages is the difference between what it would have cost Macke to perform and what it would have received had the Pizza Shops not repudiated.

We can understand why the court below was "not satisfied that the claim for damages (was) shown with reasonable certainty, since it (was) based upon conjecture." Macke attempted to prove damages by the testimony of two witnesses. The first was Arnold Harlem, the general manager of Macke's Chesapeake area, in which the Pizza Shops were located. His testimony related to gross sales figures for the cold drink vending machines at the six locations for the month of January, 1968, when the machines were still under Macke's control. . . .

. . . .

Macke then called Thomas S. Sherwood, one of the individual defendants, as an adverse witness. He testified, without objection, to the commissions received by five of the Pizza Shops during the calendar year 1967, and by the sixth shop, at Gaithersburg, for the last five months of that year. Based on this testimony, Macke's counsel prepared, and submitted to the court, a "Memorandum of Damages Claimed," an extrapolation of 1967 figures intended to show profits lost in 1968.

The fact that the projection from Harlem's testimony showed lost profits of $5,286.80, and the extrapolation from Sherwood's testimony showed lost profits of $9,047.00 was surely enough to give the lower court pause. . . .

There is ample authority for the proposition that loss of profits may be projected from past performance, assuming, of course, that past performance has continued long enough to be the best evidence of damage which is available.

We cannot agree with the lower court's conclusion that the claim for damages could not be shown with reasonable certainty because it was based on conjecture. For this reason, we propose to remand the case in order that damages may properly be assessed. On remand, the court may wish to take several factors into consideration. First, it seems clear to us that no damages should be allowed with respect to the repudiation of the agreement covering the vending machine at 16523 North Frederick Road, Gaithersburg. The uncontroverted testimony of the Pizza Shop's manager established that the agreement covering this machine was breached in January, 1968 by Macke's failure to stock and service the machine.

Then, too, the record is deficient as regards Macke's duty to mitigate damages. Harlem's testimony as to what disposition was made of the vending machines removed from the Pizza Shops was vague and inconclusive. It may well be that the machines were placed at other locations prior to the time when the agreements would have expired by their terms, and this, of course, may have to be taken into account in assessing damages, subject, however, to the limitation that gains made by Macke could not have been made, save for the breach.

Finally, it is not an implausible inference that Macke's machines were replaced in the Pizza Shops by comparable machines provided by another concern. If this is the case, a more appropriate measure of damages might be that grounded on the five Pizza Shops' actual experience for the period February through December 1968, rather than one based on extrapolating profits from the results experienced in the year 1967 or in January 1968, particularly in the light of testimony that the seating capacity of one or more of the shops may have been altered in 1967 and the conflicting testimony as to whether cold drink sales remain constant in pizza shops. Authority for the use of a defendant's future earnings as an appropriate method of determining lost profits may be found in [several cases]. . . .

Judgment reversed as to liability; judgment entered for appellant for costs, on appeal and below; case remanded for a new trial on the question of damages.

In some states the formula for damage remedies varies. As noted before, whether a state adopts a formula awarding the benefit of the bargain or whether it compensates for out of pocket losses is a matter of some importance. In the main, however, damages might be calculated variously depending upon the injuries sustained. For breach of contract for the sale of goods, damages are calculated on the replacement cost of goods, the lost profit, or the resale cost of the goods, depending on who breaches, the character of the goods sold, and the character of the breach. These questions are more particularly dealt with in Part V, covering the sale of goods.

If a party breaches a service contract, then the aggrieved party can hire a replacement and sue for the difference in salary. When a servant is fired wrongfully, but gets comparable employment elsewhere, he sues for the difference between what he now earns and what he would have earned under the agreement.

Mitigation of Damages

The doctrine of *mitigation of damages* is the basis of most damage theories in the law, with a significant exception to be discussed later. It imposes a general duty on persons suffering from breach to minimize the impact or effect of that breach. Thus, when a person is unjustly fired from his job, he is required to look for a commensurate job and, thereby, reduce his economic loss.

The courts have held that the duty to mitigate damages does not require a person to find a job unlike the job he held under the contract. Thus, a wrongfully fired college professor does not have to mitigate his damages by finding a job as a gardener. In addition, if he diligently searches for a professorial position, but is unable to find one and must take a gardener's job, then the courts have held the salary paid to him as a gardener is not considered in calculating his damages.

In the following case, the defendant contends that the plaintiff failed to minimize damages.

Schafer v. Sunset Packing Co.
Supreme Court of Oregon, 1970. 256 Or. 539, 474 P.2d 529

HOWELL, JUSTICE.
Plaintiff, a berry grower, filed an action for damages against the defendant for breach of contract for failure to provide workers to harvest plaintiff's berry crop for 1967. The case was tried before the court without a jury and a judgment entered against defendant for $17,880.

On April 7, 1967, the defendant, a processor of fruit and berries, contracted to purchase at least a portion of plaintiff's berry crop and to provide 150 to 200 laborers to harvest the crop from June 1, 1967, to the end of the season. A recruiting fee of $15 per laborer was to be paid by plaintiff to defendant, and the plaintiff gave defendant a check for $2000 as a payment on the contract. . . . On May 29, two days before the workers were due to arrive, the defendant notified plaintiff of difficulty in securing the workers. On June 7 the defendant offered the services of 100 pickers from the defendant's own labor camp, but . . . plaintiff would have to pay an additional $20 per ton for the picking, and the pickers could be used only as long as defendant had no need for them. Plaintiff rejected the offer and began hiring some workers from his neighbors. . . .

. . . .
. . . The defendant contends that the court erred in awarding damages when the evidence showed that plaintiff made no effort to minimize his damages.

. . . .
A few days before June 1, when the defendant was to deliver the pickers, it advised plaintiff of the difficulty it was having in securing pickers, but that other pickers were expected to leave Texas on June 2 and Phoenix, Arizona, on June 6. On June 8 plaintiff was advised that the pickers were on the way. The facts disclose that plaintiff could have hired pickers on the first of June, but that he did not want to fill his camps because of the assured arrival of pickers by defendant. When the defendant's pickers did not arrive, plaintiff called the employment office, advertised on the radio and solicited help from other growers who might have pickers available. He finally used what pickers were available in the neighborhood.

We conclude that the plaintiff exercised reasonable efforts and business prudence to minimize defendant's failure to provide the pickers.

However, the defendant criticizes the plaintiff for rejecting the defendant's offer of 100 pickers from its own camp and another offer from defendant of four busloads of children to pick plaintiff's berries. We have mentioned the conditions the defendant attached to its offer to supply 100 pickers from its own camp. The offer of the four busloads of children was conditioned also on plaintiff paying an extra $35 per day for each of four platoon leaders and 35 cents per mile for the buses, in addition to the picking charges. Apparently the defendant feels that the plaintiff was obliged to accept the offer regardless of the extra charges. . . .

. . . .

We conclude that plaintiff's damages were established with reasonable certainty and that the judgment of the trial court is supported by substantial evidence.

Affirmed.

Remedies and Real Property

In agreements for the sale or lease of real property, the injured party may sue for money damages, the most usual remedy in the law. Yet, certain aspects of real property damages vary from the more conventional remedies already mentioned.

The first of these variations concerns the duty to mitigate damages. Many states do not impose this obligation in real estate transactions. In those states a landlord is not required to mitigate his loss by securing another tenant if the tenant wrongfully vacates the apartment. He can keep the premises vacant and sue for the rental payments as they become due. This peculiar remedy rule is one more example of the special position occupied by real property under the law. Other unique standards involve the rules of offer and acceptance and the statutory requirements of a writing. Some states have changed the common law rule either by statute or judicial decision and now require the landlord to make a good faith effort to relet the premises, entitling the landlord to expenses resulting from the tenant's breach and from reletting.

Specific Performance

Specific performance is an equitable remedy that did not develop in the common law courts. Instead, it came from the courts of equity and was introduced to handle those situations that were not capable of conventional legal redress in the form of money damages.

The remedy of *specific performance* compels a party to live up to the terms of that agreement. Simply put, when a contract provides for the sale of a house and the seller refuses to deliver the house in accordance with the terms of the agreement, the doctrine of specific performance requires the seller to deliver the house. The purchaser may decide to sue for the dollar amount of his loss, but he can also ask the court to deliver the particular item to him. The remedy is ordinarily highly irregular because the courts usually do not enter into the direct relationship of the buyer and seller and demand a particular satisfaction. The courts entertain such remedies where the subject matter is a unique form of property, that is, when a recovery in dollars would not adequately compensate an aggrieved purchaser who had the old family homestead or a particular Picasso painting in mind when he undertook the contract.

The remedy of specific performance, then, would not be appropriate in most circumstances. For instance, if a nationally known Brand X washing machine is purchased from a local store and the store breaches the agreement by failing to deliver the machine, the customer can find another Brand X machine elsewhere. Money damages would adequately restore the purchaser to his precontract position.

Liquidated Damages

Thus far we have dealt with remedies that are determined by the jury and that restore the parties to their precontract positions or that compensate them for the loss sustained under the agreement. One important remedy, however, has little to do with a judicial determination. The *liquidated damage* remedy is the remedy the parties provide in their contract in a clause that establishes the liabilities of the parties before the actual breach occurs; the determination of damages is not decided in prolonged litigation. The parties simply insert a clause in their agreement indicating how much the injury sustained is worth if a breach of the agreement occurs.

The clause may be simply inserted, but the courts will not consider it casually. The courts have been quite firm in preventing liquidated damage clauses from serving as a penalty that results in a windfall to the injured party. If anything indicates the clause was intended as a penalty or operates as a penalty, then the court will disregard the liquidated damage clause, and the parties will have to rely upon the traditional damage remedies.

Thus, as a practical measure, when liquidated damage terms are inserted in agreements, the parties should deal with the notion of compensation for loss and not with the hope of a windfall. They should attempt to estimate the loss and not attempt to reward themselves by the misfortunes of the breaching party. A fair calculation of the damages when the contract is formed, of course, might not correspond to the damages actually sustained, which has been the source of some difficulty for the courts. For example, a business building is constructed with the builder undertaking completion by January 1. At the making of the contract, the builder agrees to pay the owner $500 for each week the construction continues after January 1, an amount representing the profit that could reasonably be expected from the operation of the building at a rate of $4.50 per square foot and with a projected occupancy of 75 percent. The price of office space, however, might climb to $5.00 per square foot, and the occupancy rate in that area might grow to 90 percent. In these circumstances, the damage estimate would be low. The occupancy rate, however, might drop to 40 percent and the rental rate to $4.00 per square foot, in which case the damage estimate would be high. There is, in short, no way to predict the actual damages with certainty. The more enlightened jurisdictions require only a reasonable and prospective estimate of the loss in the liquidated damage clause. In other jurisdictions, the liquidated damage clause must be reasonable in light of the actual damages sustained. Thus, the loss must approximate the injury resulting from the breach.

Special Remedies in the Law of Sales

The law of sales has developed a number of advanced forms of contract remedies that essentially provide flexibility for merchants who have a heavy volume of business and offer the most commercially feasible method of keeping the string of this trade unbroken. These remedies are treated extensively in Part V on the sale of goods.

Other Remedies

The recent and famous "palimony" case, which follows, involves conventional contract concepts argued in an unconventional human and economic setting. Of particular interest is the California Supreme Court's comment on the judiciary's power and responsibility to fashion new equitable remedies when conventional contract remedies are inadequate. The case's implicit reminder to look to the substance of a matter and not be distracted by its form and glitter is also an appropriate theme for our last contracts case.

Marvin v. Marvin
Supreme Court of California, 1976. 134 Cal.Rptr. 815, 557 P.2d 106

TOBRINER, JUSTICE.
During the past 15 years, there has been a substantial increase in the number of couples living together without marrying. Such nonmarital relationships lead to legal controversy when one partner dies or the couple separates. Courts of Appeal, faced with the task of determining property rights in such cases, have arrived at conflicting positions. . . . We take this opportunity to resolve that controversy and to declare the principles which should govern distribution of property acquired in a nonmarital relationship.

    . . . .

1. The Factual Setting of This Appeal.
Since the trial court rendered judgment for defendant [Lee Marvin] on the pleadings, we must accept the allegations of plaintiff's complaint as true, determining whether such allegations state, or can be amended to state, a cause of action. We turn therefore to the specific allegations of the complaint.

Plaintiff [Michelle Marvin — plaintiff acquired the name Marvin by a legal name change, not by marriage.] avers that in October of 1964 she and defendant "entered into an oral agreement" that while "the parties lived together they would combine their efforts and earnings and would share equally any and all property accumulated as a result of their efforts whether individual or combined." Furthermore, they agreed to "hold themselves out to the general public as husband and wife" and that "plaintiff would further render her services as a companion, homemaker, housekeeper and cook to . . . defendant."

Shortly thereafter plaintiff agreed to "give up her lucrative career as an entertainer [and] singer" in order to "devote her full time to defendant . . . as a companion, homemaker, housekeeper and cook"; in return defendant agreed to "provide for all of plaintiff's financial support and needs for the rest of her life."

Plaintiff alleges that she lived with defendant from October of 1964 through May of 1970 and fulfilled her obligations under the agreement. During this period the parties as a result of their efforts and earnings acquired in defendant's name substantial real and personal property, including motion picture rights worth over $1 million. In May of 1970, however, defendant compelled plaintiff to leave his household. He continued to support plaintiff until November of 1971, but thereafter refused to provide further support.

. . . .

2. Plaintiff's Complaint States a Cause of Action for Breach of an Express Contract.

. . . .

In summary, we base our opinion on the principle that adults who voluntarily live together and engage in sexual relations are nonetheless as competent as any other persons to contract respecting their earnings and property rights. Of course, they cannot lawfully contract to pay for the performance of sexual services, for such a contract is, in essence, an agreement for prostitution and unlawful for that reason. But they may agree to pool their earnings and to hold all property acquired during the relationship in accord with the law governing community property; conversely they may agree that each partner's earnings and the property acquired from those earnings remains the separate property of the earning partner.[1] So long as the agreement does not rest upon illicit meretricious consideration, the parties may order their economic affairs as they choose, and no policy precludes the courts from enforcing such agreements.

. . . .

3. Plaintiff's Complaint Can Be Amended to State a Cause of Action Founded Upon Theories of Implied Contract or Equitable Relief.

. . . .

We conclude that the judicial barriers that may stand in the way of a policy based upon the fulfillment of the reasonable expectations of the parties to a nonmarital relationship should be removed. As we have explained, the courts now hold that express agreements will be enforced unless they rest on an unlawful

---

1. A great variety of other arrangements are possible. The parties might keep their earnings and property separate, but agree to compensate one party for services which benefit the other. They may choose to pool only part of their earnings and property, to form a partnership or joint venture, or to hold property acquired as joint tenants or tenants in common, or agree to any other such arrangement. (See generally Weitzman, *Legal Regulation of Marriage: Tradition and Change* (1974) 62 Cal. L.Rev. 1169).

meretricious consideration. We add that in the absence of an express agreement, the courts may look to a variety of other remedies in order to protect the parties' lawful expectations.[2]

The courts may inquire into the conduct of the parties to determine whether that conduct demonstrates an implied contract or implied agreement of partnership or joint venture, or some other tacit understanding between the parties. The courts may, when appropriate, employ principles of constructive trust or resulting trust. Finally, a nonmarital partner may recover in quantum meruit for the reasonable value of household services rendered less the reasonable value of support received if he can show that he rendered services with the expectation of monetary reward.[3]

Since we have determined that plaintiff's complaint states a cause of action for breach of an express contract, and, as we have explained, can be amended to state a cause of action independent of allegations of express contract, we must conclude that the trial court erred in granting defendant a judgment on the pleadings.

The judgment is reversed and the cause remanded for further proceedings consistent with the views expressed herein.

WRIGHT, C. J., and McCOMB, MOSK, SULLIVAN and RICHARDSON, JJ., concur.

CLARK, Justice (concurring and dissenting).

On remand, Judge Marshall of the Los Angeles Superior Court reviewed the extensive testimony in *Marvin* v. *Marvin* and concluded that no express contract had been negotiated between the parties. He further concluded that no implied contract, partnership, joint venture, or other tacit understanding had been reached. The latter set of conclusions was based on such evidence as the following: no joint bank accounts were established; no real property was placed in joint tenancy or tenancy in common; the plaintiff used a separate account for her allowance of $400 per month, her earnings from a Hawaii engagement, and her settlement of a previous lawsuit; when the defendant bought real property, he placed it in his own name; their tax returns were separate. The court also noted that the plaintiff had resorted to unemployment insurance, that her return to a career as a singer was doubtful, and that the defendant owned property worth more than $1 million. Based on these facts and relying on the footnote renumbered as 3 in our edited version of the case, Judge Marshall awarded the plaintiff $104,000:

"... for rehabilitation purposes so that she may have the economic means to re-educate herself and to learn new, employable skills or to refurbish those utilized,

---

2. We do not seek to resurrect the doctrine of common law marriage, which was abolished in California by statute in 1895. Thus we do not hold that plaintiff and defendant were "married," nor do we extend to plaintiff the rights which the Family Law Act grants valid or putative spouses; we hold only that she has the same rights to enforce contracts and to assert her equitable interest in property acquired through her effort as does any other unmarried person.

3. Our opinion does not preclude the evolution of additional equitable remedies to protect the expectations of the parties to a nonmarital relationship in cases in which existing remedies prove inadequate; the suitability of such remedies may be determined in later cases in light of the factual setting in which they arise.

for example, during her most recent employment and so that she may return from her status as companion of a motion picture star to a separate, independent but perhaps more prosaic existence." ["*Marvin* v. *Marvin*", April 18, 1979, *Metropolitan News,* April 19, 1979, page 1.]

That part of the decision on remand awarding Ms. Marvin $104,000 for rehabilitation was reversed at the appellate level by a two-to-one vote in August 1981. Ms. Marvin appealed the reversal, and the case was once again before the California Supreme Court when this book went to press.

FINDING AN APPROPRIATE COURT

Thus far we have discussed the prospects of bringing a legal action for the redress of a wrong, but we omitted considering where the action should be brought and what law should be applied where several states have parties involved in the dispute or have contacts with the issues at hand. Citizens of New York and New Jersey could form a contract in Connecticut that provides for the shipment of goods manufactured in Maine, but warehoused in Vermont, with delivery through nine states, receipt in Illinois, and use in Indiana. Where an aggrieved party can sue, and what state's laws apply become important questions resolved by applying legal principles generally considered under the rubric of conflict of laws. (Chapter 2 on procedure contains a further discussion of this topic.)

There is an increasing tendency to permit the parties to sue in any number of states if some relationship between the parties or legal issues and that state exists. Legal claims may be pursued in the plaintiff's or defendant's state of domicile as well as the state where the injury occurred. Long-arm statutes have extended the jurisdictional claims of the courts of all the states.

The applicable law is the law of the state that has the most "significant contacts" with the claim. Thus, in the example above, if the meaning of the contract terms was disputed, then the law of Connecticut (where the contract was made) applies; if the delivery of the items was disputed, then the law of Illinois (where the delivery was to occur) applies; if the performance of the items was disputed, then the law of Indiana (where the goods were to be used) applies.

In addition to the state courts, some cases may also be brought in the federal courts under the rules of diversity of citizenship. The federal courts have jurisdiction over claims exceeding $10,000 if citizens of different states are involved. In such cases, the state law is followed by the federal courts.

PROBLEMS AND QUESTIONS

Pam Lipmann, a schoolteacher, was hired by the New York City Board of Education for a ten-month term at $500 per month. After school had gone on for two months, her little, red one-room school house — the last in the city — was destroyed in a tremendous fire. The board could not use her school house any longer, transferred the pupils to neighboring schools, and dismissed Lipmann without salary. She sued the board. Did she win?

2. Carter, a building contractor, entered into a written agreement with Adams, an owner of real property, whereby Carter agreed to build a store at a cost of $75,000 on Adams's property. Payments were to be made in installments, as the work progressed, with the work to be completed by December of 1972. In October of 1972, as the work was almost completed, a fire of undetermined origin completely destroyed the building. At that time payments totalling $60,000 had been made, and labor and materials had cost $62,000. Is Carter excused from completing the building? Who bears the loss of the partially completed building? Explain.

3. Midland Iron and Steel contracted to sell to the government of Italy 2,000 tons of steel to be used for nonstructure purposes. By the time 500 tons had been delivered, the United States government prohibited further shipments of all steel in the absence of a release to be obtained by the seller.

Releases of the kind needed were easily granted, and in fact Midland had obtained releases for steel of a similar kind sent to Canada. Midland made no attempt to secure the releases for the steel to be sent to Italy and because of the federal bar on such shipments, Midland failed to deliver the steel. The government of Italy sued for breach of contract. Decision for whom? Explain.

4. Bayer and Seymour entered into an agreement whereby Bayer agreed to purchase 100 bales of cotton to be shipped by Seymour by rail. Prior to the time for shipment, a national railroad strike occurred and Seymour was unable to ship per the contract. Although truck deliveries were available, Seymour decided to cancel the agreement on the grounds of impossibility. Is she permitted to do so? Explain.

5. Colombo Ice contracted to supply Barkley with her daily requirement of ice, needed to keep a large quantity of fish under refrigeration in her seafood restaurant; Colombo is aware of this need and also that other sources of ice and refrigeration are not available to Barkley. Colombo fails to deliver ice for three days running and Barkley loses $500 worth of fish as a result. Does she have a claim against Colombo for her loss? Explain.

6. Garner, a traveling salesman, bought an airplane ticket for a flight from New York to Cincinnati. At his request, he was scheduled for an evening flight. Because of an error at the ticket office he was not able to be seated as scheduled. His trip was delayed until the next morning and as a result he missed several appointments with customers and lost $500,000 in orders. He sued the airline for the loss he sustained as a result of their failure to fly him as scheduled. Has

the airline breached the contract? Assuming it has, would he be able to recover for the losses sustained? Explain.

7. Wilson, a contractor, agreed to build twenty houses for Avon Realty at various prices from various designs to be supplied by Avon. The contract called for full payment for each completed house to be made 30 days after the completion of each of the houses, and also provided for one house to be completed every four weeks. The total price specified in the contract was $500,000. After ten houses had been completed and $220,000 had been paid for 9 of the houses completed to date, and $10,000 worth of work had been done on the eleventh house, Wilson realized that he was operating at a loss, and walked off the job.

Avon hired a new contractor to complete the ten remaining houses at a cost of $275,000. Did Wilson commit a material breach of the contract? Is he able to recover the cost of the tenth house and the $10,000 expended on the eleventh? Does Avon have any damages? Explain.

8. On January 3, Coogan contracted to sell 3000 bushels of wheat to Clancy, delivery to be made on April 1. On March 1, Coogan notified Clancy that she could not make delivery in a month, and Clancy sued for breach of contract without waiting for the time of delivery. Could such a suit be maintained? Explain.

9. Cleary, a professor of modern languages at a prominent local university, was under a two-year contract calling for a salary of $15,000 per year. She was unjustifiably fired from her position at the college and received no salary. As a result of her being out of work, she booked passage for Europe on the very next day and took the two years off from teaching in order to study language and literature. When she returned, she sued the university for breach of contract, claiming $30,000. Decision for whom? Explain.

10. Chisolm and Beltz entered into an agreement whereby Chisolm agreed to restore and refinish antique furniture for Beltz in return for Beltz's promise to give a designated oil painting in payment. Chisolm did restore and refinish the furniture as promised, but Beltz advised him that the painting was no longer available since it had been sold to an innocent third party for value. Does Chisolm have a cause of action for breach of contract? May he recover the painting? Explain.

11. The Beetlebombs, a family of aerial artists, contracted with the Park-Miller Circus to perform for three months in the national tour of the circus during the coming year. After one month, the Beetlebombs repudiated the contract, refused to perform and signed a new agreement with the Clark Brothers Circus, a major competitor of Park-Miller.

Would Park-Miller be able to compel the Beetlebombs to refrain from performing their contract with Clark Brothers? Would they be able to compel them to perform on the national tour? Explain.

12. Morris, who owns 35 percent of the Elm Corporation, agreed to purchase an added 16 percent interest in the corporation from Vacanti, thereby giving him control. The agreed upon price was fair and satisfactory from the standpoint of the parties but Vacanti refused to conclude the transaction and deliver the stock. Would Morris be able to compel Vacanti to perform the contract? Explain.

13. In March, Cowles entered into a contract to build a cabin cruiser of certain specifications for Globe. The agreed upon price was $90,000 payable in installments, with the last installment of 25 percent upon completion. The contract provided that the boat was to be completed by August 1, and if not completed by that time there would be a charge of $100 per day for each day of delay. Discuss the validity of the damage clause.

IV

SALE OF GOODS

POTENTIAL PROBLEMS

In Part V we shall discuss the legal rules governing the distribution of goods. This material is intellectually challenging, and much of that challenge arises from the astonishing variety and volume of sales transactions generated by the American economy. Every day millions of items ranging from aspirin to airplanes are bought and sold. The sale may be for cash on the line, or payment may be postponed with a credit card. Some parties will deal face to face across a grocery counter in Sand Gap, Kentucky, while others on Fifth Avenue will deal with Paris and London via communications satellite. A buyer may either take immediate possession of his newly purchased stereo or leave it with the seller with the understanding that the seller will deliver the goods to the buyer's home. The potential number of unique situations and their permutations — and problems — is staggering. These problems may be of several types: one party reneges on the deal, deadlines are missed due to strikes or tardy suppliers, goods are inherently defective, goods are lost or damaged by plane crashes and by acts of God such as hurricanes. Our task is to acquire an understanding of the legal rules adopted to catalog this multiplicity of transactions and ensure a high degree of predictability regarding the resolution of the problems created when things go wrong.

Surprisingly, things rarely do go wrong. Almost all sales take place without incident: the seller is immediately or eventually paid, and the buyer obtains possession and satisfaction with the performance of the purchased goods. On those occasions when things do go wrong, buyers and sellers generally work out the problems without resorting to their ultimate weapon — litigation — or even their intermediate weapon — the threat of litigation. These ad hoc resolutions more often than not have little or nothing to do with statutes and the decisions of judges. They are largely the product of such factors as a sense of fairness; an assessment that the other fellow is basically honest and not trying to put one

16

INTRO-
DUCTION
TO SALES

over; a special consideration shown a good customer; a reasonable desire to protect one's goodwill; a distaste for litigation, and finally, perhaps just inertia. These nonlegal factors are very important problem solvers.

Nevertheless, a small percentage of cases requires the articulation and assertion of hard core legal rights and duties. The prudent businessperson will not willingly place himself at the mercy of another person's sense of fairness. He prefers instead to structure his transaction so that he has the security and predictability associated with a position of legal strength. Where the sale of goods is involved, the source of this legal strength is Article 2 of the Uniform Commercial Code, hereinafter referred to as the Code or UCC.

THE UNIFORM COMMERCIAL CODE: ARTICLE 2

Beginning in 1953 and culminating with a surge in the 1960s, the legislatures of all states except Louisiana adopted the Uniform Commercial Code. Article 2 of the Code embodies many new and drastically different principles and policies that bring to sales a uniformity and predictability not previously possible. The benefits of the Code to businesspeople are enormous. Visualize the confusion and uncertainty associated with a multistate manufacturing and distribution system subjected to different statutory provisions and interpretations in each state. The risks of unexpected decisions or the legal fees necessary to reduce those risks are great, especially for the small businessperson.

Prior to the nearly unanimous adoption of the UCC, such was the situation, for two major reasons and one minor one. First, the ghost of federalism, still a very real force in various state legislatures and court houses, tended to encourage disparate laws. Second, legislators and judges throughout the fifty states were understandably hard put to agree on which was the proper rule of law in a particular area of sales. A third factor, of less importance, was that the adoption of a new sales law appeared to many legislators to have little political appeal for their constituents and hence took a back seat to other issues. These problems have now been surmounted; the Code is operative and promises to reduce substantially, though not entirely eliminate, the horrors of interstate operation and many of the unexpected results that attended intrastate operation.

Though the UCC is now the law of the land, it would be myopic to think that sales law began with the Code. Despite the many bold and new concepts, most of the provisions in the Code itself have evolved from early mercantile custom into English common law on through a British codification (the Sale of Goods Act, 1893) and eventually into the hodgepodge American copy of the British approach — the Uniform Sales Act — that was the immediate predecessor of Article 2.

Let us examine these pre-Code eras in order to gain a better understanding of the workings of the Code. In the agrarian England of the eleventh and twelfth centuries, trade beyond one's hamlet took place at regional fairs. As these were temporary gatherings, the problems that arose had to be completely resolved, quickly, before the merchants scattered. Consequently, early

Norman grants of the privilege of holding a fair also contained authority to hold a court for the resolution of disputes. In these *pie poudre* ("dusty foot") courts a jury of merchants, presided over by a "mayor of the staple," decided cases in a manner consistent with commercial practices. These decisions generated a body of customs and then principles known as the *law merchant*, portions of which were subsequently adopted on a case by case basis into the more formal common law. Legal rules pertaining to sales became, in effect, a blend of the flexible law merchant with the more rigid rules governing an agrarian economy.

The Industrial Revolution of the late eighteenth and nineteenth centuries exerted considerable pressure for a body of law more responsive to the needs and expectations of merchants. In 1893, Parliament adopted the Sale of Goods Act, which became law throughout most of the British Commonwealth. Because of our business contact with the Commonwealth, the Sale of Goods Act was the model for the American codification effort beginning in 1902 that culminated in 1906 when the National Conference of Commissioners on Uniform State Laws approved the Uniform Sales Act. In the following year, state legislatures began adopting the Act. Although adoption went forward at a snail's pace, eventually over thirty states adopted it. However, a number of these states subsequently adopted amendments to specific sections, thereby reducing the Uniform Sales Act's uniformity.

In 1940, the National Conference of Commissioners on Uniform State Laws began work on a successor to the Sales Act. Sponsored by the commissioners and the American Law Institute, this project was expanded beyond sales and became the UCC. The first official draft was issued in 1952. It was followed by the official edition of 1957, which contained several important changes, and by the official texts of 1958 and 1962, which contained only minor changes. Nationwide adoption began in 1953, when Pennsylvania enacted the 1952 version, accelerated in the early 1960s, and proceeded with a rush thereafter. Today, besides being operative in all states but Louisiana, the Code is in force in the District of Columbia and the Virgin Islands. The 1972 version of the Code, which differs from the earlier versions in areas not emphasized in this book, has been adopted by several states and appears likely to replace its predecessors. It is the official text used throughout this book and is reprinted in its entirety in Appendix A.

One inconvenience of combining successive official texts with the adoption pattern sketched above is that different states use different official texts or insisted on making minor changes in the text used. Thus, the UCC is not completely uniform throughout the United States. These variations are minor and will, we hope, remain that way as courts continue the task of interpreting and applying this relatively new body of law.

THE SALES CONTRACT

For the rest of this chapter we shall consider a potpourri of preliminary topics: whether a contract is in existence, whether the contract is enforceable, and whether Article 2 is applicable. Subsequent chapters assume that the contract is enforceable and go on to explore the concepts used to identify the winning party in a dispute.

Sales Distinguished from Contracts of Sale

There is considerable difference between a sale and a contract of sale, the practical consequences of which we shall consider later. A *sale* occurs when title (ownership) to the goods passes from seller to buyer for a price. UCC § 2–106. (Without a price, the transaction would be a gift or a bailment.) A *contract of sale* involves a contract (the requisite offer, acceptance, and consideration must be present) to effect a present or future transfer of ownership.

For example, suppose that Ann Thornton orders a maroon Mercedes Benz 280 with specified options. She has made a contract of sale with the dealers — the actual sale will not occur until the car is available, Thornton has checked it out and paid for it, and the title has been signed over to her. The two events — entering into the contract and transferring ownership — may thus occur at substantially different points in time. In the interim, the parties' rights and remedies for breach of contract and their protection against damage caused by third parties and acts of God may differ from those available after ownership passes.

While the Mercedes situation represents a very common transaction, it is undoubtedly true that most sales, as measured by numbers of transactions rather than dollar volume, occur at the same time that the contract·is made, i.e., they involve an immediate transfer of ownership. For example, in buying a newspaper, ownership or title changes when one gives the person at the newsstand a quarter and receives the paper in return. Giving the money and receiving the paper constitute both the consummation of the contract and its simultaneous performance. Although most transactions are simultaneous, you must keep the distinction between contract and sale in mind as you study the material that follows, particularly the material dealing with rights, remedies, and risk of loss.

Definition of Goods

Part V deals only with the sale of goods; in other words, Article 2 does not control the sale of such nongoods as services and real estate. You will do well to remember this point and guard against the tendency of legal jargon to obscure the distinction. A lawyer will typically use the word *sale* as a shorthand equivalent of the phrase *sale of goods*. Without advance warning, the uninitiated often, and quite reasonably, take the word literally and assume the speaker's or writer's comments pertain not just to goods but also to real estate or services.

Distinguishing between goods and services tends to be more troublesome than distinguishing between goods and real estate (land and buildings). The following case is a good example.

Helvey v. Wabash County Remc
Indiana Court of Appeals (1st Dist.), 1972. 278 N.E.2d 608

[A consumer, Helvey, sued an electric company for damage caused to 110-volt household appliances because the electricity furnished allegedly had 135 volts or more. The electric company argued that electricity constituted "goods" so that the UCC's four year statute of limitations applied. The consumer argued that a six year statute of limitations applied since the purchase of electrical energy constituted purchase of a service. The court held that electricity was goods and discussed the matter as follows:]

ROBERTSON, JUDGE.
. . . .

> "(1) 'Goods' means all things (including specially manufactured goods) which are movable at the time of identification to the contract for sale other than the money in which the price is to be paid, investment securities and things in action. . . .
> (2) Goods must be both existing and identified before any interest in them can pass. . . ."

Helvey concedes that electricity is legally considered to be personal property, that it is subject to ownership, and that it may be bartered and sold. We further note that electricity may be stolen and taxed.

It is necessary for goods to be (1) a thing; (2) existing; and (3) movable, with (2) and (3) existing simultaneously. We are of the opinion that electricity qualifies in each respect. Helvey says it is not movable and in this respect we do not agree, if for no other reason than the monthly reminder from the electric company of how much current has passed through the meter. Logic would indicate that whatever can be measured in order to establish the price to be paid would be indicative of fulfilling both the existing and movable requirements of goods.

We further take note that one of the principal underlying purposes in adoption of the Uniform Commercial Code is "to make uniform the law among the various jurisdictions." With this in mind, we rely upon the authority of *Gardiner* v. *Philadelphia Gas Works* (1964), wherein natural gas was determined to be goods within the scope of the Uniform Commercial Code. . . .

In *Epstein* v. *Giannattasio*, 25 Conn. Sup. 109, 197 A.2d 342 (Com. Pleas 1963), Epstein visited Giannattasio's beauty parlor for a beauty treatment. In the course of the treatment, Giannattasio used a number of bleaches and dyes that caused all of Epstein's hair to fall out and gave her acute dermatitis. Epstein sued, alleging breach of one of the UCC's quality warranties. She was denied recovery on the ground that the transaction did not involve a sale of goods. Where service is the predominant feature of the transaction, and the transfer of title to goods is merely incidental, there is no sale of goods within the Uniform Commercial Code.

Similar issues were raised in *Aegis Productions, Inc.* v. *Arriflex Corp. of America*, 25 A.D.2d 639, 268 N.Y.S.2d 185 (App. Div. 1966). Aegis took one of its motion picture cameras to Arriflex to be repaired. Arriflex subsequently returned it, claiming that the work had been completed. However, when the camera was used, it did not function properly and an entire film was ruined. Aegis's subsequent efforts to recover for the alleged breach of a quality warranty were unsuccessful because under section 2–312 (1) "warranties are limited to sales of goods. No warranty attaches to the performance of a service."

Assume that William T. Sherman became ill after eating a hamburger at the local diner. Assuming further that the meat was foul and caused his illness, is Sherman prevented from suing under Article 2 because the transaction did not involve a sale of goods? No. The Code declares that the serving of food by a restaurant is a sale of goods. In so doing, the Code rejects two lines of earlier cases: one took the position that such transactions were services; the other thought the serving of food was not a sale. The official comments — a statement of the legislative history (objectives, rationale, choices) behind a Code provision — do not provide the drafters' reasoning, only their conclusions. This suggests that a variety of reasons persuaded individual drafters to a common conclusion.

Warranty of Title and Against Infringement

One of the warranties imposed by the Code is the *warranty of title*. This warranty constitutes a guarantee by the seller to the buyer that the seller has a right to sell the goods and that the goods are free from any undeclared charge or encumbrance of which the buyer has no actual knowledge. Should this not be the case, the buyer has recourse to the seller for damages sustained as a result of the breach, providing he notifies the seller of the breach within a reasonable time.

Both tradition and public policy have combined to produce this warranty. As the common law evolved, it became increasingly obvious that buyers and sellers rarely included in their contract a provision that the seller owned and had legal right to dispose of the goods the buyer was acquiring. The parties, while negotiating vigorously over other contract terms, typically took good title for granted and did not waste paper or effort stating the obvious. Case law and the early statutes gradually recognized this phenomenon and implied the warranty of title. The Code followed suit.

From the point of view of policy, the warranty of title has two effects. First, it causes the law to conform to the expectations of most honest businesspeople. Second, it minimizes the ability of a careless, shrewd, or downright dishonest seller — the party who normally has the most information about title — to stick the buyer with any loss occasioned by the real owner's reacquisition of the goods.

The Code has innovated in this area by expanding the buyer's protection through a new warranty guaranteeing that the goods do not infringe on any trademarks or patents held by a third person. However, this aspect of the warranty of title and against infringement applies only to a merchant seller selling standard goods. It does not apply when the buyer provides his own specifications for the goods.

While the preceding constitute the general rules, there are inevitably some exceptions. These occur where the reasonably informed person should know that seller is dealing with an unknown or limited title. Thus, when executors of estates, foreclosing lienors, or auctioneers are selling goods, the implied warranties of title do not impose a personal obligation on the seller. The seller can, however, make an *express warranty of title* in such a situation if he wishes.

Merchants and the Law of Sales

Throughout our subsequent discussion of sales, note that special rules often apply when merchants are involved, i.e., when the transaction involves a merchant dealing with another merchant or a merchant dealing with a non-merchant. The justification for these special standards is that the law should be pragmatic in reflecting the current practices used by businesspeople (merchants) when dealing with each other. It also reflects the view that a different standard should apply when the experienced businessperson (merchant) deals with the average, relatively unsophisticated consumer. Generally speaking, the UCC fosters the creation of legal rights more easily when the agreement is solely between merchants as opposed to a transaction involving a consumer and a merchant. In addition, the UCC tends to protect the consumer more fully when he deals with a merchant rather than a nonmerchant.

Who, then, is a merchant? The Code in section 2–104 (1) defines a merchant as a person with one or more of the following three characteristics:

1. A dealer in goods of the kind under discussion,
2. One who is not a dealer but who nevertheless holds himself out as having knowledge or skill peculiar to the practices or goods involved in the transaction,
3. One who employs an agent who has the knowledge or skill to qualify as a merchant.

Statute of Limitations

As discussed in Chapter 2, our system of law stipulates that claims must be prosecuted within specified periods of time or recovery will be denied. Such limitations on delay are known as *statutes of limitation*. The general rule laid down by the Code in section 2–725 is that actions for breach of contract must commence within four years of the breach, regardless of when the aggrieved party learns of the breach. This rule may be modified by the parties provided they do so at the time of the original agreement. The power to modify is, however, substantially circumscribed: the period of limitation may be reduced to a minimum of one year, but it may not be extended beyond four years.

Supplements to the Code

The drafters and adopters of the Code did not expect to embody in one document a set of rules that would dispose of every sales problem. Thus, they wisely provided that "unless displaced by the particular provisions of this Act, the principles of law and equity . . . shall supplement its provisions." UCC § 1–103.

Do not forget this important provision. In subsequent chapters we shall have recourse to supplementary state law. Unless you keep the foregoing authorization in mind, our occasional excursions beyond the Code's confines will be disconcerting.

Modifications of Common Law Contract Principles

During our consideration of contract law, we encountered several provisions of Article 2, Sales, which deviated in important respects from traditional contract rules. The more important of these provisions are summarized below. Reference back to the appropriate pages should help you remember them:

1. *Determination of price.* The parties possess the power to stipulate in their contract either the actual price or the manner in which the price is to be determined. Should they fail to exercise their power, the Code provides that the price shall be a reasonable one determined as of the time and place of delivery. For related discussion see pages 101–3.

2. *Offer and acceptance.* Where an acceptance includes additional terms, the terms are to be regarded as proposed additions to the contract. Where merchants are involved, the proposed additions will be deemed accepted unless they materially alter the contract, or the original offeror objects to the modifications within a reasonable time. For related discussion see pages 98–101 and 115–16.

3. *Options (firm offers).* When the offeror is a merchant and the offer is contained in a signed writing, the offer will be irrevocable for a reasonable time not exceeding three months, even though no consideration is given. For related discussion see pages 110–11.

4. *Statute of frauds.* Contracts for the sale of goods priced at $500 or more must be in writing. The only absolutely essential term of the signed writing is a statement of the quantity involved. A merchant who receives a letter of confirmation will be bound by its provisions unless he notifies the other party within ten days, and in writing, of his objections. Partial performance does not remove the entire contract from the signed writing requirement; only the part of the contract which has been performed will be enforceable. For related discussion see pages 177, 179, and 179–83.

5. *Parol evidence rule.* It is permissible and proper to consider evidence of the pattern of prior dealing between the parties, the meaning given to certain contract language within the trade, and the ordinary course of dealing within the trade. For related discussion see pages 183–86.

6. *Implied conditions.* A seller is excused from delivering goods when his performance has become commercially impracticable due to unforeseen supervening circumstances not contemplated when the contract was created. One is not excused from a contract because of increased cost or inconvenience, nor when a greater than normal burden was knowingly assumed. For related discussion see pages 204–6 and 222–25.

7. *Output, requirement, and exclusive dealing contracts.* Such contracts are enforceable where the parties have acted in good faith and the quantity offered or demanded is not unreasonably disproportionate to any stated estimate or previous normal requirements or output. For related discussion see page 122.

PROBLEMS AND QUESTIONS

1. What are the pros and cons of adopting a uniform body of statutes, such as the UCC? Why did some states hesitate in adopting it?

2. What was the Uniform Sales Act?

3. At what point does a sale occur?

4. Is the term *sale* really a shortened version of the term *contract of sale?*

5. In what situation is the sale of goods not within the Uniform Commercial Code?

6. We are concerned with the sale of goods. What are *goods?*

7. When, if ever, does a warranty attach to the per-

formance of a service under the provisions of the Uniform Commercial Code?

8. Joe Spencer rented the Volunteer Firemen's Hall for his daughter's wedding reception and bought chicken, shrimp, and tuna salads as the entrees. It was a hot summer day and the caterer did not provide ice trays to keep the salads cool. The salads were left at room temperature for four hours. After eating, most of the guests became ill. Do the guests have a claim under the Uniform Commercial Code? Does Joe Spencer?

9. Under the provisions of the Uniform Commercial Code is a buyer protected under all circumstances by a warranty which guarantees that the goods do not infringe upon any trademarks or patents held by a third person?

10. Anthony's Auto Repair occasionally does work on a car the owner of which does not show up to claim the car. Anthony's then sells the car for the value of the work done. Under the provisions of the Uniform Commercial Code, is Anthony's a merchant as to the sale of the car?

17

WARRANTIES OF QUALITY

WARRANTIES IN PERSPECTIVE

Definition and Types

In the sale of goods, a *warranty of quality* is a guarantee that the goods have certain characteristics or meet certain minimum standards of excellence. Although warranties may be created in several ways, the two most common are express warranty and implied warranty.

Express warranties may be created in three ways: by an affirmation of fact or promise, by a description of the goods, or by use of a sample or model. The existence of any one of the three as part of the basis of the bargain between seller and buyer creates an express warranty. *Implied warranties* are imposed where experience has shown that the parties normally intend warranties to exist even though they are not explicitly stated, or where the conduct and circumstances are such that society deems it desirable to protect the buyer.

History

Over the years, the judicial attitude toward warranties has varied enormously, parallelling the evolution in attitude toward unintentional torts. You will recall that unintentional torts evolved in a circular fashion: the old tort rule of strict liability (liability regardless of fault) gave way during the Industrial Revolution to the concept of negligence (liability only when one was at fault), a theory that now seems to be giving way in turn to strict liability, at least where injury is the consequence of defectively manufactured products. A similar pendulum effect is observable with warranties.

The medieval seller was confronted with exacting standards of quality as a consequence of the combined power of Church and guilds. This changed, however, with the Industrial Revolution. In an effort to protect infant industries, the maxim *caveat emptor* (let the buyer beware) became the embodiment of judicial attitude. The gradual swing of the pendulum away from *caveat emptor* has occurred slowly; many barriers to effective warranty protection began to crumble only during the early part of the twentieth century. Their erosion took two forms. First, the judiciary began to find warranties more readily than in the past. Second, the courts began to circumscribe severely a seller's ability to escape or limit his warranties. The Code reflects both of these avenues to consumer protection and quite clearly intends to afford greater warranty protection than existed under prior law.

CREATION OF WARRANTIES

Express Warranties

Express Warranties by Affirmation or Promise

Express warranties under the Code are created by a process of bargaining or dickering between the buyer and seller. UCC § 2–313, comment 1. More specifically, they arise from an affirmation of fact or promise made by the seller which relates to the goods and which becomes part of the basis of the bargain. UCC § 2–313(1)(a). The phrase *basis of the bargain* is not well defined in either the Code or the official comments. The official comments do state that the phrase embodies the idea that the affirmation is part of the essence of the bargain, which has been woven into the "fabric of the agreement." The concept of express warranties also suggests reliance in the sense that the statement was material or important to the buyer's decision.

A warranty can be created despite the seller's possibly strong desire not to create one. Section 2–313 and its comments make it clear that neither the seller's intention nor his use of any words of art or specific words such as *warrant* or *guarantee*, are required to create a warranty.

The Code does not, however, provide an absolute standard by which every statement a seller makes can be readily classified as a warranty or a nonwarranty. The courts are still called on to decide whether a particular statement is an affirmation of fact or a promise, and thus an express warranty, or whether it is merely the old sales pitch, i.e., "a statement purporting to be merely the seller's opinion, or commendation of the goods." Through this provision, the Code recognizes, as did the common law, that salespeople have a tendency to wax eloquent when discussing their wares — a fact of life the public is assumed to know. Statements that merely puff up the value of one's goods, and are thus within what the common law called the *puffing privilege*, do not create warranties. Pre-Code examples of such puffing have included statements that a product was "wonderful" or that "you couldn't buy a better one."

In an attempt to delineate the Code's position on warranties and the puffing privilege, the official comments to section 2–313 observe that the identification of warranties turns on the following question: "What statements of the seller have in the circumstances and in objective judgment become part of the basis of the bargain?" The comments conclude that, "All the statements of the seller do so unless good reason is shown to the contrary." The old common law distinction between opinion and fact is helpful here. Section 2–313(2) refers to this distinction by stating that a mere affirmation of the value of the goods or a statement purporting to be opinion or commendation will not create a warranty. As the line between opinion and fact is often blurry at best, the common law sought to distinguish between the two concepts on the basis of probability that the buyer had relied on the particular misstatement in question. Judge Learned Hand compared privileged puffing or opinion with the claims of campaign managers before election, which, he said, are "rather designed to allay the suspicion which would attend their absence than to be understood as having any relation to objective truth." *Vulcan Metals Co.* v. *Simmons Manufacturing Co.*, 248 Fed. 853, 856 (2d Circuit, 1918).

A case illustrating the problems in this area is set forth below.

Carpenter v. Alberto Culver Co.
Court of Appeals of Michigan, Division 3, 1970. 28 Mich. App. 399

Before FITZGERALD, P. J., and McGREGOR and O'HARA, J. J.

PER CURIAM.

This is a damage suit brought against the above named defendants, arising from personal injuries claimed to have been caused by a hair-dyeing product manufactured by defendant Alberto Culver Company, and sold to plaintiff by defendants Gardner and Janis, doing business as City Drug Store. After a jury trial in circuit court, a verdict of no cause of action was found and judgment was entered accordingly. Plaintiff's suit charged negligence and breaches of implied and express warranties. The trial judge refused to submit the count of express warranty to the jury, and from this, plaintiff appeals.

This Court confines itself to the question of any express warranty made by the City Drug Store; since plaintiff makes no argument as to the liability of defendant, Alberto Culver Company, this issue is deemed to be abandoned.

Plaintiff entered defendants' drug store with the intention of purchasing a hair dye; while she was viewing the various hair-dyeing products, of which there were more than twenty, she was offered assistance by one of the sales clerks in the store. Plaintiff claims the clerk indicated that several of her friends had used the hair-dyeing product in question, and that her own hair came out "very nice" and "very natural." Plaintiff also testified that the clerk told her she "would get very fine results." This Court notes that evidence establishes that both the package containing the solution and the bottle had cautionary instructions regarding the product.

Plaintiff claims that no instructions were enclosed and that she called the store for such instructions. She did not inquire in regard to taking a preliminary test (commonly known as a "patch" test), as she was admittedly familiar with the necessity for so doing. Plaintiff contends that she performed such a patch test and alleges that there was no adverse reaction prior to the product's use. Plaintiff ultimately used the product and suffered an adverse skin reaction.

. . . .

In determining whether a statement of the seller is to be deemed a warranty, it is important to consider whether in the statement the seller assumes to assert a fact of which the buyer is ignorant, or merely states an opinion or judgment upon a matter of which the seller has no special knowledge and on which the buyer may be expected also to have an opinion and to exercise his judgment. Representations which merely express the seller's opinion, belief, judgment, or estimate do not constitute a warranty.

In the instant case, from all the factual evidence, we cannot agree that such statements made by the retail seller can be considered that of express warranty for use by this plaintiff. From the context in which such statements were made, coupled with the cautionary instructions printed on both the bottle and the box, warning against possible adverse reaction, nothing more existed than an implied warranty that the product was reasonably fit for use as a hair dye. . . . Plaintiff did not present sufficient evidence from which a jury could have inferred an express warranty and a breach thereof.

. . . .

Affirmed. Costs to appellees.

The classification of express warranties as warranties of quality does not preclude the possibility that an attribute having little bearing on the product's quality can also be the subject of an express warranty. Assume James Conrad's purchase agreement calls for a red sports car. Delivery to him of the correct model but the wrong color — gray, for example — will amount to breach of an express warranty if the color was part of the basis of the bargain.

Express Warranties by Description or Sample

Express warranties are not limited to those created by affirmation or promise. In those sales where a sample, model, or description of the goods becomes part of the basis of the bargain, the comments to section 2–313 observe that an express warranty arises to ensure that the goods will be comparable to the description, sample, or model. Furthermore, a description need not be verbal. Technical specifications, blueprints, and the like often afford more exact descriptions than ordinary language; if they are made a part of the basis of the bargain, the goods must conform to them. For example, in *Fairbanks, Morse & Co.* v. *Consolidated Fisheries Co.*, 190 F.2d 817 (3rd Circuit, 1951), a contract for the sale of a generator contained the following technical description: "1–1420 KVA–1136 KW @ 80% Power Factor, 3 Phase, 60 Cycle, 2400 volt, 3 wire, 720 RPM, 50° Rated Fairbanks Morse Alternator with Sole Plates, Rheostats and Field Discharge Resistor." The court concluded that this description constituted an express warranty that was breached when the generator failed to produce 1136 kilowatts.

Similarly, in *Baltimore Machine & Equipment Co., Inc.* v. *Holtite Manufacturing Co., Inc.*, 241 Md. 36, 215 A.2d 458 (1965), the buyer contracted to purchase a large shipment of dowel pullers to be used by shoe repairers for pulling spike heels from ladies' shoes. The contract had been entered into only after the seller had produced a sample that was approved by the buyer. When the full shipment failed to conform to the sample, the buyer rejected it. The court upheld the buyer's right on the grounds that the seller had breached the express warranty.

Regarding warranties by sample, the question often arises whether the sample shown is intended to merely suggest or to literally represent the contract's subject matter. The UCC drafters believed that a sample drawn from an existing stock of goods should be regarded as a literal representation of the goods contracted unless the seller has indicated otherwise; in the case of a sample of merchandise not in stock, there is a weaker presumption that it is a literal description.

Implied Warranties

General Considerations

Express warranties come into existence through explicit statements or representations made by the seller. But if warranties could arise only from explicit statements, descriptions, and samples, then silence or careful wording on the seller's part could easily defeat a buyer's attempt to recover for defective goods. To preclude such conniving, the theory of implied warranties developed and has been embodied in the UCC.

There are two implied quality warranties: the *implied warranty of merchantability* and the *implied warranty of fitness* for a particular purpose. Neither entails explicit bargaining between buyer and seller. Instead, the law imposes these warranties on those sales transactions where human experience and our evolving social values have shown the buyer to particularly need protection. Since not all transactions give rise to implied warranties, you should be especially attentive to the circumstances required to create each of them and should note the ways in which the two sets of requirements differ.

Implied Warranty of Merchantability

The UCC, in section 2–314, provides an implied warranty that all goods sold by merchants shall be "merchantable." The UCC substantially improves on prior law by containing a fairly elaborate, though by no means exhaustive, definition of this standard. Particularly important is the wording that goods "pass without objection in the trade under the contract description." UCC § 2–314(2)(a). *Agoos Kid Co.* v. *Blumenthal Import Corp.*, 282 Mass. 1, 184 N.E. 279 (1932), a pre-Code example of this standard, is cited with approval in the Massachusetts comments to the Code. This case involved a contract for 4,000 dozen dry salted Baghdad goat skins, 50 percent of which were rotted upon delivery. In holding the goods unmerchantable, the court noted that if 3 percent of the skins had been rotted, the goods would have been of "merchantable quality," since that was the average incidence of rot in the trade.

Similarly, in *Mathieu* v. *George A. Moore & Co.*, 4 F.2d 251 (N.D. Cal.,

1925), the buyer contracted to purchase 200 tons of Indo-Chinese native brown sugar at a very low price. Upon delivery the buyer discovered the sugar was of exceedingly poor quality. The court, however, held that the sugar was merchantable because sugar of such poor quality was typical of Indo-Chinese sugar exportation during that particular season and one engaged in the sugar trade expected that when buying sugar of that description.

Another especially significant articulation of the merchantable standard is that the goods be "fit for the ordinary purposes for which such goods are used." UCC § 2–314(2)(c). This raises, of course, the question of what the "ordinary purposes" of any particular goods are. For instance, if a log chain breaks while being used to tow a truck and the truck is damaged as a result, is the seller of the chain liable for the damage to the truck because the chain was unmerchantable? The answer depends on whether log chains are ordinarily used to tow trucks, and this presents a question of fact to be determined from the evidence presented in the particular case.

As you read the following somewhat colorful decision, note the authorities Judge Reardon uses to bolster his decision. Do they surprise you?

Webster v. Blue Ship Tea Room, Inc.
Supreme Judicial Court of Massachusetts, 1964. 347 Mass. 421, 198 N.E.2d 309

REARDON, JUSTICE.

This is a case which by its nature evokes earnest study not only of the law but also of the culinary traditions of the Commonwealth which bear so heavily upon its outcome. It is an action to recover damages for personal injuries sustained by reason of a breach of implied warranty of food served by the defendant in its restaurant. . . .

The jury could have found the following facts: On Saturday, April 25, 1959, about 1 P.M., the plaintiff . . . entered the Blue Ship Tea Room operated by the defendant. . . .

. . . .

The plaintiff, who had been born and brought up in New England (a fact of some consequence), ordered . . . a cup of fish chowder. Presently, there was set before her "a small bowl of fish chowder." She had previously enjoyed a breakfast about 9 A.M. which had given her no difficulty. "The fish chowder contained haddock, potatoes, milk, water and seasoning. The chowder was milky in color and not clear. The haddock and potatoes were in chunks" (also a fact of consequence). It was hot when she got it, but she did not tip it with her spoon because it was hot . . . but stirred it in an up and under motion. . . . She did not see anything unusual about it. After 3 or 4 spoonfuls she was aware that something had lodged in her throat because she couldn't swallow and couldn't clear her throat by gulping and she could feel it." This misadventure led to two esophagoscopies at the Massachusetts General Hospital, in the second of which, on April 27, 1959, a fish bone was found and removed. The sequence of events produced injury to the plaintiff which was not insubstantial.

We must decide whether a fish bone lurking in a fish chowder, about the ingredients of which there is no other complaint, constitutes a breach of implied warranty under applicable provisions of the Uniform Commercial Code, the annotations to which are not helpful on this point. . . .

. . . .

The defendant asserts that here was a native New Englander eating fish chowder in a "quaint" Boston dining place where she had been before; that "[f]ish chowder, as it is served and enjoyed by New Englanders, is a hearty dish, originally designed to satisfy the appetites of our seamen and fishermen"; that "[t]his court knows well that we are not talking of some insipid broth as is customarily served to convalescents." We are asked to rule in such fashion that no chef is forced "to reduce the pieces of fish in the chowder to miniscule size in an effort to ascertain if they contained any pieces of bone." "In so ruling," we are told (in the defendant's brief), "the court will not only uphold its reputation for legal knowledge and acumen, but will, as loyal sons of Massachusetts, save our world-renowned fish chowder from degenerating into an insipid broth containing the mere essence of its former stature as a culinary masterpiece." Notwithstanding these passionate entreaties we are bound to examine with detachment the nature of fish chowder and what might happen to it under varying interpretations of the Uniform Commercial Code.

Chowder is an ancient dish preëxisting even "the appetites of our seamen and fishermen." It was perhaps the common ancestor of the "more refined cream soups, purées, and bisques." Berolzheimer, The American Woman's Cook Book (Publisher's Guild Inc., New York, 1941), p. 176. . . . Our literature over the years abounds in references not only to the delights of chowder but also to its manufacture. A namesake of the plaintiff, Daniel Webster, had a recipe for fish chowder which has survived into a number of modern cookbooks and in which the removal of fish bones is not mentioned at all. One old time recipe recited in the New English Dictionary study defines chowder as "A dish made of fresh fish (esp. cod) or clams, stewed with slices of pork or bacon, onions, and biscuit. 'Cider and champagne are sometimes added.' " Hawthorne, in The House of the Seven Gables (Allyn and Bacon, Boston, 1957) p. 8, speaks of "[a] codfish of sixty pounds caught in the bay, [which] had been dissolved into the rich liquid of a chowder." . . . The recitation of these ancient formulas suffices to indicate that in the construction of chowders in these parts in other years, worries about fish bones played no role whatsoever. This broad outlook on chowders has persisted in more modern cookbooks. "The chowder of today is much the same as the old chowder. . . ." The American Woman's Cook Book, supra, p. 176. . . .

. . . We are not inclined to tamper with age old recipes by an amendment reflecting the plaintiff's view of the effect of the Uniform Commercial Code upon them. We are aware of the heavy body of case law involving foreign substances in food, but we sense a strong distinction between them and those relative to unwholesomeness of the food itself. . . . In any event, we consider that the joys of life in New England include the ready availability of fresh fish chowder. We should be prepared to cope with the hazards of fish bones, the occasional presence of which in chowders is, it seems to us, to be anticipated, and which, in the light of a hallowed tradition, do not impair their fitness or merchantability. . . . We are most impressed by Allen v. Grafton, 170 Ohio St. 249, where in Ohio, the Midwest, in a case where the plaintiff was injured by a piece of oyster shell in an order of fried oysters, Mr. Justice Taft (now Chief Justice) in a majority opinion held that "the possible presence of a piece of oyster shell in or attached to an oyster is so well known to anyone who eats oysters that we can say as a matter of law that one who eats oysters can reasonably anticipate and guard against eating such a piece of shell. . . ."

Thus, while we sympathize with the plaintiff who has suffered a peculiarly New England injury, the order must be

Exceptions sustained.

Judgment for the defendant.

Implied Warranty of Fitness for a Particular Purpose

A warranty of fitness for a particular purpose differs from the warranty of merchantability (fitness for ordinary purposes) mentioned above. The concept of merchantability deals with the customary uses made of goods in question, whereas the concept of particular purpose refers to the buyer's use that is peculiar to his individual needs. The particular purpose warranty also aims at protecting a buyer who has little or no knowledge of the product and must therefore rely on the seller's judgment when making his purchase. As a consequence of these distinctions, there are three requisites for creating the implied warranty of fitness for a particular purpose: (1) the seller must have actual or constructive knowledge of the particular purpose for which the buyer wants the goods; (2) the seller must furnish or select the goods; and (3) the buyer must rely on the seller's choice. UCC § 2–315.

An example should make the preceding points even clearer. Suppose that Tom Wolf purchased two pounds of pork chops from Smith's Meat Market. Wolf eats the pork chops raw, gets trichinosis, and eventually tries to sue Smith's Meat Market for breach of an implied quality warranty. Since it is well known that eating uncooked pork might cause trichinosis, and since few people eat pork raw, there would be no breach of the implied warranty of merchantability. Under ordinary circumstances raw pork is merchantable if it is edible when properly cooked, even though if consumed in its original raw state it might produce trichinosis. If Wolf, the buyer, had indicated his particular and peculiar purpose — to consume the meat raw — and if Wolf had relied on Smith's Meat Market's choice of pork, then an implied warranty of fitness for a particular purpose would arise and Smith's Meat Market would be liable. See *Adams* v. *Scheib*, 408 Pa. 452, 184 A.2d 700 (1962).

Whether or not the particular purpose warranty attaches to a sale is a question of fact to be decided in each individual case. The buyer need not actually specify the particular purpose for which he is buying the goods if the circumstances are such that the seller should (or does) know this purpose. For instance, in *Brown* v. *Chapman*, 304 F.2d 149, 4 A.L.R.3d 490 (9th Cir., 1962), the plaintiff borrowed her aunt's hula skirt to wear to a costume party. At the party the skirt was ignited by a cigarette and completely burned, causing the plaintiff personal injury, not to mention embarrassment. In affirming a judgment for the plaintiff against the seller of the hula skirt, the court held that the seller should have realized that such an article of clothing would reasonably be worn at costume parties or other social gatherings where drinking and smoking would take place, and that the seller, therefore, breached his implied warranty of fitness for a particular purpose.

Under the old Uniform Sales Act, the warranty of fitness for a particular purpose had been precluded if a buyer ordered goods by a trade name, such as Wheaties, Crest, or Schlitz. The theory was that the buyer did not rely on the seller's skill and judgment if the goods were ordered by a trade name, hence, no warranty was created. Under the UCC, however, the existence of a trade name is only one fact among many to be considered in determining whether the buyer relied on the seller's skill or judgment. Clearly, though, if the buyer insists on a particular brand name, he is not relying on the seller's skill or judgment, and therefore, the warranty of fitness for a particular purpose does not arise. UCC §2–315, comment 5.

Multiple Warranties

When a fact situation gives rise to multiple warranties, the integration or ranking of these warranties can become an important issue for courts. Consider the following problem.

George Meade, having just moved from Alabama to Aspen, Colorado, decided that he would learn to ski. He went into the Schuss Ski Shop and told the saleswoman that he had never skied in his life and needed a full set of equipment designed for beginners. Having equipped him with skis, boots, and poles, Schuss's saleswoman said, "I have just the safety bindings you need." The saleswoman then picked out a pair of Austrian safety bindings designed to withstand, without releasing, the considerable pressure that an expert skier puts on bindings when racing the giant slalom at breakneck speeds. Included with the bindings was a manufacturer's guarantee that read: "These bindings are guaranteed not to release under rigorous slalom pressure."

Meade relied on the saleswoman's judgment and bought the bindings. His first day out on the beginners' slope Meade went out of control at ten miles an hour and fell in an inextricable heap, with two skis pointing in opposite directions. Because the bindings would not release, Meade suffered a compound fracture of his left leg.

It is obvious that the bindings were not fit for Meade's purpose of learning how to ski. They were, however, merchantable, since they would release under an expert's crash conditions and since they conformed to the express warranty. What are Meade's rights under the various conflicting warranties? As a general rule, under section 2–317, all warranties, express or implied, are to be considered cumulative unless such a construction is impossible or unreasonable. When such a construction is unreasonable, as in the case of the safety bindings, the intention of the parties determines which of the inconsistent warranties shall prevail.

Since it is often difficult to determine what the intention of the parties was at the time of the contract, the UCC, in section 2–317, has set forth the following presumptions regarding the parties' intentions: express warranties prevail over inconsistent implied warranties of merchantability, but express warranties give way to inconsistent implied warranties of fitness for a particular purpose. Thus, Meade would recover from Schuss Ski Shop for breach of the implied warranty of fitness for a particular purpose, despite the fact that the bindings conformed to the inconsistent merchantability and express warranties.

While the preceding covers the most important presumptions, one should also be aware that technical specifications are to be relied on over an inconsistent sample, and a sample from an existing stock of merchandise is to be relied on over inconsistent language of general description. All of these presumptions may, however, be changed by evidence showing that the intention of the parties was otherwise. UCC § 2–317, comment 2.

PROBLEMS AND QUESTIONS

What are the types of implied warranty?

What does *merchantability* mean?

Upon delivery of a shipment of speed boats, the contract for which had already been signed, the buyer, a boat renter, asked the seller, a manufacturer, "Can these hulls take choppy seas at high speeds?" Seller answered, "Don't sweat it. They'll withstand any pounding at any speed." Subsequent hard use in choppy seas caused the hulls of many of the boats to split. Does buyer have a claim on an express warranty?

As McGraw was leaving Stengel's office after preliminary negotiations for the purchase of heavy construction machinery, Stengel, the seller, called to McGraw, "Don't forget, our stuff won't need servicing for a year." McGraw was heard to retort, "Bunkum!" McGraw's company ultimately bought the machinery and incurred a sizeable servicing bill within six months. Does it have a claim against Stengel for the servicing bill?

Kaiser, a camera saleswoman, sold Fraser a camera declaring, "This little camera will give you pictures as sharp as any other box on the market, and clearer than most." The inexpensive camera did not, in fact, produce pictures with any high degree of clarity. Was there an express warranty?

Hackney sold Cartwright a five-day-old bull calf, referring to the calf's good blood lines ("the great record his relatives had made") and declaring that the calf's father was "the greatest living dairy bull." Cartwright was advised to keep the calf for breeding purposes, as he would be "a help to build up your herd." Unforeseen by both parties, the calf turned out to be sterile. Did Hackney's statements constitute an express warranty?

The City of Newark awarded a construction contract to Berlanti, but specified that she use a patented process owned by Vacuum Concrete, or an approved equivalent, in her construction. Vacuum sent Berlanti a memorandum stating its prices for leasing the equipment and hiring the personnel necessary to operate its process. Berlanti submitted a purchase order accepting Vacuum's terms provided that Vacuum strictly comply with the specifications outlined by the City of Newark. Vacuum submitted a counteroffer that mentioned the price for its personnel and outright purchase of the equipment, but nothing else. Berlanti accepted this offer. When the equipment failed to perform up to the specifications required by the City of Newark, Berlanti claimed a breach of an express warranty. What would be the result? Were the specifications in the contract between Berlanti and Newark part of the contract between Berlanti and Vacuum?

8.   Contemplating buying a shipment of apples, Kroger asked MacIntosh, "Do any of these apples have worms?" Unsure himself, MacIntosh, the seller, replied, "See for yourself," and made the whole shipment available for Kroger's inspection. After looking through two boxes, Kroger bought the whole shipment. One-third of the apples turned out to be wormy. Was there an express warranty?

Would the result be different if MacIntosh had picked out the two boxes to be inspected by Kroger?

9.   In *Webster* v. *Blue Ship Tea Room, Inc.*, would New England fish chowder be unmerchantable if it had too many fish bones in it, or must the chowder actually be adulterated before the court will impose liability on the seller? Do you think the result would have been different if Miss Webster had been from the Midwest and had never before enjoyed a bowl of New England fish chowder? Should the buyer be on the lookout for bones when the goods normally contain bones?

10.   Rhonda ordered a hamburger and a beer at Deas' restaurant and chipped her tooth when she bit into a hard substance in the hamburger that Deas served her. Deas claimed that he didn't know the hard object was there. What would be the result?

11.   Benavides bought some ivory soap labeled "99-44/100% pure" from defendant, Stop and Shop. While washing her face she accidently got some of the soap in her eye and felt an immediate sharp pain. The eye began to fill with fluids and eventually became so bad that her vision was blurred for almost a week. In suing on a breach of warranty of merchantability, she introduced no evidence other than the above. Should she be allowed to recover? Do you think there was

enough evidence to link her eye disorder to the soap or to prove that the soap was not "99-44/100% pure?"

12. Apex, a cosmetic manufacturer and retailer, sold a face cream to Mrs. Green. Upon application of the cream, Mrs. Green suffered a violent allergic reaction. In her suit for damages she proved that her particular sensitivity was shared by about 15 percent of all women. What would be the result?

What if Apex, aware of the possibility of allergic reactions to its product, recommended that consumers take a patch test prior to using it, and Mrs. Green failed to take the test?

13. Gibbs, needing a furnace to heat her four bedroom house, escorted furnace salesman Bartlett throughout the house before requesting his help in selecting an appropriate furnace. The one Bartlett chose ran properly but could not generate enough heat to reach the two most remote bedrooms. Gibbs sued for breach of warranty. What would be the result?

14. A buyer for Bunyon Logging Company told a used car salesman, Zimmer, that she needed a truck to haul boulders over particularly rough log roads but indicated that she would prefer a Ford. Zimmer, aware of the particular terrain in question, selected a Ford truck from his large stock and sold it to Bunyon. Unable to take the strain, the springs on the truck broke on the second day the truck was in use. Bunyon sued Zimmer. What would be the result?

15. Odyssey Corporation is in the exclusive business of selling fuselages to the United States Air Force. The government will buy fuselages only if they meet strict quality specifications, one of which is an extremely low porosity steel. Ludwig Steel Corporation is under contract with Odyssey to supply Odyssey's steel requirements. Since Ludwig has supplied Odyssey for many years, it is familiar with Odyssey's business and with the strict government specifications. When a delivery from Ludwig to Odyssey failed to meet government requirements because the steel porosity was too high, Odyssey incurred high costs in processing the steel to lower its porosity. Odyssey then sued Ludwig for breach of warranty. What would be the result?

Several mechanisms for limiting or attempting to limit warranties have long existed. These mechanisms and the circumstances under which they will be effective will be discussed in this chapter.

DISCLAIMERS

Definition and Perspective

Disclaimers are oral or written statements by the seller that purport to modify or completely exclude express or implied warranties. For example, the sales contract between a buyer and a used car dealer might contain a statement that "it is expressly understood by both parties that the seller makes neither express nor implied warranties as to the quality of the car." In the legal profession this is known as a disclaimer clause. The Code permits such clauses but severely circumscribes their ability to weaken or eliminate express or implied warranties. In other words, the disclaimer may not be permitted to accomplish all that it seeks to accomplish.

Disclaimers are one of several shields afforded the seller against the considerable potential liability inherent in warranties. Warranties can arise independent of any inquiry into the seller's negligence. Their effect can be the imposition of strict liability upon the seller. Such legal power in the buyer's hands requires particular attention to a fair adjustment and compromise between the competing interests of a buyer and seller. Consequently, the common law and the UCC both afford the seller certain protections against warranties.

As we have seen, not every situation gives rise to warranties: there must be statements, samples, or models for the express warranty to arise, and implied warranties arise only when a merchant is present or when the buyer has relied upon the seller's judgment in the selection of goods. In addition, the seller is protected against untrue claims of express warranties by the parol evidence rule (see UCC § 2–202 and discussion of the rule on pages 183–86 in

18
ATTEMPTS TO LIMIT WARRANTIES

Contracts), which rules out any inconsistent oral statement made prior to or contemporaneously with the document, if the document integrates the agreement. Third, even when all of the conditions prerequisite for a warranty hold, the Code permits the seller to defend himself against warranties by arguing that the warranty was not breached or that the breach did not cause the injury. Additional protections for the seller will be discussed later in this chapter.

Disclaimers Under the UCC

The Code in section 2–316(1) provides that words attempting to negate or limit an express warranty are inoperative when they violate the terms of the express warranty. When an express warranty and a disclaimer inconsistent with that warranty coexist, the express warranty overrides the disclaimer. For instance, if the salesperson for a used car dealer had stated, "We guarantee 5,000 miles of trouble-free driving with this car," this express warranty would dominate the disclaimer clause should the buyer be able to avoid the parol evidence rule. As a practical matter, the parol evidence rule or proof that the warranty was not part of the basis of the bargain, are the only two ways in which the seller can defeat an oral express warranty inconsistent with a disclaimer. To defeat a written express warranty with a written disclaimer, the seller must prove the warranty was not part of the basis of the bargain.

To disclaim the implied warranty of merchantability, the language of the disclaimer must contain the word *merchantability* or one of its variants. And if the disclaimer is written, it must be a conspicuous writing. UCC § 2–316. As a practical matter, these requirements severely hamper the seller. The prudent consumer marketing company will ponder long and hard before invoking the right to disclaim the implied warranty of merchantability. Picture the typical shopper's reaction when she picks up a can of peaches at the local supermarket and finds conspicuously displayed thereon the word *nonmerchantable*, or the phrase "the implied warranty of merchantability is hereby disclaimed." Oral disclaimers of the warranty of merchantability would be even more attention getting, in addition to being difficult to prove. To exclude the implied warranty of fitness for a particular purpose, the disclaimer must be written and conspicuous. UCC § 2–316(2). However, no special language is required.

Since a written disclaimer of either of the implied warranties must be conspicuous, the question arises as to what will be deemed conspicuous. The following case discusses the point and illustrates as well the general judicial antipathy toward disclaimers.

Hunt v. Perkins Machinery Co.
Supreme Judicial Court of Massachusetts, 1967. 352 Mas. 535, 226 N.E.2d 228

[Hunt purchased a marine engine from Perkins. On the face of the order it was stated: "BOTH THIS ORDER AND ITS ACCEPTANCE ARE SUBJECT TO 'TERMS AND CONDITIONS' STATED IN THIS ORDER." On the reverse side at the top, the words "TERMS AND CONDITIONS" appeared. Underneath these words were eleven numbered paragraphs. One of the paragraphs was printed in bold block letters. It was a disclaimer of all warranties, express and implied. Hunt did not read anything on the back of the order when he signed it. However, when the engine proved defective Hunt sued for breach of the implied warranties of merchantability and fitness for a particular purpose. The trial judge denied Perkins's motion for a directed verdict and the jury returned a verdict in favor of Hunt for $5,357. Perkins appealed, claiming that the trial judge erred in failing to decide in his favor.]

CUTLER, J.

. . . .

This case presents issues under the Uniform Commercial Code concerning excluding or modifying (a) the implied warranty of merchantability under § 2–314, and (b) the implied warranty under § 2–315, that goods shall be fit for a particular purpose. Section 2–316(2) reads, in part: "(2) . . . [T]o exclude or modify the implied warranty of merchantability or any part of it the language must mention merchantability *and in case of a writing must be conspicuous,* and to exclude or modify any implied warranty of fitness the exclusion must be by a writing and *conspicuous.* Language to exclude all implied warranties of fitness is sufficient if it states, for example, that 'There are no warranties which extend beyond the description *on the face hereof'* " (emphasis supplied). Section 2–316(2) must be read with § 1–201(10) which provides, in part: " 'Conspicuous': A term . . . is conspicuous when it is so written that a reasonable person against whom it is to operate *ought to have noticed it.* A printed heading in capitals (as: NON-NEGOTIABLE BILL OF LADING) is conspicuous. Language in the body of a form is 'conspicuous' if it is in larger or other contrasting type or color. . . . Whether a term or clause is 'conspicuous' . . . is for decision by the court" (emphasis supplied).

Hunt concedes that Perkins's disclaimer of warranties would have been effective if the disclaimer language in the "Terms and Conditions," . . . instead of being on the back of the contract form had been (a) on the face of the purchase order, or (b) had been referred to on the face of the order by words such as "see other side" or "as stated on the reverse hereof." The first question for decision is whether the disclaimer of the warranties on the back of this purchase order was "conspicuous."

Some light is shed upon the meaning of "conspicuous" in § 1–201(10) by the official comment on the subsection, which says in part, "This is intended to indicate some of the methods of making a term attention-calling. But the test is whether attention can reasonably be expected to be called to it." . . . Most commentators discuss the issue in general terms.

The decided cases are not controlling. In *Boeing Airplane Co.* v. *O'Malley,* . . . a disclaimer "merely in the same color and size of type used for the other provisions" was treated as not conspicuous. In *Minikes* v. *Admiral Corp.,* . . . a "disclaimer . . . smaller, not larger, than the rest of the purchase order" was held not conspicuous. In *Roto-Lith, Ltd.* v. *F. P. Bartlett & Co.,* . . . effect was given to a disclaimer in type "still conspicuous" on the back of the acceptance of an order, which was referred to on the front of the order in the following terms, "All goods sold without warranties, express or implied, and subject to the terms on reverse side."

Under 2–316(2) read with the last sentence of 1–201(10), it is a question of law for the court whether a provision is conspicuous. We are in as good a position to decide that issue as the trial judge, for a photographic copy of both sides of the purchase order is before us. We decide the issue by applying the statutory test under 1–201(10) of what is conspicuous, viz. whether "a reasonable person against whom . . . (the disclaimer) is to operate ought to have noticed it."

In the language of the official comment . . . the bold face printing on the front of the purchase order (although adequate in size and contrast with the rest of the printing on the form) was not in words sufficient to call attention to the language on the back of the form. That language would naturally be concealed because the forms were part of a pad of paper when Hunt signed the paper. There was no reference whatsoever on the front of the order to the "Terms and Conditions" as being on the back of the order, and the quoted words "Terms and Conditions" might have been thought to apply to other small type provisions on the front of the order unless Hunt had happened to turn over the form and look at the back of the order. His first reasonable opportunity to do this was when the executed form was returned to him.

In the opinion of a majority of the court, the provisions on the front of the purchase order did not make adequate reference to the provisions on the back of the order to draw attention to the latter. Hence the provisions on the back of the order cannot be said to be conspicuous although printed in an adequate size and style of type. The disclaimer was not effective.

Exceptions overruled.

Sale "As Is"

Two exceptions to the general rules on disclaiming warranties are the "as is" provision and the inspection provision.

If goods are sold "as is" or "with all faults," both quality warranties and the implied warranty of title are abrogated. UCC § 2–316(3)(a). Thus, if the contract between a buyer and a boatyard contains a provision that "the Lightning class sailboat that is the subject of this agreement is sold as is," the merchantability and fitness warranties are excluded without following any technical procedure. Merchantability does not have to be mentioned, and disclaimer of the fitness warranty does not have to be in writing. Words other than *as is* and *with all faults* may be substituted, but whatever the language, it must be powerful enough to call attention to the exclusion of warranties.

Note, however, that the exception is effective only against the implied warranties. It is totally ineffective against express warranties.

Inspection

Inspection of the goods by the buyer or his agent before entering into the contract is the second exception to the general rules governing modification and exclusion of warranties. This exception, like the "as is" provision, relates only to implied warranties. It differs from the "as is" exception by pertaining solely to defects that examination should reveal. Looking at the engine of a used car is not apt to disclose a hairline crack in the engine block. Suppose, though, that a glance under the hood revealed a hole in the radiator. The implied quality warranties do not protect the inspecting buyer in the situation of an obvious defect.

May the seller effectively assert that the implied quality warranties have been excluded if the buyer failed to inspect? No. The seller must demand that the buyer fully examine the goods (or the model or sample). UCC § 2–316, comment 8. Mere availability for inspection is not enough. In addition, inspection, or refusal to inspect, waives the implied warranties only with regard to those defects that inspection would or should have disclosed. UCC § 2–316(3)(b).

PRIVITY

Privity in Perspective

The word *privity* is legal shorthand for *privity of contract*, a concept which means that a direct contractual relationship exists between buyer and seller. The concept of privity is quite straightforward and easy, as the following example illustrates.

A buyer and a seller enter into a contract pursuant to which the buyer purchases from the seller a sonar depth gauge manufactured by Morrison Manufacturing. The buyer and seller are in privity of contract with each other; so are the seller and Morrison. But no privity exists between the buyer and Morrison Manufacturing.

The consequences of privity are equally simple to comprehend. Historically, and until quite recently, a plaintiff had to be in privity of contract with a defendant before the plaintiff could recover for damages caused by a defective product. In other words, warranties were only extended to and enforceable by those who were in privity of contract with the seller. To illustrate, suppose that the buyer's boat was severely damaged because of a defect in the sonar device, which amounted to a breach of a quality warranty. Basic privity doctrine would permit the buyer to recover against the retailer, but would preclude recovery against the manufacturer Morrison. Similarly, if the buyer had given the depth gauge to a friend, the friend would not be in privity of contract with either the seller or Morrison and would have no suit against either of them should her boat be damaged. The same result would have followed had the buyer loaned or resold the depth gauge to his friend. The privity of contract doctrine, when operative, is an extremely effective and important limitation on the enforcement of the quality warranties.

Privity Under the UCC

In the formative stages of Anglo-American law, privity was naturally characteristic of most sales, which were simple transactions between a craftsman (who sold his own product) and a buyer. In time, a question was raised: could a user, who was not the purchaser, recover from the artisan for injuries sustained by the user as the result of the breach of an express warranty given by the artisan to the purchaser? An analogous question, posed in the famous

English case of *Winterbottom* v. *Wright,* 10 M&W 109 (Exch. 1842) was answered, "No," and for many years, American courts followed this example.

Evolutions in business changed the relationship between consumer and manufacturer, however: products became more complicated and potentially dangerous; extensive and enthusiastic advertising emerged; liability insurance became available; a retailer and often a wholesaler were sandwiched between the consumer and the manufacturer. In the minds of many, the privity doctrine, in the face of these business changes, gave the manufacturer a disproportionately advantageous relationship with the consumer and burdened the retailer with excessive responsibility for defective goods. To adjust the balance of responsibility for defective merchandise, many judges became inventive in limiting the privity doctrine in order to extend warranty protection.

The UCC takes an intermediate position on privity. It gives states three alternatives from which to choose. Alternative C, the most protective of consumers, does not go as far as some states in restricting the privity doctrine. Neither does Alternative A, the most restrictive, codify a privity limitation as rigorous as in *Winterbottom.*

The Code's privity provision has already received considerable authoritative and useful judicial comment. The following case involves the most restrictive alternative. The opinion discusses the privity questions not covered by any of the alternatives under section 2-318 and discusses the major definitions under Alternative A (*guest, family member,* and *household*) and their relationship to the "reasonable expectation" requirement.

Miller v. Preitz

Supreme Court of Pennsylvania, 1966. 422 Pa. 383, 221 A.2d 320

COHEN, JUSTICE.

. . . .

[On October 1, 1961, Gloria Sewell purchased a vaporizer-humidifier from defendant Preitz, owner of the Hartsville Pharmacy. Miss Sewell subsequently loaned the device to her sister, who lived next door, for use in relieving the nasal congestion of Miss Sewell's infant nephew, Brian Coakley. On January 27, 1962, the vaporizer, while in use, suddenly spewed boiling water on the nephew's body, causing his death three days later. Miller, the administrator of the infant's estate, brought suit for breach of the implied warranty of merchantability against Preitz (the retailer), Rexall Drug Company (the distributor from whom Preitz acquired the vaporizer), and Northern Electric Company (the manufacturer).

Asserting that they were not in privity of contract with the infant, all three defendants sought to have the case dismissed before trial. The lower court upheld the defendants and the plaintiff appealed.

After discussing the relevant "Wrongful Death" and "Survival" statutes the court continued.]

. . . The issue remains, however, whether decedent's lack of "privity" to the warranties precludes the action.

With respect to this issue there are two main inquiries. The first is whether section 2–318 of the Commercial Code obviates the requirement of "privity" with respect to the plaintiff.

Section 2–318 provides:

"A seller's warranty whether express or implied extends to *any natural person who is in the family or household of his buyer* or who is a guest in his home if it is reasonable to expect that such person may use, consume or be affected by the goods and who is injured in person by breach of the warranty. . . ." (Emphasis supplied). Act of April 6, 1953 . . . P.S. § 2–318.

The comments to this section elaborate on its purpose and scope:

"2.   The purpose of this section is to give the buyer's family, household and guests the benefit of the same warranty which the buyer received in the contract of sale, thereby freeing any such beneficiaries from any technical rules as to 'privity.' It seeks to accomplish this purpose without any derogation of any right or remedy resting on negligence. It rests primarily upon the merchant-seller's warranty under this Article that the goods sold are merchantable and fit for the ordinary purposes for which such goods are used rather than the warranty of fitness for a particular purpose. Implicit in this section is that any beneficiary of a warranty may bring a direct action for breach of warranty against the seller whose warranty extends to him.
"3.   This section expressly includes as beneficiaries within its provisions the family, household, and guests of the purchaser. Beyond this, the section is neutral and is not intended to enlarge or restrict the developing case law on whether the seller's warranties, given to his buyer who resells, extend to other persons in the distributive chain."

. . . .

With respect to this inquiry appellant contends that the decedent, being a nephew of the "buyer," was in her "family," as that term is used in Section 2–318, and, therefore, within the benefit of defendant Hartsville Pharmacy's implied warranty. The lower court held and appellees urge that the word "family" was meant by the Legislature to be used interchangeably with the word "household" and that since the decedent, who lived next door to his aunt, was not a member of her "household" he could not be in her "family." In our opinion such a construction is erroneous. The word "family" appears in the phrase "any natural person who is in the family or household of his buyer or who is a guest in his home." Obviously, the clause "guest in his home" has significance different from and independent of the clause "person . . . in the . . . household." It would seem also that the clause "person . . . in the family" has significance different from and independent of the clause "person . . . in the . . . household" rather than being mere surplusage. The use of the conjunction "or" strengthens the natural conclusion that "family" and "household" have different meanings in this statute.

. . . .

The statute provides no clear indication of the meaning to be given to the word "family," and we have found no case on the matter. In our opinion, considering the remedial nature of the provision and the natural connotations of the word, its meaning was not intended to be unduly restrictive. Accordingly, we hold that the word "family" as used in this statute includes the nephew of the purchaser. This interpretation of the word "family" is not too burdensome on the seller who makes the warranty because not only must the beneficiary be in the buyer's family but also it must be "reasonable to expect that such person may use, consume or be affected by the goods. . . ." Whether this member of the family was also within the latter clause is a factual and objective question and depends upon all the relevant circumstances, which may include such factors as the remoteness of the family relation, the geographical connection between the buyer and the member of his family, and the nature of the product.

Because decedent was in the buyer's "family," section 2–318 supports his representative's action against defendant Preitz, notwithstanding decedent's lack of privity. Therefore, it was error to sustain said defendant's demurrer to plaintiff's second count. Of course, the pertinent factual matters must be proven before recovery may be had.

. . . .

[The court went on to hold that the suits against the distributor and manufacturer were properly dismissed.[1] The suit against Preitz was sent back to the lower court for trial.]

Supplementary State Law

Consider the following situation: Manufacturer, Inc., sells an electric waffle iron to Wholesaler, Inc., which in turn resells the waffle iron to Retailer, Inc. John Buyer then purchases the appliance. Frances Buyer, a member of John's family, is later injured because of a defect in the product. If Frances is a foreseeable user, the UCC and *Miller* v. *Preitz* make it clear that she can recover from Retailer, Inc., since she is a family member. However, suppose Retailer, Inc., is a small local store without sufficient insurance or financial resources to pay the desired judgment. Can Frances sue the manufacturer or the wholesaler, the more distant sellers? Though the Code is silent on this important question, the official comments quoted in the *Miller* case tell us to refer to supplementary state law to resolve this question.

In addition, supplementary state law governs important variations on the waffle iron situation. Suppose John Buyer had given the waffle iron to his friends Stan and Susan Strong as a wedding present. If Susan was the injured party, she would find no warranty protection in the Code. She is not in Buyer's family, nor is she in his household, nor is she a guest in his home. Her ability to sue even the retailer would depend on non-Code law. Even John Buyer might have to resort to supplementary state law. Suppose he kept the waffle iron and was injured because of the defect. Clearly he could sue the retailer; there is no privity problem here. But could he sue the manufacturer or the wholesaler? The Code itself says neither yes nor no.

The next case indicates the general response most states have given to this question. While reading it, keep these relationships in mind:

Manufacturer of component
↓
Manufacturer of the finished product
↓
Wholesaler
↓
Retailer
↓
Purchasing consumer — user — bystander

---

1. That portion of *Miller* v. *Preitz* denying the plaintiff recovery against the manufacturer was overruled in *Kassab* v. *Central Sova,* 432 Pa. 217, 246 A.2d 848 (1968). The court stated in *Kassab* that: "[T]his Court is now of the opinion that Pennsylvania should join the fast growing list of jurisdictions that have eliminated the privity requirement in assumpsit suits by purchasers against remote manufacturers for breach of implied warranty. That aspect of *Miller* must therefore be overruled."

In addition, it may facilitate understanding to view the case as asking the court either to expand the list of potential defendants (vertical privity) or to expand the list of potential plaintiffs (horizontal privity). For example, if a state permits an injured purchasing consumer to recover from the manufacturer of the finished product, should it also let her recover from the manufacturer of a component part if the component part caused the product to malfunction? As another example, should an innocent bystander injured by a defective product be permitted to recover from the manufacturer of the finished product if the purchasing consumer could have recovered had he been injured? A last point to bear in mind is the nature of the warranty. Does the court make a distinction (or should it make a distinction) on privity questions among express warranties, implied warranties or merchantability, and implied warranties of fitness for a particular purpose?

Randy Knitwear, Inc. v. American Cyanamid Co.
Court of Appeals of New York, 1962. 11 N.Y.2d 5, 181 N.E.2d 399

FULD, JUDGE.

"The assault upon the citadel of privity," Chief Judge Cardozo wrote in 1931, "is proceeding in these days apace." (*Ultramares Corp.* v. *Touche*, 255 N.Y. 170 . . .). In these days, too, for the present appeal, here by leave of the Appellate Division on a certified question, calls upon us to decide whether, under the facts disclosed, privity of contract is essential to maintenance of an action against a manufacturer for breach of express warranty.

American Cyanamid Company is the manufacturer of chemical resins, marketed under the registered trade-mark "Cyana," which are used by textile manufacturers and finishers to process fabrics in order to prevent them from shrinking. Apex Knitted Fabrics and Fairtex Mills are manufacturers of fabrics who were licensed or otherwise authorized by Cyanamid to treat their goods with "Cyana" and to sell such goods under the "Cyana" label and, with the guaranty that they were "Cyana" finished. Randy Knitwear, a manufacturer of children's knitted sportswear and play clothes, purchased large quantities of these "Cyana" treated fabrics from Apex and Fairtex. After most of such fabrics had been made up into garments and sold by Randy to customers, it was claimed that ordinary washing caused them to shrink and to lose their shape. This action for breach of express warranty followed, each of the 3 parties being made the subject of a separate count. After serving its answer, Cyanamid, urging lack of privity of contract, moved for summary judgment dismissing the cause of action asserted against it, and it is solely with this cause of action that we are concerned.

. . . .

[Our] traditional privity limitation on a seller's liability for damage resulting from breach of warranty has not, however, been adhered to with perfect logical consistency . . . and, just a year ago, in *Greenberg* v. *Lorenz*, we noted the definite shift away from the technical privity requirement and recognized that it should be dispensed with in a proper case in the interest of justice and reason. More specifically, we held in *Greenberg* that, in cases involving foodstuffs and other household goods, the implied warranties of fitness and merchantability run from the retailer to the members of the purchaser's household, regardless of privity of contract. We are now confronted with the further but related question whether the traditional privity limitation shall also be dispensed with in an action for breach of express warranty by a remote purchaser against a manufacturer who induced a purchase by representing the quality of the goods in public advertising and on labels which accompanied the goods.

. . . .

The world of merchandising is, in brief, no longer a world of direct contract; it is, rather, a world of advertising and, when representations expressed and disseminated in the mass communications media and on labels (attached to the goods themselves) prove false and the user or consumer is damaged by reason of his reliance on those representations, it is difficult to justify the manufacturer's denial of liability on the sole ground of the absence of technical privity. Manufacturers make extensive use of newspapers, periodicals and other media to call attention, in glowing terms, to the qualities and virtues of their products, and this advertising is directed at the ultimate consumer or at some manufacturer or supplier who is not in privity with them. Equally sanguine representations on packages and labels frequently accompany the article throughout its journey to the ultimate consumer and, as intended, are relied upon by remote purchasers. Under these circumstances, it is highly unrealistic to limit a purchaser's protection to warranties made directly to him by his immediate seller. The protection he really needs is against the manufacturer whose published representations caused him to make the purchase.

. . . .

It is true that in many cases the manufacturer will ultimately be held accountable for the falsity of his representations, but only after an unduly wasteful process of litigation. Thus, if the consumer or ultimate business user sues and recovers, for breach of warranty, from his immediate seller and if the latter in turn, sues and recovers against his supplier in recoupment of his damages and costs, eventually, after several separate actions by those in the chain of distribution, the manufacturer may finally be obliged "to shoulder the responsibility which should have been his in the first instance." . . .

. . . [I]nsistence upon the privity requirement may well leave the aggrieved party, whether he be ultimate business user or consumer, without a remedy in a number of situations. For instance, he would be remediless either where his immediate seller's representations as to quality were less extravagant or enthusiastic than those of the manufacturer or where — as is asserted by Fairtex in this very case . . . — there has been an effective disclaimer of any and all warranties by the plaintiff's immediate seller. Turning to the case before us, even if the representations respecting "Cyana" treated fabric were false, the plaintiff would be foreclosed of all remedy against Fairtex, if it were to succeed on its defense of disclaimer, and against Cyanamid because of a lack of privity. . . .

Although we believe that it has already been made clear, it is to be particularly remarked that in the present case the plaintiff's reliance is not on newspaper advertisements alone. It places heavy emphasis on the fact that the defendant not only made representations (as to the nonshrinkable character of "Cyana Finish" fabrics) in newspapers and periodicals, but also repeated them on its own labels and tags which accompanied the fabrics purchased by the plaintiff from Fairtex and Apex. There is little in reason or logic to support Cyanamid's submission that it should not be held liable to the plaintiff even though the representations prove false in fact and it is ultimately found that the plaintiff relied to its harm upon such representations in making its purchases.

OTHER CONTRACTUAL LIMITATIONS ON LIABILITY

The UCC allows buyers and sellers substantial — but not unlimited — freedom to contract for provisions that modify the Code's general rules. Attempts to disclaim warranties have already been discussed. With substantial frequency the contracting parties jockey for position over five other categories of UCC terms: the type of damages for which the buyer can recover; a cap or maximum dollar amount of damage recovery per incident; a modification of the standard statute of limitations; the period of time within which notice of an alleged breach of warranty must be given to the seller; and, less frequently, an indemnification provision whereby the buyer agrees that in the event of resale it will insist on similar provisions from the new buyer and will indemnify the manufacturer-seller should the limitations not be forthcoming.

The UCC is, of course, not the only body of law that exposes a manufacturer or other seller to potential liability. Typically the contract will also speak to these other topics. One such topic is liability for negligence, which is commonly addressed in a so-called *exculpatory clause* (See Chapter 3). Another topic is that of *strict liability in tort*. The circumstances under which this recently developed concept can be limited by contract are currently being worked out by the courts. The position articulated in *Southwest Forest Industries, Inc.* v. *Westinghouse Electric Corp.*, which will be considered shortly, is typical.

Especially where sophisticated parties are negotiating over unique goods, it is understandable that they should desire to confront the legal and economic risks arising under both the UCC and tort law and allocate them to one party or the other. For example, if the seller or its insurance company is to bear the risk of a substantial payment because of a broad range of potential damages, it should adjust the selling price upward to compensate for that risk, whereas if the buyer or its insurance company is to have limited access to damage theories, a lower contract price should reflect this fact.

Limitations by Dollar Amount and Category of Damages

Damages are of several types. Should an automobile wheel collapse, causing damage and provoking a law suit, *direct damages* would include such things as the broken wheel or a bent fender, had one resulted from the wheel's collapse. *Consequential damages* are more remote and less foreseeable than direct damages. For example, should a taxi's wheel collapse and its owner seek to recover for lost profits while the vehicle is out of operation, such lost profits, if recoverable at all, would fall under the heading of consequential damages. Consequential damages arise with less frequency than direct damages, but the dollar amounts they represent often dwarf the direct damages or the sale price of the goods. Understandably, then, sellers often view damages in general, and consequential damages in particular, as something of a legal and financial time bomb that needs to be defused. The cap or maximum dollar recovery for any breach of contract is one straightforward approach. An alternative, which raises several subsidiary problems, is to seek to exclude the worrisome category by specifying that there will be no recovery of consequential damages.

One's ability to predict consequential damages is limited since the actual events that are sufficiently foreseeable vary from case to case. To minimize or overcome this problem, sellers like to specify only those things for which there can be a recovery. This approach is often buttressed with an *exclusivity of remedy clause*, that is, one which states that the rights and remedies provided in the contract are the only ones the buyer has.

Another problem involves the so-called battle of the forms. Large corporations often have carefully developed boilerplate provisions in their purchase or sale documents. When negotiations and correspondence have gone on for a substantial period of time, it often becomes a very important question of fact as to whose contract terms govern. If it is unclear whose were intended to govern, courts will often apply the general rules of the UCC. Another typical issue is whether both parties had the requisite sophistication to appreciate the implications of the limitations on liability.

The following case deals primarily with an attempt to exclude recovery for consequential damages. On a secondary level, it considers a reduction in the statute of limitations and an attempt to eliminate liability for negligence and strict liability in tort. It is illustrative of judicial attitude where knowledgeable parties have entered into an agreement containing limitation of liability provisions.

Southwest Forest Industries, Inc. v. Westinghouse Electric Corp.
United States Court of Appeals, Ninth Circuit, 1970. 422 F.2d 1013, cert. denied 400 U.S. 902

DUNIWAY, CIRCUIT JUDGE.

In 1963 Southwest Forest Industries, Inc. [Southwest] brought suit against Westinghouse Electric Corp. [Westinghouse] for damages resulting from defects in a 25,000 kilowatt turbine generator sold by Westinghouse to Southwest.[1] Jurisdiction in the district court rested on diversity of citizenship. Southwest appeals from the district court's judgment for Westinghouse. We affirm.

After preliminary feasibility studies, Southwest and Rust Engineering Company [Rust] entered into an agreement under which Rust was to construct a pulp and paper mill for Southwest near Snowflake, Arizona. Pursuant to this agreement, Rust initiated negotiations with Westinghouse for the purchase of the generator in 1960. There followed a warranty battle, the outcome of which is disputed by the parties. Westinghouse built the unit and it was installed in the Southwest plant in late 1961. The bulk of the damages claimed by Southwest are for "lost time, labor, materials, and loss of business" suffered as the result of subsequent slowdowns and shutdowns in Southwest's Snowflake plant in late 1961 and 1962, allegedly caused by defects in the Westinghouse generator.

. . . .

2. The Merits.

Proceeding to the merits, there are several issues properly before this court on appeal.

a. Was There a Meeting of the Minds?

First, Southwest argues that there was never a meeting of the minds on the Westinghouse form of warranty as required by the Uniform Commercial Code,

---

1. The original claim was for $11,000,000. By the time of trial it had been reduced to approximately $2,500,000. An antitrust count in the original complaint was severed.

§§ 2–204, 2–207(3) as interpreted by the Pennsylvania courts. In light of the nature of the decision below, this must be taken as an argument that the district court's decision was clearly erroneous or unsupported by the evidence.[2] That position cannot be maintained on this record, and thus we need not go into Southwest's argument that code warranties apply in the absence of agreement on an express warranty or that Southwest's own warranty applies. We leave the "battle of the warranties" problem to another day.

b. Was the Limiting Language of the Warranty Unconscionable?

Southwest argues that the limitation of consequential damages was unconscionable, and that the limitation was not brought to the attention of Southwest. As to the latter assertion, the district court expressly found that:

> "[t] here were experienced purchasing departments, staffs of engineers, and legal departments available to all three companies. Rust has had great experience in purchasing electrical equipment from Westinghouse. . . .
> All purchasing departments involved were familiar with the Westinghouse order and acknowledgement forms."

The unconscionability argument runs as follows: under the warranty Southwest's sole remedy was repair or replacement of defective parts; Westinghouse made the repairs negligently and Southwest was thus left without any remedy at all; this makes the exculpatory clause unconscionable and therefore invalid under UCC sections 2–719(2) and 2–302.

The problem with this argument is that it was not raised properly below. As the district court noted in its opinion, "there is no evidence before the court that Westinghouse failed to perform its obligations under its warranty . . . there are no allegations of unconscionability." In rejecting the argument when it denied Southwest's motion to alter or amend, the district judge said:

> "I do not think that the question of unconscionability was ever seriously raised by counsel. No offer was ever made to make any record supporting it, and I think in the context of this case these facts and these parties, the court could not say that there was a question of unconscionability upon which evidence should be taken particularly in the absence of any offer or claim by counsel to that effect."

We agree. Certainly the district judge's refusal to entertain the argument on the post-judgment motion was not an abuse of discretion.

c. Was There Liability for Negligence?

Southwest's argument concerning liability for negligence must take the following form in light of our characterization of the proceedings below: The district court erred in its conclusion that the Westinghouse warranty was adequate as a matter

---

2. The district court said: "At all times in the negotiations and in the contract documents, and in the complaint itself, which alleges June 6, 1960, as the contract date, all of the parties operated on the assumption that the Westinghouse proposal and the Rust letter of intent, as confirmed by the Westinghouse order acknowledgement form, constituted the contract for the sale of the turbine generator unit. The conduct of the parties during the entire time and up to the filing on August 2, 1967, of plaintiff's 'Amendment of Complaint — July 29, 1967,' cannot reasonably be explained on any other basis. By every objective test there was an agreement as to the nature of the contract in effect and its terms and conditions and particularly as to the express warranty involved." (Footnotes omitted.)

of law to relieve Westinghouse from liability for (1) negligent breach of warranty and (2) negligence on a pure tort theory; therefore Southwest was entitled to a jury trial on the issue of negligence.

As to the first, Pennsylvania law applies. The district court was correct in holding that "[L]imitations of liability under Pennsylvania law are valid and enforceable. The parties to an agreement may contract as to limitation of liability resulting from breach of both express and implied warranties." Such a limitation may also preclude recovery for losses resulting from negligence.

. . . .

The general rule is to permit contracts limiting tort liability when they have been bargained between large corporate enterprises as here. . . . Thus the district court was correct in finding that the Westinghouse warranty succeeded in limiting Westinghouse's liability for consequential damages resulting from negligence.

. . . .

. . . [T]he warranty is clear both that repair and replacement are all that Westinghouse may be held responsible for and that Westinghouse may not be held liable for consequential damages.

. . . .

Finally, Southwest argues that Westinghouse should have been held liable on a theory of strict liability in tort. The district court was correct when it granted Westinghouse's pretrial motion for summary judgment on this count. As the district court said:

> "the principles underlying the doctrine of strict liability in tort for defective products were not applicable. All damages sought by Southwest in this case are consequential damages. The turbine generator is a highly specialized, custom-built piece of machinery, built to particular specifications and tested in the factory before delivery, under supervision of engineers representing both parties.
>
> The circumstances of this case do not bring the plaintiff within that class of consumers, type of transaction, or damages suffered that created the need for relief based on strict liability in tort. Neither the philosophy nor the theory of the doctrine of strict liability in tort nor the actual holdings of the cases involved support an extension of the doctrine of strict liability in tort to the present facts." (Footnotes omitted.)

Affirmed.

Buyer's Delay in Giving Notice of Breach

The buyer may be prevented from asserting an otherwise valid claim if he delays too long in apprising the seller of an alleged breach. Prompt notification is a necessary and reasonable requirement. The seller should have an opportunity to correct flaws or to resell or otherwise to dispose of his defective goods.

More difficult questions arise, though, when the buyer carelessly fails to discover a defect or when the defect is of such a nature that it is difficult to perceive. The following case summarizes the relevant provisions of the UCC and constitutes, as well, an example of a seller's attempt to limit warranties by contractually specifying the period within which notice must be given.

Q. Vanderberg & Sons, N.V. v. Siter
Superior Court of Pennsylvania, 1964. 204 Pa. Super. 392, 204 A.2d 494

[Plaintiff had sold tulip and hyacinth bulbs to the defendant. The bulbs did not flower and defendant, contending that the plaintiff had allowed them to grow beyond their capacity, refused to pay. The plaintiff sued for the price and the defendant counterclaimed for damages for breach of express warranties and implied warranties of merchantability and fitness.

The lower court entered judgment for the plaintiff after excluding the defendant's evidence as to the condition of the bulbs during the period beginning nine days after delivery. The defendant appealed and asked for a new trial arguing that the judge erred in excluding the evidence.]

The contract contained the following clause of warranty: "The seller warrants the goods to be sound and healthy at the time of shipment but does not otherwise warrant flowering or other planting, growing or forcing results. . . . All claims hereunder shall be deemed waived unless presented within eight (8) days after receipt of the goods."

. . . .

While the defendants did not present their claim until several months after they received the bulbs, it was for the jury to say, under proper instructions, whether the eight day limitation is reasonable and binding upon them under the circumstances. Several provisions of the Uniform Commercial Code affect this question. Section 2–607 (12A P.S. § 2–607) provides that the buyer must give notice of the breach of the contract of sale "within a reasonable time after he discovers or should have discovered any breach. . . ." Section 2–608 (12A P.S. § 2–608) provides: "(2) Revocation of acceptance must occur within a reasonable time after the buyer discovers or should have discovered the ground for it. . . ." Finally, § 1–204 (12A P.S. § 1–204) provides: "(1) Wherever this Act requires any action to be taken within a reasonable time, the agreement may fix any time which is not manifestly unreasonable. (2) What is a reasonable time for taking any action depends on the nature, purpose and circumstances of such action."

Under the defendants' evidence which was stricken out by the court below, the defects in the bulbs which prevented flowering, though existing at the time of delivery, were latent, and not known to the defendants at the time of planting and could not be discovered thereafter by the buyer until flowering time. The defendants argue that this makes the eight day limitation unreasonable under § 1–204 of the code, supra.

. . . .

Undoubtedly the parties may by their contract limit the time for the buyer's notice of claim for breach of warranties, but the limitation must be reasonable. A limitation which renders the warranties ineffective as regards latent defects, literally covered by the warranty but not discoverable within the limitation period of the contract, is manifestly unreasonable and therefore invalid under § 1–204 of the code. The evidence offered by the defendants on the question of the timeliness of the notice under the circumstances should have been received and left for the jury's consideration, along with the countervailing evidence of the plaintiff.

. . . .

[The judgment was reversed and a new trial ordered.]

UNCONSCIONABLE CONTRACTS

Restriction on Attempts to Limit Warranties

The unconscionable contract provision, section 2–302, is a straightforward and candid authorization to the courts to exercise their historic equitable powers to strike down contracts, or portions of contracts, which are decidedly unfair. It is not limited to antiwarranty clauses. It can be used against any grossly offensive matter, as was pointed out in our earlier discussion of duress in Chapter 6. The unconscionable contract provision states that if the court finds a contract or clause thereof unconscionable (such as the pound of Antonio's flesh Shylock demands as part of the contract in Shakespeare's *The Merchant of Venice*) at the time it was made, the court may refuse to enforce the whole contract or any unconscionable part of it in order to avoid an unconscionable result.

The inclusion in the Code of the unconscionable contract provision recognizes the fact that judges on occasion have secured what they thought were just results by manipulating the rules of offer and acceptance, or by resorting to the conclusion that a particular clause was either contrary to public policy or in violation of the dominant purpose of a contract. However laudable this pursuit of justice, it has had undesirable side effects: bending basic legal principles out of their familiar shape can diminish the predictability so important in law. By permitting the courts through the unconscionable contract provision to exercise their equitable instincts and powers in the sales area, it is hoped that the general principles of the sales contract will not be subjected to distortion and that the application of UCC principles to fact situations will thereby ensure a more uniform posture throughout the states.

The unconscionable contract provision is not intended to give the courts *carte blanche* to hand down decisions that comport with the judge's "gut feeling" sense of justice. The basic tests for application were stated in the comments to the provision earlier considered at pages 141–44. The comments go on to give examples of decisions consistent with the section:

> The underlying basis of this section is illustrated by the results in cases such as the following:
> *Kansas City Wholesale Grocery Co.* v. *Weber Packing Corporation*, 93 Utah 414, 73 P2d 1272 (1937), where a clause limiting time for complaints was held inapplicable to latent defects in a shipment of catsup which could be discovered only by microscopic analysis; *Hardy* v. *General Motors Acceptance Corporation*, 38 Ga App 463, 144 SE 327 (1928), holding that a disclaimer of warranty clause applied only to express warranties, thus letting in a fair implied warranty; *Andrews Bros.* v. *Singer & Co.* (1934 CA) 1 KB 17, holding that where a car with substantial mileage was delivered instead of a "new" car, a disclaimer of warranties, including those "implied," left unaffected an "express obligation" on the description, even though the Sale of Goods Act called such an implied warranty.

It becomes apparent that only extreme and flagrant cases are to be affected by the unconscionable contract provision. Nevertheless, a feel for the law in this area and insight into the factors that will weigh heavily with the courts can be gained by considering the very articulate and much cited opinion in the pre-Code case of *Henningsen* v. *Bloomfield Motors, Inc.* Comment 2 of the New Jersey Study of the Code states that *Henningsen* "cited 2–302 with approval and seems to be decided expressly on grounds of unconscionability."

Henningsen v. Bloomfield Motors, Inc.
Supreme Court of New Jersey, 1960. 32 N.J. 358, 161 A.2d 69
FRANCES, J.
Plaintiff Claus H. Henningsen purchased a Plymouth automobile, manufactured by defendant Chrysler Corporation, from defendant Bloomfield Motors, Inc. His wife, plaintiff Helen Henningsen, was injured while driving it and instituted suit against both defendants to recover damages on account of consequential losses. The complaint was predicated upon breach of express and implied warranties. . . . [T]he cause was submitted to the jury . . . on the issues of implied warranty of merchantability. Verdicts were returned against both defendants and in favor of the plaintiffs. Defendants appealed.

. . . .

The manufacturer agrees to replace defective parts for 90 days after the sale or until the car has been driven 4,000 miles, whichever is first to occur, *if the part is sent to the factory, transportation charges prepaid, and if examination discloses to its satisfaction that the part is defective.* It is difficult to imagine a greater burden on the consumer, or less satisfactory remedy. Aside from imposing on the buyer the trouble of removing and shipping the part, the maker has sought to retain the uncontrolled discretion to decide the issue of defectiveness. . . .

[The court held that the implied warranty of merchantability, imposed by law on the sale of the automobile from Chrysler to Mr. Henningsen, was not precluded by the absence of privity. The court then upheld the lower court's conclusion that the warranty was breached. The next question, then, was whether the disclaimer clause and express warranty, in fine print and on the back of the Henningsen's contract, effectively excluded the implied warranty and limited recovery on the express warranty to replacement of parts. The court proceeded to discuss this issue as follows:]

. . . .

[We] must keep in mind the general principle that, in the absence of fraud, one who does not choose to read a contract before signing it, cannot later relieve himself of its burdens. . . . And in applying that principle, the basic tenet of freedom of competent parties to contract is a factor of importance. But in the framework of modern commercial life and business practices, such rules cannot be applied on a strict, doctrinal basis.

. . . In a society such as ours, where the automobile is a common and necessary adjunct of daily life, and where its use is so fraught with danger to the driver, passengers and the public, the manufacturer is under a special obligation in connection with the construction, promotion and sale of his cars. Consequently, the courts must examine purchase agreements closely to see if consumer and public interests are treated fairly. . . .

. . . .

The traditional contract is the result of free bargaining of parties who are brought together by the play of the market and who meet each other on a footing of approximate economic equality. In such a society there is no danger that freedom of contract will be a threat to the social order as a whole. But in present-day commercial life the standardized mass contract has appeared. It is used primarily by enterprises with strong bargaining power and position. . . .

. . . .

The warranty before us is a standardized form designed for mass use. It is imposed upon the automobile consumer. He takes it or leaves it, and he must take it to buy an automobile. No bargaining is engaged in with respect to it. In fact, the dealer through whom it comes to the buyer is without authority to alter it; his function is ministerial — simply to deliver it. The form warranty is not only standard with Chrysler but, as mentioned above, it is the uniform warranty of the Automobile Manufacturers Association. . . .

. . . .

In the context of this warranty, only the abandonment of all sense of justice would permit us to hold that, as a matter of law, the phrase "its obligation under this warranty being limited to making good at its factory any part or parts thereof" signifies to an ordinary reasonable person that he is relinquishing any personal injury claim that might flow from the use of a defective automobile. Such claims are nowhere mentioned. The draftsmanship is reflective of the care and skill of the Automobile Manufacturers Association in undertaking to avoid warranty obligations without drawing too much attention to its effort in that regard. No one can doubt that if the will to do so were present, the ability to inform the buying public of the intention to disclaim liability for injury claims arising from breach of warranty would present no problem.

. . . .

The task of the judiciary is to administer the spirit as well as the letter of the law. On issues such as the present one, part of that burden is to protect the ordinary man against the loss of important rights through what, in effect, is the unilateral act of the manufacturer. The status of the automobile industry is unique. Manufacturers are few in number and strong in bargaining position. In the matter of warranties on the sale of their products, the Automobile Manufacturers Association has enabled them to present a united front. From the standpoint of the purchaser, there can be no arms length negotiating on the subject. Because his capacity for bargaining is so grossly unequal, the inexorable conclusion which follows is that he is not permitted to bargain at all. He must take or leave the automobile on the warranty terms dictated by the maker. He cannot turn to a competitor for better security.

Public policy is a term not easily defined. Its significance varies as the habits and needs of a people may vary. It is not static and the field of application is an ever increasing one. A contract, or a particular provision therein, valid in one era may be wholly opposed to the public policy of another. . . . Courts keep in mind the principle that the best interests of society demand that persons should not be unnecessarily restricted in their freedom to contract. But they do not hesitate to declare void as against public policy contractual provisions which clearly tend to the injury of the public in some way.

. . . .

Under all of the circumstances outlined above, the judgments in favor of the plaintiffs and against the defendants are affirmed.

PROBLEMS AND QUESTIONS

1. What is a disclaimer? What are the limits to its effectiveness?

2. What historical changes have caused courts to loosen the requirement of privity?

3. In the course of selling automobile tires the salesman stated, "These tires will keep their tread for at least 10,000 miles." The sales contract stated, "All warranties, express or implied, are disclaimed." The tires went bad within 5,000 miles of average driving and the buyer sued. What issues are raised by these facts?

What if the disclaimer had said, "Seller does not warant how long these tires will keep their tread."

4. When Minikes claimed that her refrigerator did not meet the implied warranties of merchantability, the seller said that all implied warranties had been disclaimed. To support this claim the seller exhibited the purchase order, on which the disclaimer was printed in type smaller than the type of the rest of the order. Were the warranties effectively disclaimed? How small can a disclaimer be?

5. A sales contract for a shipment of oriental fish included the words "UNMERCHANTABLE FOR CONSUMPTION PURPOSES" in large print under the heading "DISCLAIMERS." The last paragraph under that heading was the only paragraph on the back of the sheet and contained these words in medium print: "There are no warranties of merchantability on the use of this fish for any other purposes." Buyer used the fish for fertilizer and it killed his crops. Can he recover?

6. Bob Matick Chevrolet, Inc., a used car dealer, was asking $395 for a seven-year-old car. After fixing the master cylinder and other defects, Matick sold the car for $325 to a college student, but at that price the company refused to attach any guarantees. A salesperson carefully explained to the buyer that the car was being sold "as is." The student bought the car and drove it 500 miles, when she discovered a latent oil leak, which was fixed only at considerable expense. The buyer sued Matick to recover this expense on the basis of breach of warranty. What would be the result?

7. Seller left a train shipment of eggs on buyer's siding available for his inspection. Buyer bought without inspection and soon discovered that 10 percent of the eggs were broken. A train shipment of eggs is considered merchantable if there is less than 3 percent breakage. Buyer sues for breach of warranty. What would be the result?

What if seller insisted that the buyer inspect them, while assuring the buyer that they were merchantable under ordinary trade standards. The buyer briefly inspected a few boxes but, due to the size of the shipment, told the seller, "I'll rely on your word rather than any inspection." What would be the result?

8. Baxter loaned his new television set to his mother-in-law. A short circuit in the set completely destroyed it and set the mother-in-law's home on fire. The interior of one room was gutted before the flames were snuffed. Mother-in-law sued seller for breach of warranty. What would be the result?

9. Harris asked his nine-year-old son to open a bottle of beer. The boy was injured when the neck snapped off the bottle as he was attempting to uncap it. The seller of the beer maintained that the son could not bring suit against it because it was not reasonable to expect that a nine-year-old boy would be affected in any manner by a bottle of beer. What would be the result?

10. Ballard, a widow, bought her small child a paint set from Sigma. The paint was manufactured by Miller Company. Ballard was in the habit of doing live-in baby sitting, taking her own child with her. While she was baby sitting in the Smiths' home, the Smiths' child and her own child became violently ill while playing with the paint set, due to its toxic effect. Both children were hospitalized. Through their respective parents the two children sue Sigma and Miller. What would be the result?

11. The Rochester Gas & Electric Co. ran its power lines over the same utility poles used by the Rochester Telephone Co. Pimm, a telephone company employee, was doing repair work on the telephone lines when he was electrocuted by touching a faulty electrical fixture installed by Gas & Electric. This fixture had been bought by Gas & Electric from the Graybar Electric Co., a wholesale distributor of electrical products. Graybar, however, had never actually handled the fixture involved in this case. It had arranged for the manufacturer of the fixture to ship it directly to Gas & Electric. Pimm brought a suit against Graybar alleging both negligence and breach of warranty. Will his lack of privity bar the warranty action? Has Graybar been negligent?

12. Buyer bought a set of special storm windows for the purpose of wind-proofing her ski lodge in the mountains of Colorado. Seller knew buyer's purpose and knew that buyer had relied on his choice of windows for that purpose. The windows were bought in July, and the contract stated that all implied warranties were waived if seller did not receive notice of breach by August 30. The first large winter snow storm occurred the following December and blew out all the windows, causing great damage to buyer's lodge. Buyer sued for breach of warranty of fitness. What would be the result?

13. Bunyon bought a two-faced axe from Sharp. The accompanying warranty stated that the axe had a useful life of ten years but that the seller disclaimed all liability for personal injury due to defects in production. After a year of normal use the head of the axe flew off while Bunyon was cutting down a tree and imbedded itself in his ankle. The nerves, tendons, and muscles were severed by the accident, and Bunyon lost the effective use of his foot for life. He brought suit against seller Sharp for breach of implied warranty of merchantability. What would be the result?

14. Capone operated a department store in a ghetto of Washington, D.C. Aware that most of her customers were receiving welfare payments, she sold goods on a revolving credit system that had the effect of keeping many customers saddled with constant payments with interest. The standard form credit contract stated that failure to meet any payment would result in a waiver of all warranties of fitness and merchantability on all goods bought with credit. The waiver was to apply retroactively to all goods bought since the last point in time when the buyer's account was paid in full. Getty had owed Capone varying amounts since 1978, sometimes as little as $5. In June of 1981, he bought a $400 phonograph and missed his September payment. A lamp, bought with credit in 1979 exploded in October, injuring the buyer and setting fire to other of buyer's property. Getty sued Capone for breach of implied warranty of merchantability. What would be the result?

PRODUCT LIABILITY IN PERSPECTIVE

A person injured by a defective product has an arsenal of legal weapons. Understandably, it matters little to him which weapon or theory is effective so long as the desired objective — a good recovery — is secured. The UCC codifies only one recovery theory, breach of warranty. Since our investigation of sales relies primarily on the UCC, it would be easy to lose sight of the other theories. However, we would be remiss if we did not briefly review negligence and strict liability, two alternative recovery theories contained in supplementary state law. A survey of these companion theories serves to place warranties in their proper context within the product liability area.

NEGLIGENCE: A WAY AROUND PRIVITY

The classic common law theory of negligence is a subdivision of tort law, that body of case law dealing with enforcement or protection of private or civil rights which exist independent of contract. To establish negligence, as discussed in Chapter 3, a plaintiff must show the following:

1. That the defendant owed him a legal duty of due care (determined pursuant to the concept of foreseeable danger,
2. That the defendant breached that duty,
3. That the plaintiff sustained damages,
4. That the breach of duty was the proximate cause of the damage.

Shortly after *Winterbottom* v. *Wright* begat the privity requirement, attorneys recognized the potential of negligence theory to circumvent both privity and disclaimer limitations encountered in an action for breach of warranty. The negligence argument was used with considerable success. Many courts then sought to counteract this development by limiting the commercial relationships that gave rise to a duty of due care. Eventually the issue of whether or not a manufacturer or seller owed a duty to

19

NEGLIGENCE AND STRICT LIABILITY: Alternative Theories Protecting Against Defective Goods

a particular plaintiff in a product liability case depended on whether the plaintiff and the manufacturer or seller were in privity of contract. Privity of contract was thus bludgeoned into a tort concept and made a requirement for recovery in negligence actions as well as in actions for breach of warranty.

Blending the tort theory of negligence with the contract theory of privity tended to produce unjust results, parallel to the injustice arising from a similar blending of privity and warranty theories. Manufacturers responsible for the defects and financially most able to assume the liability were often shielded from liability. To mitigate these harsh results, the courts began creating exceptions to the privity limitation in negligence suits. These exceptions developed much more rapidly in negligence actions than in breach of warranty actions and became so substantial that in the landmark case of *MacPherson* v. *Buick,* the privity requirement was swallowed by its exceptions.

MacPherson imposed tort liability on a manufacturer regardless of lack of privity if his defective product was reasonably certain to cause personal injury and if it was reasonably foreseeable that the product would be used by a person such as the plaintiff who was not the immediate purchaser from the defendant. Broadening the class of consumers to whom a manufacturer or seller owed a legal duty of due care sharply curtailed the privity limitation in negligence.

MacPherson v. Buick Motor Co.
Court of Appeals of New York, 1916. 217 N.Y. 382, 111 N.E. 1050

CARDOZO, J.

The defendant is a manufacturer of automobiles. It sold an automobile to a retail dealer. The retail dealer resold to the plaintiff. While the plaintiff was in the car, it suddenly collapsed. He was thrown out and injured. One of the wheels was made of defective wood, and its spokes crumbled into fragments. The wheel was not made by the defendant; it was bought from another manufacturer. There is evidence, however, that its defects could have been discovered by reasonable inspection, and that inspection was omitted. There is no claim that the defendant knew of the defect and willfully concealed it. . . . The charge is one, not of fraud, but of negligence. . . .

The foundations of this branch of the law, at least in this state, were laid in *Thomas* v. *Winchester* (6 N.Y. 397). A poison was falsely labeled. The sale was made to a druggist, who in turn sold to a customer. The customer recovered damages from the seller who affixed the label. . . . A poison falsely labeled is likely to injure anyone who gets it. Because the danger is to be foreseen, there is a duty to avoid the injury. . . .

[Judge Cardozo reviewed a line of New York negligence cases permitting recovery against manufacturers by a plaintiff not in privity with the manufacturer. In one case workmen were injured when a defective scaffold collapsed. In another, the plaintiff was injured when a large coffee urn exploded in a restaurant.]

. . . .

We hold, then, that the principle of *Thomas* v. *Winchester* is not limited to poisons, explosives, and things of like nature, to things which in their normal operation are implements of destruction. If the nature of a thing is such that it is reasonably certain to place life and limb in peril when negligently made, it is then a thing of danger. Its nature gives warning of the consequences to be expected. If to the element of danger there is added knowledge that the thing will be used by persons other than the purchaser, and used without new tests, then, irrespective of contract, the manufacturer of this thing of danger is under a duty to make it carefully. . . . There must be knowledge of a danger, not merely possible, but probable. It is possible to use almost anything in a way that will make it dangerous if defective. That is not enough to charge the manufacturer with a duty independent of his contract. Whether a given thing is dangerous may be sometimes a question for the court and sometimes a question for the jury. There must also be knowledge that in the usual course of events the danger will be shared by others than the buyer. Such knowledge may often be inferred from the nature of the transaction. But it is possible that even knowledge of the danger and of the use will not always be enough. The proximity or remoteness of the relation is a factor to be considered. We are dealing now with the liability of the manufacturer of the finished product, who puts it on the market to be used without inspection by his customers. If he is negligent, where danger is to be foreseen, a liability will follow. . . .

[The court specifically left open the question of when the manufacturer of a component part, the wheel, could be held liable.] . . . The presence of a known danger, attendant upon a known use, makes vigilance a duty. We have put aside the notion that the duty to safeguard life and limb, when the consequences of negligence may be foreseen, grows out of contract and nothing else. We have put the source of the obligation where it ought to be. We have put its source in the law.

From this survey of the decision, there thus emerges a definition of the duty of manufacturer which enables us to measure this defendant's liability. Beyond all question, the nature of an automobile gives warning of probable danger if its construction is defective. This automobile was designed to go fifty miles an hour. Unless its wheels were sound and strong, injury was almost certain. It was as much a thing of danger as a defective engine for a railroad. The defendant knew the danger. It knew also that the car would be used by persons other than the buyer. This was apparent from its size; there were seats for three persons. It was apparent also from the fact that the buyer was a dealer in cars, who bought to resell. The maker of this car supplied it for the use of purchasers from the dealer just as plainly as the contractor in *Devlin* v. *Smith* supplied the scaffold for use by the servants of the owner. The dealer was indeed the one person of whom it might be said with some approach to certainty that by him the car would not be used. Yet the defendant would have us say that he was the one person whom it was under a legal duty to protect. The law does not lead us to so inconsequent a conclusion. Precedents drawn from the days of travel by stage coach do not fit the conditions of travel to-day. The principle that the danger must be imminent does not change, but the things subject to the principle do change. They are whatever the needs of life in a developing civilization require them to be.

. . . .

We think the defendant was not absolved from a duty of inspection because it bought the wheels from a reputable manufacturer. It was not merely a dealer in automobiles. It was a manufacturer of automobiles. It was responsible for the finished product. It was not at liberty to put the finished product on the market without subjecting the component parts to ordinary and simple tests. Under the charge of the trial judge nothing more was required of it. The obligation to inspect must vary with the nature of the thing to be inspected. The more probable the danger the greater the need of caution. . . .

The judgment should be affirmed with costs.

[A dissenting opinion is omitted.]

Today the negligence doctrine is in the process of losing its utility to plaintiffs in the product liability area. The inroads on privity in breach of warranty cases and the rapid development of the doctrine of strict liability have resulted in plaintiffs having two legal weapons with greater force than the negligence rationale. As a practical matter, it is more difficult to prove the existence of a duty and its breach in negligence than it is to prove a violation under either of the other doctrines. Negligence remains important for historical reasons and in those cases where warranties have been disclaimed or otherwise limited and the jurisdiction has not yet adopted strict liability in tort. In actual practice, the plaintiff may utilize all three theories.

STRICT LIABILITY

The idea of *strict liability* in the product liability area lurked on the periphery of common law or judge-made law for several years. During the 1960s many courts began adopting strict liability. By 1966 courts in at least half the states had expressly adopted the doctrine while many others had indicated they would follow.[1] By 1980 the number of adopting states was much in excess of one half.

In the following case Wisconsin adopts strict liability. The court discusses the justification for the doctrine, its relationship to the Code and to suits for breach of warranty, and also sets forth the conditions that must be met before a court will impose strict liability.

Dippel v. Sciano
Supreme Court of Wisconsin, 1967. 37 Wis.2d 443, 155 N.W.2d 55

The order appealed from sustained a demurrer, upon the ground of no privity, to the third cause of action of the plaintiff's complaint which alleges breach of express and implied warranty.

[The plaintiff-appellant, Donald Dippel, brought this action to recover for personal injuries sustained when the front leg assembly of a large coin-operated pool table collapsed, crushing his left foot. The accident happened on January 1, 1964, in a tavern operated by the defendants, Tony and Dottie Sciano in the city of Milwaukee.]

The injury occurred when plaintiff, a patron of the Scianos' tavern, and two other men were moving the pool table to a position where it could be used. Plaintiff alleges that the table was moved at the request and with the consent of the tavernkeepers' agent and employee. The table weighed about 750 pounds. While moving it, the front leg assembly collapsed and the table top fell on plaintiff's foot, traumatically amputating two of his toes.

The plaintiff brought the action against the following defendants: Fisher Manufacturing Company, a Missouri corporation; Pioneer Sales and Service, Inc.; Carl J. Dentice, doing business as City-Wide Amusement Company; and Tony and Dottie Sciano, doing business as Tony and Dottie's Tavern.

---

1. Prosser, "The Fall of the Citadel (Strict Liability to the Consumer)," 50 Minn. L. Rev. 791, 794 *et. seq.* (1966).

Fisher manufactured the coin-operated table; Pioneer, the sole respondent in this appeal, was the sales distributor; City-Wide Amusement purchased the table and leased it to the Scianos; and the Scianos displayed the table and offered its use to its patrons for a fee.

   . . . .

BEILFUSS, JUSTICE.

The plaintiff-appellant states the issue to be:

> "Does a cause of action based upon breach of implied warranty, arising from the sale of a product intended for use by the general public, exist in the absence of privity of contract between the seller and the ultimate user?"

Under the facts alleged and our view of the law to be applied, we deem the issue to be: Is the lack of privity of contract between the seller of the offending product and its ultimate user or consumer fatal to the injured user's claim of strict liability in tort against the seller?

The plaintiff concedes that the law of Wisconsin has always required privity of contract in an action for a breach of implied warranty. . . .

During the past several years few legal subjects in the field of civil liability have undergone such change and variety of change as products-liability. In addition to the case law and statutory change, products-liability has been the topic of discussion and comment by many authoritative text writers and eminent authors of law review articles.

   . . . .

[The court extensively discussed the origin of the privity limitation and the reasons for abandoning it. The major points of that discussion follow. The notion that there can be no liability upon warranty without privity was an outgrowth of attempts to protect fledgling industries in the early part of the Industrial Revolution. Most jurisdictions in the United States have now abandoned the concept since the modern seller can distribute the costs of the risks created by defective products through price increases or through insurance coverage. Moreover, since manufacturers have some ability through quality control to limit the defects in products, abandoning privity will encourage them to do so. Finally, the abolition of privity or the imposition of strict liability avoids circuity of action. In a single suit, the plaintiff may proceed against all or the most affluent member in the distribution chain.

Discussing the recently adopted UCC, the court noted that it had broadened the scope of implied warranty in Sec. 2–318, but really did not do much to change the privity doctrine. There still existed a requirement that the injured user or consumer notify the seller of an alleged breach of warranty within a reasonable time after the buyer knows or should know of the breach. The court viewed this requirement as unrealistic when applied to the relationship of injured consumer and remote seller of a product.

Another problem the court perceived was the ability of the seller to issue a disclaimer. A disclaimer may be reasonable if the seller is uncertain of the quality of the product and is involved in face to face negotiations with the buyer. It is unreasonable, the court concluded, when a retail buyer is bound by a manufacturer's disclaimer which comes as a part of the purchase.

Use of the word "warranty" is also part of the problem since "warranty" is a contract concept requiring privity. The court then made the choice to treat product liability cases in terms of the concept of strict liability in tort.]

California explicitly abandoned the use of warranty concepts in 1962. *Greenman* v. *Yuba Power Products, Inc.* (1962), 59 Cal.2d 57, 377 P.2d 897. Justice Traynor speaking for the court set forth the rule:

". . . A manufacturer is strictly liable in tort when an article he places on the market, knowing that it is to be used without inspection for defects, proves to have a defect that causes injury to a human being." P. 62, 27 Cal. Rprt. p. 700, 377 P.2d p. 900.

Under this rule ". . . it was sufficient that plaintiff proved that he was injured while using [the product] . . . in a way it was intended to be used as a result of a defect in design and manufacture of which plaintiff was not aware that made the product . . . unsafe for its intended use." P. 64, 27 Cal. Rptr. p. 701, 377 P.2d p. 901.

The approach has been lauded:

". . . This innovation avoids the need for making apologies to warranty doctrine for each abrogation of the privity requirement to permit another, more remote, class of plaintiffs to recover. The plaintiff's status prior to his injury is irrelevant under the new dispensation; he need only be 'a human being,' . . ." Schreiber and Rheingold, Products Liability, 4:26, 4:27. Reprinted from Columbia Law Review (1964), Vol. 64, p. 916.

. . . .

The abrogation of the privity requirement is not strictly and exclusively a matter of sales and contract law. When the manufacturer or the seller offers a product for sale which he expects to be used by the consuming public within its intended use and such product is defective and injures the consumer, his liability in tort can be based upon a breach of duty quite apart from contract obligations. In these situations the Uniform Commercial Code is inapplicable.

We are of the opinion that the rule which requires privity of contract in products-liability cases should not be used to defeat a claim based upon a defective product unreasonably dangerous to a nonprivity user. For products-liability cases we adopt the rule of strict liability in tort as set forth in sec. 402 A of Restatement, 2 Torts (2d), pp. 347, 348. . . .

. . . .

The term *strict* liability in tort might be misconstrued and, if so would be a misnomer. Strict liability does not make the manufacturer or seller an insurer nor does it impose absolute liability. From the plaintiff's point of view the most beneficial aspect of the rule is that it relieves him of proving specific acts of negligence and protects him from the defenses of notice of breach, disclaimer, and lack of privity in the implied warranty concepts of sales and contracts.

From a reading of the plain language of the rule, the plaintiff must prove (1) that the product was in defective condition when it left the possession or control of the seller, (2) that it was unreasonably dangerous to the user or consumer, (3) that the defect was a cause (a substantial factor) of the plaintiff's injuries or damages, (4) that the seller engaged in the business of selling such product or, put negatively, that this is not an isolated or infrequent transaction not related to the principal business of the seller, and (5) that the product was one which the seller expected to and did reach the user or consumer without substantial change in the condition it was in when he sold it.

The defense of contributory negligence is available to the seller. The plaintiff has the duty to use ordinary care to protect himself from known or readily apparent danger. Defenses among others that suggest themselves are that the product must be reasonably used for the purpose for which it was intended; abuse or alteration of the product may relieve or limit liability; some products just naturally wear out in such a manner as to render them unsafe and as to others, the intended use can be coupled with inherent danger — anyone can cut his finger with a sharp knife or puncture it with a fish-hook, and teeth can be damaged by the sugar in the consumption of soft drinks.

Another defense that may be available in some jurisdictions so as to bar recovery is assumption of risk . . . .

The third cause of action of the plaintiff's complaint is grounded upon a theory of an abolition of the rule of privity of contract in actions for breach of implied warranty. Because we have determined that physically injured users or consumers of unreasonably dangerous defective products should pursue their remedy under the rule of strict liability in tort, we conclude that the third cause of action in the complaint does not state facts sufficient to constitute a cause of action and the order sustaining the demurrer should be affirmed but with leave to plead over.

Order affirmed, with leave to the plaintiff to amend the third cause of action of the complaint within 20 days of remittitur. No costs to be taxed on this appeal.

CURRIE, Chief Justice (concurring).

. . . .

HALLOWS, Justice (concurring).

Justice Traynor, author of the landmark *Greenman* v. *Yuba Power Products* case quoted in *Dippel*, expressed the reasons for imposing strict liability in tort in a concurring opinion in 1944. Nearly two decades later, Justice Traynor finally had enough judicial support so that his rationale was promoted in the *Greenman* case. The following passages from Justice Traynor's concurring opinion in *Escola* v. *Coca Cola Bottling Co. of Fresno*, 24 Cal.2d 453, 150 P.2d 436 (1944) will be useful:

> I concur in the judgment, but I believe the manufacturer's negligence should no longer be singled out as the basis of a plaintiff's right to recover in cases like the present one. In my opinion it should now be recognized that a manufacturer incurs an absolute liability when an article that he has placed on the market, knowing that it is to be used without inspection, proves to have a defect that causes injury to human beings. *MacPherson* v. *Buick Motor Co.* . . . . established the principle, recognized by this court, that irrespective of privity of contract, the manufacturer is responsible for an injury caused by such an article to any person who comes in lawful contact with it. *Sheward* v. *Virtue*, 20 Cal.2d 410 . . . *Kalash* v. *Los Angeles Ladder Co.*, 1 Cal.2d 229. . . . In these cases the source of the manufacturer's liability was his negligence in the manufacturing process or in the inspection of component parts supplied by others. Even if there is no negligence, however, public policy demands that responsibility be fixed wherever it will most effectively reduce the hazards to life and health inherent in defective products that reach the market. It is evident that the manufacturer can anticipate some hazards and guard against the recurrence of others, as the public cannot. Those who suffer injury from defective products are unprepared to meet its consequences. The cost of an injury and the loss of time or health may be an overwhelming misfortune to the person injured, and a needless one, for the risk of injury can be insured by the manufacturer and distributed among the public as a cost of doing business. It is to the public interest to discourage the marketing

of products having defects that are a menace to the public. If such products nevertheless find their way into the market it is to the public interest to place the responsibility for whatever injury they may cause upon the manufacturer, who, even if he is not negligent in the manufacture of the product, is responsible for its reaching the market. However intermittently such injuries may occur and however haphazardly they may strike, the risk of their occurrence is a constant risk and a general one. Against such a risk there should be general and constant protection and the manufacturer is best situated to afford such protection.

. . . .

As handicrafts have been replaced by mass production with its great markets and transportation facilities, the close relationship between the producer and consumer of a product has been altered. Manufacturing processes, frequently valuable secrets, are ordinarily either inaccessible to or beyond the ken of the general public. The consumer no longer has means or skill enough to investigate for himself the soundness of a product, even when it is not contained in a sealed package, and his erstwhile vigilance has been lulled by the steady efforts of manufacturers to build up confidence by advertising and marketing devices such as trade-marks. . . . Manufacturers have sought to justify that faith by increasingly high standards of inspection and a readiness to make good on defective products by way of replacements and refunds. See Bogert and Fink, Business Practices Regarding Warranties In The Sale Of Goods, 25 Ill.L.Rev. 400. The manufacturer's obligation to the consumer must keep pace with the changing relationship between them; it cannot be escaped because the marketing of a product has become so complicated as to require one or more intermediaries. Certainly there is greater reason to impose liability on the manufacturer than on the retailer who is but a conduit of a product that he is not himself able to test. . . .

The manufacturer's liability should, of course, be defined in terms of the safety of the product in normal and proper use, and should not extend to injuries that cannot be traced to the product as it reached the market.

PROBLEMS AND QUESTIONS

1. In *MacPherson* v. *Buick Motor Co.*, did Judge Cardozo base his decision of liability on a holding that the manufacturer must have knowledge of a probable danger to the user before he will be held liable?

2. Does the manufacturer of a finished product, which is found to be defective due to negligence on the part of a component parts supplier, have his liability covered by the component supplier?

3. Does the rule of strict liability make the manufacturer of a product the equivalent of an insurer of his product?

4. In *Dippel* v. *Sciano*, Wisconsin adopted strict liability rather than breach of warranty with relaxed privity requirements. What advantages did the Wisconsin Supreme Court perceive strict liability to have over breach of warranty?

5. Harmon manufactures and sells hair dye. Mrs. Jones bought three bottles from a retailer. The warranty accompanying these bottles stated that the product would dye hair black. Mrs. Jones applied the dye according to the instructions, but her hair turned bright green and stayed that way for six months. Neither her scalp nor the texture of her hair was harmed. It was found that green clothing dye had been mistakenly added during the manufacturing process. Would Mrs. Jones recover on a negligence action against Harmon in a state which has not adopted strict liability? Would she win her suit in a strict liability state?

6. In the previous case, what if instead of merely dying Mrs. Jones's hair the wrong color, the green clothing dye resulted in Mrs. Jones's losing her hair and sustaining serious burns on her scalp requiring hospitalization? Would she recover on a negligence action against Harmon in a state which has not adopted strict liability? In a strict liability state?

7. Again varying the facts, now assume that though

the dye left Harmon's factory in the same condition in which it ultimately reached Mrs. Jones, no specific act of negligence on the part of Harmon could be found. Assume that Mrs. Jones suffered baldness and burns rather than just miscoloring. Would she win her negligence action against Harmon in a state which does not follow strict liability? In a strict liability state?

8. Mrs. Jackson bought through a retailer a washing machine manufactured by Polk Co. Due to a faulty water intake regulator the machine burst while in operation, severely burning Mrs. Jackson's small child in a spray of hot water. The child, through its mother, sued the retailer and Polk for both negligence and breach of warranty. What would be the four results in a state which does not follow strict liability? In a strict liability state? Assume state warranty law in both states has not progressed beyond UCC 2–318.

9. A skier went to his favorite ski resort and rented a pair of skis for the day. He was properly fitted for skis, and the bindings were adjusted properly according to his height, weight, and ability level. The skier, while coming rapidly down a narrow trail, fell and skidded. The ski binding released properly, but also snapped off the ski, causing the ski to continue down the trail. A bystander, who was waiting at the bottom of the trail, was injured by the errant ski. Under Justice Traynor's definition of strict liability in *Greenman*, is the manufacturer of the binding liable for the bystander's injury?

10. Varying the facts in the preceding question, what if the skier had failed to adjust the bindings and the safety strap properly, causing the ski to come loose and injure the bystander?

20

RISK
OF LOSS

NATURE OF THE PROBLEM

On November 9, 1940, Bragmus, a poultry processor, purchased a flock of 700 turkeys from Radloff, a poultry farmer, to meet the Thanksgiving demand. The contract stated that Bragmus was to pick up the birds on November 13 at Radloff's turkey farm. Unfortunately, a violent snowstorm on November 11 destroyed or damaged the entire flock.

A situation like this presents the businessperson and his lawyer with several practical questions. Who must bear the loss represented by the turkeys' diminished value? Must the buyer pay for goods now defective and nearly worthless? Alternatively, must the seller forego his profit and bear the out-of-pocket loss of raising the birds? Regardless of which party bears the loss of the birds, which one is responsible for paying for the turkeys Bragmus, the buyer, still needs to meet his customers' Thanksgiving demands? If no replacement turkeys can be found, can Bragmus recover from Radloff for the lost profit and goodwill he will have incurred? The answers to these vexing questions hinge on interrelated concepts grouped under risk of loss, performance, and damages. The bulk of this chapter will deal with risk of loss. Damage questions will be considered in the following two chapters.

Performance

The term *performance*[1] encompasses those concepts which determine whether a party has done that which the contract contemplated or law required and if not, whether the deviation was justified. The UCC does little either to abrogate or to codify common law principles dealing with performance. Instead, it relies heavily on supplementary state law with which the reader is

---

1. The term *performance* is not a legal word of art; it has no one immutable meaning. The topic under discussion could equally well be designated *excuse for nonperformance* or *discharge*.

generally familiar through the material on common law contracts. Common law concepts that bear on this topic are impossibility of performance, frustration of purpose, substantial performance, materiality of breach, constructive condition of cooperation, mutual mistake, and unilateral mistake, among others.

The Code does speak to the performance problem involved in the frost-bitten turkey case in two overlapping provisions. Section 2–615, the commercial impracticability provision discussed in Chapters 6, 11, and 12, provides that ordinarily delay or nondelivery is not a breach by the seller if his performance "has been made impracticable by the occurrence of a contingency the nonoccurrence of which was a basic assumption on which the contract was made. . . ." Thus, since the goods were clearly identified as Radloff's flock and since the nonoccurrence of the particularly vicious snowstorm was presumably a basic assumption for the contract for the flock of turkeys, Radloff's nonperformance, specifically nondelivery, was not a breach, and he is discharged.

Section 2–613, the companion provision, provides that:

> [W]here the contract requires for its performance goods identified when the contract is made, and the goods suffer casualty without fault of either party before the risk of loss passes to the buyer . . . (a) if the loss is total the contract is avoided; and (b) if the loss is partial the buyer may inspect and either avoid the contract or accept the goods with due allowance for the deterioration or deficiency in quantity.

Since, as we shall shortly see, risk of loss under the UCC generally follows possession, the risk of loss would still be borne by the seller and Radloff's nonperformance, specifically nondelivery, would not constitute a breach.

Under either of these Code provisions, it is Bragmus who must locate new birds (perhaps at a higher price) and pay for them if he is to supply his customers' Thanksgiving needs. Moreover, since Radloff's nondelivery was justified, Bragmus cannot recover damages for the higher price he may pay for turkeys or for lost profits or injury to goodwill if he does not secure an alternative source of supply.

The relationship between performance and damages should now be clear. Given the unexpected destruction or damage of goods, the issue of performance deals with whether there has been a breach of the contract. Damages start from the assumption that there has been a breach and focus on the types of injury for which recovery is permitted and the method of determining the amount of that injury. Viewed another way, performance determines who is responsible for solving the problems created by the casualty (such as who must secure replacement turkeys so the buyer can meet commitments to his customers), and damages quantifies the cost of the solution. In contrast, risk of loss concepts determine who bears loss for the casualty (the destroyed flock of turkeys) that gave rise to the performance and damage issues.

Risk of Loss Before the UCC

Pre-Code law held that title or ownership to the turkeys passed when the contract was signed on November 9 and further provided that risk of loss passed with title or ownership. Under that law Bragmus, the turkey buyer, was forced to pay for the birds that he never had nor would have in his possession. *Radloff* v. *Bragmus*, 214 Minn. 130, 7 N.W.2d 491 (1943).

Although abstractly it might seem appropriate that the party possessing title to the goods, i.e., having legal ownership, should bear the responsibility for the loss, the turkey case illustrates that such a resolution may in practice create unexpected hardships. Few businesspeople are pessimistic or cautious enough to expect violent snowstorms, fires, and floods. Consequently, few appreciate and provide for passage of title and its consequences.

IF NEITHER PARTY HAS BREACHED THE CONTRACT

Although in section 2–106 the UCC defines a sale as "the passing of title from the seller to the buyer for a price," it does not use the technical and legalistic concept of title as a device for determining who has the risk of loss. The Code bypasses title and focuses first on the question of whether either party has breached the contract. It then asks the eminently practical question of whose insurance is likely to cover the damaged goods. This pragmatic approach, though more complicated, appears more in step with the businessperson's expectations and his sense of justice.

The Code provides three rules for allocating the risk of loss. The first rule applies when the contract authorizes or requires the seller to ship the goods by common carrier such as a commercial railroad, airline, or trucking company; the second rule applies where the goods are held by a third party bailee such as a warehouse; the third is a general or catchall rule applicable in those cases not covered by the first two.

General Rule

The turkeys were not held by a bailee, nor was the seller called upon to ship them by common carrier; therefore, the catchall rule would apply in the turkey case were it to be decided under the Code. The risk of loss passes to the buyer when he takes possession of the goods if the seller is a merchant, as was the turkey seller. Thus, under the Code, the turkey case would have been decided differently. The seller, Radloff, would have absorbed the loss since Bragmus had not received the goods. This disposition would justify one's reasonable expectation that a merchant, here one who raises and sells turkeys for a living, would continue to look after them while they were in his possession. Being professionally familiar with the hazards of turkey raising, he would be likely to have all merchandise in his possession covered by appropriate insurance. Conversely, it would be unusual for the buyer to have an insurance policy covering goods not yet in his possession: an insurance company would want a substantial premium for a policy committing it in advance to the risk inherent in insuring unknown quantities of goods located on unknown premises. Indeed, these considerations, comporting with common sense, comprise the underlying theory of the Code's general rule on risk of loss.

It should be stressed that where the seller is a merchant, actual possession of the goods must be obtained by buyer before the risk of loss passes. UCC sections 2–509(3), 2–103(1)(c). Thus, according to the Code's comments, even where the buyer has made full payment and been notified that the goods are at his disposal, the risk remains with the merchant seller until the buyer actually receives the merchandise.

If the seller is not a merchant, under the general rule the risk passes to the buyer when the seller properly tenders the goods, i.e., when the seller holds conforming goods at the buyer's disposition at a reasonable hour for the period reasonably necessary to enable the buyer to take possession. UCC sections 2–509(3), 2–503.

The following case considers a nonmerchant seller under the general rule. Note the imaginative and technically plausible bailment argument the seller makes. Had the court accepted the bailment argument, a major exception to the Code's approach to risk of loss would have been created. In basing its decision on policy considerations, the opinion supplements our text in a valuable way concerning the problems of pre-Code law and the reason for the UCC's new approach.

Martin v. Melland's Inc.
Supreme Court of North Dakota, 1979. 283 N.W.2d 76

ERICKSTAD, CHIEF JUSTICE.

. . . .

On June 11, 1974, Martin entered into a written agreement with Melland's, a farm implement dealer, to purchase a truck and attached haystack mover for the total purchase price of $35,389. Martin was given a trade-in allowance of $17,389 on his old unit, leaving a balance owing of $18,000 plus sales tax of $720 or a total balance of $18,720. The agreement provided that Martin "mail or bring title" to the old unit to Melland's "this week." Martin mailed the certificate of title to Melland's pursuant to the agreement, but he was allowed to retain the use and possession of the old unit "until they had the new one ready." The new unit was not expected to be ready for two to three months because it required certain modifications. . . .

Fire destroyed the truck and the haymoving unit in early August, 1974, while Martin was moving hay. The parties did not have any agreement regarding insurance or risk of loss on the unit and Martin's insurance on the trade-in unit had lapsed. . . .

. . . .

One of the hallmarks of the pre-Code law of sales was its emphasis on the concept of title. The location of title was used to determine, among other things, risk of loss, insurable interest, place and time for measuring damages, and the applicable law in an interstate transaction. This single title or "lump" title concept proved unsatisfactory because of the different policy considerations involved in each of the situations that title was made to govern. Furthermore, the concept of single title did not reflect modern commercial practices, i.e., although the single title concept worked well for "cash-on-the-barrelhead sales," the introduction of deferred payments, security agreements, financing from third parties, or delivery by carrier required a fluid concept of title with bits and pieces held by all parties to the transaction.

Thus the concept of title under the U.C.C. is of decreased importance. The official comment to Section 2–101 U.C.C. provides in part:

"The arrangement of the present Article is in terms of contract for sale and the various steps of its performance. The legal consequences are stated as following directly from the contract and action taken under it without resorting to the idea of when property or title passed or was to pass as being the determining factor. The purpose is to avoid making practical issues between practical men turn upon the location of an intangible something, the passing of which no man can prove by evidence and to substitute for such abstractions proof of words and actions of a tangible character."

. . . .

. . . [T]he question in this case is not answered by a determination of the location of title,[1] but by the risk of loss provisions in Section 2–509. Before addressing the risk of loss question, it is necessary to determine the posture of the parties with regard to the trade-in unit, *i.e.*, who is the buyer and the seller and how are the responsibilities allocated. It is clear that a barter or trade-in is considered a sale and is therefore subject to the Uniform Commercial Code. It is also clear that the party who owns the trade-in is considered the seller. . . .

Martin argues that he had already sold the trade-in unit to Melland's and, although he retained possession, he did so in the capacity of a bailee. White and Summers in their hornbook on the Uniform Commercial Code argue that the seller who retains possession should not be considered bailee within Section 2–509:

. . . .

". . . [E]xcept in circumstances which we cannot now conceive, a seller should not ever be regarded as a bailee. To allow sellers in possession of goods already sold to argue that they are bailees and that the risk of loss in such cases is governed by subsection (2), [governing bailees] would undermine one of the basic policies of the Code's risk of loss scheme. . . . [T]he draftsmen intended to leave the risk on the seller in many circumstances in which the risk would have jumped to the buyer under prior law. The theory was that a seller with possession should have the burden ot taking care of the goods and is more likely to insure them against loss.

"If we accept such sellers' arguments, that is, that they are bailees under subsection (2) because of their possession of the goods sold or because of a clause in the sale's agreement, we will be back where we started from, for in bailee cases the risk jumps under (2)(b) on his 'acknowledgment' of the buyer's right to possession. By hypothesis our seller has acknowledged the buyer's right and is simply holding the goods at buyer's disposal. Thus, to accomplish the draftsmen's purpose and leave risk on the seller in possession, we believe that one should find only non-sellers to be 'bailees' as that term is used in 2–509(2). Notwithstanding the fact that a seller retains possession of goods already sold and that he has a term in his sales contract which characterizes him as a 'bailee', we would argue that he is not a bailee for the purposes of subsection (2) of 2–509. . . ."

The courts that have addressed this issue have agreed with White and Summers.

---

1. While the role of title has been diminished under the U.C.C., it has not been entirely excluded. . . . Generally, it is still necessary to consider title in two broad contexts:

(1) For purposes outside the law of sales, *e.g.* criminal law, taxation, and public regulation; and (2) where the final question is ownership, not merely some incident of the sale, *e.g.* liability insurance coverage.

It is undisputed that the contract did not require or authorize shipment by carrier . . . ; therefore, the residue section, subsection 3 is applicable:

> "In any case not within subsection 1 or 2, the risk of loss passes to the buyer on his receipt of the goods if the seller is a merchant; otherwise the risk passes to the buyer on tender of delivery."

. . . .

It is clear that the trade-in unit was not tendered to Melland's in this case. The parties agreed that Martin would keep the old unit "until they had the new one ready."

. . . .

. . . Martin must bear the loss.

We affirm the district court judgment.

SAND, PAULSON, PEDERSON and VANDE WALLE, JJ., concur.

If the Goods Are Shipped by Carrier

Risk of loss problems become considerably more complex when we insert an independent third party, such as a common carrier, between the buyer and seller. Suppose, for example, that the seller operated a large apple orchard in Ohio and that the buyer was a grocery chain in Los Angeles. It would be unlikely that the pickup and delivery facilities of these businesses would overlap. The sales contract would require or authorize shipment by carrier. However, assume that through an "act of God" the apples are frozen crossing the Rocky Mountains. Who bears the loss, the buyer or the seller?

The Code ties risk of loss to the delivery arrangement agreed upon by buyer and seller. The buyer and seller really have only two practical alternatives, a *shipment contract* or a *destination contract*. Either the buyer takes delivery and assumes responsibility for shipping in Ohio, or the seller has responsibility for transportation and buyer takes delivery in Los Angeles. The parties could arrange to effect delivery at Omaha or Denver if they desired, but they would not ordinarily do this since it tends to complicate rather than simplify the problems. If the orchard's responsibility for delivery terminates when the apples are turned over to the carrier in Ohio, the contract is a *shipment contract*. Since risk of loss under the Code follows the parties' agreement, risk of loss in a shipment contract passes from seller to buyer when seller delivers the goods to the carrier. In our hypothetical case buyer would bear the loss of the apples through freezing. Had the parties worked out a *destination contract*, i.e., one where the seller is charged with delivering the goods to the buyer at the destination point (Los Angeles), the risk of loss would not pass until tender was made in Los Angeles. Thus, in the destination contract the seller would bear the loss associated with the "act of God."

Over the years, businesspeople and their lawyers have developed several technical terms to be used when goods are transported. The most important of these are F.O.B., F.A.S., and C.I.F.

The term *F.O.B.* stands for *free on board*. It is used with either the place of shipment or the place of destination; it may also be used with the name or number of a designated vessel, car, or other vehicle. When used with the place of shipment, e.g., F.O.B. *SS Trader,* Charleston, seller must bear the risk and expense of putting the goods on board the *SS Trader* in Charleston Harbor. This accomplished, risk of loss then passes to buyer. When F.O.B. is used with the place of destination, e.g., F.O.B. San Francisco, the contract is a destination contract, and the seller bears the expense of shipment and the risk of loss until the goods are properly tendered for delivery at San Francisco. UCC sections 2–319(1)(b), 2–509(1)(b).

The term *F.A.S.* means *free alongside.* It is used with the name of a vessel and the port from which the vessel will sail. Thus, a contract might specify F.A.S. *Great Lakes Queen,* Duluth. Such a contract requires the seller to deliver the goods alongside the vessel at his own expense and risk and to obtain the proper documents in receipt. Once this has been done, buyer assumes the risk of loss.

C.I.F. means *cost, insurance, and freight.* Under a C.I.F. contract the seller extends credit to the buyer for cost, insurance, and freight by paying all these expenses to the place of destination. The seller is reimbursed for these expenses, however, since he adds them to the total price which buyer must pay. The fact of reimbursement implies that the buyer has assumed financial responsibility for the goods at the start of the voyage. The contract, therefore, is still considered a *shipment* contract with risk of loss passing to buyer when seller delivers the goods to the carrier. UCC sections 2–320(2); 2–320, comment 1.

Unless specific contractual language indicates otherwise, all contracts bearing the delivery terms discussed above are shipment contracts, except those contracts bearing the term *F.O.B.* followed by the point of destination. The F.O.B. point of destination contract, then, is the only one is which the risk of loss stays with the seller beyond the point of delivery of the goods to the carrier.

A Bailment Situation

The Code provision on risk of loss where a bailee has control of the goods being sold is also treated as an exception to the general rule. Consider the following example of such a situation.

Competitive emphasis on quick delivery requires that Shaw, a bicycle manufacturer, keep an inventory of vehicles in the major U.S. cities. Shaw cannot afford to own facilities in each city. Shaw stores his bicycles in a warehouse and effects transfer of the goods by requiring buyers to pick them up at the warehouse.

If Shaw sells to Benttenhausen twelve bicycles stored in Olfield's warehouse, and if these bicycles are stolen or destroyed prior to pickup, the law must allocate the loss to either the seller, Shaw, or the buyer, Benttenhausen. Under the Code risk of loss will shift from seller to buyer in either one of two events: acknowledgement by the bailee that buyer has a right to the goods, or receipt by buyer of a document of title to the goods. In selecting these as the risk-shifting events, the drafters of the Code were trying to utilize events whose occurrence would suggest to the buyer that his obligations toward the goods had increased while seller's responsibilities had decreased or ceased.

IF THE CONTRACT HAS BEEN BREACHED

Loss, in the phrase *risk of loss*, refers to a loss wherein buyer and seller are both faultless. If a loss occurs through the fault of either party, the matter is one of breach of contract.

Occasionally both situations characterize a transaction, i.e., one party has breached the contract and there is also a loss resulting from some "act of God." The Code provides that in cases of risk of loss where the contract has been breached, the party at fault assumes a greater proportion of the burden of risk than when he is not in breach. The UCC distinguishes also between a breach by the seller and a breach by the buyer. In the case of a seller's breach, the Code further distinguishes a situation wherein discovery occurs after acceptance. Although calculated to produce just and predictable results, this high concentration of distinctions usually makes mastery of the material difficult.

Seller's Breach: Buyer Rejecting Before Acceptance

If the goods or tender of delivery fail in any respect to conform to the contract[2] the buyer may reject the goods. UCC section 2–601. Should the buyer do this, the risk of loss remains with the seller until the defects are cured or until the buyer accepts them despite the defects. This rule applies regardless of the physical location of the goods during correction, i.e., during the time the seller repairs, partially substitutes, or sorts out improper goods.

Thus, if Stover delivers walnut paneling for Burroughs's library and Burroughs rejects it because several panels are warped, Stover has the risk of loss even if Stover, for convenience, leaves the panels at Burroughs's home.

Seller's Breach: Buyer Revoking Acceptance

In some cases a buyer will accept nonconforming goods either without knowledge of their nonconformity or on the assumption that the seller intends to cure this nonconformity. When the buyer discovers the defects, or, in the

---

2. Reasons goods might not conform to the contract include the following: an express or implied quality warranty was breached; the warranty of title and against infringement was breached; the goods were not as described in the contract even though that description was not part of the basis of the bargain and therefore did not create an express warranty; the quantity tendered was less than specified. Reasons tender of delivery might not conform to the contract even though the goods were conforming include the following: the manner, time, and place for tender specified in the contract were not adhered to; any necessary documents were not provided.

second case, if the seller fails to cure the defects, the buyer may revoke his acceptance. UCC section 2–608. If such a revocation is made, the faultless buyer must bear the risk of loss to the extent that his insurance covers the goods. The rest of the loss falls upon the breaching seller. UCC section 2–510(2).

For illustration, suppose in the turkey case that the seller had delivered the turkeys to the buyer's slaughterhouse on November 13. Thereafter, the buyer discovered that the birds were grossly underweight and rightfully revoked his acceptance because of breach of a quality warranty. The snowstorm then occurred and destroyed the turkeys while they were in buyer's pens awaiting repossession by the seller. If the faultless buyer has insurance adequate to cover the loss of all the turkeys, he must apply this to the entire loss. If his insurance covers only half of the turkeys, the seller bears the loss of the other half. Note that this rule does not force the buyer to pay any of his own money upon destruction of the nonconforming goods. If the innocent buyer has no insurance, he bears no liability. In most cases, however, the buyer, as we have seen, will carry some insurance for goods in his possession since, absent seller's breach, the entire risk of loss would have been on him.

Buyer's Breach

In some cases loss will occur after the seller has identified, i.e., set aside or earmarked, certain conforming goods as the subject matter of the contract but prior to the passage of ownership to the buyer. If the buyer repudiates or otherwise breaches the contract after the making of this identification, the innocent seller will bear the risk of loss to the extent that his insurance covers the goods; the rest of the loss will fall on the breaching buyer. This insurance-oriented allocation is analogous to that required where the seller is the breaching party.

The breaching buyer does not retain the partial risk indefinitely. Since the seller has possession of goods identified for the buyer but no longer wanted by the buyer, the seller must make an alternative disposition of the goods in such a way as to minimize his immediate monetary loss and to minimize the buyer's eventual monetary responsibility for that loss. Should the seller not make this alternative disposition within a commercially reasonable period of time, his delay will cause the entire risk of loss to shift back to him; the breaching buyer is left with no risk of loss, although he may still be subject to a suit for damages. The question of what constitutes a commercially reasonable period of time varies depending upon the facts of the particular situation.

To illustrate the basic rule, assume in the turkey case that on November 9, when the contract was signed, the seller had separately penned 700 plump turkeys, thereby identifying them as the ones to go to the buyer, who was to pick them up on November 13. On November 10, the buyer called the seller and repudiated the whole contract, saying he did not need any turkeys after all. The snowstorm occurred on November 11. Had the buyer not repudiated, the seller would have borne the entire loss under the Code. Buyer's repudiation, in effect, puts the risk of loss on the innocent seller only to the extent of his insurance coverage. The rest of the loss, if any, is borne by the breaching buyer.

SPECIAL SITUATIONS

The Code in section 2–326 gives special consideration to the problem of risk of loss in two common business situations. The first situation is one with which the reader is doubtlessly personally familiar: the buyer is permitted to use the goods in his house for a trial period — say, thirty days — and "if you are not completely satisfied, return it with no questions asked." This circumstance, where a buyer may return conforming goods delivered to him primarily for his use, is called a *sale on approval*. Where the sale is on approval, the risk of loss does not pass to the buyer until acceptance, and use of goods consistent with the purpose of the trial is not acceptance. The rationale for placing the risk of loss on the seller appears to pivot on the fact that most sales on approval are to individuals who are unlikely to have insurance coverage.

A *sale or return* occurs when the buyer may return conforming goods delivered to him primarily for the purpose of resale. A typical example would be the probable arrangement between the publisher of this textbook and bookstores where it is sold; usually bookstores can return unsold books to the publisher. Where the circumstance is one of sale or return, the risk of loss is on the buyer. This allocation of risk is consistent with the premise that one holding for resale is most likely a merchant with insurance coverage for goods on his premises.

CONCLUSION

Since states began adopting the Code, very few cases have arisen under sections 2–509 or 2–510, the risk of loss provisions. Loss of goods certainly has not ceased; only litigation has virtually ceased. It seems reasonable to attribute this absence of litigation to the Code. The risk of loss provisions are clear, precise, and thorough, leaving little doubt as to who bears the risk of loss in almost any given situation. With such predictability there seems no point in carrying on costly litigation. In addition, the risk of loss has been made to coincide with insurance coverage. Consequently, the businessperson can recoup the loss through insurance rather than through litigation.

PROBLEMS AND QUESTIONS

1. Why does the UCC relate risk of loss to the possession of insurance coverage? Do you feel this is fair? What is the justification for it?

2. What is the difference between a shipment contract and a destination contract?

3. National Paper Company contracted to sell four tons of white paper to Scribe's Stationery Company. Scribe's paid the contract price. Prior to its receipt of

the paper, National's warehouse, which stored the paper, was struck by lightning and burned to the ground. Scribe's sues National for refund of the purchase price. What would be the result?

4. Grant purchased Jones's 21-foot inboard speedboat for $35,000. The boat was docked at Surfside Marina. Jones issued Grant a document of title to facilitate his taking possession. Subsequent to the issuance, but before Grant picked the boat up, a tidal wave destroyed the marina and demolished the boat. Grant sues Jones for return of the $35,000. What would be the result?

5. Brown contracted to sell his golf clubs to Duff for $150. Brown told Duff that the clubs were in his garage and asked that Duff come by and pick them up as soon as he could. Duff procrastinated for over a month. When he finally arrived, Duff learned that Brown's garage had burned down the night before and the clubs were destroyed. Brown claims that Duff owes him $150 anyway and sues him for that amount. What would be the result?

6. Ace Meat Company in Chicago contracted to purchase a car of frozen beef from the O-K Cattle Ranch in Amarillo, Texas. The contract required that the meat be shipped F.O.B. Amarillo. En route to Chicago, refrigeration in the railroad car failed and the meat was completely spoiled. O-K sued Ace Meat for the balance of the purchase price and Ace Meat counterclaimed for a refund of the money paid. What would be the results? Does the party which bears the risk of loss have a claim against the railroad?

Would the results differ if the contract had read F.O.B. Chicago? To whom, if anyone, would the railroad be liable under these circumstances?

7. Goodwin's Brewing Company, a St. Louis outfit, contracted to purchase 5000 aluminum half-keg containers from Hardy Aluminum Company in Tucson, Ariz. The contract called for the kegs to be shipped C.I.F. St. Louis. Hardy paid for the freight and insurance, delivered the kegs to the carrier, and received a bill of lading in return. It thereupon drew a draft on Goodwin's and sent the documents to its bank in St. Louis. Goodwin's paid the draft, which included the cost of the kegs, freight, and insurance, and received the bill of lading and other necessary documents in return. The kegs, however, never arrived. A train wreck totally destroyed them en route. Goodwin's sued Hardy for a refund of the contract price. What would be the result? Who is the beneficiary of the insurance policy? After paying the beneficiary, does the insurance company have a claim against the railroad?

8. The University Bookstore contracted to purchase from Quality Publishing Company 500 copies of *Alice in Wonderland*. Quality, however, confused its orders and delivered to the carrier 500 copies of *Smut*. While the carrier was passing through Boston, the attorney general confiscated the books and destroyed them as pornography. The bookstore sued Quality for the return of the purchase price. What would be the result?

9. Pursuant to a contract for forty new truck tires, Shad Rubber Company delivered forty tires to Bend Truck Company. At the time of delivery Bend's agent at the receiving platform was assured the tires were new, and, indeed, they were wrapped as though new. After only 100 miles of normal use one of the tires blew out. Bend investigated and discovered that all forty tires were recaps. Bend immediately revoked its acceptance and sought instructions from Shad regarding disposal of the tires. While awaiting the instructions, Bend stored the tires in its garage. The garage was broken into by vandals and those tires which were not stolen were slashed. Bend's insurance covered only one-half the loss. Since Shad had already refunded the contract price and paid damages, it now sues Bend for the value of the forty recaps. What would be the result?

10. Baker's Bread Company contracted with McClellan, a wheat farmer, to purchase McClellan's total wheat crop, to be delivered in the fall. McClellan had planted his fields to full capacity and was raising a good crop of wheat when Baker's Bread repudiated the contract in mid-August. Four days later, before McClellan could find another buyer, the wheat crop was destroyed by a grasshopper invasion. McClellan had carried no insurance and now sues Baker's Bread for the contract price. What would be the result?

If Baker's Bread had not repudiated the contract, who would have borne the loss? Under these circumstances, could Baker's Bread have recovered damages from McClellan for failure to deliver?

21

BUYER'S RIGHTS AND REMEDIES

OVERVIEW

The UCC affords the buyer an arsenal of legal weapons with which to defend himself against a seller who has breached his contract. The extent of this protection makes somewhat difficult our task of identifying and understanding the protections and the circumstances under which they may be used. Perhaps the simplest way to meet this difficulty is to identify the more common ways in which sellers breach their contracts and then to consider the alternative courses of action afforded the buyer. We shall discuss breaches in the chronological order in which they would occur with respect to a single contract. We shall assume that the seller in fact breached the contract, i.e., that nothing in the buyer's conduct and nothing such as an "act of God" justifies or excuses the seller's action.

ANTICIPATORY REPUDIATION

Suppose that on January 1, Wine Cellar Accessories Corp. contracted with Bacchus Vintage Wine Shop to sell Bacchus twenty-four wooden wine racks which Bacchus planned to resell to customers. The contract calls for Wine Cellar to deliver the racks to Bacchus's place of business on July 1.

The first way in which Wine Cellar can breach is to repudiate the contract anticipatorily, i.e., to disclaim the contract in advance of the delivery time. Wine Cellar can, for example, write Bacchus prior to July 1 and inform it that Wine Cellar will not perform the contract when the time for performance arrives (perhaps Wine Cellar has arranged a better price elsewhere). Since the seller has clearly shown unwillingness or inability to perform, section 2–610 permits, but does not require, the buyer to treat the repudiation as final and to act immediately to protect itself. In other words, Bacchus does not have to wait until July 1 to see whether Wine Cellar has changed its mind and decided to perform. The buyer has the time between repudiation and delivery to ponder its rights and remedies, as well as some flexibility in timing their implementation.

The most commonly used and taken for granted rights are the right to cancel the contract — thereby suspending the buyer's own obligation to perform — and the right to recover any part of the purchase price already paid. It would obviously be unjust to make Bacchus pay for wine racks it will never receive. It would be equally unfair to permit Wine Cellar to keep any down payment or advance.

These rights of cancellation and recovery of the purchase price are rather modest. They return the buyer to the position he occupied prior to contract. However, a buyer must be able to go beyond these rights and resort to remedies that will secure him the benefits of the contract. Such remedies are provided by the Code. The most frequently used are *cover* and *damages*. Less often available but especially powerful are the remedies of *specific performance* and *replevin*. A *liquidated damages* provision may also be used if inserted into the sales contract. Finally, *punitive damages* may be recovered where supplementary state law authorizes them. Those remedies will be discussed in turn, stressing cover and damages in particular.

Cover

Cover, a remedy first introduced by the UCC in section 2–712, authorizes the buyer to enter the market and procure goods in lieu of those which the seller will not deliver. The buyer can then recover from seller the difference in price between the substitute goods and the price called for in the contract. Assume, for example, that Wine Cellar's selling price for the wine racks was $100 per rack. If the price of a substitute was $125 per rack, Bacchus could move immediately to purchase the substitute and recover the difference of $25 per rack from Cellar. This speed in protecting oneself and the unequivocal right to recovery are the especially attractive features of cover. Bacchus acted to forestall loss of the goodwill of customers whose orders he had already taken. If Wine Cellar is solvent, Bacchus will not have to foot the bill for the increased cost of the substitutes.

Cover does not place the seller totally at the buyer's mercy. The test for determining whether the buyer has correctly comported himself is:

> . . . whether at the time and place the buyer acted in good faith and in a reasonable manner, and it is immaterial that hindsight may later prove that the method of cover used was not the cheapest or most effective. UCC § 2–712, comment 2.

The substitute goods need not be identical to the goods originally ordered. It suffices that they are commercially reasonable substitutes. Thus, the standards of conduct the buyer must meet permit reasonable latitude.

Cover offers additional flexibility in that it is not an exclusive remedy. Section 2–712 authorizes its use with a combination of other remedies. As we have already discussed, the buyer can recover any part of the purchase price already paid. If the buyer has sustained incidental or consequential damages (discussed in more detail further on), he can recover for them also. But the buyer's recovery will be reduced by any expenses the buyer avoids as a consequence of the seller's breach. Finally, the buyer does not have to utilize cover at all. He can, for example, rely exclusively on his damage remedy.

Damages

The damages authorized by the Code have three components. First, the buyer may recover the difference between the contract price (in our hypothetical case, $100 per rack) and the market price ($125 per rack) of the goods at the time he learned of the breach and at the place where the goods were to be accepted or tendered. Second, the buyer may recover any incidental and consequential damages he sustained. Third, the sum of money produced by the preceding two components must be reduced by the expenses that the buyer saved as a result of the breach. The result of these computations is the sum the buyer should receive.

With regard to the first component, the drafters of the UCC selected market price at the time the buyer learns of the breach, rather than market price at the time for performance, in order both to permit and to encourage the buyer to cover. Should the buyer not cover at the time he learns of the breach and should the price of substitute goods thereafter increase, the securing of substitutes near the performance date will be more expensive than their acquisition at the time buyer learned of the breach. This increased cost cannot be recovered from the seller since the measure of damages is the difference between contract price and market price at the time buyer learns of the breach. Thus, the buyer is encouraged to cover because he will otherwise assume the risk of a subsequent increase in the cost of substitute goods. Cover is the favored remedy because it minimizes the effect of a breach on the continuing flow of commerce by encouraging the prompt acquisition of substitutes. It tends, moreover, to make determination of the amount of damage easy, thereby reducing the need for litigation.

One notable problem in assessing the difference between contract and market price is the occasional lack of readily available evidence for determining the market price for goods at a particular time and place. For example, should a seller not deliver a frozen food display case to an independent grocer in a small town, the injured grocer would have little evidence of the goods' market value there, since such goods are rarely purchased in that town. The Code provides that when the necessary evidence is not readily available, the price prevailing within any reasonable time before or after the time of tender or at any other place that in commercial judgment or under trade usage would serve as a reasonable substitute for the actual place of tender may be used. UCC § 2–723(2).

The second component of damage has two subdivisions, incidental and consequential damages, both of which were considered in Chapter 12. In a sale of goods context, incidental damages include any reasonable expense arising due to the breach, such as tne charges and commissions incurred in effecting cover, or the costs of determining market value when it is not immediately ascertainable. UCC § 2–715(1). Consequential damages have the greatest dollar producing potential to the buyer. Under consequential damages the buyer will recover for the personal injuries and property damage directly resulting from breach of contract. UCC § 2–715. It is unlikely, though, that there would be a recovery for personal injury and property damage when the seller anticipatorily repudiates the contract. Such damages usually occur as a result of the malfunctioning of goods, as opposed to the nonreceipt of goods, which is characteristic of repudiation.

Consequential damages also include any loss resulting from particular requirements and needs of the buyer of which the seller had knowledge at the time of contracting, providing those needs are incapable of being satisfied with cover.

Useful insight into both the damage and cover remedies can be gained by comparing the buyer's economic position after using each. Were Bacchus to cover, it would own substitute goods worth $125 per rack at a net cost to it of $100 per rack: the cost would be computed by paying $125 per rack for the substitute goods and then recovering $25 per rack from Wine Cellar. Were Bacchus to rely solely on the damage remedy, it would end up in the same economic position though his value would be in money, not in wine racks. It would recover $25 per rack from Wine Cellar and would have, in addition, the $100 per rack which it did not spend for wine racks. Thus, cover would reduce Bacchus's cash position by $100 per rack and increase the fair market value of its inventory by $125, thereby giving the $25 benefit inherent in the initial bargain. Damages would not affect Bacchus's inventory but would increase its cash by $25 per rack without reducing it by any expenditure, thereby giving the same $25 benefit of the bargain as did cover. Incidental and consequential damages can be recovered under both alternatives.

This comparison should illustrate that Bacchus, in choosing its remedy, is deciding whether it prefers wine racks, which it could sell to another retailer for $125 per rack, or $125 cash, which it could spend to purchase wine racks or anything else.

Replevin and Specific Performance

Both *replevin* and *specific performance* result in the buyer obtaining physical possession of the goods in question from the seller. *Replevin* refers to a court order directing an official such as a sheriff to take physical possession of the goods and turn them over to the party requesting the order. Historically the order was particularly powerful because the person who had the goods was not first given an opportunity to object: his objection came later. Since the order was issued after only one party had been heard, a criterion for the replevin order was that the judge be persuaded that there was a strong likelihood the goods would be damaged, destroyed, or hidden if left where they were. Furthermore, it had to be shown that destruction, the expected action, would deprive the party seeking replevin of any effective remedy. Today most states also require the party seeking replevin to post a bond, oftentimes in an amount greater than the value of the goods for which recovery is sought. In addition, since experience indicates replevin is more frequently used against consumer goods than commercial goods, increasing sensitivity to consumers' rights requires that one possessing goods receive an early hearing in a replevin action. The hearing often precedes, but may in some cases immediately follow, the seizure of property.

Specific performance, as discussed in Chapter 12, is a judicial decree that directs someone to fulfill his contract. It is a remedy that operates directly against the person of the seller and causes him to do something. Should the seller refuse, he can be held in contempt of court and imprisoned until he complies. Specific performance deviates sharply from the general common law damage rules that attack one's pocketbook rather than one's person, on the theory that every injury has a monetary equivalent. The official comments to section 2–716 encourage greater use of specific performance, especially where unique goods are involved. Otherwise, the comments indicate that this remedy is intended to be applied according to the general principles of common law existing prior to the UCC.

Specific performance is appropriate where the property in question has a "peculiar, unique or sentimental value to the buyer not measurable in money damages." *McCallister* v. *Patton*, 214 Ark. 293, 215 S.W.2d 701 (1948). If substitute goods are available, the buyer has an effective remedy in cover and thus replevin would not be appropriate. The availability of substitutes also indicates the goods are not unique and, therefore, specific performance would also not be appropriate. If substitute goods are not available, cover would be ineffective and the buyer would have to resort to replevin and specific performance if he wants goods rather than money damages. Replevin and specific performance both require the buyer to secure a court order to obtain possession of the goods. The order requires an appearance in court, which in turn involves nuisance, delay, and legal costs. Thus, replevin and specific performance require a court appearance and may produce physical possession, whereas cover produces physical possession of similar goods and does not require a court appearance unless the seller denies there was a contract or for some other reason refuses to pay the difference between the contract price and the cost of the substitute goods.

Liquidated Damages

Under UCC section 2–719 the parties to a contract are allowed to provide their own remedies in addition to or in substitution for the remedies listed above. In many contracts the parties exercise this option by *liquidating* their damages, expressly stipulating in their agreement the amount of damages to be recovered by either party for a breach of the agreement by the other. Damages may be liquidated only at an amount that is reasonable in light of the anticipated harm to be caused by the breach, the difficulties of proof of loss, and the inconvenience or nonfeasibility of otherwise obtaining an adequate remedy. A term fixing unreasonably large liquidated damages is void as a penalty under section 2–718(1).

Punitive Damages

The Code has no provision regarding punitive damages. Their availability depends on supplementary state law. As the material on common law contracts has shown, punitive damages are appropriate only when conduct is malicious, wanton, or intentionally wrongful. Consequently, such damages are unusual.

NONDELIVERY

A second way in which a seller such as Wine Cellar Accessories might breach a contract is by nondelivery, i.e., by a failure to deliver the goods at the appointed time. July 1 comes and goes and the wine racks do not appear. Nor do they appear on subsequent days. As a practical matter, this type of breach seems to occur less frequently than others. Usually a seller will be thoughtful enough to let a buyer know in advance if he is unable to perform. In addition to being thoughtful, such notice is often to the seller's advantage. It tends to minimize his loss of goodwill. In addition, by giving the buyer time to make alternative arrangements, it tends to minimize the buyer's injury and thus the damages the seller must pay.

When nondelivery does occur, section 2–711 provides that a buyer such as Bacchus Vintage Wine Shop has recourse to the remedies just discussed under anticipatory repudiation. These remedies include:

1. Cover plus incidental or consequential damages
2. Recovery of damages equal to the difference between the contract price and the market price at the time the buyer learned of the breach (here, the time of delivery), together with any incidental or consequential damages
3. Specific performance or replevin
4. Liquidated damages
5. Occasionally, punitive damages

REJECTION BY BUYER OF NONCONFORMING GOODS OR TENDER

General Observations

A third way a seller may breach a sales contract is by providing goods that do not conform to the contract or by making a tender[1] that does not conform to the contract. Let us assume the goods in our hypothetical wine rack case are nonconforming, specifically because express warranties are breached: the

---

1. "Tender of delivery requires that the seller put and hold conforming goods at the buyer's disposition and give the buyer any notification reasonably necessary to enable him to take delivery. The manner, time and place for tender are determined by the agreement . . . and in particular (a) tender must be at a reasonable hour, and . . . goods . . . must be kept available for the period reasonably necessary to enable the buyer to take possession. . . ." UCC § 2–502.

wine racks only hold half-bottles, not regular wine bottles; the racks are made of the wrong wood; they are of rickety construction. By way of contrast with repudiation and nondelivery, note that Wine Cellar has gone further toward performance than in either of those situations: goods are actually made available to Bacchus. Note also that if Wine Cellar tenders or delivers goods that conform to the contract, Bacchus is under an obligation to accept them. Failure to accept will give the seller immediate remedies for breach of contract.

When a seller tenders or delivers nonconforming goods, the buyer is presented with three alternatives. He may accept the whole, reject the whole, or accept any commercial unit or units and reject the rest. His choice of action at this point will determine the contractual obligations he must continue to follow and the remedies he is entitled to utilize.

The Code requires that rejection occur in a particular manner in order to be effective. If these requirements are not met, rejection will be ineffective and the buyer may find to his chagrin that he has lost his right to object and, in so doing, has accepted the goods. Because of the importance of an effective rejection to the preservation of the buyer's remedies, we will consider his responsibilities here before proceeding to discuss his remedies.

Rejection

To ensure that the seller has a fair opportunity to cure defects, resell, or otherwise dispose of his rejected goods, section 2–606 calls for affirmative action by the buyer. If he does nothing, an effective rejection cannot occur; his silence constitutes an acceptance of the goods.

His affirmative responsibilities are threefold. First, he must notify the seller of his rejection: this requirement is met when the buyer takes such steps as would reasonably be required to impart notice in the ordinary course of events. UCC §§ 2–602(1); 1–201(26). Second, the rejection must be made within a reasonable time after tender or delivery; the reasonableness of the time depends upon the circumstances of the case. UCC §§ 2–602(1); 1–204(2). Third, if the seller would have time to correct the defect before the time for performance passed, the buyer must specify all defects that are ascertainable upon reasonable examination and, if the seller so chooses, the buyer, before seeking further remedies, must give the seller a chance to correct the defect. UCC §§ 2–605; 2–508.

In addition to these affirmative responsibilities, the buyer has two further duties when the goods remain in his possession for a period of time after rejection. First, he must not utilize them in any manner inconsistent with the seller's ownership. UCC §§ 2–606(1)(c); 2–602(2)(a). Second, he must exercise reasonable care toward them and must hold them sufficiently long to permit the seller to remove them. UCC § 2–602(2)(b). Should the buyer be a merchant, and should the seller not have a local agent, the merchant buyer must carry out the seller's reasonable instructions with regard to the goods. The merchant buyer is also under a duty to sell the goods for the seller's account if they are perishable or apt to decline rapidly in value. UCC § 2–603(1). Subject to these responsibilities, a final option of both merchant and nonmerchant buyers is to store, reship, or sell the goods for the seller if no instructions are received within a reasonable time after notification. UCC § 2–604.

Buyer's Remedies

Where the buyer rightfully rejects all of the tendered goods and the defects are not or cannot be cured, section 2–711 provides the same remedies as those for repudiation and nondelivery. Replevin would, of course, be an unlikely remedy since it would only give the buyer possession of goods he has already rejected.

ACCEPTANCE BY BUYER OF NONCONFORMING GOODS

General Observations

In this situation the seller has again breached his contract; he has tendered or delivered nonconforming goods. The only factual difference between this situation and the preceding one is that the buyer, Bacchus, elected the alternative not discussed there: he accepted the goods rather than rejecting them.

Let us assume the nonconformity in the wine racks had to do with the type and color of the wood. The racks are nearly blond in color instead of the rich dark tone called for in the contract. Bacchus inspects the goods when they arrive and is aware of the nonconformity, but it decides to accept them anyway. It may figure that having blond wine racks delivered on time is more desirable than having dark wine racks delivered two weeks later.

Should it accept the goods, Bacchus is precluded from rejecting them later but is permitted by section 2–607(2) to sue for damages (if there are any) arising from the breach of contract. This is true whether it inspects the goods and knowingly accepts the nonconforming ones, or whether it does not inspect, discovers the nonconformity later, and yet decides to keep the goods.

Had Bacchus accepted the wine racks without knowing of the nonconformity because its agents either did not inspect the racks or inspected them but did not detect the flaw, Bacchus may still be able to avoid ownership of the blond wine racks. It may be able to revoke its acceptance and pursue the remedies already discussed in connection with rejection and repudiation.

While the preceding discussion should give a sense of the buyer's remedies when he knowingly or unknowingly accepts nonconforming goods, that sense will be more complete after consideration of two further questions. What constitutes acceptance? How does one revoke acceptance?

Acceptance

Section 2–606 of the UCC states that acceptance of goods has occurred when the buyer specifically informs the seller that he has accepted them; the buyer, without rejecting the goods, keeps them beyond the time that he "has had a reasonable opportunity to inspect them"; or the buyer does anything "inconsistent with the seller's ownership."

The third of these tests, inconsistent usage, has posed a number of interpretive problems. The following case identifies some of the relevant policy questions and gives an impression of where the line is drawn between permissible and impermissible conduct.

Can-Key Indus. v. Industrial Leasing Corp.
Supreme Court of Oregon, 1979. 286 Or. 173, 593 P.2d 1125

HOWELL, JUSTICE.

. . . Plaintiff Can-key Industries, Inc., manufactured a turkey hatching unit which it sold to defendant Industrial Leasing Corporation (ILC) which in turn leased it to Rose-A-Linda Turkey Farms, a California corporation. ILC's purchase order conditioned its final acceptance on Rose-A-Linda's willingness to accept the equipment. When Rose-A-Linda indicated that it was dissatisfied with the equipment, defendant refused to proceed with the contract of sale and plaintiff brought this action against ILC. From a judgment for plaintiff, defendant appeals.

. . . .

The sole issue in this case is whether defendant "accepted" the equipment manufactured by plaintiff. The contract between plaintiff and defendant provided that defendant's obligation to pay would be conditioned upon acceptance of the equipment by its lessee. Consequently, the trial court could properly find that defendant accepted the equipment only if there is evidence that Rose-A-Linda, the lessee, accepted the equipment.

. . . .

[Section 606(1)] provides:

"Acceptance of goods occurs when the buyer:

"(a) After a reasonable opportunity to inspect the goods signifies to the seller that the goods are conforming or that he will take or retain them in spite of their nonconformity; or
"(b) Fails to make an effective rejection. . . , but such acceptance does not occur until the buyer has had a reasonable opportunity to inspect them; or
"(c) Does any act inconsistent with the seller's ownership; but if such act is wrongful as against the seller it is an acceptance only if ratified by him."

No contention is made that . . . (a) is applicable in this case. . . .

. . . .

[After rejecting plaintiff's argument regarding subsection (b) the court continued as follows.]

. . . .

. . . Plaintiff's evidence that Rose-A-Linda accepted the equipment is therefore sufficient only if it shows that Rose-A-Linda performed acts inconsistent with the seller's ownership under the terms of . . . [subsection (c)].

What constitutes "any act inconsistent with the seller's ownership" has proved to be one of the trouble areas under Article 2 of the Uniform Commercial Code. Courts that have applied the provision have reached inconsistent results and commentators have termed the provision an "obstreperous" one. J. White and R. Summers, Uniform Commercial Code 251 (1972). It has been suggested that "courts are first deciding upon the merits of the buyer's claim and then reasoning backwards to the determination of whether there has been an acceptance because of an inconsistent act." White & Summers, supra at 253.

A reasoned application of the section requires that the court recognize the existence of two competing policies. A buyer who verbally rejects goods should not in all cases be allowed to use the goods as if he were the owner and effectively "have it both ways." On the other hand, there are many cases in which use of the goods after rejection is not only reasonable in that it minimizes economic waste, but may be required under the buyer's statutory duty to mitigate consequential damages. The court must consider both policies when defining the scope of "any act inconsistent with the seller's ownership."

. . . .

Nearly all the evidence plaintiff relies upon to demonstrate that Rose-A-Linda performed acts inconsistent with plaintiff's ownership was provided by Gibson, Rose-A-Linda's president. Plaintiff did introduce testimony that Rose-A-Linda used the equipment in March and April of 1976, but it is clear from the record that these uses related to Rose-A-Linda's initial inspection of the equipment and plaintiff's efforts to solve the "problems" with the equipment that it recognized in its April letter to Rose-A-Linda. Neither of these uses was inconsistent with plaintiff's ownership of the equipment. Rose-A-Linda's initial inspection cannot be considered inconsistent with plaintiff's ownership because . . . [subsection] (b) assures a buyer of goods a "reasonable opportunity to inspect them." Nor can the use of the equipment during April be considered inconsistent, because that use was approved by plaintiff, which was attempting to solve the problems with the equipment.

Plaintiff's primary reliance is on the modifications and alterations performed by Rose-A-Linda "after the equipment was installed and functioning." These acts all occurred after Gibson notified plaintiff that the equipment was unacceptable and asked that it be removed. The only testimony concerning these acts is Gibson's. That testimony shows that Rose-A-Linda employed the original developer of the equipment in an attempt to remedy the defects. It used the equipment four times during 1977. Three of those uses followed modifications or suggestions for modifications by the developer, and the final use was for the purpose of conducting a comparative test. Although the equipment apparently remains in Rose-A-Linda's possession, it has not been used since May of 1977.

We hold that this evidence does not demonstrate a use inconsistent with the seller's ownership under the terms of . . . [subsection] (c). To hold otherwise would have the effect of penalizing Rose-A-Linda for its apparent good faith efforts to cure the defects in the equipment. We do not believe such a holding is compelled by the language of . . . [subsection] (c). On the contrary, we think such a holding might be inconsistent with other provisions of the Code, specifically the statutory duty to mitigate consequential damages and the statutory obligation of good faith.

It must be remembered that this transaction involved a newly developed product, the first of its kind manufactured by plaintiff. All parties to the transaction undoubtedly expected that the equipment would have some initial "bugs." After an initial test, Rose-A-Linda found the equipment unsatisfactory and notified plaintiff to that effect. Plaintiff then attempted to remedy the problems, and Rose-A-Linda again found the equipment unsatisfactory. Rose-A-Linda asked plaintiff to remove the equipment and plaintiff refused. Plaintiff did not instruct Rose-A-Linda to refrain from using the equipment and plaintiff has not demonstrated that Rose-A-Linda's testing and modifications damaged the equipment in any way.

. . . [The Court considered its holding consistent with cases involving the following facts:] (continued occupancy of mobile home held not inconsistent with seller's ownership); (use of pleasure boat for fishing trips up until time of trial held to constitute an acceptance); (use of motor and pump to irrigate property held to constitute acceptance).

Because there is no evidence that Rose-A-Linda ever accepted the equipment in this case, the judgment against the defendant Industrial Leasing must be reversed.

Reversed.

As a result of acceptance the buyer becomes obligated to pay for the goods. He can no longer reject them, but he may be able either to revoke his acceptance, return the goods, and recover damages, or to keep the goods and recover damages.

Revocation of Acceptance

In many cases the nonconformity will not be apparent upon reasonable inspection, and the buyer will, therefore, accept the goods without knowledge of their defects. Similarly, the seller might make a misrepresentation to the buyer that causes the buyer to accept defective goods, or the buyer may knowingly accept nonconforming goods, on the understanding that the seller will correct the defects in the future. The Code provides for revocation of acceptance in such cases.

Cases involving revocation of acceptance have been relatively frequent under the Code. The case presented is included partly because of its discussion of revocation of acceptance and partly because of its discussion of incidental and punitive damages as they relate to the Code. The plaintiffs in *Grandi* seek to revoke acceptance, cancel, recover their purchase price, and, in addition, recover incidental damages, such as the cost of the care, feeding, and maintenance of a race horse, plus punitive damages.

Grandi v. LeSage
Supreme Court of New Mexico, 1965. 74 N.M. 799, 399 P.2d 285

CHAVEZ, JUSTICE.

The facts found by the trial court, stated in narrative form, are as follows: The horse in question, Cur-Non, was foaled on April 19, 1957, in Kentucky, and on November 1, 1957, was registered with the jockey club which issued its certificate of registration showing Cur-Non to be a chestnut colt. Defendant LeSage purchased Cur-Non from the breeder in July of 1958, and in 1960, at the direction of a former trainer, Cur-Non was gelded . . . and LeSage knew the operation had been performed. . . . LeSage shipped Cur-Non to Claggett [LeSage's horse trainer] and directed him to enter Cur-Non in the racing meet in the Fall of 1961 and Spring of 1962 at Sunland Park Race Track, Sunland Park, New Mexico. At this time, Claggett, although knowing that Cur-Non was a gelding, registered Cur-Non as a four-year-old chestnut colt, thus indicating his sex to be that of a stallion. At the same time, Claggett deposited the "Jockey Club Certificate of Foal Registration" showing Cur-Non to be a four-year-old colt, and at no time did he advise the race officials that Cur-Non was a gelding.

[Each day Sunland Park racetrack publishes information in its program about the horses racing that day. The information includes the sex of the horse. This information was relied upon by plaintiffs, since custom dictates that claimants in a claims race are not allowed to inspect the horses prior to the race. Plaintiffs needed a stallion for breeding purposes and were the successful claimants of Cur-Non in a January 6, 1962 race. They paid the $3,500 claiming price to R. S. LeSage. Following the claims race, plaintiffs' veterinarian discovered a leg injury and had an operation performed, not to improve Cur-Non's racing ability but rather to ease the pain in the hope he would be a better breeder. The operation was unsuccessful, and Cur-Non was returned to plaintiffs' ranch when it was discovered that Cur-Non was a gelding.

When plaintiffs were finally able to notify LeSage that Cur-Non was claimed for breeding purposes, he informed them that he did not consider himself liable and refused their offer to return Cur-Non.]

    . . . .

Sections 2–711(1)(b), 713 and 715(1), N.M.S.A., 1953 Comp., give a buyer, who rightfully rejects or justifiably revokes acceptance of the goods, the right not only to rescind and recover back the purchase price paid, but, in addition, the right to recover incidental damages resulting from the seller's breach, including expenses reasonably incurred in the care and custody of such goods. . . .

By his point VI, appellant LeSage argues:

"VI. That under the provisions of Article 2, Chapter 50A, New Mexico Statutes Annotated, 1953 Compilation, as Amended and Supplemented, the plaintiffs accepted delivery of Cur-Non since after reasonable opportunity to inspect him:

"(a) They did not reject Cur-Non within a reasonable time after they had taken delivery from the defendant LeSage; and

"(b) They had him treated, removed from the State of New Mexico to the State of Arizona, and there caused him to be operated upon by a veterinarian, and all said acts being inconsistent with the ownership of defendant LeSage."

Notwithstanding there may have been an acceptance within the meaning of § 2–606, N.M.S.A., 1953 Comp., under § 2–608, a buyer who justifiably revokes his acceptance has the same right to rescission as though he had rejected the goods in the first place. Such revocation is justifiable if he accepted them:

"(b) without discovery of such nonconformity if his acceptance was reasonably induced either by the difficulty of discovery before acceptance or by the seller's assurances.

"(2) Revocation of acceptance must occur within a reasonable time after the buyer discovers or should have discovered the ground for it and before any substantial change in condition of the goods which is not caused by their own defects. It is not effective until the buyer notifies the seller of it."

Even assuming an acceptance by the buyer, such acceptance was effectively revoked in accordance with § 2–608, supra.

LeSage argues that plaintiffs had been guilty of laches in failing to promptly examine Cur-Non and asserts that plaintiffs had no right to rely on representations made in the racing form. The trial court specifically found otherwise. A review of the record convinces us that the contrary findings by the trial court are supported by the evidence and, consequently, they will not be disturbed on appeal. *Bogle* v. *Potter*, 72 N.M. 99, 380 P.2d 839.

. . . .

. . . Since the Commercial Code, § 2–711, N.M.S.A., 1953 Comp., permits recovery of damages in an action for rescission, punitive damages may likewise be recovered in such action where the breach is accompanied by fraudulent acts which are wanton, malicious and intentional. . . . It is apparent to us that LeSage had knowledge of the agent's unauthorized action and failed promptly to repudiate it and, that having received the benefits of the sale by his acceptance and retention of the consideration, he cannot now reject the burdens incident thereto. The award of punitive damages was not error.

It follows from what has been said that the judgment . . . must be affirmed in all respects as to the appellant LeSage. [The judgment affirmed was for: 1) return of the $3,500 purchase price; 2) the expense incurred by plaintiffs in the care, feeding and maintenance of the horse; and 3) punitive damages in the sum of $2,500.] The cause is remanded to the district court with instructions to proceed in a manner not inconsistent with what has been said.

It is so ordered.

NOBLE and MOISE, JJ., concur.

BUYER'S REMEDY WHEN TIME FOR REVOCATION HAS PASSED

We are here concerned with the remedies available even after the time for revocation of acceptance has expired. On the seller's side, the situation again involves breach by the tendering of goods which are nonconforming. The breach may have involved violation of a quality warranty, of a title warranty, or of any other contractual obligation of the seller.

On the buyer's side, Bacchus has accepted the goods but has subsequently become aware of the breach or, having known of the breach upon acceptance, has just become convinced that Wine Cellar is not going to cure the defect. We assume that the proper notice of the breach required for any recovery was given within a reasonable time after the breach was discovered or should have been discovered. Up to this point Bacchus has proceeded properly and can either revoke acceptance, thereby avoiding ownership of the goods, and sue for damages, or it can keep the goods and sue for damages. Suppose Bacchus now for any number of reasons puts off beyond a reasonable time notifying Wine Cellar that it does not want the goods. Alternatively, suppose Bacchus has an opportunity to act within a reasonable time but there has been a substantial change in the condition of the goods for some reason not caused by the defect: the goods may have been damaged by a ruptured water pipe in the storeroom. Either reason — unreasonable delay or change in condition — will preclude Bacchus from revoking acceptance. In other words, Bacchus is stuck with the goods.

Since the buyer has the goods, cover, replevin, and specific performance are inappropriate. Bacchus is not, however, deprived of its damage remedy. It may under section 2–714 recover whatever loss resulted from the seller's breach, including incidental and consequential damages.

PROBLEMS AND QUESTIONS

1. List and briefly describe the five types of buyer's remedies. What are the factors that would lead a buyer to seek each of these remedies? What is the reason for the latitude in choice of remedy?

2. Castor ordered a quantity of hula hoops from Standard Pipe. When Standard Pipe failed to deliver part of the order, Castor claimed as part of its consequential damages loss of goodwill as a result of the orders it was not able to fill. What would be the result?

3. McCormick contracted to buy a trucking business, including goodwill, real estate, and the transfer of Interstate Commerce Commission and Public Utilities Commission certificates which were necessary to operate the business. Would any of these items be the proper subject for specific performance?

4. Bounce Seat Co. is in the business of manufacturing automobile seats and is under long-term contract to sell them to Tucker Motors. Bounce contracted with Super Spring Corp. to purchase an order of springs for $5,000. Super was aware that Bounce needed the springs in order to meet its contract with Tucker. Prior to the performance date, however, the market price for springs rose to $6,500 and Super repudiated its contract with Bounce. Bounce immediately purchased springs from Atlas Spring Company for $6,500 in time to meet its Tucker Motors contract. Bounce had to pay an additional $700 for transportation costs from Atlas's place of business. Bounce sues Super. How much will Bounce recover?

5. Assume the same facts as in problem 4, except that after reasonable but unsuccessful efforts to purchase springs elsewhere, Bounce was forced by Super's repudiation to breach its contract with Tucker Motors, for which it had to pay $15,000 in damages. Bounce sues Super. How much will Bounce recover?

Assume now that although Atlas was able and willing to sell Bounce the springs it needed for $6,500, Bounce chose not to cover but to pursue alternate remedies against Super. Again, Bounce's breach of its Tucker Motors contract cost it $15,000. How much will Bounce recover from Super?

6. Bates contracted to buy 5,000 laying hens from Sanders for $25,000. Bates prepaid $1,000. When the hens were delivered, he discovered that they were game hens. Bates immediately notified Sanders of this nonconformity and rejected them all. The cost of penning them until Sanders repossessed them was $500. Bates thereupon purchased 5,000 laying hens from Adams for $28,000. In a suit for breach of contract, how much will Bates recover from Sanders?

7. Baxter bought a secondhand truck and immediately noticed that the two-speed transmission was not functioning properly and that the truck consumed too much oil. He attempted to contact the dealer who sold him the truck but was unsuccessful. He did, however, contact one of the dealer's mechanics, who stated that there was nothing wrong with the vehicle. Five months later the truck exploded while being driven, but there was no direct proof that the explosion was due to a defect which existed when Baxter made his purchase. Baxter refused to pay any further installments on the vehicle and sued to cancel the contract on grounds of breach of warranty. What would be the result?

8. Byways Transporting Co. contracted to purchase a fleet of trucks from Sanford Retail Truck Outlet for $100,000. The contract required that the trucks bear the inscription "Byways" on the cab doors. One week before the performance date, Sanford delivered the trucks, but it had neglected to paint the inscriptions. The cost of painting would have been $50 and Sanford had easy access to a painter. Byways, however, chose to reject the trucks and telegraphed Sanford, "Goods are nonconforming and are hereby rejected." Sanford sued Byways for breach. Does Byways have a good defense?

9. Fleet bought an ice cream freezer and refrigeration unit from Lang. Later Fleet moved his business and the ice cream freezer to a new location without informing Lang. When Lang finally repossessed the machinery because of Fleet's lack of payment, Fleet was using the machinery to operate his air-conditioning unit. Fleet sued to cancel the contract and recover his down payment, alleging that the unit was defective. What would be the result?

10. Marks had her house covered with an artificial stone which the seller claimed would never lose its color. After two years all the color had disappeared from the stone, which was also seriously cracking. Marks sued for return of her purchase price and consequential damages. Is two years more than a reasonable time in which revocation of acceptance can be made? The stone would have been reduced to rubble had it been removed from the house. Does this make any difference?

11. In September Bowers Corp. purchased an air-conditioning system from Sayers, Inc. The system was guaranteed to cool all ten of the rooms in Bowers's office complex. The purchase price was $5,000. One month after installing the system, Bowers's purchasing agent became convinced that it was incapable of cooling more than eight of the ten rooms. By that time (mid-October) the market value of the air-conditioning unit had dropped to $4,500, as retailers made end-

of-season reductions. The October market value of a larger unit, adequate to cool all ten rooms, was found to be $5,500, down from $6,000 in September. Bowers chose not to revoke its acceptance and sued Sayers for damages. What amount will Bowers recover?

Suppose the overworked air conditioner sprayed a thin mist into the office, rusting Bowers's metal office furniture. Could Bowers recover for this property damage?

12. Bradley contracted to buy 100 fully equipped typewriters from Spires Typewriter Co. to stock his newly opened newspaper office. The contract price was $15,000. Although the contract called for blue ink ribbons, Spires delivered the typewriters with black ribbons. The cost of 100 blue ribbons would have been $25. Bradley telegraphed Spires, "Please provide blue ink ribbons as per our contract; the present ribbons are black." Bradley then proceeded to use the typewriters as they were since "black ribbons were better than none." Spires made no reply and no effort to cure. A month later Bradley telegraphed, "Goods are rejected for reasons specified last month." Is Bradley's rejection effective? What would you advise Bradley to do?

22

SELLER'S RIGHTS AND REMEDIES

OVERVIEW

Although a buyer may breach a sales contract in a variety of ways, the four most common forms of breach, and the ones specifically mentioned in the UCC, are as follows: buyer repudiates the contract; buyer rejects the goods but is not justified in doing so (wrongful rejection); buyer revokes acceptance but is not justified in doing so (wrongful revocation of acceptance); buyer fails to make payments. Repudiation, rejection, and revocation of acceptance were all discussed in Chapter 21. Nonpayment is self-evident. We shall now consider the options available to the seller when the buyer breaches in any one of these ways or in any other less frequently occurring manner.

The UCC provides the seller with the following rights and remedies as protection against the buyer's breach. The seller may:

1. Cancel
2. Withhold or stop delivery of the goods if delivery has not taken place
3. Resell the goods and recover damages
4. Recover damages for nonacceptance or (in a proper case) the price of the goods
5. Salvage unfinished goods or, if the goods are finished but have not yet been identified to the contract (set aside for the buyer), identify them to the contract and resell them
6. Recover damages pursuant to a liquidated damage provision if there is one in the sales contract

These remedies are essentially cumulative in nature, and the seller does not have to select only one. For instance, if a buyer repudiates the contract, the seller can both withhold delivery of any goods identified to the contract and recover damages for nonacceptance. This chapter will be devoted to an analysis of the available remedies.

CANCEL

The right to cancel because of the buyer's breach enables the seller to terminate the contract and thereby free himself of any ongoing obligations under the contract. For example, the contract might have specified that seller deliver ten dozen footballs to buyer's sporting goods shop on September 1, ten dozen more on October 1, and a final ten dozen on November 1. Cancellation would free the seller of this commitment to make future deliveries. The buyer had this same right to cancel when it was the seller who had breached.

WITHHOLDING AND STOPPING DELIVERY

Suppose that Rally Pro Shop contracted to purchase 500 unstrung metal tennis rackets from Ideal Manufacturing. Should Rally, the retailer, repudiate or otherwise breach the contract, Ideal would obviously gain nothing and perhaps lose much by giving Rally possession of the tennis rackets. The Code in section 2–703(a) therefore permits Ideal to withhold delivery of any goods still in its possession when breach occurs.

Conceivably, knowledge of Rally's breach could reach Ideal when the rackets are speeding along a highway in the possession of a trucking company, or the goods might be in a warehouse waiting to be picked up by the trucking company or by the buyer. In such circumstances the seller has a limited right to stop delivery. If the seller discovers that the buyer has become insolvent, section 2–705(1) confers the right to stop delivery of any size shipment of goods. However, in order to minimize the burden on carriers, warehousers, and other bailees, the right to stop delivery for any reason other than the buyer's insolvency is limited to carload, truckload, planeload, or larger shipments. Thus, on smaller shipments the seller must protect himself either by shipping C.O.D. or by inserting a provision for prepayment in the contract.

The right to stop delivery extends only until the buyer or a representative of the buyer, such as a subpurchaser, receives the goods. Furthermore, if the bailee holding the goods acknowledges the buyer's right to them, or if the buyer receives a negotiable document of title to the goods, the seller may no longer hold up delivery. UCC § 2–705(2).

DAMAGES WHERE GOODS ARE RESOLD

The seller's right to resell the goods on a buyer's breach is analogous to the buyer's right to cover on a seller's breach. In cover, the buyer acquires substitute goods at the prevailing market price and recovers any adverse difference in price from the seller. In *resale*, the seller makes a substitute disposition of the goods at the prevailing market price and recovers from the buyer any adverse difference between the contract price and the disposition price. The analogy goes one step further. Whereas cover is the buyer's primary remedy, resale is the seller's primary remedy. The reasons for the primacy of resale among remedies for the seller are quite practical.

Suppose a wholesaler has ordered goods from a manufacturer in order to fill the contract of a customer. The customer then repudiates or wrongfully rejects and leaves the wholesaler with goods on hand that he would not have had but for the buyer's contract. A similar situation exists with regard to a manufacturer-seller. The buyer's contract may have affected the seller's estimate of demand and thus his production. In either situation, the buyer's breach leaves the seller with goods he would not otherwise have had. To minimize the potential inconvenience to the seller in these situations, the Code authorizes the seller to resell in good faith and in a commercially reasonable manner in order to dispose of the excess goods quickly and at the same time to fix the precise amount to be recovered from the buyer in damages, which will be the unfavorable difference between contract price and the proceeds from the sale.

If the seller acts in a commercially unreasonable manner, he loses his right to this measure of damages. Unreasonable resale would entitle the seller to recover only the difference between the contract price and the market price at the time and place of tender, or, if that measure of damages is inadequate to put the seller in as good a position as performance would have done, the profit he would have made had the buyer performed. UCC § 2–706, comment 2. This measure of damages encourages the seller to use reasonable resale, just as the buyer is encouraged to use cover. Should the seller act unreasonably, as by waiting too long to resell, he is forced to assume the risk that the market price of the goods will increase between the date of unreasonable resale and the date of tender. Thus, if the contract price is $100, the goods are unreasonably resold for $50, and their market price on the date of tender is $75, the seller recovers only $25 rather than $50. Should the seller not resell the goods at all, his recovery is still only $25, based on value on the date of tender.

Let us assume a reasonable resale in the hypothetical tennis racket case. With a contract price of $30 per tennis racket, Ideal would have received $15,000 for its 500 rackets if the contract had not been breached. Given the breach and assuming that Ideal can make an alternative disposition of the rackets for $20 each, the seller will still end up in the same position as if the contract had not been breached, i.e., without the rackets but with $15,000. The alternative disposition of 500 rackets at $20 each will yield $10,000; the $5,000 balance can be recovered in damages from the buyer, providing he has the money. As in the case of most buyer's remedies, the expenses seller can save as a result of buyer's breach are deducted from the recovery.

The seller's remedy of resale and damages differs from cover, however, in the area of incidental and consequential damages. Whereas an injured buyer could recover for both, an injured seller can recover only his incidental damages. He cannot recover consequential damages. Consequential damages are by nature a buyer's remedy; they compensate the buyer for losses due to his particular needs and requirements in connection with the goods, as well as compensate him for personal injury and property damage resulting from defects. The seller's needs and requirements in connection with the contract price are satisfied when he collects interest on the judgment in his favor.

In some cases the seller will make a greater profit on his resale of the goods than he would have made selling the goods under the original contract. For instance, Ideal might be able to sell the 500 tennis rackets to Ace Sports Shop at $34 per racket. Should Ideal be required to give Rally all or a part of the additional profit made possible by his breach? The Code in section 2–706(6) says no. Ideal is not accountable to Rally for any part of this excess. This is fair since Ideal might have been able to secure additional tennis rackets and sell to Ace at the same price even if Rally had not breached.

Any resale must be made in good faith in a commercially reasonable manner and after reasonable notice to the original buyer. An indication of what these standards mean can be gathered from the following case.

Coast Trading Co. v. Cudahy Co.
United States Court of Appeals, Ninth Circuit, 1978. 592 F.2d 1074

[Over an eight month period plaintiff, Coast Trading Company (CTC) a grain merchant, sold the unprecedented sum of 10,000 tons of barley to a long-standing customer, defendant Cudahy Co. Cudahy operated a cattle feedlot at Sunnyside, Washington. Robin Van Woerden was general manager of the feedlot and the person who placed the orders. When Van Woerden's supervisors learned of the purchases, they considered them excessive and speculative and tried to cancel them. CTC refused. Cudahy then repudiated on the grounds that Van Woerden had no authority to bind defendant. CTC sued for damages.

At trial, the court found that Van Woerden had the apparent authority of an agent to bind the defendant for reasonable amounts amounting to 4,500 tons of barley. Fifteen hundred of these tons had been sold at a private sale without proper notice to the defendant. Consequently seller was entitled to damages on only 3,000 tons.]

GRANT, J.

. . . .

Damages
The second and more difficult issue is whether the trial court correctly measured the damages. . . . The seller in the case at bar has asserted that § 2–706 should be the measure of damages. Under § 2–706, if the resale is made in good faith and in a commercially reasonable manner, the seller may recover the difference between the resale price and the contract price. . . .

. . . [W]e conclude that the trial court erred in allowing damages under Section 2–706 of the Oregon Uniform Commercial Code. In its 12 April 1976 Memorandum Opinion, the trial court insisted upon the reasonable notification requirement of Section 2–706, but failed to address the question of whether the other prerequisites had been fulfilled by the plaintiff. We find that, as a matter of law, the plaintiff did not satisfy the elements of good faith and commercial reasonableness, required in every aspect of every sale. The most striking example of commercial unreasonableness that suggests bad faith is the alleged resale contract between the plaintiff and a corporate purchaser entitled Montana Merchandisers, Inc. The total amount of barley involved in the repudiated contracts equals 10,343.11 tons. Of the 10,343.11 tons resold by plaintiff, 5,293.11 tons were supposedly sold to Montana Merchandisers, Inc., on 19 June 1974, as part of a 6,000-ton transaction. The sale price was $100 per ton, although the pertinent market price was $105 per ton. Nine days later, on 28 June 1974, the plaintiff signed a contract to purchase an identical amount (6,000 tons) of barley from Montana Merchandisers, Inc. This purchase agreement for the identical amount of grain stated only a $0.25 per ton increase in price and the instrument negated the earlier sale before any grain exchanged hands and even before written confirmation of the 18 June sale was received by plaintiff from Montana Merchandisers, Inc. The trial court admitted defendant's exhibit showing what actually happened to the next 5,293.11 tons of barley that were sold by plaintiff after 28 June 1974. That exhibit reveals actual receipt of $133,566 more than that reported by plaintiff as receipts from the alleged sale to Montana Merchandisers, Inc. The defendant has characterized this sale to Montana Merchandisers, Inc., as a fictitious "wash" sale designed to inflate plaintiff's damage claim. We agree. The uncontroverted evidence has established that the Montana Merchandisers transaction was little more than a paper contract apparently intended to serve only as a basis for calculating resale damages under Section 2–706. The commercial unreasonableness is obvious and raises questions of bad faith. Plaintiff contends that it was totally independent of Montana Merchandisers, Inc., because their relationship had terminated a year earlier. We are not persuaded. . . .

. . . .

We . . . hold that the commercial unreasonableness of the resale of over fifty per cent of the barley involved in the repudiated contracts is of such magnitude that we need not further examine whether other aspects[1] of the resales were in derogation of the safeguards required under Section 2–706. The plaintiff may not recover under Section 2–706.

The condition of the goods (i.e., whether they are perishable or subject to swift decline in value) and the condition of the market are additional factors bearing on whether the sale is conducted in a commercially reasonable manner. Failure to comply with the good faith, commercially reasonable, or notice standards deprives the seller of the measure of damages provided in this section of the UCC and relegates him to damages for nonacceptance, a remedy which will be discussed shortly.

DAMAGES WHERE GOODS ARE NOT RESOLD OR ARE RESOLD UNREASONABLY

General Rule

If the buyer repudiates the contract or refuses to accept the goods when tendered, the goods, of course, remain in the seller's possession or under his control. The Code gives the seller in this situation the option to resell the goods and recover any unfavorable difference between the sales price and the price specified in the breached contract. Suppose, though, that the seller forfeits the resale remedy because he resells in an unreasonable manner. Or suppose he decides not to resort to resale. What then should be the nature

---

1. *E.g.*, whether plaintiff properly identified the resale contracts to the repudiated contracts, and whether the plaintiff fulfilled its duty to realize as high a price as possible under the circumstances. *Columbia Nitrogen Corp.* v. *Royster Co.*, 451 F.2d 3 (4th Cir. 1971).

of his remedy? The Code's rule is twofold. Section 2–708(1) states that the seller's damages will be the difference between the market price at the time and place for tender and the unpaid contract price plus any incidental damages but less expenses saved. However, should this measure of damages be inadequate to put the seller in as good a position as performance would have done, the amount of damages should be the profit the seller would have made from full performance plus incidental damages but less expenses saved.

Let us assume that at the time suit is brought or the matter is settled out of court, Ideal has not resold the tennis rackets. This situation poses the following question: what amount of money should a seller receive from the buyer as damages when the seller has retained possession of the goods? Ideal would obviously enjoy a windfall if it were permitted to recover the full contract price from the breaching buyer; it would still have possession of the tennis rackets, which it could later sell to generate additional cash.

The Code takes the position that reasonable resale is the fairest procedure all around. To encourage the seller in this direction, his damages are computed as if he had resold even though in fact he did not. For example, if the market price of the tennis rackets was $20 cash at the time and place of tender, Ideal's quantum of damages would be the difference between the $20 market price and the $30 contract price, i.e., $10 per racket. The analogy to resale should be clear. If Ideal had resold the rackets at the time and place of tender, it would have received $20 each for them. This coupled with $10 per racket of damages would put Ideal in the same position it would have occupied had the contract been performed or had Ideal resold at the contract price.

Assume now that instead of keeping the goods, Ideal resells them, but does so at the unreasonably low price of $12 each, $8 below the market price for the goods. The Code takes the position that it would be unfair to permit the seller to saddle the breaching buyer with this unnecessary $8 of lost revenue. When the seller unreasonably resells, he is precluded from computing damages according to the regular resale procedure, i.e., he cannot recover the difference between actual sales price and the contract price. He can, however, recover the difference between the market price and contract price. Assuming the market price of tennis rackets at the time and place of tender was $20 each, Ideal can recover as damages the $10 difference between that figure and the $30 contract price. Thus, Ideal receives $10 in damages from Rally plus $12 per racket from the unreasonable resale for a total of only $22. The $8 difference between this cash inflow and the $30 contract price represents the amount Ideal must absorb because of its irresponsible conduct in reselling at an unreasonable price.

When damages are computed by reference to the market price instead of an actual sales price, as in the two situations just discussed, there is occasional disagreement as to what the market price is. These problems have already been discussed with reference to buyer's damages for seller's breach (pages 359–60). The same alternatives available to the buyer for proving market price may be utilized by the seller. That is, reference may be made to the price prevailing at a reasonable time before or after that specified and at a place which is a reasonable substitute for the place in question. UCC § 2–723(2).

Recovery of Profit

The profit measure of damages is appropriate only when the general rule of contract price minus market price does not put the seller in as good a position as would performance. In the tennis racket situations, the profit measure of damages would not be appropriate. Assuming Ideal could have sold the goods for $20 each had it chosen to do so, the $10 of damages would have put it in the same financial position as performance. Ideal's unreasonable resale was certainly not as remunerative a course of action as performance would have been. The reason for this was not the inadequacy of the general rule. The inadequacy resulted instead from Ideal's unreasonable decision to sell at the price it did.

There are situations, however, in which the general rule, even though properly applied, would be inadequate. These involve goods which are sold at standard prices. If Ideal maintains a standard or list price of $30 for its tennis rackets, profit (i.e., the list price minus manufacturing costs including reasonable overhead) would be the proper measure of damages. Here Rally's breach will have injured Ideal even if Ideal can resell the 500 rackets to another purchaser at the identical $30 per racket price. Ideal has been able to sell only 500 rackets, whereas Ideal would have sold 1,000 if Rally had performed; the other buyer would have taken 500 rackets whether Rally breached or performed. In other words, at a standard price of $30 per racket it is assumed that only a fixed number of rackets will be sold. If one of the purchasers breaches his contract, the sale is deemed lost forever. This situation does not exist if the price is subject to negotiation and varies over the short term in response to different competitive pressures. Here a drop in price is deemed capable of eliciting a purchase which otherwise would not have occurred.

The profit approach poses problems only when the seller is in a new business. In such a case there is no evidence of the seller's previous manufacturing costs, overhead, or previous profits to aid in measuring what the lost profits should be. Because of this, a rule evolved under common law to the effect that lost profits cannot be the measure of damages in a new business. The Code is endeavoring to change the law in this area; the official comments to section 2–708 state it is not necessary to a recovery of profit to show a history of earnings, even in the case of a new business.

ACTION FOR THE PRICE

In an *action for the price* the seller seeks to recover from the buyer the amount stipulated in the contract as the price which the buyer must pay for the goods. The seller may also recover his incidental damages.

An action for the price is intended to produce the same dollar value for the seller as would the remedies of resale and damages. In our hypothetical tennis racket case, the seller recovered the $30 per racket contract price through a combination of selling the goods and recovering the balance due from the buyer. An action for the price is slightly less complicated. The seller seeks the entire $30 per racket from the buyer; the seller does not have to bother with selling the goods.

An action for the price is authorized by section 2–709 only in those situations where the seller's ability to sell the goods has been impaired. There are three such situations. One occurs where the buyer has accepted the goods and has possession of them. The buyer's possession obviously makes it impracticable for the seller to dispose of the goods.

An action for the price is also appropriate if the goods are lost or damaged within a commercially reasonable time after risk of their loss has passed to the buyer. In this case, possession of the goods will typically have passed from the seller to a common carrier. Alternatively, the seller will have possession but the buyer will have breached the contract and the seller will not have insurance coverage for the damage sustained. Here the impairment of the seller's ability to sell rests in the lack of possession or the lost or damaged character of the goods.

In this second situation, unfairness to the buyer is prevented through two built-in safeguards. First, no action for the price may be maintained unless the goods conformed to the standards required by the contract. Second, the seller bears the risk of loss when he waits longer than a commercially reasonable period of time after the buyer's breach before making an alternative disposition of the goods. Thus, the period of time during which an action for the price is justified on this ground is limited.

The third situation in which an action for the price can be brought occurs where the buyer has breached the contract before delivery and the seller has been unable to resell the goods at a reasonable price. The goods must have been identified to the contract before the breach and the right to the price arises only after a reasonable but unsuccessful effort to resell has been made or the circumstances indicate that such an effort to resell would be futile.

The buyer is entitled to possession of the goods once he has paid the price. Nevertheless, if resale of the goods becomes possible before the defaulting buyer pays the judgment, the seller may resell the goods and credit the buyer with the proceeds.

SALVAGE OF UNFINISHED GOODS AND IDENTIFICATION OF GOODS TO THE CONTRACT

Prior to the Code the resale remedy presented problems in two common situations: when the buyer breached after the goods had gone into production but before they were finished; and when the seller, especially a wholesaler or retailer, had the goods on hand but had not specifically earmarked them for the buyer. In the first situation, the seller had to decide whether to complete production and sell, or whether to sell partially finished goods. In court, the buyer was apt to disagree with his decision whichever way he opted. In the second situation, a buyer might complain that goods had been sold at a variety of prices and that it was thus impossible to tell which price was applicable to goods for which the buyer was responsible.

To resolve these problems, the Code provides in section 2–704 that when the goods are still in the process of manufacture when the buyer breaches, the seller is allowed to exercise a commercially reasonable judgment whether to complete the unfinished product. In most cases damages will be kept to a minimum if the goods are completed and sold to another party. In some instances resale will be virtually impossible and completion of manufacture will only add to the damages; the manufacturer should obviously cease work on the goods in the latter case. Where manufacture has been stopped the seller can sell the unfinished goods for scrap or salvage value or dispose of them in any other reasonable manner.

When the buyer breaches after manufacture has been completed but before the seller has specifically identified goods as the subject matter of the contract, the Code gives the seller the right to identify or earmark the goods provided that they conform to requirements of the contract and were in the possession and control of the seller at the time of the breach. Once this identification has been made, the seller can resort to his primary remedy, resale. However, in those special situations where resale as salvage or finished goods is not practicable, the Code, in section 2–704, allows the seller to seek the contract price so he can receive the value of the contract.

LIQUIDATED DAMAGES

As discussed in Chapter 12's coverage of common law contracts and buyer's remedies, a liquidated damage provision is one wherein the parties have expressly stipulated the amount of damages to be recovered for a breach of the agreement. The Code treats buyer and seller equally by permitting the seller to rely on such a contractual provision when it is reasonable and not a penalty.

SELLER EXCUSED BY FAILURE OF PRESUPPOSED CONDITION

The seller has one final right granted by the Code: the right to justify non-performance of the contract by the occurrence of a contingency the nonoccurrence of which was a basic assumption on which the contract was made. This material was discussed as part of impossibility of performance and commercial impracticability in Chapter 12.

PROBLEMS AND QUESTIONS

1. List the remedies a seller has against the buyer's breach of contract. What factors would govern a seller's choice of remedy?

2. Star, Inc., a sailboat manufacturer, contracted to sell a boat to Bradshaw equipped with special sails which Star would have to import from England at a cost to it of $500 above what domestic sails would cost. The contract price for the fully equipped boat was $10,000. Before Star ordered the sails from Eng-

land, Bradshaw repudiated the contract. Star properly notified Bradshaw of its intention to sell the boat elsewhere, equipped it with domestic sails, and sold it to Anderson for $9,000. In a suit for breach how much will Star recover from Bradshaw?

3. Bob's Body Shop, Inc., contracted to purchase 15 rolls of fiberglass cloth from Safety Glass Company. The contract price was $1,500. Upon tender of delivery the buyer wrongfully rejected the rolls, putting Safety Glass through the expense of transporting them back to its plant, at a cost of $25. Upon proper notification to Bob's, Safety resold the rolls to a toy manufacturer for $1,300. The cost of commissions in effecting the resale was $50. Assuming the resale to have been commercially reasonable, what amount will Safety Glass recover from Bob's?

Had the resale price to the toy manufacturer been $1,600, would Safety Glass have recovered anything?

4. Stonefeller, Inc., contracted to sell 10 tank truckloads of petroleum to Bingham Petroleum Products Corporation for $10,000. On the date of performance the market price of 10 tank truckloads of petroleum fell to $7,500. Upon Stonefeller's tender of delivery, Bingham wrongfully rejected the goods. The cost to Stonefeller of shipping the goods back to its plant was $500. In its suit for damages, how much will Stonefeller recover from Bingham?

5. Seed and Grain Cooperative contracted to sell a truckload of feed grain to Benson for $1,000. Before delivery Benson repudiated the contract. Without notifying Benson, Seed and Grain sold the grain to Akers for $800. The market price of the grain at the time and place of tender was $900. In a suit for damages for breach of contract, how much will Seed and Grain recover from Benson?

6. Sears Co. contracted to sell a matched set of living room furniture to Bowden for $2000. Prior to delivery Bowden repudiated the contract. The prevailing market price at the time and place of tender was $2000. The cost to Sears of the furniture had been $1700. In a suit for damages how much will Sears recover from Bowden?

7. Brown Brothers Shoe Company contracted to purchase alligator hide boots to be manufactured according to its specifications by the seller, Simpson Manufacturing Company, for $1,000. In addition to its normal production overhead, the cost to Simpson of obtaining the materials and manufacturing the boots would have been $500. Before Simpson had incurred any expenses, however, Brown repudiated the contract and informed Simpson not to start pro-

duction as it was not able to accept delivery. Accepting Brown's advice Simpson did not start production but, alleging its own willingness and ability to perform, sued Brown for damages. The market value of alligator boots at the time and place of tender (the action came to trial after the due date) was found to have dropped to $600. How much will Simpson recover?

8. The Sunshine Citrus Fruit Co. contracted to sell three carloads of frozen orange juice to Luther Foods. The contract required that the goods be shipped C.I.F. Hamburg. Upon prepaying the insurance and freight charges Sunshine duly delivered conforming goods to the carrier. On its way to Hamburg, however, the carrier's refrigeration equipment failed, spoiling the entire shipment. Sunshine immediately sued Luther Foods for the full contract price. What would be the result?

9. The Brawn Construction Co. contracted to purchase a bulldozer from Sampson Co. for $30,000. In addition to its normal production overhead, the cost to Sampson of manufacturing the bulldozer would have been $20,000. After expending $8,000 in the production process for material which had a salvage value of $7,000, Sampson was informed by Brawn that the contract was repudiated and that delivery would not be accepted. Sampson chose to complete production and incurred the expected additional cost of $12,000. Upon notice to Brown and following standards of commercial reasonableness, Sampson sold the finished product to Aztec Construction Co. for $24,000, the prevailing market price. Sampson sued Brawn for $6,000, the difference between the contract price and the resale price. Brawn defended on the ground that Sampson's continuing to spend money on a breached contract unreasonably increased the damages. What would be the result?

10. The Supervisors of Babcock County contracted with Stevens Construction Co. to purchase a dome scaled after the U.S. Capitol to be placed by crane on the Babcock County Courthouse. The contract price was $40,000. In addition to its normal production overhead, the cost to Stevens of constructing the dome would be $30,000. After Stevens had expended $10,000 for material with a salvage value of $8,000, Babcock County repudiated the contract, informing Stevens that it would not accept delivery. Stevens chose to complete production and now, holding the dome available for Babcock's acceptance, sued the county for the contract price. Since there is no demand for such a product the dome has no market value. What is the result?

23

GOOD FAITH PURCHASERS

In this chapter, ownership of goods is the focal point of our foray into sales law. We shall consider the various circumstances in which a buyer claims ownership as the adversary of either the seller or an owner whose alleged interest predates that of the seller. A buyer may desire to establish his ownership to goods in a variety of situations, but the four listed below probably occur most frequently.

The first situation arises when seller and buyer who have dealt directly with each other have conflicting claims. For example, seller Sothesby contracts with buyer Bennet to sell a Rembrandt painting. Sothesby then changes his mind and desires to keep it instead. Both parties desire the painting but only one can have it. Which one should be the eventual owner?

The second situation arises where a previous owner demands goods from a subsequent buyer and bases his demand on the fact that a third party acquired the goods illegally and thereafter improperly sold them to the buyer. For example, Burr illegally acquires Harrison's electric typewriter and sells it to an honest and innocent purchaser, the Collegiate Supply Shop. Who should be the owner, Harrison or the Collegiate Supply Shop?

In the third situation, two innocent purchasers have conflicting claims. For example, Shuldane sells a desk to Borg but before delivering it to Borg sells the same desk again to Carmody. Both buyers, Borg and Carmody, want the desk, especially if Shuldane has either spent or run off with their money.

The fourth situation occurs where a seller retains a security interest in goods and the buyer resells the goods to a third party, contrary to the original seller's security interest. The conflict then arises between the original owner and the ultimate buyer.

The principles necessary to resolve the first situation, the reneging seller, have already been discussed in Chapter 21. Assuming that the buyer can prove that a contract exists, he can acquire ownership of the goods if he can also show that he is entitled to specific performance of the contract.

The remaining three situations will be the focus of this chapter. Generally speaking, all three devolve upon the interests of two comparatively innocent parties in conflict with each other. While it is desirable to mete out justice to each simultaneously, this is often impossible; one innocent party usually sustains a loss. The law faces a difficult task in this area. It is necessary to be sensitive to the factors which cause legislatures and courts to allocate the loss as they do, and to consider whether this allocation comports with your own equitable instincts.

VICTIMIZED OWNER VERSUS INNOCENT BUYER

In the electric typewriter situation, there are several ways in which the machine could be illegally acquired. Burr might be a thief who broke into Harrison's room to steal the typewriter. Alternatively, Burr might be a swindler who talked Harrison into selling him the machine on credit and then absconded without paying or paid with a bad check before disappearing. Assume in either case that Burr then took the typewriter to the Collegiate Supply Shop and, posing as the owner of the typewriter, sold the machine. If Harrison subsequently demanded return of the typewriter, who should be declared the owner of the machine, Collegiate — the innocent buyer — or Harrison — the victimized owner?

Good, Void, and Voidable Title

The Code makes ownership of goods turn on whether the purchaser (Collegiate Supply Shop) has a title that is *good, void,* or *voidable.* If Collegiate has good title, it can keep the typewriter, whereas if it has void title, Harrison can reacquire the machine. If Collegiate has voidable title, Harrison may or may not be able to recover the typewriter, depending on circumstances to be discussed shortly. Since the Code provides in section 2–403 that a purchaser acquires all title which his transferor had, we must first determine which of the three types of title Burr possessed.

Good title exists when one actually owns goods. *Void title,* on the other hand, is one without any legal effect, i.e., it is no title at all. *Voidable title* has some characteristics of both good and void title. Voidable title is good subject to a condition; when that condition takes place voidable title becomes absolutely void. That condition is the exercise by another person (usually the original owner) of the right and power to treat the voidable title as void.

Good and voidable title may be acquired either pursuant to Article 2 or as conferred by supplementary state law. Under Article 2, it is a precondition to acquisition of both good and voidable title that the transaction in question at least purport to be a sale by one party and a purchase by the other of goods. Good title will arise only if the transaction is lawful; voidable title will arise when goods have been delivered under a purchase transaction that is in some way fraudulent or felonious. UCC § 2–403.

In the hypothetical case, where Burr entered Harrison's room and stole the typewriter, there was not even a charade of a purchase. As a result, Burr acquired no title pursuant to the Code. Supplementary state law provides that good or voidable title may be acquired in nonpurchase circumstances (for example, where an owner makes a completed gift of the goods), but none of those circumstances is present here. As a matter of fact, it is a general rule of common law that a thief acquires void title to goods. Thus, resort to both the Code and supplementary state law gives Burr neither good nor voidable title. Therefore, Collegiate acquires void title, and Harrison will succeed in repossessing the typewriter regardless of whether Collegiate purchased without knowledge of the theft. Although Burr, when he sold the typewriter to the shop, expressly or impliedly warranted that he had good title to the machine,[1] the shop's claim against a common thief for breach of warranty usually has little real value. The thief will be hard to find and in many cases will have few assets.

Had Burr swindled Harrison by inducing him to sell the typewriter and then disappeared without paying, Burr would have acquired a voidable title to the typewriter. The key to the distinctions between the void title in the theft and the voidable title in the swindle is the transaction of purchase. If the swindler accomplishes his larceny by means of a fraudulent transaction of purchase, he receives voidable title. If he perpetrates an outright theft, he receives void title. The distinction is particularly important, since the Code provides in section 2–403(1) that one who has voidable title has power to transfer good title to a good faith purchaser for value.

Good Faith Purchasers for Value

In order to comprehend the concept of good faith purchaser for value it is first necessary to understand three corollary concepts: purchaser, good faith, and value.

A *purchaser* is an individual or organization that takes the goods in any voluntary transaction creating in the taker an interest in the property. UCC § 1–201(30), (32), and (33). A sale is the most common example of such a voluntary transaction. *Good faith* means "honesty in fact in the conduct or transaction concerned." UCC § 1–201(19). We will again confront this concept when considering negotiable instruments; there, good faith is referred to as "the pure heart and empty head test." *Value* means generally "any consideration sufficient to support a simple contract." UCC § 1–201(44) (d). Thus, a good faith purchaser for value is one who receives the goods in a voluntary transaction in return for consideration without knowledge or strong suspicion that the goods were acquired by means of fraud.

---

1. Implied warranties of title are discussed at page 302.

If the Collegiate Supply Shop satisfies these requirements when it purchases the typewriter from the swindler Burr, it receives good title to the machine, and Harrison will fail in his suit to recover the typewriter. All Harrison can salvage out of his loss is a claim against Burr for damages. Since Burr will probably be prosecuted and imprisoned for larceny if apprehended, a claim against him for damages is not apt to produce any money and is, therefore, a poor substitute for possession of the typewriter.

Asserting the Right to Make Voidable Title Void

You will recall that Harrison recovered the typewriter from Collegiate in the first hypothetical case, in which Burr committed theft. Harrison recovers there regardless of whether the shop was a good faith purchaser for value. However, where the larceny is in the form of a fraudulent transaction of purchase rather than a theft, the shop keeps the typewriter if it is a good faith purchaser for value.

What happens if Collegiate fails for some reason to qualify as a good faith purchaser for value? Alternatively, what happens if Harrison traces Burr before he has disposed of the typewriter?

In the case of larceny, as long as Burr possesses the typewriter he has voidable title to it. If Harrison acts within a reasonable time after his discovery of the fraud, he may rescind (cancel) the fraudulent transaction of purchase and recover possession of the machine, i.e., Harrison may void Burr's voidable title. Recovery of the goods is usually accomplished by an action in replevin.

If Harrison fails to track down the typewriter until after Burr has sold it to Collegiate, he is precluded from recovering the machine if the shop is a good faith purchaser for value. On the other hand, if Collegiate fails to qualify as a good faith purchaser, it acquires only the voidable title Burr had. Thus, again, if Harrison acts within a reasonable time he can void the shop's voidable title by rescinding (cancelling) the original transaction of purchase and suing the shop in replevin.

CONFLICTING CLAIMS OF TWO INNOCENT PURCHASERS

At the outset of this chapter we identified an ownership problem where Shuldane wrongfully contracts to sell a desk to two different buyers, Borg and Carmody. This situation does not present a problem unless the first purchaser has left the goods in the possession of the seller. Obviously, if Borg, the first purchaser, paid for the desk and took possession immediately, his contract with Shuldane would have been performed by both parties, and Carmody would have to proceed against Shuldane for failure to deliver. Retention of possession by the seller is the hitch. The drafters of the Code make the relevant statutory provision hinge upon this point. The drafters use the phrase *entrusting* to embody the idea of retention of possession by the seller.

Where there has been an entrusting, as, for example, if Borg acquiesced in Shuldane's retention of possession of the desk, the Code permits "a merchant who deals in goods of that kind . . . to transfer all rights of the entruster to a buyer in ordinary course of business." UCC § 2–401(3). Thus, the practical question of whether Borg or Carmody will get the desk turns upon the legal questions of whether Borg acquiesced in Shuldane's retention of possession, whether Shuldane was a merchant, and whether Carmody purchased the goods in the ordinary course of business. Carmody's failure to establish any one of these requirements will entitle Borg to the goods. If Carmody establishes each of these points and in addition establishes that he has taken possession of the goods, the desk will be his. However, the Code does not deal with the issue of who gets the goods when the legal questions involving acquiescence, merchant status, and purchase in the ordinary course of business are answered in favor of Carmody but Carmody does not obtain possession of the goods. Since the Code does not treat this question, it will be decided according to the supplementary law of the relevant jurisdiction, and the various states go both ways.

So far the factual background against which we have discussed entrusting has involved a scalawag and two innocent purchasers. Entrusting can, however, involve other situations. One such variant is where an owner takes his goods, say, an antique grandfather clock, to be repaired, but is unable to recover the clock because it has been deliberately or mistakenly sold to a third party. Here only one of the innocent parties is a purchaser; the other is an earlier owner. In reviewing the three key entrusting concepts, note that the innocent purchaser can acquire rights superior to those of the original owner.

The following case discusses the entrusting provision and its purpose in a factual context that gives us insight into the "ordinary course of business" requirement.

DePaulo v. Williams Chevrolet-Cadillac

Pennsylvania Court of Common Pleas, Lebanon County, 1966. 10 Lebanon County Legal J. 465, 3 UCC Rep. Serv. 601

[Joseph Aldio, an unfranchised dealer in new and used cars, had agreed with plaintiff Frank DePaulo to obtain for him a 1963 white Chevrolet Impala for $2,800. The car and the documents of title were delivered to DePaulo. DePaulo filled out the documents and they were returned to the defendant Chevrolet dealer, who signed and delivered them together with Aldio's check for $2,665 to Aldio's bank, the drawee of the check, with instructions to the bank not to deliver the documents of title to plaintiff DePaulo until Aldio's check was accepted by the bank.

Aldio's check was returned because of insufficient funds and Aldio has since disappeared. Criminal warrants were issued for his arrest. Since the check was not accepted, the documents of title were returned to the defendant Chevrolet dealer. The defendant thereupon demanded that DePaulo return the car or pay the sum of $2,665. DePaulo refused and filed, instead, a suit in equity asking that the court direct the defendant to deliver the document of title. The defendant has counterclaimed asking that DePaulo be directed to return the car to the defendant.]

Discussion

It is said to be a fundamental principle of our law of personal property that no man can be divested of it without his own consent; and, consequently, even an honest purchaser under a defective title cannot resist a claim of the true proprietor. It is a well recognized legal maxim that, "No one can transfer to another a better title than he has himself." More simply put, even a bona fide purchaser succeeds only to the rights of his vendor.

While the legal foundation is well settled, there are certain recognized exceptions. One of these is where the owner has so acted with reference to his property as to invest another with such evidence of ownership or apparent authority to deal with and dispose of it as is calculated to mislead or does mislead a good faith purchaser for value. . . . Actually, this is merely a special application of the broad equitable principle that where one of two innocent persons must suffer loss by reasons of the fraud or deceit of another, the loss should rightly fall upon him by whose act or omission the wrongdoer has been enabled to commit the fraud.

The Uniform Commercial Code as adopted in Pennsylvania provides another exception to the fundamental rule of law that mere possession of a chattel entrusted by the owner does not enable the possessor to give a good title to a purchaser. The Code, however, specifically provides that, unless displaced by the particular provisions of the Code, the principles of law and equity, including the law merchant and the law relative to principal and agent, fraud, misrepresentation or other validating or invalidating causes shall supplement the provisions of the Code. It is the apparent legislative intention, subject to commercial standards, of course, to re-introduce the general use of equitable principles into the law governing commercial transactions. Thus, the Commercial Code considers equity in all of its aspects as an inherent part of the law in commercial cases. The exception to which we have referred is not new in perspective but merely new in nomenclature. The provision [§ 2–403(2), (3)] is as follows: —

> "Any entrusting of possession of goods to a merchant who deals in goods of that kind gives him power to transfer all rights of the entruster to a buyer in the ordinary course of business. 'Entrusting' includes any delivery and any acquiescence in retention of possession regardless of any condition expressed between the parties to the delivery or acquiescence and regardless of whether the procurement of the entrusting or the possessor's disposition of the goods have been such as to be larcenous under the criminal law."

. . . .

We do not believe that this plaintiff was a buyer in the ordinary course of business. Under circumstances which should have caused him to hesitate, he was approached by the seller concerning the purchase of a new automobile. The plaintiff knew at that time that the seller did not have the vehicle he was bargaining for in his possession. The seller agreed to obtain one for the buyer. Even at a later and more critical time, he knew that the seller did not have the vehicle available for delivery, because the seller called him on the telephone and told him that he needed the purchase price before he could make delivery. We do not believe this to be in the ordinary course of business. . . .

. . . .

[Having held that DePaulo's transaction with Aldio was not in the ordinary course of business by virtue of the fact that Aldio did not even have possession of the car when DePaulo paid him for it, the court went on to explain the policy behind the requirement that the purchase transaction be "in the ordinary course of business": if the merchant dealer in goods of that kind has possession of the goods when he wrongly sells it, the original owner can be said to have occasioned the wrong to the buyer by having entrusted the good to the unethical merchant. In this situation the buyer would get good title as opposed to the entruster assuming that the sale was "in the ordinary course of business" in all other respects. Here, however, since Aldio did not have possession of the car when DePaulo paid for it, the wrong to DePaulo could not have been occasioned by the defendant's hasty entrusting. Thus between the two relatively innocent parties the defendant original owner must prevail.

The court further indicated that the same result would be reached under the law of principal and agent, i.e., DePaulo would be bound by the agreement his agent Aldio made with the defendant.]

Conclusions of Law

1. The defendant is the owner of the 1963 white Impala Chevrolet . . . which is now in the possession of the plaintiff.

BUYER VERSUS PRIOR SELLER HAVING A SECURITY INTEREST

A seller will often sell goods on credit and, to protect himself, retain a residual ownership interest called a security interest until he is paid in full. The Code, in section 1–201(37), specifically defines *security interest* as "an interest in personal property or fixtures which secures payment or performance of an obligation." When a seller possesses such an interest there arises a potential conflict with the interests of a subsequent buyer.

Suppose, for example, Minor Manufacturing Company, reserving a security interest, sells gyroscopes to Ragnar & Sons. Ragnar subsequently sells the goods to Bailey, who is not aware that Minor has a security interest in the gyroscopes. Since the Code imposes an implied warranty of title upon Ragnar, and since the security interest limits Ragnar to an incomplete title, the result is a breach of contract by Ragnar. Bailey, of course, has a suit for breach of warranty of title, but it will be of little utility if Ragnar is bankrupt. Bailey's greatest protection is to possess the goods. Predictably, Minor Manufacturing has similar ideas; it desires to use its security interest to recover the gyroscopes and thereby minimize its losses. The law again has the task of balancing and compromising the conflicting interests of two innocent parties.

The compromise of interests adopted by the Code gives ownership to one who buys in the ordinary course of business, i.e., to one "who in good faith and without knowledge that the sale to him is in violation of the ownership rights or security interest of a third party in the goods buys in ordinary course from a person in the business of selling goods of that kind." UCC §§ 9–307(1), 1–201(9). In the typical sale of goods out of inventory or off the shelf these conditions would ordinarily be met and the purchaser in Bailey's position would win.

Where the purchase is not in the ordinary course of business, it is possible for the party with the security interest (Minor Manufacturing) to reacquire the goods. Such a party will be able to do this if it has fulfilled the technical requirement of filing a financing statement covering the goods with a public office designated by statute for that purpose. If Minor has not filed, a different compromise is made: the purchaser, Bailey, keeps the goods if they are consumer goods purchased without knowledge of the security interest, for value, and for his own personal, family, or household use. UCC § 9–307(2). If Bailey does not meet all three of these requirements, the party with the security interest may reacquire the goods under section 9–503, even if it has not filed its financing statement.

IMPORTANCE OF OWNERSHIP TO RIGHTS OF UNSECURED CREDITORS

The question of whether a buyer owns the goods he purchases is important to parties other than those identified above. The rights of the buyer's (or seller's) unsecured creditors may turn on the question. Although this topic will be discussed more extensively in Chapter 40, a brief comment here will give us perspective on the general topic of ownership and will help to highlight those few situations where the Code attaches significance to the technical location of title or ownership.

Those to whom a buyer owes money will occasionally desire to lay hands on goods in the buyer's possession to help pay off the debt. For example, Llewellyn Fuel Company might seek to possess O'Toole's tugboat in order to satisfy a large and long outstanding bill for marine fuel. This would not necessarily be in the best interests of McKay Shipbuilding, which sold O'Toole the tug; McKay may have sold on credit and may not yet have been fully paid. In such a circumstance, McKay would certainly prefer to have a claim on a specific asset, such as the tug, rather than occupy the status of an unsecured or general creditor. Consequently, McKay would likely object to Llewellyn satisfying its debt from the goods McKay had transferred to O'Toole.

The law's posture in this area enables the creditor, Llewellyn, to attach only property that is owned by the debtor, O'Toole. Therefore, Llewellyn will be seeking to establish that O'Toole acquired ownership of the goods, whereas McKay will argue that title — and thus ownership — had not technically passed from seller to buyer.

PROBLEMS AND QUESTIONS

1. Describe the meaning of the phrase "in the ordinary course of business."

2. What is the difference between void title and voidable title? What is the rationale for the distinction?

3. James agreed to purchase a Jaguar from the Fitzhugh Importing Co. When the car arrived, James paid for it with his personal check and drove away with all the required documents in order. Posing as an importer, James then sold the Jaguar to Abrams, who bought in good faith. Fitzhugh subsequently discovered the check James had given was no good. James was finally apprehended by the police and convicted of grand larceny. Fitzhugh sues Abrams in replevin. What would be the result?

4. Murphy, a dairy farmer, owned a prize stud bull worth $15,000. Her neighbor, Plunkett, wanted the bull, but Murphy had rejected all his offers, declaring that it was not for sale. Plunkett thereupon approached Stiles and told her that he would be willing

to pay her $15,000 for the bull if Stiles could succeed in purchasing it from Murphy. Stiles, posing as a veterinarian, told Murphy that the animal had a rare terminal disease but that she, Stiles, would pay $5,000 for it since it was of value to medical science. Murphy was deceived by the hoax and sold the bull to Stiles, who sold it to Plunkett for $15,000 without saying how she had procured it. When Murphy discovered that the bull was well and in Plunkett's possession, she rescinded the contract and sued Plunkett in replevin for its return. What would be the result?

5. Darrow stole a diamond pendant from Alcott and sold it to Hood, a good faith purchaser for value. Hood subsequently sold the pendant to Vinton, also a good faith purchaser for value. Should Vinton be allowed to keep the goods if Alcott sues for their recovery?

6. Ambrose & Finch, a prestigious sporting goods store, advertised that it had seventy-five specially crafted spinning rods for sale. On the day the advertisement appeared in the newspapers, sixty of the rods were sold for cash and taken from the store by purchasers. In addition, due to a communication breakdown and the unexpected demand, orders were taken over the telephone from charge account customers for an additional twenty-five rods. The callers were told that the rods were available, that the caller's offer to purchase was accepted, and that the goods would be shipped within 48 hours. Since only fifteen of the twenty-five callers will receive spinning rods, what rights and remedies do the remaining ten customers have?

7. Moran, falsely posing as a sales representative for Muir Appliance Co. persuaded Bryan to let him take her portable television to the shop for repairs. Once in possession of the set, Moran sold it to Maloney, a secondhand appliance dealer, and disappeared. Bryan traced the set to Maloney and demanded its return. When Maloney refused, Bryan brought an action in replevin. What would be the result?

8. Zendman bought a diamond ring from Brand, a diamond merchant, at one of Brand's regular auctions held on the Boardwalk in Atlantic City. Zendman acted in good faith, paid full value, and received a certificate of title from Brand. Unbeknownst to Zendman, however, Brand did not have title to the ring. It was owned by Winston, another diamond merchant, and had been left in Brand's possession so that Brand could solicit bids on the stone on behalf of Winston. Winston sought to recover her ring from Zendman. Were this case to arise under the UCC, who should win it? Why?

9. King Bed Manufacturing Company sold a double bed complete with vibrator to the Irving Furniture Co. King properly reserved a security interest in the bed, the terms of which denied Irving's right to resell until it was one-half paid for. After paying only one-quarter of the contract price, Irving sold the bed to Harbor View Motel. The purchasing agent of the motel was unaware of any restrictions on Irving's right to resell. Irving subsequently defaulted in its payments to King and declared bankruptcy. King brought a replevin action against the Harbor View Motel for recovery of the bed. What would be the result?

If Harbor View was not a buyer in the ordinary course of business, would it make any difference whether King had filed its financing statement?

10. Suppose Irving Furniture Company had sold the bed, contrary to its security agreement with King, not to a motel but to Cummings for his own personal use. Cummings had no knowledge of any security interest in the bed but did strongly suspect from Irving's weak financial position that Irving did not have good title. If Irving defaults and subsequently declares bankruptcy, can King recover the bed from Cummings?